CW00544600

# IMAGE AND DEVOTION

## IN LATE MEDIEVAL ENGLAND

*'La sélection des monuments supprime à la fois la réalité de la terre et celle des hommes, elle ne rend compte de rien de present, c'est à dire d'historique et par là, le monument lui-même devient indéchiffrable, donc stupide.'*

Roland Barthes, 'Le *Guide bleu*', in idem, *Mythologies* (*Oeuvres complètes*, I, *1942–1965*), ed. E. Marty, Paris, 1993, p. 638

(*'To select only monuments suppresses at one stroke the reality of the land and that of its people, it accounts for nothing of the present, that is, nothing historical, and, as a consequence, the monuments themselves become undecipherable, therefore senseless.'* Roland Barthes, *Mythologies*, London, 1972 (trans. A. Lavers), p. 76)

# IMAGE AND DEVOTION

## IN LATE MEDIEVAL ENGLAND

RICHARD MARKS

SUTTON PUBLISHING

First published in the United Kingdom in 2004 by
Sutton Publishing Limited · Phoenix Mill
Thrupp · Stroud · Gloucestershire · GL5 2BU

Copyright © Richard Marks, 2004

All rights reserved. No part of this publication may be reproduced, stored in a retrieval system, or
transmitted, in any form, or by any means, electronic, mechanical, photocopying, recording or
otherwise, without the prior permission of the publisher and copyright holders.

The author has asserted the moral right to be identified as the author of this work.

British Library Cataloguing in Publication Data
A catalogue record for this book is available from the British Library.

ISBN 0-7509-1466–I

For Lady Katherine Bray, Alys Cooke, John Rudde, Cuthbert Cutlat
and their fellow-parishioners in Eaton Bray and elsewhere, without
whom this book would not have been possible.

Typeset in 10/13 pt Bembo.
Typesetting and origination by
Sutton Publishing Limited.
Printed in Great Britain by
J.H. Haynes & Co., Ltd, Sparkford, England.

# CONTENTS

# ACKNOWLEDGEMENTS

Two inanimate features have been powerful influences on the gestation of this book. My interest in Orthodox spirituality and use of images has led to several sojourns on the Holy Mountain of Athos. These have enabled me to experience an intensely sacred landscape, one in which the saints are perceived to be present, as active friends and helpers, and made visible through their representation as icons. For an art historian, it has been enlightening to view the numerous ancient icons of the Mother of God, which are valued by the monks not for their contribution to our understanding of Byzantine art but as functioning images associated with the miraculous. Of course, the devotional fervency of Athos is far removed from that of ordinary English men and women of medieval times, but the Athonite experience has provided insights into the past spiritual topography of Bedfordshire and Buckinghamshire, the churches of which feature prominently in the following pages.

Landscapes, whether sacred or not, lack meaning without the people who have dwelt in them and still do. I am indebted to the monks and hermits of Athos, and especially the *higoumeni* and brothers of the Great and Holy Monasteries of Iveron and Vatopedi, for their hospitality, kindness and willingness to allow me to glimpse something of their world. From my mother has come a sense of the past, and to her I am eternally grateful for introducing me as a boy to so many of the local churches and so much local lore.

Margaret Aston, John Bossy and Alexandrina Buchanan kindly gave up their time to read drafts of the entire book; I have profited from their criticisms and suggestions and also from those of Eamon Duffy, Charles Phythian-Adams and Beth Williamson, who have commented on individual chapters. I owe much to my colleagues (notably Simon Ditchfield, Amanda Lillie and Bill Sheils), and to my undergraduate and postgraduate students in the History of Art Department and the Centre for Medieval Studies at York for their insights; also for the responses of those who heard parts of this book presented as seminar and conference papers both in England and abroad. I have benefited too from conversations, bibliographical suggestions and publications sent by continental colleagues, above all my dear and learned friends Peter and Brigitte Kurmann, but also Thomas Lentes, Hartmut Scholz and Catherine Vincent. Jim Binns and Gabriella Corona have produced polished translations from medieval Latin and saved me from unpardonable error. Jemma Street compiled the Bibliography and checked footnote references in draft stage and Jen Harland converted my crude cartographic efforts into decent maps. Margaret Condon made available her unpublished work on Sir Reynold Bray's activities at Eaton Bray. Peter Northeast and Simon Cotton have generously shared the fruits of their prodigious researches on East Anglian late medieval wills, and Aidan Hart and Father John Baggley have provided contemporary spiritual perspectives. Less quantifiable but equally important has been the influence of George Zarnecki, who first opened my eyes to medieval sculpture; similarly Michael Baxandall, who in the 1970s aroused my interest in the glories of Late Gothic sculpture and showed how the material can be interrogated in new and exciting ways. The engagement and enthusiasm of Malcolm Baker has been a constant source of inspiration. Sutton Publishing and Christopher Feeney in particular have been patience personified in awaiting delivery of this manuscript and their tolerance has extended to accepting a much larger tome than was first envisaged. To all of the above I am deeply grateful and I hope that anyone whose name is missing but should have appeared will accept my apologies for the inadvertent oversight. A general acknowledgement is due to the incumbents and churchwardens of the churches visited during the research for this book and also to the archivists and curators for access to the collections in their care. A last and special debt of gratitude is owed to my wife Rita, who has seen this project through from the beginning to the end and without whose encouragement and advice, both tangible and intangible, as well as palaeographical skills, this book would not have been completed. Responsibility for errors of fact and interpretation rests firmly on the author's shoulders.

The photographs are reproduced by kind permission of the following: Institut Amatller d'Art Hispànic (Arxiu Mas), Barcelona (VIII), Antivarisk-topografiska arkivet, Stockholm (26), Ashmolean Museum, Oxford (170), Peter Bartlett, Ludlow (173), Basque Museum, Bilbao (69), Bayerisches Nationalmuseum, Munich (100), Bedfordshire & Luton Archives and Record Service (4), Bergen University Historical Museum (35), P. Bossard, Service des biens culturels du canton de Fribourg (114), The British Library Board (I, XIV, 27, 37, 38, 74, 134 (left), 163), Trustees of the British Museum (113, 158 (left)), John Vere Brown, Newhaven, Sussex (148), Buckinghamshire County Museum Service (18), Catharijneconvent Museum, Utrecht (151), Conway Library, Courtauld Institute of Art (13, 14, 23, 44, 95, 117, 129), The Master and Fellows of Corpus Christi College, Cambridge (112), F.H. Crossley (78, 80, 86, 102), Domschatzkammer, Aachen (150), Erfurt Cathedral (30), Exeter Cathedral Library (147), Exeter Museums (11), Fitzwilliam Museum, Cambridge (106), Gerd Gering, Aachen (XX), Germanisches Nationalmuseum, Nuremberg (XXI), Glasgow Museums, The Burrell Collection (15, 72, 77, 81, 162), Green and Whittingham, *Norfolk Archaeology* 1968 (132, 133); F.A. Greenhill (96), The Revd Murray Haig (156), The Master and Fellows of Keble College, Oxford (83), A.F. Kersting (32, 125), King's Lynn Museums (153 (d)), Professor Peter Kurmann (47), Lambeth Palace Library (XV, 39), John Larson (XI), Luton Museum Service (64), The Metropolitan Museum of Art, New York (VI, 41), Musée national du Moyen Age, Thermes de Cluny, Paris (88, 103), Museo d'Arte Antica, Milan (31), The Museum of Fine Arts, Boston, USA (124), The Museum of London (17, 153 (c), 158 (right)), The National Gallery of Art, Washington (79), National Monuments Record (XII, 5, 8, 12, 40, 43, 48, 50, 53, 61, 84, 85, 92, 98, 99, 101, 109, 110, 131, 136, 138, 139, 140, 146, 149, 152, 161 (b, c), 164, 174), Norwich Castle Museum & Art Gallery (56, 153 (d), 157), Phillimore & Co. (66), Rheinisches Bildarchiv, Cologne (2, 28), Rheinisches Landesmuseum, Bonn (XVIII, 94), Crown copyright, The Royal Commission on Historical Monuments of Wales (36, 143), Society of Antiquaries of London (76, 104, 105), the late Brian Spencer (134 (right), 153 (a, b)), Martin Stuchfield (20, 59, 62, 172), The Master and Fellows of Trinity College, Cambridge (XVI, 91), The Trustees of the Victoria & Albert Museum (IV, XIII, 9, 10, 16, 24, 42, 51, 54, 63, 68, 89, 107, 159, 160, 167, 168), Victoria County History (111), Winchester Cathedral (V), Paul Woodfield (135), York Glaziers Trust (152), York Minster Archives (71), York Museums Trust (165), Professor George Zarnecki (22, 25), Horst Ziethen, Cologne (XXII). The following were taken by the author: II, III, VII, IX, X, XVII, XIX, XXIII, XXIV, 1, 3, 6, 7, 19, 21, 29, 33, 34, 45, 46, 49, 52, 55, 57, 58, 60, 65, 67, 70, 73, 75, 82, 87, 90, 93, 97, 108, 115, 116, 118, 119, 120, 121, 122, 123, 126, 127, 128, 137, 142, 144, 145, 154, 155, 161 (a), 166, 169, 171, 175, 176.

Richard Marks,
Department of the History of Art
University of York
May 2003

# ABBREVIATIONS

| | |
|---|---|
| Beds. & Luton Archives: | Bedfordshire and Luton Archives and Record Service |
| BHRS: | Bedfordshire Historical Record Society |
| Bucks. RO: | Buckinghamshire Record Office |
| EETS: | The Early English Text Society |
| JBAA: | *The Journal of the British Archaeological Association* |
| PRO: | London, Public Record Office |
| RCHM: | Royal Commission on Historical Monuments (England) |
| VCH: | Victoria County History |

CHAPTER ONE

# INTRODUCTION

This is a book about images without images. Or almost so. It is concerned with what, for historical reasons, can no longer be seen, yet is about a period when what was seen was considered paramount: '. . . often man is more steryd [stirred] be syghte than be heryng or redyngge', observes one of the protagonists in an early fifteenth-century dialogue.[1] More precisely, it is about a ubiquitous kind of representation which is defined neither by medium nor form, but by function; this representation I have termed the devotional image.[2]

The premises of this book are firstly, that devotional images are incomprehensible without considering the communities and individuals that used them, and secondly, that the images can tell us something about social bodies and those who constituted them. The primary emphasis is on the kinds of devotional images accessible to the non-elites and therefore, for the most part, located in the public space of the parish church. Although Bishop Pecock, writing in the fifteenth century, allowed that images might be venerated in any location – 'bifore a bare wal in a chirche, or in a corner of a chirche or of an other hous, or in the feeld' – his principal focus (also that of the author of the late fourteenth-century *De Adoracione Ymaginum*) was on 'ymagis sett up in the chirche'.[3] Indeed it is impossible to understand the physical and social fabric of the late medieval parish church without reference to the devotional image. I am not attempting to write a social history of art along Hauserian lines, still less will it be argued that the visual material is a passive 'reflection' of society; on the contrary, devotional images occupied an active place in individual and collective religio-cultural responses and were one of the means by which selfhood and communal identities were constructed. My approach is perhaps best described by appropriating a phrase used by Amos Rapaport: 'a series of relationships between things and things, things and people and people and people'.[4] Here this is defined as the interactions between devotional images and their locations and presentation; between these artefacts and their makers, commissioners and, above all, users (these categories are not mutually exclusive); and between users as members of their communities and as individuals. The devotional image is seen as a cultural object firmly embedded in the socio-economic fabric of the parish and rooted in communal and individual life.

The medieval devotional image on the continent has attracted growing attention from art historians in recent years. Following the pioneering studies of Panofsky and then Ringbom, the emphasis has been on the private or personal devotional image, although not exclusively so. Three important exhibitions on the subject have been held within the last few years: Amsterdam (1994–5), Nuremberg (2000) and Berne/Strasbourg (2001).[5] The works of Baxandall, Belting, Camille, Cormack (on Byzantium), Freedberg, Hamburger and Van Os *inter alia* have enriched our understanding of the devotional image, with much of the impetus stemming from the broadening of art-historical methodologies to embrace issues of audience and reception. The devotional image is also a field which lends itself to cross-disciplinary approaches. Scribner, Trexler, Vauchez, Jean-Claude Schmitt and Jean Wirth have contributed the historian's perspective and in the 1970s the anthropological methodologies of Victor and Edith Turner offered new insights on the phenomenon of pilgrimage.

English devotional images have not generated the same level of scholarly interest. Their wholesale destruction or erasure during the Reformation meant that no early antiquarian historiography was generated, apart from one or two notices in the *Gentleman's Magazine*. It was only with the discoveries made during Victorian church restorations that individual images, principally in wall-painting and alabaster, began to be published. The latter medium has been studied extensively in a series of important articles on carvings in this medium, firstly by St John Hope, Hildburgh and Nelson and latterly by Cheetham, whose catalogue of the Victoria & Albert Museum's holdings (founded on the gift of Hildburgh's collection) is invaluable. Recently the contentious ground of the Reformation has been re-evaluated by historians, who, in the process of offering reinterpretations of its causes and impact, have paid much attention to late medieval religion. In this, discussion of images has been unavoidable and in the case of the first volume of Margaret Aston's *England's Iconoclasts*, it has been central. Likewise, Eamon Duffy's influential *Stripping of the Altars*, Kathleen Kamerick's *Popular Piety and Art in the Late Middle Ages* and regional studies by Robert Whiting and Andrew Brown have all considered the controversies over the use and alleged abuse of images. For the most part, the approaches have been predicated on texts, rather than on using the documentary sources in conjunction with surviving images. As a consequence, there has been a tendency to treat every image as though its significance was the same, irrespective of whether it is a mural, a screen- or glass-painting, or a carving mounted on a bracket. The chronology of the devotional image has also not been explored in great depth, nor has much attention been paid to England in the wider context of developments within western Christianity. Visitors to European museums and churches with an interest in medieval art or iconography cannot fail to observe the plethora of carved representations of the same sacred personages who populate the pages of English wills, demonstrating the ties that bound this country to the continent in so many matters devotional.

In order to try to address some of the *lacunae*, I have borrowed tools from a range of disciplines, including theology, folklore, social history and local history. Gender studies have been illuminating and the researches by the anthropologist William Christian Jr. on past and recent 'popular religion' in Spain have provided some helpful models and insights. I am conscious of not being a trained operator in any of these specialized fields and am thus open to the charge of wielding a blunt or even the wrong instrument. Nevertheless, I feel that it is only through adopting a multi-disciplinary approach that the subject can be illuminated across all its facets.

The problematics are numerous. Of the countless images defined here as 'devotional', those in wall-painting have survived in greater numbers than those in statuary. While the former were often merely whitewashed or plastered over, three-dimensional images were almost all smashed or destroyed. The minute and unrepresentative fraction of extant carved representations rules out a formalist approach; to pursue this methodology would be akin to attempting a jigsaw puzzle with 99 per cent of the pieces missing. Those that remain for the most part consist of a few battered *membra disjecta*. None can be anchored either specifically or ideologically to its original context and uses. Conjunction between documentation and extant imagery is very rare: heads at Whittlesford (Cambs.) and Cobham (Kent) are among the very few instances where surviving images can be linked with wills (**166**; **XIX**). In the case of the latter, the wills date from long after the images were created. As a result, for dating of extant images recourse has to be made to stylistic comparison, to say the least an inexact science. As a rough rule of thumb, for the purposes of this exercise, *c.* 1400 can be taken to mean within about ten years either side and 'early', 'middle', 'late' and 'end' correspond with the quarterly division of a century.

The detritus also distorts. Almost no carved devotional image exists from before 1300, although there are a number of earlier murals. If conclusions were to be drawn from surviving images, it might be assumed that alabaster was the most popular medium, followed by stone. Of wooden images (known from texts to have been the most ubiquitous) only a handful remain, and none of the richest images encased in gold or silver. Even where they still stand in their parish churches, carved images are mere shadows of their former selves. The vast majority have been decapitated, truncated or otherwise mutilated, stripped of colour and gilding and wrenched from their original settings (**1**). The elaborate gilded wooden canopies or tabernacles which framed so many images have vanished (apart from the modest little housings of some alabasters) and so have the rich fabrics in which many images of the Virgin were clad. Also absent are the candlesticks or 'braunches' which held wax candles or tapers, those most common material manifestations of devotion.

The architectural settings too have suffered severely, with the transformation of church interiors through religious changes and restoration. The Reformation, the Civil War and Commonwealth, and the ecclesiological zeal of the nineteenth century are not the sole explanations. In many areas, notably East Anglia, the Cotswolds, and Devon and Somerset, the widespread reconstruction of parish churches during the fifteenth and early sixteenth centuries effaced evidence of previous image display and location. Over the course of time image-brackets too have been removed or relocated. Mural images, of course, have remained *in situ*, but other fittings which shed light on the relationships between venerators and an image have suffered: medieval seating has often gone and sepulchral monuments, especially brasses, placed before an image have mostly been moved. The very significance of certain images has been concealed through changes in church dedications since the Reformation.

None the less, the canvas is far from blank. Considering the severity of governmental proscriptions under Henry VIII, Edward VI and Elizabeth I, the number of surviving three-dimensional images is quite surprising. Almost every county in England can claim a few, in addition to the quantity of alabaster images to be found on the continent, either as a result of demand in pre-Reformation times or through post-Reformation export. Discoveries are still being made, such as the mutilated but still attractive St Margaret at Fingringhoe (Essex), which was found immured in its elaborate stone niche in 1968 (**X**). The frame for this image is but one of many stone corbels, brackets and niches remaining in parish churches throughout England, which are highly informative about the relative importance and accessibility of the images they supported or enclosed.

The absence of the vast majority of carved images, especially almost all those which were executed for the most prestigious institutions and individuals, has one advantage: there is no canon predicated on artificial hierarchies of importance imposed by the *diktats* of connoisseurship. Images can therefore be studied relatively free from the colouring of antiquarian and art-historical scholarship. Instead, the approach adopted in this book is to examine the function of images in society and the beliefs and practices which surrounded them; it is also concerned with the ways in which the forms of certain images were determined by the society which used them.

*1. Whittlesford (Cambs.), St Mary and St Andrew's church: display of alabaster fragments*

*2. Cologne, Schnütgen Museum: display of medieval sculpture, 1932*

It has long been the practice of museums, both within and outside the United Kingdom, to present carved images as art objects, usually arranged taxonomically either as part of a chronological sequence to demonstrate stylistic evolution or grouped by iconography. In such settings they are invested with a set of meanings radically different from their original ones (**2**).[6] In contrast, the Roman Catholic cathedral of Westminster possesses a medieval alabaster image of the Virgin and Child, which, placed against a pillar not far from the high altar and elevated on a corbel, is one of the few English examples retaining its function as an object of devotion (**3**). Its suppliants perform the same outward gestures and actions as their medieval predecessors, albeit perhaps without some of the latter's more excessively emotive practices. It may even be the case that the internalized devotions of today's venerators may not be so far removed from their counterparts of half a millennium ago. Yet the Westminster image, like those in museums, experiences a continuing life within cultural parameters very different from its original context.

Margaret Miles has observed that in the absence of the original worshipper all we are left with is the image itself.[7] In England this is not strictly true. There might be comparatively few images extant which fall into the category of devotional, but there are a large number of wills and the voices of image users are heard occasionally through such documents as churchwardens' accounts and fraternity records. These sources need to be interrogated with circumspection. They are often legalistic documents or records couched in the phraseology and terms of reference of

*3. Westminster Roman Catholic Cathedral: a medieval English alabaster Virgin and Child in use as a devotional image*

clerics or accountants. They were shaped to what their compilers and readers needed to know, which is not necessarily what the historian or art historian would like to know.

There is no textual indication of lay attitudes to images prior to the fourteenth century. From then on, the voices we hear are neither neutral nor unmediated and the evidence is both occasional and ambiguous. Do the exhortations to provide, repaint or repair the patronal and Marian images in the early fourteenth-century Devon diocesan visitations point to a deep well of lay indifference, or even to hostility towards images? Or is the fact that in only nine of the forty-four churches within the archdeaconry of Totnes in this diocese was the condition of the principal images remarked upon in 1342 a sign of lay fervour (or conversely, a lack of clerical concern)?[8]

Although partly dealing with the policing of morality, visitations were also concerned with enforcing lay responsibilities for the enhancement and upkeep of the fabric and fittings of parish churches.[9] This needs to be borne in mind before reading into the refusal of the parishioners of Shillington and Swineshead (Beds.) to contribute to the new fabric of their churches anything more than a natural reluctance to part with hard-earned cash or kind.[10] At most, such references hint that, below the bland record of fabric and image endowment, things were not always what they seemed. Dean Chandler's concern for the good repair of the principal images in the churches of the Salisbury diocese was repeated in identical language by Archbishop Warham in Kent a century later. Reading the two accounts, it is easy to forget that Kentish social structures and economic conditions were very different from those of the south-west of England, conditions which were bound to have had an effect on images. The language is consensual, filtered and homogenized.[11]

Only from the second half of the fifteenth century is there a sufficiently large *corpus* of written evidence to shed light on images and their use (and abuse). These sources provide a mine of information on image iconography, distribution, production and externalized devotional practices. Nevertheless, they still require careful evaluation.

Churchwardens' accounts are usually records of income and expenditure, in which offerings to images and their lights feature frequently, as well as direct outlays on the images themselves. Sometimes these documents are fair copies and prepared for specific reasons. For example, Clive Burgess has shown how the highly informative Church Book of Bristol All Saints, compiled in the 1480s, was shaped by its particular function, namely to act as a bederoll of past and present benefactors to the fabric and furnishings.[12] To write about parish devotion in late medieval England solely from such sources would therefore be akin to telling the history of Barings Bank in the 1990s from the annual audited accounts.

The most common written sources are wills, which from the late fifteenth century began to be made by artisans, yeomen and husbandmen and their widows.[13] The wills of such people provide a rich seam of information on images; without them, this study would not have been possible. One has, however, to be aware of their limitations for this purpose.[14] They represent only testators' desires on the eve of their death or in old age, and consequently the arrangements for the well-being of their souls feature prominently. They give no indications of the scale of lifetime benefactions. Where it is possible to compare wills with churchwardens' accounts, a very different picture can emerge.[15] For example, the early sixteenth-century accounts for Bassingbourn (Cambs.) reveal considerable investment in new images of St Margaret and St George, yet the sole testamentary references are only to the latter and occur in just two wills. Wills are far less helpful than material objects in the form of pilgrim badges and amulets when it comes to evaluating pilgrimage cults, for the obvious reason that this was a lifetime activity (unless it was done posthumously by proxy).

The parishioners of late medieval England were framed by their own temporal parameters and *mentalités* as well as by our own perceptions. Peasants, even the will-making yeomen and husbandmen, did not articulate their own thoughts in their wills any more than they did in any other document. To borrow Andrew Brown's nice turn of phrase, wills are 'less windows on to the soul than mirrors of social convention'.[16] By their nature wills are positive documents, in that they record an action which either is desired or has occurred. They are rhetorical in that they are official statements of record or intent; they are also constrained by custom and practice.

Wills do provide insights into the relationship between images and place and occupation, but in general they present a homogeneous appearance stemming from their formulaic nature: it is only the choice of certain saints' images which might distinguish the wishes of a Devon testator from his or her counterpart in Kent. This cloak of uniformity fits ill with the observation by two economic historians that the medieval scene was characterized by variety.[17] In considering wills *en bloc* there is a high risk of picking and mixing, resulting in insensitivity to the inner histories of regions and communities as well as to individuals.

None the less, differences do exist. Bedfordshire wills in general are more informative about images and lights than the earliest surviving collection of wills from the archdeaconry of Sudbury.[18] Between 1480 and 1530 only about 40 per cent of testators in the Bedford archdeaconry failed to leave cash or kind to some feature of their parish church, be it the fabric, the rood or Sepulchre light, or the images and their lights. By contrast, in the deanery of Dunwich within the archdeaconry of Suffolk between 1420 and 1530 the number of wills mentioning images and lights never rose above 10 per cent of the total.[19] Did Suffolk testators care less about the images in their parish churches? Churchwardens' accounts and other records suggest not; it is merely that the testamentary format adopted within the two archdeaconries differed. The Bedfordshire wills are invaluable for providing some indication of the numbers and subject-matter of images in individual churches, but even here they need to be treated with caution. The extent to which wills were determined by parish custom even within this archdeaconry is demonstrated by comparing the villages of Eaton Bray and Blunham. Almost all of the eighteen wills from the latter made in the period 1501–40 mentioned the Sepulchre light, the parochial fraternity of the Holy Trinity and the bells, but not one referred to the images, which included the fine alabaster figures of the Virgin and Child and Our Lady of Pity (**IX, VII**). In contrast, the nine Eaton Bray will-makers in the years 1509–39 between them endowed a whole range of images. Quantitative analysis too has its limitations and cannot be used as a measure for the devotional commitment of the community as a whole. Nine swallows do not make a summer at Eaton Bray and nine wills of the better-off elements do not add up to a fervent, as opposed to a conventional, laity in matters religious. In such matters, it cannot be assumed that testators were always free agents. The pattern of bequests in the Suffolk parish of Blythburgh points to a managed programme of embellishment for the magnificent parish church. Donations to images and their lights ceased while the chancel was under construction and resumed when it was completed; this suggests that testators were steered in their endowments, no doubt by the parish clergy and/or churchwardens.[20]

The selective and fragmentary nature of the empirical evidence rules out any attempt to write grand narrative, even if one were so inclined. Like the medieval Church itself, image-use was not monolithic; it operated at different levels, reflected different interests and took place in different contexts. An interpretation is offered here, not a survey. A study based on microhistories and polysemic readings in time and place precludes the shoe-horning of the relationships between medieval people and their images into inappropriate and therefore unhistorical structures. It is neither desirable nor possible to generalize over such a *longue durée* as five centuries or so and over such a wide and diverse geographical area as the whole of England. Wherever possible, examples of devotional images in three-dimensional or painted form are called upon, especially where there is evidence for their original provenance. The survivors are important. Carvings and pictures convey their own messages and meanings and can form a corrective to the traditional primacy of texts.

The book's structure is thematic, although discussion of chronology is included where it is relevant to demonstrate significant innovations or changes. Chapter Two is concerned with defining the devotional image in the public space of the parish church. In Chapter Three the rise to prominence of images of the Virgin is examined and in Chapter Six the expansion and diversification of her representations is explored. Chapter Four is devoted to patronal images and Chapter Five to the proliferation of images of specialist saintly helpers. Liturgical and individual devotional and social practices surrounding images are discussed in Chapter Seven. Chapter Eight looks at the kinds of cult images in vogue during the later Middle Ages and the ways in which they were presented to their devotees. The subject of Chapter Nine is the production of images, including their commissioning and cost. The debates about and destruction of devotional images in the parish church during the Reformation comprise the last chapter (Ten).

The main focus is on the late fifteenth century and onwards, although not to the exclusion of earlier periods. In more than half the chapters discussion is hung on a series of pegs. The choice of case-studies needs some explanation, perhaps even justification. They are selected from parish churches in the adjoining archdeaconries of Bedford and Buckingham (**Maps 1, 2, p. 277**). These are not intended to be paradigms: there is no such thing as a typical English parish church. The choice was in part motivated by the wish to make the point that devotional images could be found in every parish church, however humble – and in both these archdeaconries the commonplace is more frequently encountered than the spectacular in respect of parish church architecture. Between them they possess a number of churches of various dates, which retain traces of the former emplacement of their images. Examples of images themselves survive in surprising numbers. The two archdeaconries are well served by a *corpus* of wills with many references to images. The parishes were of varying size and social composition. The diversity of landscapes resulted in differences in means of livelihood and economic conditions as well as church building and design and provides a testing-ground for the examination of the relationship between images and locality. Lastly, the churches of both Bedfordshire and Buckinghamshire have been familiar and easily accessible to me since childhood.

None of the case-studies is treated in isolation; around them material from other locations is grouped, sometimes in support (without I hope creating an unhistorical hybrid), sometimes to offer contrasts and differences. The selection is open to the charge that the principal examples are drawn neither from the north of England nor, with one exception, from an urban centre. Images from both these contexts, however, do feature throughout the text. In addition to calling on work that has been done in the field on the continent, as occasion demands the subject is examined in relation to western Christendom as a whole, seeking to draw out what is distinctive and what is different about images and their use in England. In a few instances continental images are illustrated where no relevant English example survives; the same applies to the occasional forays into Wales.

In the process of interrogating both texts and extant images, I have endeavoured to be sensitive to diversity rather than to homogeneity, to change and flux rather than to seamless continuity. This study focuses on the practice of medieval piety as it related to images through individual and collective prayer, donations and commissions. It is not concerned with measuring the spirituality of medieval users of images. Some readers may object that this dimension has been neglected in favour of socio-economic, demographic and political readings. A reviewer of the book associated with the Amsterdam *Art of Devotion* exhibition questioned the extent to which images perceived in religious terms by their users is reconstructable in an age principally concerned with their aesthetic appeal.[21] I would only add that the religious perspective is best left to those more qualified than me to write with authority (and conviction).

One further *caveat*: that most universal of images, the rood, found in every church throughout the land, lies outside the parameters of this study; so too do the Easter Sepulchre, the Man of Sorrows and the image generally known as St 'Sunday', perceived to have been associated with the Sunday Christ or the Warning to Sabbath-breakers (**21, 22**).[22] The very ubiquity and centrality of the rood, as a focus for both collective and personal devotion, make it worthy of its own monograph. The rood and other images with the Saviour as the central focus underline the Christocentric nature of late medieval religion, but it was one in which the saints as represented by their images provided an ever-increasing and active supporting cast.

Whether this book attempts to make bricks without straw is left to the reader to determine. This study claims neither total objectivity nor closure. To offer a 'social history of the medieval image' does not mean that the past is any more recoverable by this than by any other methodology. It is impossible not to concur with an eminent historian of the Reformation:

> even if the art historian turns to the discipline of historical context and begins to probe local knowledge in the mode of the historical ethnographer, even if the historian attempts to attune his or her visual perception to the level of sophistication of the art historian, the task of unravelling images as historical evidence is still far from easy.[23]

# CHAPTER TWO

# SEABLE REMEMORATIJF SIGNES: DEFINING THE DEVOTIONAL IMAGE

The parish church of St Mary at Eaton Bray is situated in the far south of Bedfordshire, on the border with Buckinghamshire. The unremarkable exterior with its Perpendicular fenestration gives no hint of either the beauty or the antiquity of the interior (**4–6**; **II**). The structure is basically of the first half of the thirteenth century, and is notable for the nave arcades, resplendent with an array of stiff-leaf capitals and, on the north side, with clustered piers; all this must be the work of masons from the neighbouring parish of Totternhoe, with its famous limestone quarries, who were responsible for the construction of several local churches in the same period. Contemporary with the arcades are the font, the chancel piscina and the magnificent iron scrollwork of the nave south door, attributed to the local craftsman Thomas of Leighton (Buzzard), who made the ironwork for Eleanor of Castile's tomb in Westminster Abbey.[1]

Pictorially, nothing medieval remains, with mainly clear glass in the windows and whitewashed walls. The rood and Easter Sepulchre have vanished; absent too are the roodscreen (removed in 1972) and any pre-Reformation figural glass and wall-paintings. The church is not entirely devoid of medieval fixtures. Apart from the font, there are Perpendicular stone retables in the two projecting nave chapels; the retable in the south chapel is surmounted by an elaborate canopied niche occupying the middle light of the east window, accompanied by a smaller canopied niche set high and abutting the north jamb of the window; on the south side of the window is a moulded bracket supported by a man's head (**II**). A shallower niche with a cinquefoil cusped head is adjacent to the east window of the north chapel. Two small niches with cusped ogee heads and crocketed gables are located below and on either side of the chancel arch on the nave side. Two more brackets are inserted into the nave piers adjacent to the south door. Altogether in the nave there are eight frames and supports, several of which are visible in **5** and **6**. What was the purpose of these elevated and framed niches and corbels? What occupied the spaces within and above them?

For answers to these questions we can turn to the wills of two early sixteenth-century parishioners of Eaton Bray. Late in November 1515 John Rudde composed his last will and testament, disposing of his property and making provision for good works, especially in his parish church. Apart from donations to the rood and Sepulchre lights, he bequeathed small sums to a number of dedicated lights: 4*d* to the 'gaudys of our lady', 12*d* to the Trinity, 8*d* to each of the lights of SS Anthony, Nicholas, Christopher and Our Lady; and 6*d* to each of St George, St Erasmus and Our Lady of Pity. Three more lights, associated with SS Eligius, Sunday and Thomas, are mentioned in Cuthbert Cutlat's will of six years later.[2]

Each of these twelve lights had a visual focus and their names were derived from the representations of the sacred personages before whom they burned. No indication is given in

4. Eaton Bray (Beds.), St Mary's church from the south-east; watercolour by Thomas Fisher, c. 1815 (County Hall, Bedford)

5. Eaton Bray (Beds.), St Mary's church, interior looking east (before the removal of the rood screen)

*6. Eaton Bray (Beds.), St Mary's church, image-corbels on nave south aisle piers*

Rudde and Cutlat's wills and those of their fellow-parishioners of the location of the individual images, but it can be assumed that some of them occupied the frames and supports described above. Hard though it is to imagine today, in Rudde and Cutlat's era their church was peopled by multiple images, around which took place devotional practices of a kind prevalent in Catholic Europe from medieval times until the Second Vatican Council, and still familiar in some areas. In this respect Eaton Bray is representative of England as a whole.

There is nothing remarkable about John Rudde's will. Its formulaic structure is indistinguishable from thousands of late medieval wills of the middling and lower ranks of society. Neither Eaton Bray church nor Rudde's will can be taken as exemplary, but to link them is a helpful starting point in defining the nature of and the role played by the images which formerly occupied the brackets and niches.

Rudde's testamentary bequests expressed his lifetime veneration of the saintly recipients and his continued desire for their intercessory aid after his death. For him and his peers, his attitude to and use of images was determined by what they heard (the liturgy and perhaps sermons), what they experienced (in life and labour) and what they viewed (the images). Each of the Eaton Bray saints acted as a devotional image, an artefact defined by its relationship with its viewers. The devotional image does not enjoy an autonomous existence, but only derives meaning – as in the label – from the process of its cultural use by the devotee.[3] Actions took place before these images which were prompted by their presence. Interaction with an audience distinguishes this kind of representation from the vast majority of English imagery in screen-paintings, murals and stained glass. The light of St Erasmus was a signifier that this was a devotional image. Rudde would have been able to identify the image of St Erasmus on the screen at Roxton, east of Bedford, from its resemblance to

*7. Roxton (Beds.), St Mary's church, painting of St Erasmus on the rood screen, early sixteenth century*

the image of the same saint in his own church, and there was nothing to prevent him from treating it as an object of veneration in the same way (**7**). However, the Roxton representation is only one of a row of figures and there is not a single specific reference to a bequest to a light or any gesture of devotion in Bedfordshire wills to imagery on screens.

The suggestion that the lost Eaton Bray images should be included within the category of devotional images marks the introduction of English material into a debate which hitherto has been conducted primarily in terms of continental visual production. Art-historical scholarship has concentrated either on cult images or on the *Andachtsbild*.[4] The latter term has been seen as the equivalent of the 'devotional image' in English but, as Ringbom observed, this equation can be misleading.[5] The label *Andachtsbild* was coined by German scholars as a means of categorizing several new kinds of carved images, including Our Lady of Pity and the Man of Sorrows, which first manifested themselves in fourteenth-century Germany. To qualify as *Andachtsbilder*, they had to be 'certain sculptural representations which did not suit the liturgical conditions of the altar service'.[6] In his discussion of the Man of Sorrows, Panofsky broadened the definition, firstly by including painting as well as sculpture and secondly by distinguishing them from narrative images; he also differentiated them from the cult image as they provided an opportunity for contemplation or interiorized religious experience.[7] Ringbom argued that a distinction can be made between the *Andachtsbild* and the category of religious images as a whole:

> Devotional images are simply distinguished from the liturgical and didactical compositions of ecclesiastical decoration by their intended function in connection with *private edification, prayer and meditation*. 'Devotional image' is thus a functional term, while the *Andachtsbild* . . . should be defined by formal and iconographical criteria alone.[8]

His reasoning was based on the premise that the differences between devotional images and 'public art' were those of function and scale. However, he accepted that devotional images might be located in the chapels of a church as well as in a house and that subjects used in 'official church decoration', including narrative scenes, could easily serve as devotional images.[9] He did not define the purpose of these chapels, but the context indicates that they were essentially private spaces such as chantry or family chapels.

Ringbom's stance has found wide acceptance; for example, Belting sees the 'private' cult image, as opposed to the 'public' version controlled by the Church, as the site where, from the thirteenth century, innovation and development took place:

> As soon as the portable image spread to all the property-owning classes of society, whether lay or clerical, the church authorities were driven to keep things under control. The old [i.e. the public image] now took on the appearance of a deliberate archaism, which was meant to counterbalance the continuous disintegration of what previously had been the norm of images.[10]

The concept of meaning residing in use was adopted by Belting and both he and Ringbom, as well as Panofsky, drew a line between cult images, i.e. images with miraculous powers, and a kind of personal image which 'forsook its traditional aloofness and was ready to address the beholder in a way that produced a private dialogue. . . . The old cult image, in contrast, steadfastly refused to allow its content to be manipulated by the wishes of the beholder.'[11]

The emphasis on private devotion by both Ringbom and Belting makes assumptions about the intended audience. Despite a few woodcuts and engravings of the kind which eventually became accessible to a broader social spectrum, most of the exhibits in the 1994 Amsterdam exhibition, *The Art of Devotion in the Late Middle Ages*, were small-scale artefacts of high quality and expensive materials, made for use in the private chapels and oratories, or carried about the persons, of the elites of society.[12] In short, the usual perception is that the devotional image was the preserve of the wealthy and powerful; the images accessible to the masses consisted of the monumental narrative pictorial cycles which had a didactic function and were controlled by the church authorities. Belting voices this explicitly ('property-owning classes') and it is implicit in Ringbom's definition of the 'public art of ecclesiastical decoration', which (he argued contentiously) took the form of the retable standing on the high altar and having a liturgical function, and of narrative cycles on walls and windows 'which are the "letters of the unlettered"'.[13] In respect of the latter, he was of course repeating Gregory the Great's dictum about the didactic function of images as bibles for the poor (although, as we have seen, he accepted that narrative scenes themselves could function as foci for devotion).

The Eaton Bray material adds new dimensions to the concept of the devotional image. The argument advanced here is that the English devotional image flourished in the public space of the parish church and was often on a monumental scale. The individual's interiorized religious experience, which focused on the devotional image, was not limited to the upper echelons of society; indeed, everyone might share in its patronage and use. For the laity as a whole, the devotional images in their parish church remained the principal focus of affective piety until the Reformation. The saints through their images also participated in collective worship within the *teatrum sacrum* of the parish church, hence the uses to which these images were put straddled the private and public and the social and spiritual spheres.[14] Finally, the history of the devotional image is not static, but dynamic; the period between the tenth century and the Reformation witnessed evolution and change, during which the devotional image at times, and with varying degrees of intensity, was a contested object. In England devotional images in churches usually took the form of carved statues or reliefs, although paintings on walls and piers were also common. England was far from being unique in its predilection for sculpture. Scholarly focus on panel painting may indeed be valid for Italy, but it betrays an ultramontane view of the world of images and fails to take into account the scores of three-dimensional representations to be found in the churches and cathedrals of northern Europe as well as in museums and even in the chapels and chambers of the lay and clerical elites. North of the Alps the carved image proliferated until the Reformation.[15]

Bishop Reginald Pecock, writing in the vernacular during the middle of the fifteenth century, expressed the orthodox definition of images as signs of the saintly personages represented in material form, whose purpose was to 'be had and usid as rememoratijf signes of God, and of hise benefetis, and of his holi lijf and passioun, and of Seintis and of her [their] holi conversacioun'.[16] Pecock was one of a number of English theologians who from the late fourteenth century countered Lollard attacks on images as idolatrous. Their defence centred on a tripartite justification for the use of images, expressed succinctly in *Dives and Pauper*, an early fifteenth-century tract:

> they been ordeynyd to steryn manys mende [man's mind] to thynkyn of Cristys incarnacioun and of his passioun and of holye seyntys lyvys. Also they been ordeynyd to

steryn mannys affeccioun and his herte to devocioun, for often man is more steryd be [stirred by] syghte than be heryng or redyngge. Also they been ordeynyd to been a tokene and a book to the lewyd peple, that they moun [may] redyn in ymagerye and peynture that clerks redyn in boke. . . .[17]

The same justification is repeated in the canonist William Lyndewood's *Provinciale seu constitutiones Anglie*, of about the same date as *Dives and Pauper*.[18] The argument was an ancient *topos*. The image as a didactic tool, as a means of inspiring devotion through the visual and as a mnemonic aid, stood in a long tradition of theological formulations on the subject. In the treatise *De Adoracione Ymaginum* of the 1380s or early 1390s, and long attributed to the Cambridge theologian Walter Hilton, the author drew upon Gregory the Great and the eighth-century Byzantine theologian St John of Damascus as well as the thirteenth-century authorities St Thomas Aquinas and St Bonaventure.[19] Images were justified by the Incarnation, which marked a fundamental shift in the relationship between God and the material world. In the words of St John of Damascus:

Of old, God the incorporeal and formless was never depicted, but now that God has been seen in the flesh and has associated with human kind, I depict what I have seen of God. I do not venerate matter, I venerate the fashioner of matter, who became matter for my sake and accepted to dwell in matter and through matter worked my salvation . . .

This defence remained a commonplace down to the Reformation.[20]

St John of Damascus also stressed the power of seeing: 'the word appeals to hearing, the image appeals to sight; it conveys understanding . . . the image was devised to guide us to knowledge and to make manifest and open what is hidden, certainly for our profit and well-doing and salvation . . .'[21]

A distinction is made between two kinds of visual experience of a religious nature in *The Book of Margery Kempe*. The interiorized visions of sacred events were described variously as forming 'in her mind', in 'the sight of her soul' or with her 'spiritual eye'; through these the eponymous character has visions of the Passion and engages in dialogue with Christ or Our Lady. The second encounter sprang from her viewing of a physical object or experience with her 'bodily eye', which inspired a visualization of the spiritual signified.[22] This dichotomy was neither unique to Margery Kempe, nor new in her time.

The use of mental and material images is expounded pictorially in a French miniature of *c.* 1310 (**I**). The page is divided into four tableaux and depicts the pathway to achieving mystical unity with the Godhead. In the first a female religious kneels before her Dominican confessor, seeking absolution for her sins. The second vignette depicts her venerating with her 'bodily eye' an image of the Coronation of the Virgin placed on an altar; significantly, this is the only one of the quartet in which a speech scroll, representing a dialogue between the suppliant and the object of devotion, is absent. The more elevated stages of devotion are illustrated in the last two scenes. The almost prostrate nun meditates on the Eucharist, seeing in her 'mind's eye' Christ as the Man of Sorrows with the blood from his wounds dripping into the chalice on the altar. In the last 'scene' the nun has passed beyond the world of matter and achieves mystical union with the Trinity. Meditation with the aid of a devotional image, i.e. the Coronation, thus is shown as a step on the road to spiritual perfection, not an end in itself. An exchange takes place between the suppliant and the sacred through the latter's representation; the image is the material focus of prayer and supplication and in return the signified may bestow grace on the suppliant.[23] In this miniature the image is contemplated and not used as a teaching aid and thus is experienced sensually rather than intellectually.

The function of images as pictorial 'texts' for the instruction of the illiterate faithful was certainly a primary purpose (possibly the only purpose) of images in Christian worship when formulated. However, a shift away from their didactic function towards that of a more affective, personal piety is perhaps exemplified by the supplanting of the kinds of narrative Christological cycles seen in late eleventh- and twelfth-century parish churches like Kempley (Glos.) and the group in Sussex by single mural and carved images. The use of images as vehicles for intercession made them more problematic as they were more likely to be seen as idolatrous. If a saint was invoked via his or her image for a particular outcome, the image may have been seen as a channel of grace and may be venerated.

The unequivocal distinction between sign and signified was expounded by the author of *De Adoracione Ymaginum* and also Pecock: 'the likenes of a signe to his significat, (that is to seie [say], to the thing signified bi him,) wole helpe the signe forto signifie and forto make remembraunce the bettir upon the thing signified'.[24] This was a fundamental issue in the debate over images, as both the defenders and their Lollard and reformist opponents recognized. The former drew on Aquinas in stressing that *latria* (worship due to God), *hyperdulia* (reverence due to Christ and the Virgin as the Mother of God) and *dulia* (reverence due to certain individuals exercising lordship as God's representatives – prelates and secular rulers – and those such as the saints in whom God's grace was manifested) were very different from *idolatria* (improper worship of the sign or material object itself).[25] Thus Pecock stressed that 'it is leeful [lawful] . . . forto knele and preie and bere light and sette up candelis bifore an ymage, whilis these deedis ben not doon to the ymage but to God or to a Seint'.[26] Pecock went further than the other writers in his defence of the devotional importance of images. He believed that God and the saints might be better loved through their representations and the physical gestures of devotion (touching and kissing) addressed to them, which provided a means of tangible contact with the holy – a simulacrum of familial signs of affection.[27]

## YMAGIS/PICTURIS

To separate form from function in defining the devotional image is impossible because the dialectic between the two is so fundamental yet unstable.[28] The terms 'ymage' and sometimes 'pictour' were applied by Pecock, the author of *Dives and Pauper* and other writers to works in various media. The devotional image therefore was defined neither by material nor form, nor by subject and size. It might be a mural, a piece of clay, an altarpiece, or an artefact cast in metal – even a miniature in a Book of Hours or a woodcut. It could be found in the private as well as the public sphere and comprised items of jewellery and personal adornment as much as images in architectural space (**III, XII, XVI; 8, 13, 14, 41, 43, 157, 158, 160**).

As a consequence, the devotional image does not lend itself easily to taxonomy. The apologists for images, their Lollard opponents and the hostile tracts of the Reformation period focused principally on the three-dimensional carved ('graved') and polychromed image in 'stoon' and 'stok' or 'tre', although Pecock also included mural images and those painted on cloths.[29] The Elizabethan *Homilies* were unequivocal on the greater affective power of the sculpted and embellished image:

. . . men are not so ready to worship a picture on a wall or in a window, as an embossed and gilt image, set with pearl and stone. And a process of a story painted with the gestures and actions of many persons, and commonly the sum of the story written withal, hath another use in it than one dumb idol or image standing by itself.[30]

The testimony of these adversarial texts is confirmed by Eaton Bray's niches and corbels, and similar frames and supports can be found in churches the length and breadth of the country. The carved image was the norm in this context, albeit never exclusively so. In 1513 a Norfolk gentleman gave equal weight to painting when he left money to lights in Outwell church standing before the images 'upon piler or wall peynted'.[31] Nor was the distinction between the media hard and fast. Most, if not all, carved images were painted (or intended to be painted) to some degree, as were the tabernacles housing them; sometimes subsidiary imagery was also rendered in paint only (**161 (b)**, **164**). Mural images were both cheaper and quicker to execute. The shallowness of the two niches flanking the Eaton Bray chancel arch suggests that these enclosed mural paintings. The back of the north chapel niche has been roughly chipped away, perhaps to remove a mural image. A number of mural images dating from the thirteenth century still exist, including several patronal images (**43**).[32] Fingringhoe (Essex) preserves images in sculpture and painting (St Margaret and the Holy Trinity in freestone, murals of the Virgin and Child, the Man of Sorrows, St Michael and a lost St Christopher) (**X**). The monumental scale of the St Christophers at Horley (Oxon.) and Houghton Conquest (Beds.) – the latter nearly 5 metres high – is typical of representations of this saint, who therefore was more easily rendered on a wall than three-dimensionally, although carved images exist (**8**, **68**, **III**, **XI**). Both the Horley and Houghton Conquest representations are in their customary position by the north door. A bequest of a sheep to the light of St Christopher at Houghton Conquest in 1508/9 presumably relates to this mural.[33] The Horley image and the smaller representation of St Sitha on an adjacent pillar are important evidence for the location and accessibility of devotional imagery. Sometimes murals acted as surrogate sculpture. Early fourteenth-century paintings of the Virgin and Child and St Margaret at South Newington even stand on fictive corbels (**XII**).[34] The Elizabethan *Homilies* also referred to images in stained glass; in 1533 William Barnewell left 4*d* to 'our Lady light in the window' of Eversholt church (Beds.). That he was referring to a glazed image finds confirmation in a Kent testator, who bequeathed a taper to burn before the image of St Christopher in a glass window in Lyminge church in 1511; such references are not common.[35]

As Ringbom observed, there was nothing to prevent either a single figure in a historiated cycle or the narrative as a whole serving as a focus for devotion. The Shelfanger wall-painting of *c.* 1260–80 depicts an enthroned Virgin and Child flanked by diminutive figures of the Magi and the Shepherds (**43**). This works both as a narrative and as a single image. To a greater or lesser extent it could remain within a narrative generated by its representation and/or by the viewer; saints like Eligius and Erasmus were often defined visually in terms of their presence in a narrative (**75**, **76**).[36] The same might apply to altarpieces. The Virgin in the centre of the Sutton Valence (Kent) altarpiece no doubt represented the dedicatee of a particular altar, but it could also have functioned as a personal and collective devotional image (**10**).[37]

In the Middle Ages sight was the most highly rated of the senses, so the physical appearance of images, their surroundings and trappings was of great significance. The fourteenth-century theologian Thomas Bradwardine stressed that images, whether pictorial or in words, had to

*8. Houghton Conquest (Beds.), All Saints' church: St Christopher mural over nave north aisle door, fifteenth century*

impress themselves on the memory of the viewer/reader: 'For a thing entirely abstract, of the sort as God, an angel, infinite space, and such matters are, place an image as the painters make it.'[38] It has been argued that the limewood sculptures of early sixteenth-century South Germany, in their dynamic rendering of bodily form and capacity to express individuality of character and mood, contrast starkly with the static poses and formulaic treatment of faces of their mid-fifteenth-century predecessors. The result was 'a contradiction between the religious image and the most accomplished art that was very difficult to evade: the greater the skill, the greater the distraction from devotion'.[39] The loss of all wooden imagery from the same period makes it impossible to gauge whether the same applied in England, apart from observing that the limestone head of a prelate in Westminster Abbey (early sixteenth century) manifests a marked interest in physiognomy and individual character compared with the blandness of the late fourteenth-century alabaster St Peter from Flawford (Notts.) (**9**, **54**).[40] The Flawford figure is one of three statues from this church, the others being a Virgin and Child and another prelate. Three freestone mid-fourteenth-century heads of crowned female saints from Cobham (Kent) and an All Saints' image, also in alabaster, of *c.* 1400 in Boston Museum (USA) provide a useful group for the investigation of the materiality and visuality of English three-dimensional images (**XIX**; **124**).[41] The Boston and Flawford statues are the best preserved, although the latter have lost almost all traces of their original polychromy. One Cobham head retains extensive traces of its colouring and gilding. Originally all three formed part of standing images like those at Flawford. All were intended to be viewed from the front. Their plastic quality, therefore, is – or rather was – expressed by means of the shadows cast by their settings and the lights which illuminated them from below. The rich robes, mannered disposition of drapery on the Flawford and Boston figures and their elegance create an impression of magisterial otherworldliness, reinforced by their polychromy and gilding, which translated the work of their respective carvers and their humble materials into worthy simulacra of the saints. The transcendent power of painting was acknowledged by the Lollard opponents of images: 'The peyntour makith an ymage forgid with diverse colours til it seme in foolis iyen [fools' eyes] as a lyveli [living] creature. This is sett in the chirche in a solempne place. . . .'[42] The 'diverse colours' resulted in the regal, powdered and rouged visages of the three Cobham images. From their original positions at the east end of the chancel and (possibly) the end of the nave north aisle, they faced their audiences, both clerical and lay, and cast 'arcs of address', to use Michael Baxandall's term.[43] Their gaze might be directed above the heads of the assembled faithful and into the middle distance, but the careful delineation of the eyes permitted the individual the possibility of direct engagement with them. These images provided a visual focus for interiorized and externalized devotion and through their agency they held out both to the faithful assembled for the liturgy and to the individual the promise of salvation through their intercession. The *Salve regina* antiphon beseeches Our Lady to 'turne to vsward thy merciful eyen & schewe to us ihesu, ye blessid fruyt of thi wombe' (**XVI**).[44]

The Cobham saints were distant but attainable. The more pronounced smile on the lips of one of the Cobham heads makes comprehensible Thomas More's comment that some women he had observed adoring an image of the Virgin imagined that it smiled at them.[45] This might be an expression of inner radiance, achieved by membership of the company of heaven, yet it also signalled the saints' humanity and approachability to the venerator. The other heads (also those at Boston and Flawford) are more impassive. Their aloofness finds expression not merely through the regal symbol of the crown or by clerical authority, but by means of a certain *hauteur*, enhanced in the cases of Cobham and Flawford by their location at the high altar in the chancel.

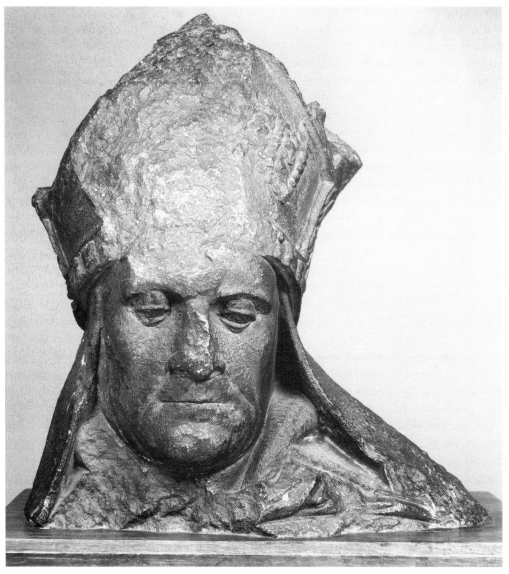

*9. Westminster Abbey Museum: limestone head of a prelate, early sixteenth century*

## IN A SOLEMPNE PLACE

The 'solempne place' at Eaton Bray was the public space of the parish church. Its images may be absent, but their mode and location of display are informative about their size and presentation; they could also engender different meanings according to their emplacement and design. For prayer and other acts of devotion an appropriate setting for the object of veneration was desirable, if not essential. This was partly a matter of decorum, partly one of convenience. The niches and brackets at Eaton Bray show that the images they supported and framed varied in scale. Most must have been around a metre in height and the smallest (on the south nave pillars) no more than 50cm. The pair occupying the niches flanking the chancel arch were of median height (approximately 80cm). Size seems to have been of less significance than location as a determinant of precedence. The image had to be both accessible and sufficiently distanced from the beholder to inspire respect as well as love for the prototype. All the Eaton Bray image supports and frames are raised and the images were set in a variety of positions: in the chancel, above or in proximity to altars, flanking the roodscreen on the nave side, and on the nave piers adjacent to the principal lay entrance to the church. Apart from the rood and Easter Sepulchre, the highest place of honour in St Mary's church was the north side of the high altar, where the patronal image was sited. Otherwise the hierarchy is less clearly defined. Thomas Ashwell left 2*d* to the five principal lights, which presumably included the Sepulchre and rood. Cuthbert Cutlat, Alys Cooke and John Collens all left sums to the lights of the Trinity and St Nicholas and to three unnamed lights, described as 'small' by Cuthbert Cutlat and Alys Cooke. Cutlat confuses the picture further by bequests of tapers to the lights of SS Thomas, Eligius, Erasmus and Sunday; Alys Cooke bequeathed a further 1*d* to each of the small lights.[46]

It is likely that the titular saints of the two nave altars at Eaton Bray took precedence over those set on the nave piers. In the Sarum rite, which was used at Eaton Bray, images at dedicated altars were censed. At Syon Abbey it was a stipulation that a taper was to be lit during the feast-day services 'of eche seynt [th]at hathe an autyr [altar]'.[47] The siting of an image in proximity to an altar enhanced the former's sanctity. At least three of the Eaton Bray images were grouped around the nave south altar (**II**). The image of the titular saint of an altar might also be placed directly on the altar itself and/or on the altar frontal or retable/altarpiece (**10, 112**).[48] A disposition approaching these was adopted in the Eaton Bray south chapel, with the central window light occupied by the image above the stone retable. This arrangement, by which the image overhangs the middle of the *mensa* and permits the titular saint to be associated with the altar, can be traced back to the thirteenth-century refurbishment of the altars at Saint-Denis Abbey in France and probably even earlier. It was known in Germany and England by the end of that century.[49] The parish church at Hartwell (Bucks.), a few miles from Eaton Bray, possessed an image of the Virgin 'standynge upon St John's ault[er]', which was the joint beneficiary of a bequest of a swarm of bees in 1532; even more explicit was John Baret's bequest of a new crown of gilt-metal or wood for the titular image in the 'housyng of ye rerdoos' of Our Lady's altar in St Mary's church, Bury St Edmunds (Suffolk).[50]

At Eaton Bray the three most elaborate frames or niches (tabernacles in medieval parlance) are those in the south and north chapels. In the Scriptures the tabernacle held the Ark of the Covenant and was used as a visual metaphor – 'In my Father's house are many mansions' – and the canopied niches presented the saints in their celestial dwelling-places.[51] Although not a prerequisite, tabernacles played a key role in the viewing of devotional images. The stone niches at Eaton Bray are part of the fabric and originally were painted and gilded. Most image-tabernacles, however, were wooden and also polychromed.[52] It was common practice to add new frames or replace existing ones around images. Between 1521 and 1537 five parishioners at Houghton Regis, near Eaton Bray, made bequests to the making, painting and gilding of a new tabernacle for the patronal image of All Saints.[53]

Today we might frame or reframe a picture to match it to a series or to the decor of our living space; this act inevitably alters our perception of that image. The French seventeenth-century painter Nicholas Poussin might have been echoing the words of a late medieval carver when pleading with a purchaser of one of his paintings that it required a frame 'so that when looking at it from all angles the eye is held by what is depicted, not distracted, its glance muddled by the

*10. Stone altarpiece of the Virgin from St Mary's church, Sutton Valence (Kent), mid-fourteenth century (London, Victoria & Albert Museum, inv. no. A58-1921)*

pell-mell intrusion of other neighbouring objects'.[54] The tabernacle enhances the space, and therefore the contents of that space which it encloses; it directs the viewer to the image and imparts a sense of reverence; it signifies the special nature of the representation.[55]

The design of the Eaton Bray tabernacles must have been settled when the nave walls were rebuilt in the fifteenth or early sixteenth centuries; presumably there was agreement among the parish authorities of the time that the images so treated were of particular significance. The greatest importance of all is accorded to the image formerly in the middle light of the Eaton Bray south chapel and is signified by the elaboration of its canopied niche. The image so enclosed was not liturgically the most important, but its canopied covering gave it particular prominence.

As well as the image deriving importance from its position, the 'solempne place' could be created by the presence of an image. Bedfordshire testators were aware that the space in front of an image was sanctified by it. In 1519 Richard Spayne of Luton desired burial in the great space before the image of Our Lady in St Nicholas's Chapel in his parish church.[56] Of course, space does not have to be internal, circumscribed by walls or screens. Images were set up on pedestals outdoors (**163**). A Dunstable testator requested his body to be buried before an image of the Virgin which stood in the churchyard.[57] Images were also located on the façades of houses and especially at street corners; a rare large-scale hagiographical survival is the monumental oak St Peter at Exeter (**11**).[58]

## ALLE PEPLE

Because the definition of a devotional image is dependent on its use, some discussion of its usership is also necessary. In his case-study of the role of religion in northern Spain forty years ago, William Christian argued that '. . . the work of historians is unnecessarily impoverished when they are unaware that their living contemporaries still do things similar to what they describe in past societies'.[59] In terms of outward forms, this observation is indeed of value. None the less, seeking to understand *how* people venerated images is more problematic when it comes to using contemporary models. Images did not function in a vacuum, but were framed by current ideologies and local power structures, whether clerical or lay (or both), by their environment and by the particular historical moment they occupied. John Rudde of Eaton Bray was not Everyman. The devotional image was multivalent and its reception by its venerator depended upon a whole range of cultural determinants affecting both the image (locality, display, appearance, embellishment) and the viewer (age, social status, gender, occupation, health, wealth or poverty, literacy or illiteracy, personal history). Not only were the early

11. Polychromed oak St Peter from the High Street, Exeter, c. 1500 (Royal Albert Memorial Museum, Exeter)

sixteenth-century villagers of Eaton Bray far removed geographically and temporally from Christian's Spanish counterparts, but they also inhabited a world which was very different from that of their twelfth-century predecessors in their own village.[60]

Both Pecock's text and the French manuscript illumination described above were produced for literate and elite audiences (in the latter's case, one which had taken religious vows). The author of *De Adoracione Ymaginum* divided society into the literate and illiterate in respect of image-use. For the former, images acted as 'commemorative tokens of the departed', i.e., the saints:

> The literate and the learned, and devout laymen who truly realise that images are nothing but wood and stone . . . are moved by no desire or reverence towards the wood itself, in as much as it is the material of the wood, or in as much as it is carefully painted. They think nothing of such things but they use images as it were for remembrance, and lying down in front of the images they forget them and send out prayers to God and his saints. . . . And if all the faithful were as strengthened and instructed by grace as these are, it would not be necessary to place images in churches.[61]

The *simplices laici* (simple laity), by contrast, although they did not err in so doing, were incapable of distinguishing between the signifier and the sign, between the material and the immaterial:

> . . . because although their mind is actively directed towards the images which they see, and not towards God – as simple people are wont to do when they see a beautiful image artfully depicted and preciously adorned – straightaway their mind is moved by carnal reverence to the adoration . . . of one image more rather than the other, and their intellect and devotion are wrapped up more in the outward appearance than spiritually, to God.[62]

In other words, the contemporary definition of an image as a 'commemorative token' depended on the audience, which was in turn defined by its attitude to and use of images. The argument presupposed a difference between the religion of the educated minority and that of the ignorant masses (*simplices et laici*). This was not a binary constructed on class and wealth, although often it must have meant the same thing. If the author of *De Adoracione*'s criterion were to be applied, Margery Kempe's illiteracy would consign her to the ranks of the 'populus', whereas by birth and marriage she belonged among the urban elite of King's Lynn. The distinction between *literatus* and *illiteratus* itself is problematic. Illiteracy transcended social strata, and there was no blanket definition of the word. There were degrees of illiteracy, ranging from those who could not read a word to those who were unable to read well or could only comprehend the vernacular. The label *illiterates* might also extend to those in holy orders who were ignorant of the central tenets of the faith.[63] The author of *Dives and Pauper* contrasted the use of images by the educated parish priest and his flock:

> PAUPER. Oft thou seeist that the preist in chirche hath his book aforn hym on the deske. He knelyth, he staryth, he lokyth on his book, he heldyth up hese hondys [his hands] for devocioun in caas he wepyth and makyth devowte preyerys. To qhom, wenyst thu [to whom, do you think], the prest doth al this wurshepe?
> DIVES. To God and nought to the book.

PAUPER. On the same maner shulde the lewyd man usyn [use] his book that is ymagerye and peynture and thynkyn that he wurshepyth nought his book, ymagerye and peynture but that he wurshepyth God abouyn [above] alle thyngge and seyntys in here [their] degree, and that al the wurshepe that he doth aforn the ymage he doth it nought to the ymage but to hym that the ymage representyth hym [to him that the image represents].[64]

It was, however, a fine point to get across in the parishes, as the author of *Dives and Pauper* saw, especially as the vernacular did not allow for a distinction between *latria* and *dulia*, in the way that it was defined in *De Adoracione Ymaginum*.[65] As the theologians were at pains to stress, when it came to lay devotion what was written did not enjoy primacy over what was seen. The ancient Gregorian dictum about images being bibles for the poor was a *topos* no longer exclusively applicable in the sixteenth century, if indeed it had ever been valid.[66] The existence of an image with its attributes presupposes knowledge by the viewer of the biography of the saintly person portrayed, knowledge which in the parishes would have been transmitted by the clergy by means of sermons and collects. Any of the denizens of Eaton Bray looking at the representation of St Christopher in their church would have been likely to have described a rather large man carrying a young child across a river, unless they were already familiar with the legend. Their devotions would have been facilitated by the image rather than its serving a primarily didactic function.[67]

The Church as well as its Lollard and, later, reformist opponents, was concerned that, during the act of veneration or supplication, the image and the saint represented might elide in the mind of the ordinary, illiterate parishioner. Though this was denied by Thomas More ('the simplest fool [interestingly categorized as female] will tell you that our Lady herself is in heaven', it was acknowledged by the less sanguine Polydore Vergil as well as by the authors of *De Adoracione Ymaginum* and *Dives and Pauper*.[68] While the infrequent use of the prefix 'image' before the names of the saints in Eaton Bray wills might be put down to scribal abbreviation, its absence also reflects the ambiguous nature of the relationship which might exist between image and prototype at parish level.[69]

The personal histories of the Eaton Bray parishioners were embedded in their community, from which they derived their identity, which itself was further shaped by their place in that society. Medieval individuals and groups can be classified in various ways: by wealth or occupation, marital status, family, gender, age, social affinity, etc. These are not watertight compartments; they formed, overlapped, dissolved and re-formed in different configurations over the centuries. As such, the application of binaries like popular/elite to a community like that of Eaton Bray is problematic.

The perceptions of individuals might have shaped their attitudes, but the former were also circumscribed by and therefore subordinate to the conventions and assumptions of the social unit(s), whether familial, occupational or whatever, to which the individuals belonged. Each of these groups might be constrained within its own *mentalités*, or, to use Stanley Fish's term, constitute an interpretive community.[70] John Rudde or Cuthbert Cutlat did not have to be exclusively a member of one interpretive community and their image-use might take on different meanings depending on the various communities to which they belonged. For example, a parishioner might view the patronal image in their parish church in much the same way as his or her neighbour, but if, like Alys Cooke and several other parishioners, they were also a member of a guild (the Dunstable fraternity of St John the Baptist), they might also enjoy a relationship with the titular saint of that guild which was exclusive to that body.

Correct and incorrect uses of images were the subject of theological debates, but John Rudde and his peer-group at Eaton Bray were not participants in these discussions. For them, like their Orthodox counterparts in the Balkans as recently as the last century, practice was of greater concern than doctrine or dogma. Religion was not so much 'a matter of the private, reflective conscience . . . [as] of collective beliefs and practices'.[71] How divergent was the religion as practised by Rudde and his ilk, not only from that described by Pecock and More, but also from that of other elements of the Eaton Bray community? In broad outline, late medieval Eaton Bray still conformed to the ancient tripartite classification of society into those who prayed, those who fought and those who laboured. Looked at in detail, these divisions become more varied and fluid. The advowson to the living had been held by Merton Priory since the twelfth century and the vicarage was instated before 1300. At the end of the fourteenth century the clerical establishment in the parish comprised two chaplains and a clerk as well as the vicar. The clerk was probably only in minor orders and the chaplains may have been associated with the manorial chapel of St Nicholas, which was already in existence in 1210 and was served by two chaplains.[72] Even within this one parish, the clergy were not homogeneous. The endowment of the non-stipendiary clergy is not known, but it cannot have come anywhere near the annual income of £12 16s 2d enjoyed by the vicar. Within the ranks of the beneficed clergy in the Bedford archdeaconry there was a vast gap in financial rewards between the richest and the poorest. The vicar of Eaton Bray was better provided for than his neighbours at Totternhoe (£10) and Whipsnade (£7 13s 4d), but poor in comparison with the £40 and more enjoyed by the incumbents of Blunham, Shillington and Luton.

Eaton Bray comprised a single manor estate, which in the first half of the thirteenth century was held by William de Cantelupe (who we may hypothesize played some part in the rebuilding of the church) and his heirs, until it passed by marriage at the end of the century into the hands of the Zouche family; they remained in possession until 1486. In this year, on the attainder of Lord Zouche after the battle of Bosworth, Lady Margaret Beaufort's *protégé* Sir Reynold Bray (**12**), was made steward, receiver and surveyor of the manor by her son Henry VII, together with adjoining Zouche manors in Houghton Regis and Totternhoe, plus Ledburn and Mentmore in Buckinghamshire. Less than a decade later Lord Zouche sold these lands to Bray at a price very favourable to the latter. Eaton formed the *caput* of an estate which eventually stretched from south Bedfordshire into Northamptonshire. Bray spent more than £1,800 between 1496 and 1497 and 1499 and 1500 on reconstructing or augmenting the ancient Cantelupe and Zouche residences at Eaton Bray. The work was on a scale commensurate with his new status and the extent of the building can be seen from the well-preserved moated site north of Eaton Bray church. On Reynold's death in 1509 the manor passed to his nephew Edmund Lord Bray (d. 1539) and afterwards to his son John (d. 1557). It is from its association with this family that 'Bray' was added to the village name, although this did not occur until later.[73]

Knowledge of the third category, those who laboured, is derived from wills and the 1539 Muster Roll. The latter lists sixty able-bodied men for Eaton Bray. Lord Bray and his servants comprised thirteen; the other forty-seven were all worth between £5 and £10 and included several families who are represented among the will-makers.[74] The surviving wills from before the beginning of what was to be the Reformation are for six men and three widows and date between 1515 and 1538. Prosopography reveals that this was a closely knit group, with numerous networks created through kinship, marriage, livelihood and friendship.[75] John Rudde and Cuthbert Cutlat had cash in hand to dispose of and property outside as well as within the parish. Widows Alys Cooke and Elizabeth Fox also possessed goods, property and money. They were

12. *Sir Reynold Bray in the* Magnificat *window, Great Malvern Priory (Worcs.), north transept, c. 1501–2*

the well-heeled members of the community, a status they shared with their executors and witnesses. The wills represent only the upper stratum and some of the more elderly of the villagers. This is thus a very small sample of the parish population and one from which the vast majority, including most women, the poor and the young, are excluded. Even within the 'labouring' category, therefore, there were variations in wealth and, no doubt, a range of voices. None the less, Rudde and Cutlat and their peers were still people of the nave; they inhabited a social and intellectual sphere remote from that of Bishop Pecock and Thomas More's cerebral scholarship. As such, they fell into the category defined variously by theologians as 'lewyd' (*Dives and Pauper*), *simplices* (*De Adoracione Ymaginum*), or 'unlettrid men and wommen' (Pecock).

The validity of an elite/popular dichotomy has exercised the minds of many scholars in recent years. Natalie Zemon Davis neatly encapsulated the consensus that the label 'popular religion' refers to 'religion as practised and experienced and not merely as defined and prescribed', adding the rider that this is the limit of scholarly agreement on this issue.[76] The problem remains, however, that historical dynamics are explained in terms of positive innovation and change by intellectual or political leaders; or, if that outcome or process is deemed to be reactionary or backward-looking, it is presented in terms of regression from an ideal. Peter Brown's trenchant critique of this vision in respect of Late Antiquity is equally valid for the later Middle Ages:

> . . . the basic weakness of the 'two-tiered' model is that it is rarely, if ever, concerned to explain religious change other than among the elite. The religion of 'the vulgar' is assumed to be uniform. It is timeless and faceless. It can cause changes by imposing its modes of thought on the elite; but in itself it does not change.[77]

Agency is denied to the masses by the assumption that they were incapable of formulating an interiorized spiritual response, either in the presence of, or without, images. In other words, the religion of the common folk was not reflective but reflexive.

Even within our small group of Eaton Bray will-makers, the blanket conventional testamentary phraseology and homogenized nature of devotional practices must not lead us to assume that every one was a committed and fervent believer. Not every parishioner would have been a paragon of godly virtue; like all communities, Eaton Bray would have encompassed within its boundaries the good, the bad and the ugly. Yet it is difficult to sustain an argument that the religion as practised by Rudde and his peers was in essence different from that of Reynold Bray and his family. The wills both of these villagers and of their overlords spoke the same discourse of conventional piety. With the exception of a small minority of dissidents (the Lollards), all classes subscribed to the same set of orthodox beliefs and practices, encompassing the liturgy, the sacraments and veneration of the saints.

No mention is made of Eaton Bray church and its devotional trappings in the wills of Reynold Bray and his wife Katherine, who were both buried in St George's Chapel, Windsor.[78] This cannot be read as indifference to Eaton Bray. As we have seen, his residence there was of prime importance and both he and Lady Katherine can be assumed to have spent time there. During his lifetime Reynold established a chantry in the manorial chapel to pray for his soul, and those of his wife, his parents and benefactors. Like Alys Cooke and a number of other villagers, Lord Edmund Bray and his wife Jane were members of the Dunstable fraternity of St John the Baptist.[79]

Lady Katherine's Book of Hours includes miniatures of the Crucifixion, Our Lady and St Anthony, which were all represented by images in the parish church (**13, 14**).[80] She also possessed devotional aids and adornments in the form of gold crucifixes and tablets (including one of the Trinity) and sets of rosary beads in gold and silver. The last occur in the wills of non-elite Bedfordshire folk and appear on the monumental brasses of the social equivalents of our Eaton Bray testators; several have been found in excavations. A gold crucifix contemporary with Lady Bray's time, found at Shenley Brook End, some miles north of Eaton Bray, and the Langdale rosary give some idea of the appearance of the devotional devices mentioned in her will (**18**, **16**). John Rudde is most unlikely to have been able to read or write and yet he was accustomed to using images. He may even have had devotional images at home, in base-metal or earthenware, perhaps even an alabaster St John's head, which occur occasionally in contemporary documents (**157**, **158**, **162**).[81] Some of the poorest parishioners may have possessed rosaries made up of wooden beads (**17**).

This all seems to bear out the official clerical view that, like the ritual of the Mass, the use of images in churches was socially inclusive. As Pecock expressed it: 'Also here with al into the open sight of ymagis in open chirchis alle peple (men and wommen and children) mowe come whanne evere thei wolen [they wish] in ech tyme of the day.' Pecock's 'alle peple' included those who studied as much as those who laboured with their hands, those who were ill and those who were in their dotage. He distinguished between literate and illiterate, but held that both could learn from images. For both groups 'the ise sight [eyesight] schewith and bringith into the ymaginacioun and into the mynde withynne in the heed [head] of a man myche mater and long mater sooner, and with lasse [less] labour and traveil and peine [travail and pain], than the heering of the eere dooth'.[82] Even those like Lady Bray who had the means to possess their own Books of Hours might be expected to make use of images in public spaces. Vernacular rubrics found in some early sixteenth-century printed primers refer to indulgences to be earned through prayers said before images.[83]

The author of *De Adoracione Ymaginum* also sought to reconcile the differences by maintaining that, although the experience of simple folk was focused on the corporeal, rather than on what the images represented, this was excusable because of their faith, humility and charity.[84]

The differences in matters spiritual between the Brays and the village community might be one of degree rather than substance, yet the degree was considerable. By rank and wealth the Brays occupied a social sphere far removed from that of even the wealthiest of the parishioners. Reynold's endowment of trentals for his soul to be sung by every mendicant house was in a different league from the three trentals to be sung in three years in Eaton Bray church for the soul of William Burre.[85] Whenever they visited their demesne here and worshipped in the parish church, their exclusivity would have been signalled by separate seating, most probably in the chancel. Katherine Bray's crucifixes, beads and gold tablets might have been aids to devotion, but they would have been superior in quality as well as materials to any possessed by the likes of Rudde and Cutlat. As such, they also served as fashion accessories and symbols of status. Socially inclusive as parish church images might have been in theory, the omission of those in Eaton Bray and all the churches endowed by Sir Reynold and Lady Bray is typical of their caste. For the latter the images in their local church were not the main focus for their piety, although we shall see that frequently the seigneurial class exercised the right to be buried in the place of honour in the chancel, sometimes before or in proximity to the patronal image. It was also in this space that the two female members of the family to be buried here were laid to rest (**19**, **20**).[86] Unlike the villagers, the Brays enjoyed private access to the sacred images which would have embellished the manorial chapel of St Nicholas, even if it perhaps lacked the proliferation of images in the chapel of their patroness Lady Margaret Beaufort, which included representations of her name-saint and St Mary Magdalen, St George, St Anne, St Peter and St Anthony.[87] More personal still were the miniatures in Katherine's Book of Hours, a manuscript of

13. *Virgin and Child in the* Bray Hours, *c. 1490 (Stonyhurst College Library, Lancs., MS 60, f. 42v)*

14. *St Anthony in the* Bray Hours, *c. 1490 (Stonyhurst College Library, Lancs., MS 60, f. 53v)*

15. *Alabaster image of St Anthony, c. 1500 (Glasgow, Burrell Collection, inv. no. 1/38)*

the highest quality and characteristic of the contemporary vogue among the English elite for Netherlandish *ars nova*. The pages include 'state of the art' devotional imagery. With the aid of the imitation pilgrim badges in the borders of one page, Lady Bray could undertake virtual pilgrimages to their cult sites (**129**). The Virgin and St John the Baptist are portrayed in half-length, bringing them closer to the edge of the picture-plane and therefore into closer proximity to the beholder, a pictorial device introduced in the Netherlands to facilitate a more intimate association with the sacred (**13**).[88] The images in this book could be contemplated exclusively by Katherine and were her constant companions; the miniature of St Anthony may even have borne different meanings to her than the representation of the same saint in Eaton Bray church did for the villagers (**14, 15**). The saint is depicted on the page as a portly figure, placed in a sylvan landscape and with his attribute of a pig grazing in the foreground. The picture is framed by exquisitely executed flowers in *trompe l'oeil* and the whole represents a comfortable image for a comfortably off consumer, one in which a fourth-century desert father has been metamorphosized into a well-fed late medieval religious in a verdant northern idiom. Like the other images, the saint has been assimilated into Katherine's personal environment. The accompanying Suffrage is couched in general terms and includes no special supplicatory prayers. Of course, the same image might operate on a number of different

16. *The Langdale rosary, gold engraved and enamelled, c. 1500 (London, Victoria & Albert Museum, inv. no.M 30-1934)*

17. *Wooden rosary beads, c. 1500 (Museum of London, inv. no. 5079)*

18. *Gold cross, c. 1470–1540, found at Shenley Brook End (Buckinghamshire County Museum, Aylesbury)*

levels, depending on the background and life-experience of the viewer and the circumstances in which it was viewed. For someone in clerical orders, St Anthony might provide a model of eremitical perfection. What motivated John Rudde, alone of the Eaton Bray testators, to endow St Anthony's light in his will is unrecorded. However, by the presence of his image in the parish church St Anthony was absorbed into the *locus* of Eaton Bray and could be viewed within the landscape of the parish. It was installed presumably because his particular powers were considered germane to the

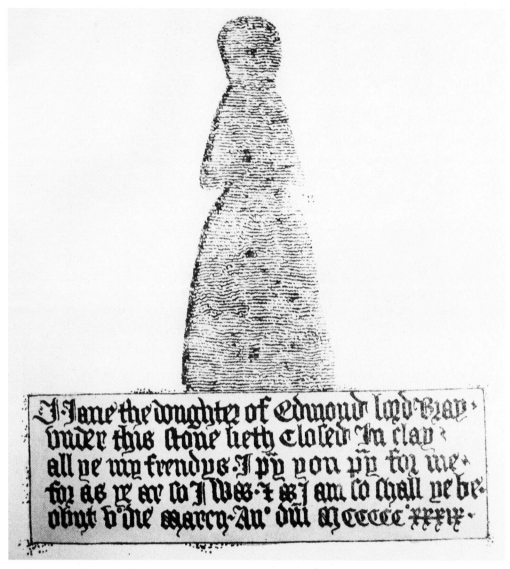

*19. Eaton Bray (Beds.), St Mary's church: brass of Lady Jane Bray (d. 1539); from Thomas Fisher,* Monumental Remains and Antiquities in Bedfordshire *(London, 1828), no. 33*

needs of the parishioners. Thus the saint's special efficacy in relation to the well-being of livestock is likely to have been of more quotidian relevance for them than for Lady Bray. Yet it was also in a public space and probably without any explicatory text; by this, and (judging by extant examples) by size, medium and elevation, it was more distanced from its venerators than its counterpart in the *Bray Hours*. The practice of investing in images of saints like Anthony (and also Eligius and Erasmus who could be called upon to assist with the everyday concerns of the ordinary parishioner) may be a manifestation of a site-specific agenda alongside those dictated by the Church hierarchy and codified in the liturgical Calendar. This might indicate a kind of religion which functioned at two levels within the same community: the Church Universal with its sacraments and liturgy, and practices

*20. Eaton Bray (Beds.), St Mary's church: brass of Jane (d. 1558), wife of Edmund Lord Bray, with her one son and ten daughters*

rooted in local custom, but the two should be seen as complementary rather than adversarial.[89] However, perhaps the initiative behind the introduction of SS Anthony, Eligius and Erasmus might just as plausibly have come from the vicar as from the likes of Rudde, Cutlat and Cooke.

Of one thing we can be sure: when Rudde, Cooke and Cutlat made their wills, the topography of Eaton Bray church was very different from what it had been when the church was rebuilt in the thirteenth century. No provision for images was made at that time in the form of brackets and niches. These were introduced in piecemeal fashion over the succeeding centuries. The earliest are the shallow ogee niches flanking the chancel arch, which date from the fourteenth century. The other frames and supports were added during the following two centuries as new images were commissioned. By Rudde, Cooke and Cutlat's day, Eaton Bray had probably attained its maximum devotional complement. How the kinds of images found here were used, the range of meanings they bore, who they represented and the circumstances of their production are examined in the following chapters.

CHAPTER THREE

# *ELEGENTISSIMA MARIOLA:* EARLY IMAGES OF OUR LADY

Eaton Bray is one of numerous medieval parish churches dedicated to the Virgin; indeed, Our Lady was by far the most common patronal saint. Bond gives a total of 2,335 and a sampling of several counties largely endorses his statistics (Table I, p. 68).[1] In Bedfordshire, Buckinghamshire, Devon and Kent she accounts for more than 25 per cent of patronal dedications. Of these, Bedfordshire is the highest, with 30.6 per cent. The Northamptonshire percentage is only slightly lower (22.7 per cent), followed by Leicestershire (18.2 per cent). In all of these counties, the Virgin occurs more frequently than any other dedication. The exception is the diocese of Carlisle, where she occurs only in 10.8 per cent of the dedications and is exceeded in quantity by two other saints, Cuthbert and Michael (both at 13.3 per cent). One difficulty with church dedications is establishing when they occurred. They have been prone to change and often the earliest record is in wills dating from the late fifteenth and early sixteenth centuries. Bond observed that in early Anglo-Saxon times Our Lady was not the most common dedication, but that from the end of the twelfth and through the thirteenth centuries more and more churches were consecrated to her. Recent research has also revealed that the twelfth century saw a considerable number of rededications of churches to the Virgin.[2] Was this burgeoning popularity of Our Lady marked – even fostered – by her visual representation at parish level?

As we have seen, the present structure of Eaton Bray church dates from the thirteenth century. An earlier structure was in existence by 1126–35.[3] Apart from wall-paintings, little is known of the internal imagery of twelfth-century parish churches. Halford (Warwicks.) is a rare case which has left traces of what must have been the dominant image of Christ on the cross (the rood), flanked by the Virgin and St John and placed between the chancel and the nave (**21**).[4] The rood itself probably resembled the unique but fragmentary wooden survival from South Cerney (Glos.) (**22**).[5] There is precious little English evidence of any other devotional imagery in the twelfth century; however, the images of Our Lady enthroned which occur in English manuscripts and *Kleinkunst* of the twelfth and early thirteenth centuries bear close iconographical affinities with the numerous Marian statues of the period which survive from various European countries, some with parish provenances. The indications are that such images began to appear in English parish churches from the twelfth century and during the following century became widespread; in the process their representations underwent transformations and took on new meanings. If much of what developed did so without leaving much evidence as to how and why

21. *Halford (Warwicks.), St Mary's church: the chancel arch with traces of the figure of St John the Evangelist (right) and a niche for the Virgin (left) from the rood group, early twelfth century*

it occurred, this expansion and shift in visual representation of the Virgin could not have taken place in a vacuum. This chapter will examine how the cult of Our Lady and her images developed in England and will explore the factors which determined the shift from a formal, hieratic image to a more empathetic representation.

The cult of the Virgin was a comparatively late development in Christian theology, only gaining momentum after the Council of Ephesus (431) proclaimed Mary as the Mother of God

22. Polychromed wooden head of Christ from a rood in All Saints' church, South Cerney (Glos.), c. 1130 (British Museum, Dept of Prehistory and Europe, reg. no. MLA 1994, 10-8, 1)

(*Theotokos*).[6] Churches with relics were founded in Constantinople and Rome and popular devotion increased over the next two centuries. In the latter part of the seventh century the feasts of the Purification, Assumption, Annunciation and Nativity of Christ were introduced into the calendars of the western church, including England. Saxon writers like Aldhelm and Bede contributed to the growing body of Marian texts and the first known representations in England occur in the seventh and eighth centuries, including St Cuthbert's coffin and the *Book of Kells*.[7] The post-Viking monastic reforms marked a dramatic expansion in the cult of Our Lady in England, measurable by the introduction from the continent of new feasts and offices, and also by the increased numbers of monasteries dedicated to her. All the Cistercian houses so rapidly established in the twelfth century were dedicated to Our Lady. Of other monasteries founded between 1066 and 1216, the proportion of those with the Virgin Mary as their titular saint rises from 34 per cent in 1066–1100, 38 per cent in 1101–50 to about 44 per cent in 1151–1216.[8] This interest triggered an outburst of Marian visual imagery in manuscript illumination, monumental and miniature sculpture and metalwork.

Marian statues were known in Carolingian times and spread throughout Europe in the succeeding centuries.[9] In England tenth- and eleventh-century stone representations of the Virgin and Child survive in a few locations, including Deerhurst (Glos.), Inglesham (Wilts.) and Langridge (Somerset) (**23**).[10] Inglesham and Langridge both have the Child shown seated on the Virgin's left knee, a pose resembling that of the famous tenth-century *Goldene Madonna* at Essen. The Deerhurst relief is placed on the east wall of the tower and is probably *in situ*. Neither Inglesham nor Langridge is in its original location. The former may have formed part of a frieze and the Langridge Virgin and Child now occupies a niche above the Norman chancel arch. In all three cases their precise function is unknown. More significant for our purposes are the references to images of the Virgin and Child at Canterbury in Archbishop Dunstan's time (d. 988) and Ely. The latter was commissioned by Abbot Aelfsige (996/9–1012/16 (or 1019)). Its description as an enthroned Virgin and Child, *mirabiliter fabrefactam* and made of gold and silver, evokes the Essen image.[11]

The twelfth century witnessed a proliferation of pictorial imagery in churches throughout northern Europe. The most costly and extensive schemes were of course in the great churches, the cathedrals and the monasteries of the Benedictines and Cluniacs. The ubiquity of representations of Christ, the Virgin and the saints and the events of Holy Scripture in the twelfth century should be connected in some way with the desire of the faithful in western

*23. Langridge (Som.), St Mary Magdalen's church: stone relief of the Virgin and Child, mid-eleventh century*

Christendom for direct contact with the sacred. It is in this period that the Church began to emphasize the Real Presence in the Eucharist and, at the end of the twelfth and early thirteenth centuries, introduced the elevation of the consecrated Host so that Christ's body could be seen by the congregation. This was a period when providing an embodiment of the sacred through pictorial representation became commonplace.[12] At the same time the visual arts responded to a desire for a greater sense of identity between the individual and the sacred, for exemplary models straddling earth and heaven; this need was met by increasing emphasis on the saints and above all on the Virgin.

The ultimate sources of inspiration for the burgeoning Marian devotion were monastic spiritual writings. In the words of Nigel Morgan: 'The Benedictines and the Cistercians of the eleventh and twelfth centuries were indeed the twin fountains from which most of the hymns and prayers to Mary flowed into the devotional life of the wider society of the church.'[13] By the end of the twelfth century images of Our Lady could be found all over western Europe and, except in England, numerous examples are extant.[14] St Anselm, Dominic of Evesham and William of Malmesbury were in the van of those writers who promoted the Virgin through theology and the compilation of miracle-texts associated with her; their works and the fact that the earliest known example of the depiction of her coronation occurred in sculpture at Reading Abbey in about 1125 together suggest that England was not slow to develop her cult in words and images.[15] There are only a handful of survivals of representations of the Virgin and Child in three-dimensional form from the twelfth century. The best preserved are the stone Virgin in York Minster and the column-figure of the Virgin from Minster-in-Sheppey (Kent) (**25, 24**), which have been dated to *c.* 1155 and *c.* 1170–80 respectively.[16] The York Virgin is a relief and the Sheppey figure is the earliest known standing Virgin in English post-Conquest sculpture, stemming from its function as a column-figure. The lack of weathering on either image points to an internal location; the York figure has a slab as backing, perhaps indicating that it formed a reredos to an altar. It has been suggested that the Sheppey image formed part of a screen in conjunction with the image of the co-patroness, St Sexburga; it is just as likely to have come from a porch. Together with the more plentiful evidence of manuscript illuminations and seals, both conform to the type identified as the *Maiestas* or *sedes sapientiae*. The sideways emplacement of the Child – awkwardly so on the Sheppey figure – echoes the disposition of the Anglo-Saxon reliefs, but is also found in the twelfth century on the continent. Although none of the monumental images has the frontal and symmetrical pose of the Virgin and Child found on the majority of the French, German and Swedish wooden images of the period (**26, 30**), it occurs in manuscripts and on a number of seals dating from the second quarter of the century, so we can assume that this type was represented in the carved versions.[17] Giraldus Cambrensis has left an account of an image of Our Lady in the monastery church of Monks Kirkby (Warwicks.). Between 1161 and 1181 some thieves attempted to rob this church:

> And finally they came to the image of the Blessed Virgin, carved in wood and adorned as is fitting with gold and silver, and, having stripped her of the gems and the gold, planning their flight while they prepared themselves to tear away and to steal the child sitting on his mother's lap, the mother who had previously had both arms stretched out towards the front, *as is usual* [author's emphasis], locked her right arm around the child and held him . . . indeed until today, as a token of such great miracle, the mother embraces her son with her locked arm.[18]

24. Stone column-figure of the Virgin and Child from Minster-in-Sheppey, St Mary and St Sexburga's church (Kent), c. 1170–80 (London, Victoria & Albert Museum, inv. no. A17-1973)

25. York Minster: stone relief of the enthroned Virgin and Child, c. 1155

A comparison to this lost Virgin is provided by the contemporary Viklau Madonna in Stockholm, probably the work of a German carver, or alternatively by the *Shaftesbury Psalter* (**26, 27**).[19]

The seigneurial aloofness of these images suggests that the growing perception of the Virgin as an emulative representation of the sacred, 'where the individual seeks from the supernatural invisible companionship with all that is most tender, most pure, most unambivalently good in his own imagination', took time to filter through from monastic texts into artistic expression.[20] One reason for this may have been the fact that many, probably the majority, of these images still functioned as reliquaries, as is evident from an example at Orcival (Puy-de-Dôme) and

*26. Painted and gilded wooden enthroned Virgin from Viklau church, Gotland, late twelfth century (National Museum of Antiquities, Stockholm)*

contemporary documents. Abbot Faritius (1100–15) had an image of the Virgin made for his monastic church at Abingdon (Berks.), which contained space for relics.[21] An ancient image of Our Lady at Thetford Priory was also found to have relics of the Passion and of several saints as well as fragments from the Virgin's girdle and her tomb.[22] By the 1160s it was no longer a *sine qua non* for Marian images to contain relics and most surviving twelfth-century French and German examples do not make provision for them; there are, however, a number of images as late as the fourteenth century with cavities presumably for relics (**28**).[23] This separation of image from image-reliquary may be plausibly connected with the appearance of the *Maiestas* statues beyond monasteries and cathedrals.

The provenance of many of the surviving French images cannot be established beyond doubt as far back as the twelfth century, but a considerable number are located today in parish churches and chapels.[24] Given the theological primacy enjoyed by the Virgin over other saints in twelfth-century England, it is not surprising to find that her pictorial representation appeared in parish churches during this century. On the chancel ceiling at Kempley (Glos.), of *c.* 1130–40, in the company of the impressive Christ in Majesty, are paintings of St Peter and the Virgin, the latter apparently holding a model of a church. This attribute might signify Our Lady as *mater ecclesiae*; alternatively (or additionally) she may be representing her role as patron saint of Kempley. The lost chancel wall-painting scheme at Barfreston in Kent of the 1170s affords evidence for the centrality of the Virgin by the late twelfth century. The subject-matter on the window-splays in the east wall included the Adoration of the Magi, which may well have acted as a supporting cast to a three-dimensional image of Our Lady placed on or over the high altar.[25] Such representations were not always carved. The Norman east end of St Mary's church at Great Canfield (Essex) is lit by two windows, with the blind recess between them filled by a niche now containing a mid-thirteenth-century mural of a *Maria lactans* (**29**). The disposition suggests that this image was a replacement for an earlier Virgin and Child. Great Canfield may therefore provide the first evidence for *sedes sapientiae* images in an English parish church.[26] Towards the end of the twelfth century St Mary's church in Bedford had a Marian image associated with an altar dedicated to her.[27]

Great Canfield also indicates where such images were placed in English parish churches. A common location for the *sedes sapientiae* in the Romanesque period in northern Europe was on

27. *Enthroned Virgin and Child with kneeling book owner in the* Shaftesbury Psalter, c.
*1130–60 (London, British Library, MS Lansdowne 383, f. 165v)*

*28. Reverse of a wooden enthroned Virgin and Child showing cavity for relics, German, c. 1230 (Schnütgen Museum, Cologne, inv. no. A15)*

or above the altar. The former is suggested by the survival of twelfth- and thirteenth-century Scandinavian Marian image-tabernacles with doors, which acted as a kind of retable in this position.[28] A mid-twelfth-century stucco enthroned Virgin is set in an arched recess embellished with more imagery in Erfurt Cathedral and analogous arrangements in the form of a freestone retable exist from Oberpleis and Carrières-Saint-Denis (**30**).[29] Such emplacements continued into later centuries. Erfurt and the French examples provide a possible context for the York Virgin and Child relief (**25**). An image of the Virgin finished during the abbacy of Abbot Robert of Gorham (1151–66) of St Albans and a replacement, carved by Walter of Colchester between 1214 and 1235, are both described as standing *supra* (on, above or behind) altars.[30] Thirteenth-century murals of the Virgin and Child on the western faces of several nave piers at St Albans were almost certainly above altars originally.[31] In twelfth-century Catalonia the Virgin and Child appears quite frequently in the mural decoration of the apse and on painted altar frontals; regrettably, none of the latter survives from this period in England.[32]

The association of images with altars was not fixed. Forsyth has produced evidence to show that sometimes the former were exhibited in spaces where they could be viewed by large numbers; they might also be carried in processions within and outside the church – this may have been the practice on feast-days of the Virgin at St Albans from at least the early thirteenth century (**31**).[33]

There are references to the provision of new Marian images in Henry III's residences, but the evidence for the occurrence of Virgin and Child images in parish churches remains sparse before the middle of the thirteenth century.[34] Obsolescence, plus the thorough-going destruction of English devotional images during the Reformation, has left only two examples, both coincidentally from Essex. One is the existing mural at Great Canfield (**29**) and the other is the polychromed oak group from Langham church, now in the Victoria & Albert Museum (**IV**); for the latter, comparisons with the Virgin and Child roof boss in the Lady Chapel of Worcester Cathedral suggest a likely date of *c.* 1220–30.[35] Of slightly later date is the battered and decapitated slender stone Virgin and Child built into a wall of St Bartholomew's Hospital in Bristol; however, its original location and function are unknown (**32**). Two early thirteenth-century chancels in Buckinghamshire retain evidence indicating the former presence of a Virgin and Child image. At Radnage an early thirteenth-century Annunciation is painted on the jambs of the central lancet of the chancel east wall, while above are angels censing Christ in Majesty; the church is dedicated to the Virgin and the scheme is reminiscent of the earlier Barfreston

29. *Great Canfield (Essex), St Mary's church: chancel east wall with* Maria lactans *mural, mid-thirteenth century*

decoration (**33**).[36] The stringcourse with projecting bracket above the altar in the chancel at Upper Winchendon looks as if it was designed to support an image (**34**). It would comfortably have held the Langham Virgin and its location is analogous to the Great Canfield mural.[37] A number of wooden groups in Norway are likely to have been either English imports or the work of English carvers working in Norway, which at the time enjoyed close political and cultural ties with England; an example is the Marian image from Hove (**35**).[38]

The Hove Virgin is exhibited in a contemporary tabernacle originally housing another Marian image, from Hopperstad church.[39] Framing was a sign of status. Both monumental sculpture and *Kleinkunst* indicate that the enclosing of the principal images within a niche or under a canopy

30. *Erfurt Cathedral (Germany): stucco enthroned Virgin and Child, with enclosing relief carvings, c. 1150*

31. *Stone relief showing the procession of an image of the Virgin and Child, from the church of S. Maria Beltrade, Milan, twelfth century (Museo d'Arte Antica del Castello Sforzense, Milan)*

was commonplace from at least the twelfth century and was of increasing importance. As was mentioned earlier, frames for Marian images exist from the twelfth century in Scandinavia. The column figures on the flanking doorways of the Royal Portal of Chartres Cathedral, *c.* 1145–50, are surmounted by multi-turreted constructions of the kind familiar from Ottonian manuscripts; this applies also to images of the Virgin in similar monumental contexts and on retables. The solitary monumental instance in English art is the column-figure from Minster-in-Sheppey (**24**); examples occur in early twelfth-century English ivories and in illuminations (**27, 44**).[40] Shortly after its creation Walter of Colchester's statue of Our Lady at St Albans was overhung by a *tegmine* or *caelatura*, evidently some kind of canopy or ceiling. In 1238 Henry III ordered an image of the Virgin and Child with a tabernacle to be made for Winchester Castle, and three years later another image of the Virgin and Child and its tabernacle in the chapel of St Peter ad Vincula in the Tower of London was to be repainted.[41] Some of the early Scandinavian Marian images are enclosed in tabernacles with wings painted with Christological and other narrative scenes, suggesting that they functioned both as devotional images and as altarpieces. A framing design which is integrated iconographically with the image survives at Llantwit Major church in South Glamorgan (**36**). The fine stone canopied recess re-set into the south aisle east wall has carvings of the Tree of Jesse, with Jesse reclining on the projecting base and heads of the kings enmeshed in the vine leaves. The mouldings and foliage details point to a date in the first half of the thirteenth century and the iconography of the niche suggests that it enclosed an image of the Virgin and Child, either a mural or a low relief. In the fifteenth century St Mary's Abbey in York possessed an image of the Virgin 'cum alto tabernaculo cum radice Jesse'.[42]

The extent to which non-cult representations of the Virgin functioned as devotional images, i.e. as foci for individual veneration by the laity, in parish churches before 1200 is uncertain. It has been claimed that a shift in sculptural focus from the grouping of saints and other celestial figures around the entrance to French churches to the interior was linked to a move from the public towards a more private sphere. Some scholars

*32. Bristol, St Bartholomew's Hospital: stone enthroned Virgin and Child, c. 1220–40*

perceive this as a fourteenth-century innovation, intimately connected with a changing perception of the role of the saints in which they adopted a more personalized, protective relationship with their suppliants.[43] However, Freedberg is surely right to see the beginning of the widespread use of images for meditation and private devotion as a thirteenth-century phenomenon.[44]

In this, devotion to the Virgin was pre-eminent. Thomas Aquinas acknowledged that, as the Mother of God, the Virgin should be accorded the level of veneration enjoyed by Christ (*hyperdulia*).[45] One indication of burgeoning affective devotion to the Virgin was the proliferation of compilations of miracle narratives. Such texts began to appear in the monastic sphere during the early twelfth century and emphasized her roles both as *mediatrix*, interceding for humanity, and as Queen of Heaven, whose grace is efficacious everywhere.[46] Initially confined to Latin, by the end of the twelfth century these collections were being translated into Anglo-Norman; in the following century versions appeared in French and Castilian, the most famous being Gautier de Coinci's verse *Miracles de Nostre Dame* (*c.* 1220). Inclusion of tales such as the apparition of Our Lady to a nobleman saying 150 *Aves* before her image would have encouraged the use of such

33. *Radnage (Bucks.), St Mary's church: chancel east wall with mural of the Annunciation and Christ in Majesty in the jambs of the central lancet, c. 1225–50*

*34. Upper Winchendon (Bucks.), St Mary Magdalen's church: chancel east end, early thirteenth century*

*35. Polychromed and gilded wooden enthroned Virgin and Child from Hove church, Norway, within a tabernacle from Hopperstad, c. 1225–50 (Bergen University Historical Museum, Norway, inv. no. Ma-27)*

*36. Llantwit Major (South Glamorgan, Wales), St Illtud's church: stone canopied niche carved with the Tree of Jesse, c. 1200–50*

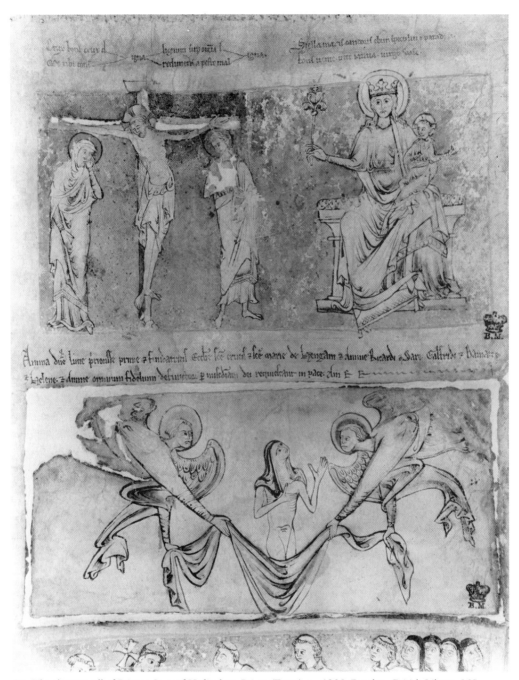

*37. The obituary roll of Prioress Lucy of Hedingham Priory (Essex), c. 1230 (London, British Library, MS Egerton 2849)*

prayers. Similarly, accounts of images of the Virgin which come to life in the hagiography of St Mary of Egypt and in the legend of Theophilus – stories known in England since the tenth century – must have enhanced the appeal of her pictorial representations. The audience for these compendia was predominantly lay.[47] The Virgin as intercessor is depicted in the obituary roll of Lucy, prioress of Hedingham (Essex), dating from *c.* 1230 (**37**); her soul is borne heavenwards in a napkin by two angels and her gaze is directed upwards to an image of the enthroned Virgin, to the left of which is the rood, flanked by the Virgin and St John.[48]

This shift was manifested iconographically in a gradual transformation of pictorial representations of the Virgin. A more empathetic, smiling image of mother and child replaced the stiff and remote hierarchism of the Romanesque *sedes sapientiae*. The majestic, frontal gaze of Romanesque images like the Viklau and *Shaftesbury Psalter* Madonnas (**26, 27**), already softening in the Langham Virgin, is absent in Matthew Paris's miniature. In this, the Virgin presses her cheek against the face of the Child and holds Him in a maternal embrace: the Child is a real infant and it is His mother with whom He engages, not the viewer (**38**). This type originated in Byzantine Mother of God *Eleoussa* images, which first appeared in the tenth century and enjoyed wide popularity from the twelfth century.[49] The lactating Virgin at Great Canfield also bears witness to the maternal nature of the Mother of God as well as emphasizing the Eucharist celebrated on the altar below (**29**).[50]

The humanization of the sacred was connected with the movement towards greater lay participation in terms of public and private devotion, which received its decisive *imprimatur* in the provisions of the Fourth Lateran Council of 1215.[51] The codification of existing liturgical practices in the cathedral and diocese of Salisbury, almost certainly the work of Richard Poore, later bishop but at that time dean of Salisbury (1197–1215), gave increasing liturgical prominence to the Virgin. During the twelfth century, some Benedictine monasteries began to celebrate a daily mass of the Virgin; and between 1214 and 1235 St Albans Abbey introduced this liturgical celebration. From the late twelfth century this devotion was accompanied by the construction of Lady Chapels in many of the greater churches.[52] A new kind of devotional text, the Joys of Mary, arranged as a series of liturgical offices and designed for private use, occurs in psalters and, from the second half of the thirteenth century, in books of hours; the latter proliferated in the following centuries.[53] Non-liturgical devotional works such as the late thirteenth-century *Meditationes Vitae Christi*, erroneously attributed to St Bonaventure but in fact the product of a Franciscan milieu in Tuscany and no doubt disseminated by the friars, also fostered this new kind of interiorized spirituality beyond those in holy orders who could read Latin.

The Hours of the Virgin might be read at home or in the church. In the *Shaftesbury Psalter* a nun or high-born lady connected with Shaftesbury Abbey prays to the Virgin without a book (**27**).[54] The growth of literacy among the upper echelons of lay society during the second half of the thirteenth century is illustrated by representations of female lay manuscript owners kneeling before the enthroned Virgin and Child and holding books.[55] In the *Lambeth Apocalypse* the owner contemplates a large image of the Virgin and Child, visualizing in her 'mind's eye' the devotional text she is reading (**39**). For the more exalted echelons of lay society, who could afford luxury items like illuminated books, such images were not just literally to hand on the manuscript pages but also accessible in their private chapels and oratories. The chapel of Little Wenham Hall (Suff.) retains a pair of brackets for monumental images on either side of the east window (**40**). Almost certainly the large numbers of exquisite ivory images of the Virgin and Child which survive from between *c.* 1250 and *c.* 1350 began life as prized objects of personal devotion in a domestic

38. *Matthew Paris kneeling before the enthroned Virgin and Child, c. 1250–9 (London, British Library, MS Royal 14. C. VII, f. 6)*

*39. The book owner kneeling before the enthroned Virgin and Child, from the* Lambeth Apocalypse,
*c. 1260–7 (London, Lambeth Palace Library, MS 209, f. 48)*

*40. Little Wenham Hall (Suff.): interior of chapel, c. 1285*

context. The majority are considered to be French and some may well have been imported into England; a number have been claimed to be the work of English craftsmen (**41**). In 1251–3 Queen Eleanor, wife of Henry III, purchased 3½lb of ivory 'ad faciendos imagines'; the carving of course might have been done by a peripatetic Parisian carver rather than by an Englishman, but the text indicates that ivory carving was carried out here by the middle of the thirteenth century.[56]

What impact did this shift towards a more affective, personalized piety have at parish level? For the tillers of the soil, the artisans and their families, the parish church was the main, if not the sole, arena in which the visual could offer a route to the transcendent.[57] The ecclesiastical authorities saw the new devotional emphasis on the Virgin as universal in its application. By the middle of the thirteenth century it was established practice, in non-monastic as well as monastic churches, for the office of Our Lady to be recited daily and the *Ave Maria* and *Salve Regina* antiphons were in use by the laity.[58] Archbishop Pecham's famous *Ignorantia Sacerdotum* of 1281 included the *Ave Maria* with the Creed and *Pater noster* and other central tenets of Christian faith and conduct which were to be expounded orally by the clergy to the laity four times a year in the parishes. Even for the illiterate and those ignorant of Latin, such prayers were easy to memorize and provided a structure for private devotion before images of Our Lady.[59] The legend of Theophilus and other tales of miraculous Marian images were portrayed from the thirteenth century in parish churches, suggesting that their communities were aware of the potential power of images already familiar to the elite from their chapels and books (**42**).[60] By the early thirteenth

*41. Ivory Virgin and Child, English (?), c. 1300 (The Metropolitan Museum of Art, The Cloisters Collection, New York, inv. no. 1979.402)*

*42. Chalfont St Giles (Bucks.), St Giles's church: mural of Theophilus and the image of the Virgin, early fourteenth century (watercolour copy by E.W. Tristram)*

century images of the Virgin were endowed with a range of functions, both individual and collective. As a young man St Edmund Rich (d. 1240) placed a ring engraved with *Ave Maria* on an image of Our Lady in an Oxford church as a sign of his symbolic marriage to the Virgin (through his vow of celibacy), a gesture echoed in one of De Coinci's compilations.[61] It was also becoming common for lights to be given and maintained by parishioners before Marian images in parish churches. A fraternity in honour of the Virgin was founded at Tilney (Norf.) in 1235–6, which supplied a candle to burn before the image. At Kirby in Essex a formal structure of support for images was in existence by 1251, with a *custos* and a group of parishioners who were obliged to contribute to the maintenance of each of the lights of the Virgin, St Peter and St Michael. This was not the case everywhere; at Pelham Arsa and Pelham Furneaux (Herts.) the provision and maintenance of lights was voluntary: 'totum votivum et nichil certum'.[62]

The imposition of responsibility for the maintenance of the church fabric and ornaments (including lights) was a feature of the thirteenth century and was established as much by case law in the form of local agreements as by the likes of the 1287 synodal statutes of Bishop Peter Quinel of Exeter, which unequivocally laid down that parishioners had to contribute to church repairs. In particular, Quinel's statutes demanded that the ornaments of each church in the diocese must include 'ymago beate virginis et sancti loci eiusdem'.[63]

Such edicts indicate the growing presence and significance of images in parish churches. They were not confined to the Virgin, as we shall see in due course, but they make clear that every church was obliged to have and maintain a Marian image, either in its own right or as the patron saint. If the argument advanced above holds water, then already by the early thirteenth century images of Our Lady were common in parish churches and by the 1240s were becoming *de rigueur*. No longer was it customary for the image to be placed on, above or behind the altar, but at the side of it – to the north if it was the patronal image, to the south if she was not the titular saint of the church. This is not made explicit in the episcopal documents of the period, but the arrangement was functioning in 1240 at St Peter ad Vincula in the Tower of London, where new images of the patronal saint and of the Virgin were to be made and set up respectively on the north and south sides of the high altar by order of Henry III.[64] This relocation was dictated primarily by the new emphasis on the patronal image, as will be discussed in the next chapter; the new image supports in the form of elevated corbels and brackets (and later niches) facilitated access to the image for private devotion (**46**, **57**, **58**) and permitted images of larger size (often standing) than the Romanesque *sedes sapientiae* (**54**).[65]

Dating from *c.* 1260–80 is the first surviving *in situ* image from this period, the mural of the enthroned Virgin and Child painted on the chancel east wall to the south of the altar at Shelfanger in Norfolk (**43**).[66] The group is accompanied by diminutive figures of the Adoration of the Magi and of the Shepherds. The gifts of the Magi were considered to have eucharistic connotations and linked the Mass with the Incarnation, so the location of this mural adjacent to the high altar was especially significant. In common with some twelfth-century representations (**44**), the Shelfanger mural has a kneeling king offering a ring, symbolizing the marriage of Christ and Holy Church; by depicting the Virgin as a *Maria lactans*, the Shelfanger painting underscores further the eucharistic message. The presence of the Magi might also have had an exemplary function, encouraging the parishioners to make mimetic offerings to the image; together with the Shepherds they demonstrated the universality of the Virgin's appeal.[67] The church of St James at Bramley in Hampshire preserves the new arrangement, also in the medium of wall-painting and of about the same date as Shelfanger. There the Virgin and Child image is located on the chancel east wall elevated above and to the south of the altar, with primacy of place to the north side ceded to the patronal image.[68]

The written and visual evidence indicates therefore that the new arrangement of high altar images was beginning in the first half of the thirteenth century, but with episcopal encouragement, gathered pace as the century progressed. The second half of the thirteenth century emerges as a critical period in the history of the parochial devotional image, one in which not only the Virgin but also iconic

*43. Shelfanger (Norf.), All Saints' church: mural of enthroned Virgin and Child with the Adoration of the Magi, c. 1260–80*

representations of other saints began to proliferate. Moreover, an important consequence of the growing Marian-focused affective devotion was the multiplication of her images beyond the chancel. By 1249–52 Willesden (Middlesex) and Thorpe (Essex) had each acquired two images of the Virgin; the former were described as 'sculpte'. Aldbury (Herts.) had two images of the Virgin, one 'cum tabernaculo' in the chancel and another in the nave north aisle.[69]

The shift towards more empathetic imagery, stressing the Virgin's role as *mediatrix*, was pan-European. Nevertheless, there are signs that Marian devotion in England was both extensive and, in certain respects, distinctive. The erection of Lady Chapels is one manifestation and the musical output of Marian antiphons was without parallel on the continent.[70] During the thirteenth and fourteenth centuries, in both England and northern Europe, there was a multiplication of images of Our Lady; throughout the northern hemisphere, there seems to have been little short of a stampede to acquire the latest models of the Virgin. This phenomenon, and the introduction and diffusion of new iconographical types, will be the subject of Chapter Six.

*44. The Journey and Adoration of the Magi in the* Winchester Psalter, c. *1150 (London, British Library, MS Cotton Nero C.IV, f. 12r)*

CHAPTER FOUR

# *YMAGO SANCTI LOCI:* THE PATRONAL IMAGE

The last chapter traced the growing presence of images of the Virgin in parish churches. Our Lady was the most popular titular saint, but she was far from alone. This chapter will examine the place of the patronal image in the English parish church, looking at questions of choice, meaning and status. The point of departure is a village church in the archdeaconry of Buckingham.[1]

## PETER DE WINTONIA, ST FIRMIN AND NORTH CRAWLEY

About 750 years ago the decision was made to undertake a wholesale rebuilding of North Crawley church on a handsome scale. Below the exterior of the chancel east window runs a Latin inscription: PETRUS CANCELLUM TIBI DAT FIRMINE NOVELLUM UT CUM LAUDERIS DEO PETRI MEMORERIS ('Peter gives you, O Firmin, a new chancel, so that, when you praise God, you may remember Peter').

Peter was Peter de Wintonia, rector between 1249 and 1289. As well as the builder of the chancel, he was probably the prime mover behind the church's entire reconstruction. He was an important royal clerk and his involvement with Henry III's rebuilding of Westminster Abbey accounts for royal patronage towards the church (oaks from the royal forest of Salcey were granted to Wintonia in 1253 and 1256) and its fenestral indebtedness to the Abbey (**45**).[2] Inside the chancel provision was made for the physical presence of St Firmin by the installation of brackets to support his image and that of the Virgin on either side of the high altar (**46**).

Why was North Crawley dedicated to St Firmin (**47**)? What was the relationship between the rector and the parish and their patronal saint? St Firmin was a fourth-century bishop of Amiens and was a very unusual dedication for an English parish church; the only other occurrence is Thurlby (Lincs.).[3] North Crawley's dedication was already ancient when Peter and the parishioners came to rebuild their church. The Domesday survey recorded that half a virgate of land was held of St Firmin's monastery here; the parish church took over the titular saint from this establishment.[4]

A dedication which can be traced back so far is unusual. Since the acceptance of the Christian religion in the fourth century, churches had been consecrated to particular saints. Initially the dedication was often determined by the relics enshrined in the high altar, but with the growth of parish churches in the eleventh and twelfth centuries, this was no longer feasible.[5]

**Table I (p. 68)** sets out the names and frequency of the most common titular saints of parish churches and parochial chapels in the archdeaconries of Buckingham, Bedford and Northampton and in counties drawn from the West Country, the north-west and the south-east. As far as possible they represent the dedications known in the later Middle Ages.

*45. North Crawley (Bucks.), St Firmin's church: chancel exterior, c. 1253–60*

A rationale for this selection is that it includes recent research, which has refined the pioneering work of Frances Arnold-Forster and Francis Bond through access to a greater body of documentary evidence.[6] Bond showed that, in England as a whole, after Our Lady, All Saints was the most popular dedication, with 1,255 instances, compared with 2,335 for the Virgin. Then comes St Peter (1,140); other titular saints trail a long way behind, with St Michael leading the field with 687.[7] Female saints other than Our Lady were very much in the minority. While the figures largely endorse Bond's totals, **Table I (p. 68)** shows that they conceal distinctive regional patterns. This is evident not only in the case of Our Lady, but with other dedications too. In the diocese of Carlisle only 2.4 per cent of churches were dedicated to All Saints. The Devon and Kent figures are more substantial but still quite low: 8.3 per cent and 8.5 per cent respectively,

*46. North Crawley (Bucks.), St Firmin's church: chancel east end interior, c. 1253–60*

placing All Saints third in the list. By contrast, in the archdeaconries of Bedford and Northampton this dedication was second only to the Virgin: 21.7 per cent (Beds.), 17 per cent (Northants.). It was also so in the Buckingham archdeaconry, but there it accounted for only 10.5 per cent of the total. Orme has observed that in Devon, All Saints was a common dedication in small or sparsely populated parishes.[8] This is not true of Buckinghamshire, where there are rural churches which have this dedication, but also some populous places, including High Wycombe and Great Marlow. It has been argued in Kent that All Saints is indicative of a late medieval foundation date for the church, i.e., from the late Saxon period at the earliest.[9]

Plotting patronal dedications is one thing, explaining them another. The histories of most individual dedications are too deeply interred and obscure to be recoverable. A further problem is that many church dedications are unrecorded before the thirteenth century. In Devon, for example, only eighteen monastic and parochial dedications are securely documented by 1086.[10] Indeed, the vast majority of patronal saints are known only from wills dating from the fifteenth and sixteenth centuries. It is by no means certain that the same dedication was retained throughout the Middle Ages and there have also been changes since the Reformation.[11]

Of this sample only Kent and the far West Country have been subject to detailed analysis. Alan Everitt has identified five factors which influenced the choice of patronal saints: the foundation date of the church, monastic or royal possession of churches, the evolution of cults, links with Anglo-Saxon minster

47. *Amiens Cathedral (France) west portal: stone statue of St Firmin, c. 1230–40*

churches and geography.[12] Kentish dedications are given a distinctive flavour by the number of saints and cults associated with the establishment of Christianity in the seventh century. The sea-girt nature of the county is also reflected in the popularity of St Nicholas, particularly favoured by mariners as a patronal saint. One-third of the churches dedicated to him were in places served by tidal water and another eight were within 3 miles of the sea (**Maps 8, 9, p. 281**).

That some Saxon and early Norman parish churches had patronal saints is demonstrated by a few extant dedicatory inscriptions, sometimes prefixed by Christ's name.[13] Although these inscriptions are too few to furnish conclusive proof, they are one of several indications that the eleventh and twelfth centuries were of considerable importance in the history of church dedications. As we saw in the last chapter, this period saw the Virgin eclipse all other dedications for monasteries; even excluding the Marian-focused Cistercians, the years between 1086 and 1216 witnessed no fewer than 235 dedications to Our Lady in religious houses, followed by a mere 47 for SS Peter and Paul.[14] The Norman Conquest and changing ethnic settlement also impacted on titular saints in some areas. In the Carlisle diocese the continuing popularity in post-Conquest times of St Cuthbert bore witness to the new regime's respect for and appropriation of

TABLE I: MEDIEVAL PARISH CHURCH PATRONAL SAINTS

| | Beds. Archd. | Bucks Archd. | Northants Archd. | Carlisle Dioc | Devon | Kent |
|---|---|---|---|---|---|---|
| BVM | 37 | 54 | 63 | 8 | 57 | 109 |
| BVM joint | 1 | – | 1 | 1 | 22 | 6 |
| All Saints | 27 | 20 | 48 | 2 | 32 | 38 |
| Trinity | – | 6 | 6 | 3 | 7 | 3 |
| Andrew | 3 | 3 | 21 | 7 | 28 | 6 |
| Cuthbert | 1 | – | – | 11 | 2 | – |
| Dunstan | 1 | – | – | – | – | 5 |
| George | 2 | – | 2 | – | 16 | 7 |
| Giles | 2 | 5 | 3 | – | 5 | 3 |
| Helena | 1 | – | 6 | – | 2 | 1 |
| James | 1 | 9 | 4 | 2 | 7 | 9 |
| John the Baptist | 4 | 6 | 20 | 2 | 14 | 21 |
| Lawrence | 2 | 8 | 6 | 3 | 5 | 14 |
| Leonard | 2 | 5 | 6 | – | 3 | 4 |
| Mary Magdalen | 2 | 9 | 2 | – | 3 | 10 |
| Michael | 5 | 13 | 7 | 11 | 32 | 16 |
| Nicholas | 7 | 13 | 11 | – | 4 | 30 |
| Peter | 11 | 11 | 18 | 3 | 23 | 20 |
| Peter & Paul | 4 | 8 | 22 | – | 15 | 22 |
| Petroc | – | – | – | – | 14 | – |

NB Monasteries where the parishioners had rights of worship are included. Some single dedications are excluded, notably in the Devon list with twenty-four other saints each with a single dedication.

Sources:

*Bedfordshire*: wills (see printed and MS sources under Bedfordshire in the Bibliography).

*Buckinghamshire*: wills (see printed and MS sources under Buckinghamshire in the Bibliography).

*Northamptonshire*: R.M. Serjeantson and H. Isham Longden, 'The Parish Churches and Religious Houses of Northamptonshire: Their Dedications, Altars, Images and Lights', *Archaeological Journal*, 70 (1913), 217–452.

*Carlisle Diocese*: T.H.B. Graham and W.G. Collingwood, 'Patron Saints of the Diocese of Carlisle', *Transactions of the Cumberland and Westmorland Antiquarian and Archaeological Society*, new series, 25 (1925), 1–27.

*Devon*: N. Orme, *English Church Dedications with a Survey of Cornwall and Devon*, Exeter, 1996, p. 31, Table 5.

*Kent*: L.L. Duncan, 'Ecclesiological Notes respecting the Deanery of Shoreham, Kent', *Archaeologia Cantiana*, 23 (1898), 134–49; *idem*, 'West Kent'; *idem* and Hussey (East Kent/West Kent). The figures differ in a number of cases from those in A. Everitt, *Continuity and Colonization. The Evolution of Kentish Settlement*, Leicester, 1986, pp. 228–9, Table 11, as he included monasteries, hospitals, chantries and chapels.

the most revered saint of the north.[15] Conversely, in Cornwall the local Celtic holy figures sometimes had to share space with Latin saints. In north Cornwall the increasing Anglicization of the countryside was a process which had already begun before 1066 and may explain the relative lack of Celtic titular saints. Further west indigenous saints were either given a new name which approximated to that of a Latin personage or, less commonly, were replaced by an internationally revered figure. These examples should not be over-stated. For the most part the long-hallowed local venerations continued in place and an accommodation seems to have been reached between the Church universal and the Church in Cornwall; only twelve instances have been noted where the Celtic patronal saint was given a companion and some of these did not occur until well into the fifteenth century.[16]

The archdeaconries of Buckingham and Bedford did not enjoy such a long and distinctive history of Christianity as the far west, the north-west and Kent. It is hard to plot any local pattern either here or in the Midland county of Northamptonshire. Clerical planning has been discerned in the distinctive pattern of church dedications in the Nansa valley of northern Spain, in order that groups of settlements did not share the same patronal feast-day.[17] The dominance and distribution of Our Lady and All Saints show that no such programme is detectable in medieval Bedfordshire (**Map 3, p. 278**). Apart from the Virgin and All Saints, only twenty-five saints were called upon to act as patrons, none of them more recent than Dunstan and Swithun; a similar figure (twenty-six) applies to Buckinghamshire. Generally, *pays*, settlement and land ownership patterns were too diverse and random for any rationale to be identified. The Augustinian priory of Dunstable possessed fourteen churches, mainly in Bedfordshire, but only two replicated its titular saints Peter and Paul, probably because the churches in question were in existence before Dunstable was established. The hilltop locations of Billington and Millbrook might account for the dedication to St Michael. The dedications of Astwick and Blunham to SS Guthlac and Edmund respectively represent the gravitational pull exerted by south Lincolnshire and East Anglia on churches on the eastern edge of the county. Blunham's dedication must have come about through the holding of the manor by the abbey of Bury St Edmunds from at least 1086. Thorney Abbey (Cambs.) was in possession of the manor and advowson of Bolnhurst and its dedication to St Dunstan is likely to be connected with the fact that this saint was in the van of the tenth-century monastic reforms, when this house was founded. The dedication of Sandy to St Swithun, Dunstan's co-reformer, also points to a late Saxon foundation. The seven churches dedicated to St Nicholas can only date from the late eleventh or twelfth centuries, after his relics had been taken to Bari and he became popular in the west.[18]

To what extent late Saxon and Norman interest in parochial dedications is connected with the unmatched investment in parish church building in England, which took place in the period *c.* 1050–1150, is unclear. The church-building boom has been seen as a consequence of the emergence of coherent local communities during the tenth and early eleventh centuries. Hitherto, minster churches had served the devotional needs of a locality; now a sense of place and of community, a desire to worship with neighbours and kin, becomes manifest in the new focus on the parish church.[19]

If the picture before 1200 remains obscure, the extensive episcopal campaign in the middle of the thirteenth century to dedicate churches, cathedrals and monasteries as well as parish churches is well documented. Many churches remained undedicated in the twelfth and thirteenth centuries, and a legatine council held in London in 1237 decreed that all such buildings had to be hallowed within two years.[20] This edict seems to have marked a point in a campaign which

*48. Church Hanborough (Oxon.), St Peter's church: tympanum of St Peter, early twelfth century*

was already up and running, rather than its beginning. Already in 1231–2 the bishop of Exeter had issued an indulgence associated with the dedication of St Mary Arches in Exeter. The Council of London spurred Bishop Robert Grosseteste into action: in 1238–40 he is chronicled as dedicating numerous churches in his Lincoln diocese.[21] One of these may have been Bradwell, not far from North Crawley; its thirteenth-century chancel arch refers to the day of its dedication to St Lawrence and associated indulgences. The wording (and date) of Peter de Wintonia's patronal inscription perhaps suggests that his construction of the new North Crawley chancel was also connected with this programme.

The absence of a formal dedication did not mean that a church lacked a patronal saint. By the twelfth century patronal saints were being invoked as protectors of Italian cities, usually those where the principal relics were held.[22] Sometimes a carved representation of that saint might be placed on the exterior of their church, as at S. Zeno in Verona. From at least the second quarter of the century in northern Europe titular images appeared on the tympanum or trumeau of the principal entrance.[23] Romanesque tympana with the image of the patronal saint occur in England at Fownhope, Herefordshire (Virgin and Child), Fordington, Dorset (St George) and Church Hanborough, Oxfordshire (St Peter) (**48**). Titular imagery could feature more prominently on major churches, such as the trumeau Virgin from St Mary's Abbey, York, of *c.* 1160–70. As was observed in the last chapter, a porch is a possible location for the column-figure(s) from Minster-in-Sheppey (**24**). Towers were used to proclaim the dedication until the end of the Middle Ages (**49**). Not all of these may have represented the patronal saint at the time of their creation, for quite a number of tympana depict a saint other than the titular. An example is St Michael on the tympanum of SS Peter and Paul's church at Dinton (Bucks.). The possibility has also to be entertained that an external Romanesque carved figure might not be evidence for the longevity of a titular saint, but instead could have furnished a convenient, ready-made identity when it became necessary to dedicate the church.

External location might signal identity, but does it indicate that the patronal saint was central to the spiritual and social life of the parish? The key development was the appearance of the image *inside* the church. Apart from the late tenth-century relic-statues of patronal saints in the Auvergne, there is little or no record of titular images as objects of internal significance before the twelfth century.[24] In Catalonia the patronal saint is the central focus on one of the seven earliest painted altar frontals, dating from the first half

*49. Holme-on-Spalding-Moor (Yorks., East Riding), All Saints' church: image of All Saints on the west tower, fifteenth century*

of the twelfth century (Durro). An attached stone statue of St Martin is placed on the left side of the apse entrance in the church of St Martin at Fuentidueña, near Segovia; this dates from *c.* 1175–1200.[25] The inclusion of the patronal saint on frontals or *antependia* was not confined to northern Spain in the twelfth century: St Walpurgis is depicted to the left of Christ in Majesty on the frontal of *c.* 1170–80 from the church dedicated to her at Soest, Westphalia.[26] The titular saint sometimes appears on choir wall-paintings in Romanesque churches in France, but is overshadowed by Christological narratives.[27]

No comparable English furnishings survive from this period, so establishing precisely when the patronal image began to appear inside the parish church is impossible. A few Romanesque fonts in Yorkshire include figures of what may have been the patronal saint in their imagery, but a serendipitous sampling over a wide area of well-preserved Norman chancels has produced no examples of provision in the forms of contemporary corbels or niches for carved images; their absence cannot be entirely placed at the door of over-zealous church restorers.[28] In the Romanesque wall-paintings at Kempley (Glos.) a pair of bishops without haloes and with hands raised in benediction occupy the chancel east wall and the patronal image of St Peter is placed on the ceiling (**50**). At Hardham (Sussex) the murals which cover the east wall are devoted to Christ's Passion, the apostles, elders of the Apocalypse and Christ in Majesty; St Botolph, the titular saint, is not represented. In the Barfreston (Kent) chancel scheme (1170s) primacy is accorded to the Virgin. In the light of subsequent developments it may be significant that Nicholas, the patronal saint, was depicted on the chancel north wall, performing one of his miracles.

50. Kempley (Glos.), St Peter's church: murals of bishops on chancel east wall, c. 1130–40

51. Checkendon (Oxon.), SS Peter and Paul's church: murals of apostles on chancel apse, c. 1260–70 (watercolour copy by E.W. Tristram)

As was argued in Chapter Three, if there were any image inside the parish church prior to 1200 (and even for a while thereafter) it was the *sedes sapiaentiae*, located on or above the altar. This may not be a purely insular phenomenon (**IV**; **26**). Hazardous though it is to flirt with the randomness of survival, it is noteworthy that in France, Scandinavia and Germany, extant pre-1200 images of saints other than the Virgin are few and far between.[29]

What impact did the thirteenth-century campaign to consecrate churches have on the setting up of patronal images as well as the representations of the Virgin and Child at the high altar? Every church was dedicated to God, as was made explicit in the Order for Church Dedications, but the Order also addressed the patronal saint.[30] No mention was made of an image, nor was there any such mention in Bishop William of Blois's instructions of 1229 for his Worcester diocese: '. . . the year and the date of consecration, the names of the dedicator, and the name of the saint to which the church is dedicated, should be clearly set out in a suitable place near the high altar. The same should be done for the minor altars.'[31] This rubric thus merely referred to the name of the patronal saint, yet by this date its images could already be found in English parish churches. In *c.* 1224 a figure of St Paul was present in the Bedford church dedicated to him.[32] We saw in the last chapter that the first reference to what became the standard arrangement, with the patronal saint to the left of the high altar and the Virgin on the right, was in 1240, when new images of St Peter and Our Lady were to be made and set up by royal order in these positions in St Peter's in the Tower of London. There were existing images of the titular saint and the Virgin in this church at this time; their locations were not stated, whereas that of the new images is, suggesting that the latter was innovatory. Placing the *patronus loci* in close proximity to the high altar no doubt was a practice borrowed from the great church. By *c.* 1179 an image of the Virgin was in existence at the high altar of Old Sarum Cathedral.[33] The mid-thirteenth-century wall-painting of St James the Greater at Bramley (Hants.) appears to be the first surviving example of a patronal image in the position of honour to the north of the chancel altar, accompanied by Our Lady on the south side.[34] The murals of *c.* 1260–70 at Checkendon (Oxon.) show a variant of the disposition, with the apse window flanked by SS Peter and Paul leading processions of the apostles. The two senior apostles are the titular saints and they are marked out and honoured by tabernacle (**51**).[35] In contrast to Bramley and Checkendon, the two North Crawley images in Peter de Wintonia's chancel were statues, as the pair of corbels in the east wall show (**46**). Elsewhere at this time provision for carved images was more rough and ready. The remarkably complete Early English parish church of St Giles at Skelton, near York, was built around 1240; subsequently a late twelfth-century capital was inserted into the east wall on the north side, presumably to support the patronal image; an identical capital served the same purpose in the same position in the church at Alne, also near York (**52**).[36] If Our Lady was the patronal saint, she occupied the place of honour on the north side, as can be observed from the traces in the church dedicated to her at Brent Eleigh (Suff.) (**164**). There does not appear to have been any hard and fast rule for the occupant of the south side in these circumstances. At Little Brickhill (Bucks.) the Trinity was placed on the south side. The high altar of Burnham Abbey in the same county was flanked by two Marian images.[37]

Quinel's injunctions of 1287 that every church in his Exeter diocese had to have images of the patronal saint and the Virgin ('ymago beate virginis et sancti loci') thus appear less innovation than a reflection of well-established practice.[38] The early fourteenth-century visitations in this diocese reveal that Quinel's efforts appear to have been generally successful.[39] While in 1301 the patronal images at Stoke Canon and Salcombe Regis had evidently been in place for some time

*52. Alne (N. Yorks), St Mary's church: late twelfth-century capital reused as a base for the patronal image*

(they are both described as old), Staverton (1314) and Axminster (1315) lacked their equivalents. The Stoke Canon and Salcombe Regis patronal images were not in good condition; that of St Gregory at Dawlish was poorly painted and lacked a hand. A visitation of the archdeaconry of Totnes in 1342 also revealed defects in patronal and Virgin images in a number of churches.[40] The various deficiencies indicated wear and tear on images which had been in place for some time. By the early fourteenth century the presence of the patronal image and principal image of the Virgin had become the norm, as the supports or tabernacles flanking the chancel east windows of churches the length and breadth of England testify (**57, 58**).[41]

Here and there the chancel images – or parts of them – have survived. In addition to Bramley and Checkendon, there are splendid early fourteenth-century murals of the Virgin and three saints (representing All Saints?) at Little Wenham (Suff.) (**53**) and traces of cruder murals of the patronal St Andrew and the Virgin at Stoke Dry (Rutland) of similar date.[42] Of the carved images (likely to have been the norm), none in wood has survived, with the possible exception of a St Michael at Stoke Charity (Hants.). All the others are of polychromed stone or alabaster. In the former medium are the matching heads of St Mary Magdalen and Our Lady from the collegiate church at Cobham (Kent) (**XIX**). The best preserved and most accomplished, albeit lacking almost all their pigmentation, are the alabaster statues of St Peter and the Virgin from Flawford (Notts.) (**54**).[43] These and other surviving patronal images are of varying dimensions. The Flawford St Peter is 82.5cm high and the Magdalen at Cobham must have been of comparable size. An image of St Nicholas commissioned for Thanington (Kent) in 1532 was to be 1.5m (5 ft) tall.[44] Monumentality was not mandatory for patronal images. The alabaster relief of the Virgin and Child at Stewkley

53. *Little Wenham (Suff.), All Saints' church: chancel east wall with murals of the Virgin and Child (left) and three saints (right), early fourteenth century*

(Bucks.) is no more than 51.5cm in height and yet almost certainly was the patronal image (**55**).[45] Its counterpart (St Paul) from Bergh Apton (Norf.) is even smaller, at 45cm high (**56**).

More important than scale was the degree of elaboration with which patronal images were displayed. Most seem to have been framed in richly gilded wooden tabernacles, all of which have vanished. Some stone versions survive, like the splendid niches at Harlington (Beds.), carved when its chancel was erected in the early fourteenth century and notable for their lavish detail (**57**). By contrast, the parish community at Hales (Norf.) was not prepared, or lacked the resources, to rebuild its chancel and was content to insert plain corbels into the Norman apse and hack rough niches into the wall; at the same time the wall around the altar and niches was repainted and a new east window inserted to provide better lighting of this area (**58**). The greater honour due to the patronal image is underlined at Harlington by the degree of elaboration accorded to its canopied niche compared with its companion; both retain traces of polychromed and gilded decoration. At Hales too the niche on the south side for Our Lady lacks the fictive crocketed canopy painted over the recess for the patronal image of St Margaret. The primacy of the patronal saint was also emphasized by the number of lights burning before it; in 1520 6*s* 8*d* was bequeathed by Alice Wilde, a parishioner of Iver (Bucks.), to buy a latten (copper alloy) candlestick of three lights for the patronal image of St Peter.[46]

*54. Alabaster statues of St Peter (left) and the Virgin and Child from St Peter's church, Flawford (Notts.), c. 1380–90 (Nottingham Castle Museum)*

Broadly speaking, English emphasis on the patronal image is in accordance with contemporary continental developments. In Catalonia the patronal saint became the most popular subject for altar frontals from the middle of the thirteenth century.[47] Images made of wood other than of the Virgin, and therefore almost certainly internal, are rare before *c.* 1250.[48] Between then and the end of the century they occur with steadily increasing frequency, notably images of St Michael in Scandinavia and Germany – also St Olav in the former and some female saints in the latter. These support Vauchez's contention that between *c.* 1250 and 1350 images became of prime importance.[49] Were they patronal images? A rare instance of an image whose provenance can be traced to a known dedication is the limewood St Michael of *c.* 1260 from Jena, but its original location in this church is unknown.[50] Serendipitous explorations in France and Germany have not revealed any comparable provision in the form of brackets or niches flanking the high altar. A number of village churches in Denmark and Sweden, especially those on the island of Gotland, have some of the best-preserved medieval interiors in Europe. Several retain evidence for the emplacement in the thirteenth and fourteenth centuries of an image of Our Lady on or behind the nave altar, often accompanied, where there is a second altar, by St Olav. It is not clear whether either represented the titular saint, although no trace of provision for Marian images in the chancel remains.[51] The late twelfth-century German practice of featuring the patronal saint on retables continued into the sixteenth century. It seems that the patronal image was displayed in various ways throughout western Christendom, its pairing with the Virgin on either side of the high altar apparently being peculiar to England. The qualification 'apparently' is necessary as so much evidence for emplacement on the continent has been lost.

*55. Stewkley (Bucks.), St Michael's (formerly St Mary's) church: alabaster relief of the Virgin and Child censed by angels, c. 1400*

## THE PATRONAL IMAGE AND THE PARISH

What functions did the image of the patronal saint perform for the individual parishioner and the parish community? What kinds of meanings did it bear?

The shift in representation of the Virgin charted in the last chapter coincided with this emphasis on the titular saint. The two images functioned in tandem, with complementary roles. In the post-Fourth Lateran Council campaign to bring the Church to the people, Our Lady may be seen as personifying the Church Universal as well as providing an affective model for the individual. By contrast, the patronal image represented the Local Church, the *genius loci* of the community. During the thirteenth century the titular image and its associated feast took on the role played by a saint's relics in early Christian times, when

> . . . the festival of a saint was conceived of as a moment of ideal consensus on a deeper level. It made plain God's acceptance of the community as a whole: his mercy embraced all its disparate members, and could reintegrate all who had stood outside in the previous year.[52]

56. *Alabaster statuette of St Paul from SS Peter and Paul's church, Bergh Apton (Norf.), late fourteenth century (Norwich Castle Museum and Art Gallery)*

The patronal and the Marian images both enhanced and were enhanced by their location. The former personified communal identity and linked the chancel to a particular saintly personage. The two images occupied the most exclusive space in the church and participated in the rites celebrated at the high altar. Through the installation and veneration of images of the titular saint and of the Virgin, the presence of the sacred was made manifest in every community, whether large or small, urban or rural. Vauchez argues that the Church encouraged the replacement of relics by images as a means of dissociating the cult of the saints from that of relics. The intention was to de-localize the cult of the saints and thus to make it an integral part of pastoral mission throughout Europe.[53] While in a general sense this may have been so, the new emphasis on the patronal saint was not about de-localization but rather the opposite: it was concerned with giving a sacred identity to every church and by extension to the community which worshipped in it, hence Bishop Quinel's 'ymago sancti loci' label. Instead of one *locus* exclusively associated with a saint through possession of his or her relics, there were multiple microlocalities – for example, the thirteen Buckinghamshire parishes whose patron was St Nicholas could all claim a special relationship with that saint.

Peter de Wintonia's inscription at North Crawley epitomizes the special relationship which existed between the medieval parish clergy and their patronal saints. The wording associates the chancel with St Firmin; by rebuilding it so sumptuously Peter de Wintonia signalled the saint's importance. In 1530 the vicar of St Mary's at Stowting (Kent) referred to the image of Our Lady as 'my patroness'.[54] The chancel was the preserve of the earthly individuals who had the right to occupy and use it. The campaign for patronal images occurred in a century when the institutional authority of the Church was promoted more vigorously than at any other time. It was also a period which saw many of Peter de Wintonia's fellow-rectors rebuild their chancels on a grand scale.[55] Endowment by parish priests of patronal images took a variety of forms. Sometimes they

57. *Harlington (Beds.), St Mary's church: chancel east end interior, early fourteenth century*

were the providers of the images, as is indicated by the clerical figures kneeling at the feet of SS Andrew and Peter at Stoke Dry and Flawford respectively (**54**). Often clerical *largesse* was directed towards the embellishment of an existing patronal image. In 1415–16 one of Peter de Wintonia's successors at North Crawley, William Hunden, Archdeacon of Totnes and canon of Exeter and Lincoln Cathedrals, left £5 for a tabernacle to be painted, or some other ornament, for St Firmin's image.[56] Maurice Hardwicke, vicar of All Saints', Bristol, from 1455, gave a velvet cloth embroidered with fleurs-de-lis, the inscription 'Hymnus omnibus sanctis' and his initials. This was to be hung behind the image of All Saints on every principal feast-day, together with a cloth of gold for the image's head; Hardwicke also paid for the gilding of the image.[57]

The special relationship between priest and patron extended beyond death. Christopher Conyers, rector of Rudby in Yorkshire, stipulated that on the day of his burial five candles were to be burned above his tomb between the high altar and the patronal image of All Saints; thereafter three candles were to be lit before the image of All Saints and two before the Virgin on the other side.[58] Peter de Wintonia's inscription was an unusual manifestation of post-mortem commemoration. The fine brass of an early fifteenth-century incumbent at Upper Hardres (Kent) shows him kneeling with a scroll bearing a bidding prayer to Peter and Paul, the patronal saints, who are depicted above on a bracket (**59**). The Latin text on the scroll may be translated as 'Keybearer of heaven and Paul, the teacher of the people, intercede for me to the king of angels that I may be worthy'.[59] In the Buckingham archdeaconry five late medieval clergy and four members of the laity desired burial before the patronal image; in the Bedford archdeaconry the figures are four and one (**118**). Wills stipulating chancel burial, together with the evidence of

*58. Hales (Norf.), St Margaret's church: chancel east end interior, remodelled in the early fourteenth century*

brasses and tombs in the chancel, show that it was the clerical estate which dominated in both archdeaconries; there is no reason to suppose that this pattern was unusual.

The chancel, however, was not the exclusive domain of the clergy. In 1229 the synodal statutes for the diocese of Worcester excluded laity from the chancel; this suggests that the latter were already infiltrating into this part of the church and in 1240 exemptions were made for patrons and 'sublime persons'. Subsequently the gentry were increasingly granted burial there, sometimes in front of the patronal image.[60] One Buckinghamshire example is Thomas Hampden, who in

1482 wished to be interred before the image of St Mary Magdalen in the chancel of Great Hampden church.[61] The lay elites may not always have been free agents in matters of burial. Thomas Hanchich, gentleman (d. 1509), was one of a handful of Bedfordshire laity who secured burial in the chancel, in his case in St Paul's church, Bedford, 'under the keeping and protection of St Paul the holy apostle'.[62] He was only accorded this honour with the permission of the prior of Newnham Priory, the holder of the advowson.

Those who governed the community shared the clergy's affinity with the saint. The discursive language of feudalism described the saints as 'our dukes and leaders' and their images were robed in the garments and trappings of power. The patronal saint was equated by John Mirk with secular authority:

> For ryght as a temporall lord helpyth and defendyth all that byn parcchons or tenantys, ryght soo the saynt that ys patron of the chyrche helpyth and defendyth all that byn paryschons to hym, and don hym worschyp halowyng his day, and offyrne to hym.[63]

At North Crawley the image of St Firmin and accompanying figure of the Queen of Heaven would have been identifiable instantly as the sacred equivalents of the twin arms of earthly lordship (**47**). Other Buckinghamshire parochial patrons included the Trinity, a king, a pope, an archbishop, a bishop, two abbots and a cavalryman; in their images they too would have been portrayed in robes reflecting their high status.[64] Authority and rank are stressed in the surviving patronal images at Cobham and Flawford. The head of St Mary Magdalen at the former is crowned, a reference to her allegedly royal ancestry as recounted in the *Golden Legend* and an aspect of her life rarely portrayed in English representations. At Cobham her social rank may have been considered appropriate for the patronal saint and matched the image of the Virgin as Queen of Heaven on the other side of the high altar (**XIX**).[65] The Flawford Virgin is also crowned as Queen of Heaven and there her heavenly status is matched by St Peter's papal tiara and other trappings of spiritual supremacy (**54**).

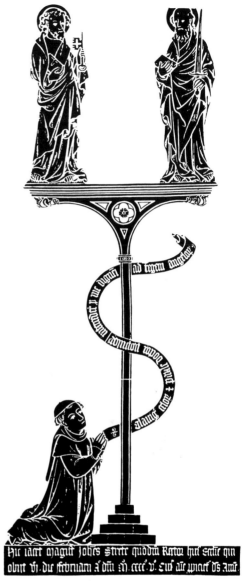

*59. Upper Hardres (Kent), SS Peter and Paul's church: brass of rector John Strete (d. 1405) with the patronal saints*

The emphasis placed on the provision of the patronal image occurred in a period which witnessed, at least in the south of England and the Midlands, the burgeoning of a sense of *locus*, or local identity, among the knightly class; the two developments can be assumed to have been related.[66] This suggests that at this time there were shared attitudes between the secular and ecclesiastical spheres concerning land and title and a sensed need for overlordship and protection over place and building. Heraldry in the east window glazing or painted on the east wall of fourteenth-century churches underlined the association of the chancel with lay as well as clerical lordship.[67]

The relationship between the patronal image and the ordinary parishioners was framed by the structures of feudal society. They were the vassals of the patronal saint, to whom obligations were due in return for his or her protection and intercession.[68] A collection of memoranda for the diocese of Salisbury (1228–56?) stipulated that parishioners should provide the images.[69] That maintenance of chancel as well as nave images was a parochial responsibility was laid down by Archbishop Winchelsey: '. . . the repair of the interior and exterior of the church nave inside and outside established by law and custom, both of images (especially the chief image in the chancel) and also of altars and window glazing'.[70] This did not apply universally and in the fifteenth century there was still wide diversity of custom regarding the respective obligations of laity and clergy in respect of the church fabric and its fittings and furnishings; as a result disputes were not unknown.[71]

The patronal image was firmly embedded in the communal and social fabric of the parish. It was used both as 'social glue' and as a means of enabling each member of a community to engage directly with the supernatural. Enshrined in the most sacred place in the church, the patronal image embodied community identity and bound together all social groups. As a result it is impossible to separate the secular from the spiritual in the relationship between parishioners and their titular image. Thomas Crypps's bequest of a bushel of malt to the image of Our Lady in Stewkley church may be seen as much a social act as a pious gesture of redemption, in that by endowing the image he was alleviating the parish's obligation to maintain it (**55**).[72] The festivals of the three most popular patronal dedications apart from the Virgin all marked major moments in the farming year. All Saints (1 November) signified the start of winter, when cattle were brought in from the fields. The feast of St Peter ad Vincula (1 August) signified the beginning of harvest, the completion of which ideally coincided with St Michael's day, or Michaelmas (29 September); the latter also saw the commencement of autumn tasks in the fields, thus simultaneously linking the beginning and the end of the agricultural cycle.[73] On the patronal festival and other important occasions lay access to the image must have been permitted for adornment and veneration. Outside service times, there was no reason to deny access to laity wishing to use the patronal image or chancel Virgin as a vehicle for counsel or intercession. Margery Kempe regularly entered the choir of St Margaret's, King's Lynn, to pray and engage in spiritual dialogue with Christ and Our Lady, although this may have been a privilege extended to her because of her exceptional religiosity, rather than representing the norm.[74]

In 1408–9 only one church visited by Dean Chandler in the Salisbury diocese lacked a patronal image while in another six they needed repainting. Of the 260 churches inspected by Archbishop Warham and his deputies in 1511–12, only Lydd was without an image of the patronal saint while that at Staplehurst was in poor condition.[75] A similar picture emerges from the visitations of the Bedford archdeaconry in 1518 and 1530, where no patronal images were identified as lacking or needing repair.[76] Provision of new patronal images during the late fifteenth and early sixteenth centuries in the Bedford and Buckingham archdeaconries is absent from wills. Even the much larger area of Kent only yields eight testamentary commissions. Two totally opposite interpretations can be put on this data: the dearth of new images and the paucity of references in the visitations suggest either that, in the century and a half preceding the Reformation, the titular images were in place and were well maintained, or that they had ceased to be of prime importance. It has been observed that in the towns and villages of late sixteenth-century central Spain, 'titular saints . . . were no more actively used for practical devotion than they are today'.[77] Similarly, it has been suggested that in the fifteenth and early sixteenth centuries the patronal image was of no great concern to the ordinary laity in England.[78]

One of the arguments in support of this view is that there were not many bequests to patronal images in the later Middle Ages. None of the North Crawley parishioners whose wills survive from 1488 mentioned St Firmin; instead, their bequests were directed towards the altars of Our Lady and the Holy Trinity, presumably in the nave aisles and with associated imagery.[79] This absence, however, is not typical for Buckinghamshire, Bedfordshire and Kent in this period and may reflect the fact that St Firmin was not a popular saint in England. Nearly twice as many parish churches in the Buckingham archdeaconry received bequests to the patronal image in the form of lights (the vast majority) and embellishments than those which did not. In Kent the figure is about 50 per cent and there is a slightly lower proportion in the Bedfordshire churches. If, like Rector Hunden at North Crawley, most of the individual bequests for the embellishment of images of titular saints came from incumbents and lay elites, there are also examples of individual and collective endowment by parishioners. The making, painting and gilding of the tabernacle for the titular image of All Saints at Houghton Regis (Beds.) was partly financed by bequests from three laymen and two women between 1521 and 1537. Women also featured among the benefactors of the patronal light of Our Lady in the neighbouring town of Luton, along with a lord of the manor and a husbandman.[80] Identification with the titular saint, therefore, was not the exclusive preserve of the lay and clerical elites. Nicholas John of Hythe (Kent) evidently believed in the protective powers of the titular saint of his place of worship as his fishing boat was named not after his name-saint and patron of sailors but as the *Leonard of Hythe*.[81]

Patronal feast-days remained highpoints in the ritual year to the Reformation. They were classified as Principal Doubles, one of eight feasts in the highest category of liturgical commemoration.[82] They may not have enjoyed the centrality to communal life of patronal festivals in Sicily during the 1950s, when preparations for the next one began as soon as the present celebration had finished, but late medieval patronal feasts could be elaborate affairs which, as in earlier times, offered opportunities for the exercise of commensality.[83] On such occasions garlands of real or imitation flowers might be placed on the patronal image. That of St Stephen at St Stephen's Walbrook in London was honoured with 'a garlonde of flowris for his hed of wyre and silke of the p'sons [parson's] yifte'; in 1534–5 14*d* was spent on the St Stephen's day garland. Some years later an ex-religious came to the attention of the Henrician authorities because he went to the church of Milton by Canterbury on the patronal feast of St Margaret, placed a garland of flowers on her image (which seems to have attracted considerable veneration) and celebrated Mass.[84] Processions might involve taking the patronal image or its replica outside the church, as at St George's in Canterbury, where the image was accompanied by civic dignitaries, their wives and the common folk, marshalled according to the social pecking-order.[85] St Andrew's, another Canterbury parish, used the patronal festival for fund-raising by the sale of badges or 'scuchons', probably in the shape of the saltire cross attribute of the saint. In 1519–20

*60. North Crawley (Bucks.), St Firmin's church: chancel interior seen through the rood screen*

four leaves of gold paper for the badges cost 4*d* and a painter was paid 13*d* for making them; receipts totalled 3*s* 5*d*. In other years the profit-margin was even higher.[86]

The patronal festivities of the wealthy and well-connected parish of St Margaret's, Westminster are described in some detail in the churchwardens' accounts. As a preliminary, the high altar was embellished with rich Arras cloths and silk hangings. The patronal image was adorned with a coral rosary on a silver chain with a pearl clasp, a gift from a parishioner to be used on feast days. On 19 July, the eve of St Margaret's day, a bonfire was lit in front of the church door and a vigil was observed by the parishioners until dawn. The feast-day proper began with a solemn Mass, followed by a procession around the parish of maidens dressed specially for the occasion. Afterwards there was a performance of a St Margaret play.[87]

In image-rich parishes like Wing (Bucks.) the esteem in which the patronal saint was held might have been affected by the presence of specialist saintly helpers (**169**). The multiplication of devotional images in parish churches was already under way by the middle of the thirteenth century and gathered pace thereafter. A related change in the internal topography of parish churches which had an impact on the patronal image was the erection of rood screens. The introduction in the early sixteenth century of the screen at North Crawley meant that St Firmin's image quite literally was not viewed at the end of the Middle Ages in the same way that it had been in Peter de Wintonia's time. The screen distanced the image (as well as the clergy and lay elites) from the parishioners and interrupted the main sightlines from the nave into the chancel (**60**). The construction of screens between chancel and nave appears to have become widespread only in the fourteenth century; many churches did not have them until the end of the fifteenth and early sixteenth centuries.

How the patronal saint was perceived by parishioners ultimately defies generalization. If the formal system of provision and maintenance guaranteed a degree of primacy, this does not mean that it inspired the same level of personal and collective devotion everywhere. The late medieval patronal festivals just described are all from urban parishes; it may be that in cities and large towns with several churches the patronal image remained a primary focus of parish identity. The silver shoes belonging to the patronal image in the London church of St Christopher-le-Stocks reveal both the extent to which it was venerated and its institutional primacy over the numerous other images here.[88] In Devon and Cornwall especially, the Celtic patron saints seem to have retained popularity until the Reformation.[89] Very occasionally laypeople addressed the titular saint using the same possessive epithet as the clergy. The 5ft-high new alabaster image of St Nicholas at Thanington, mentioned above, was described by John Marten as 'my patron'.[90] The number of bequests to the patronal light by individuals like Thomas Crypps of Stewkley suggest that in some parishes the titular image was a focus of individual lay affective piety. Stewkley seems to have possessed only one other image (of St George), so there was much less choice available to Crypps and his fellow-parishioners than to their counterparts in the neighbouring parish of Wing, with its nine or ten images.[91] Attitudes to the parochial image are likely to have varied from community to community, and depended on a range of factors. Each parish has its own history in this as in so much else concerning images.[92]

CHAPTER FIVE

# *THE HOLIE COMPANIE*
# *OF HEVEN*

Living as we do in an age saturated with visual imagery of every kind, it is easy to underestimate the impact of the growth of the devotional image on a largely illiterate laity. As has been observed, 'One of the most important defining characteristics of late medieval popular culture was that it was intensely visual.'[1] This was a world where the corporeality of the sacred through pictorial representation was commonplace.

As the wills of the Eaton Bray parishioners showed in Chapter Two, by the early sixteenth century their parish church contained at least twelve images which functioned as devotional. There are no indications as to when they were commissioned and set up, but it is a reasonable assumption that it was the result of an incremental process of addition and replacement. This chapter will trace the diffusion of the saints into the urban and rural communities of England and their relationships with the society that used them.

The infiltration of devotional images into the townscape and landscape marked a profound transfer, whereby the efficacy of a saint was spread far from his or her cult centre and relics by means of representations of that saint in the form of images. What were the imperatives which lay behind this substitution? Vauchez seeks a causal explanation in the combat of those heresies which denied the validity of representing the sacred by images.[2] But heresy can hardly be an explanation of the multiplication of images in England, which remained free of Catharism, during the course of the thirteenth century. More pertinent perhaps was the fact that the making accessible of representations of God's chosen to the populace at large accorded with the tenets of the 1215 Lateran Council.

The thirteenth century was of crucial importance in the history of the devotional image in the parish church.[3] What had previously been a restricted artefact now became ubiquitous and had multiple identities. This impetus stemmed from a change in the function of sacred representations. In place of remote, celestial beings, the saints came to play roles more closely related to the everyday concerns of the faithful. They acted as their personal intercessors and helpers, in return for which, through their images, they received prayers and offerings.[4] It was during this century that a profound shift in the relationship between pictorial imagery and its viewers, prompted by a new emphasis on the Host and on distance between officiating clergy and the congregation, reduced active lay participation in ritual to passive observation. Increasingly the images of the saints filled the void by becoming the focus of individual devotion. Of course, this was not a purely insular phenomenon.

Through texts like the very popular *Legenda Aurea* (*Golden Legend*) and the miraculous Marian image-tales of Gautier de Coinci, the power of images was stressed (**42, 149**).[5] The dissemination of images affected every community through the consequent transformation of its only public space, the nave of the parish church. The rood remained the central focus, but it was joined by a new and increasingly numerous supporting cast of images of the saints, grouped not merely around the high altar in the chancel, but also on, or in close proximity to, nave and chantry altars and on pillars, whether in the form of a carved image or a mural. Figurative stained glass too in this period became standard in the parish church.[6] These images were the centres of various identities and the focus of social and economic as well as religious acts.

The first indication of the image-complement of a non-cathedral or monastic church is that of the chapel of St Peter ad Vincula in the Tower of London. As we saw in the last chapter, in 1240 Henry III commissioned new images of the titular saint and the Virgin for the chancel. At that date the church already possessed images of St Peter and the Virgin, also of St Nicholas and St Katherine, both of whom had altars. To these the king also added a new image of St Christopher carrying the child Christ.[7] The 1249–52 inspection of churches belonging to St Paul's Cathedral in the diocese of London shows that, by the middle of the century, images were occurring in rural churches. Although neither images nor their lights were mentioned in several of this group, Barling (Essex) had images of the Virgin, St Giles and St Nicholas. At Willesden (Middlesex) there were 'due magne iconee et sculpte de beata Virgine'. Thorpe-le-Soken (Essex) possessed 'ij yconie beate Marie honeste ad majus altare' and one 'ymago linea', as well as lights of the Virgin and St Margaret in chapels beyond the church. No reference was made to the condition of the images, but, wherever known, the subscribers to the lights associated with the images are named.[8] A comparison of these visitations with another series carried out in the same churches in 1297 is instructive.[9]

| TABLE II: IMAGES IN FIVE ESSEX CHURCHES | | |
|---|---|---|
| | 1249–52 | 1297 |
| Barling | 3 | 3★ |
| Tillingham | 2 | 12 |
| Thorpe-le-Soken | 4 | 6 |
| Walton-on-the Naze | 2 | 8 |
| Kirby-le-Soken | 3 | 10 |

★ The Barling figures for 1297 do not include the nave images, which are not mentioned. NB The figures include patronal saints; the rood and its associated figures are excluded.

In 1249–52 only Thorpe-le-Soken had more than three images; by 1297 most had considerably expanded their stock. In 1249 only lights of the Virgin and St Michael were mentioned at Tillingham (Essex); in 1297 in the chancel there were 'ymagines de Sancta Cruce, de Sancto Paolo, Sancto Nicholao [the patronal saint] et Sancto Stephano'; the nave had 'Item beate Virginis cum tabernaculo, beati Andree, Sancti Eadmundi, beati Nicholai, Sancte Katerine, beate Margarete, beati Petri, beate Michaelis, et Jacobi.'[10] Sometimes the location of nave images is specified in the later visitation. Flanking the rood at Aldbury (Herts.) were the Virgin, Nicholas and James on the right, and St John the Evangelist and two images of St Margaret on the left. Presumably these were all on the rood beam. There were also images of Mary Magdalen and Katherine in the angle on the north side (the north aisle).[11] Repairs to, or repainting of, images are specified in several churches visited in 1297.

*61. Hauxton (Cambs.), St Edmund's church: interior looking east*

The fabrics of these churches which survive from the time of the 1249–52 visitation retain no trace of settings for the images listed. St Edmund's at Hauxton (Cambs.) may provide some idea of their original dispositions (**61**). During the early thirteenth century a pair of recesses were cut into the east end of the Norman nave on either side of the chancel arch. On the upper part of the southern one is a contemporary mural of St Thomas Becket, which must have been above an altar dedicated to him; the north recess can be presumed to have also had an altar and titular image on the back wall. It is impossible to say whether Hauxton's was a common arrangement, although it resembles very closely the nave altars found in thirteenth-century parish churches on the island of Gotland, Sweden. St Peter ad Vincula had two altars dedicated to saints with images and Barling possessed both an altar and an image of St Giles. In these instances the image may have functioned as both a devotional image and an altar image. The 1249–52 visitation sometimes mentions carved images, implying that if no medium is specified, they were not statuary and therefore were probably paintings. The 1229 edict for the diocese of Worcester referred only to the need to have the name of the titular saint of each altar, but the documentary references and the Hauxton niches demonstrate that before the middle of the century altar saints were being represented in pictorial form.[12] The ecclesiastical enactments of the end of the thirteenth and early fourteenth centuries prescribing the presence of titular images for altars thus reiterated what was already practice. For example, the Synod of Trier (1310) laid down that each altar should have its titular saint indicated either by an inscription or by a representation.[13]

The process of image accumulation continued into the following centuries, together with the wholesale rebuilding and enlargement of parish churches and the increased numbers of ancillary altars, both public and chantry, all of which demanded images. That the acquisition and installation of the latter was encouraged by the clergy is indicated by the wording of Bishop Trillek's indulgence issued on the occasion of his consecration of the high altar and two nave altars at Vowchurch (Herefs.) in 1348; included in the good works which would earn indulgence was assisting 'at the establishment or painting of images' of the saints to whom the altars were dedicated – and each had multiple dedications.[14]

Space had to be found for every fresh addition to the stock of images. The statutes for Bishop Grandisson's collegiate foundation of Ottery St Mary in Devon included a clause forbidding the placing of images other than the titular saint(s) on altars, as was done in disorderly fashion in rural churches; perhaps this was the case at Culmstock in 1303, where images of Our Lady and St Nicholas were sited at the north nave altar and St Katherine by the corresponding altar on the south side.[15] The desire for a seemly display of images might explain the cluster of brackets and niches around altars in numerous churches (**II**). Such decorum was impossible to maintain as images multiplied. Eaton Bray is far from alone in its apparently random insertion of image supports in nave pillars and walls (**5, 6**). In East Anglia there was a predilection for placing images in window embrasures (**X**).[16] With or without additional altars, there was a more or less constant flow of new recruits. This was a pan-European phenomenon, as is testified by the large numbers of surviving images in churches and museums.[17] The factors behind this expansion were the same throughout western Christendom, even if the particular contexts were determined by local traditions and circumstances.

The 1417 inventory for the Exeter church of St Kerrian's provides a catalogue of the entire image stock of a parish church, apart from the patronal image and companion figure of Our Lady:

Item, one small alabaster image of the Trinity [this item crossed thro']. Item, one small alabaster image of the Blessed Mary known as the Pity. Item one roundel with St John the Baptist's head . . . Item, one alabaster image of St Christopher. Item, one alabaster image of St Mary of the Assumption. Item, one old picture with the image of St Michael. Item, one image of St John the Baptist with a tabernacle. Item, one image of St Anne, with a tabernacle. Item, one image of St John the Baptist with a tabernacle. Item, one table with the image of St Erasmus. Item, one table with the image of St Christopher.[18]

Allowance has to be made for the fact that St Kerrian's was an urban church; none the less, the increase in numbers is marked compared with the 1297 St Paul's visitation data. In addition to the cast of saints familiar from the St Paul's lists, there were diversified representations of the Virgin as Our Lady of Pity and her Assumption and a new addition in the person of St Erasmus.

The inventory was taken at a time when images were continuing to proliferate. The contemporary moralizing tract *Dives and Pauper* observed that 'meen doon makyn these dayis ymagys gret plente bothin cherche and out of cherche'.[19] Image expansion may have been given renewed impetus by the early fifteenth-century campaign by the English ecclesiastical hierarchy to combat the Lollard heresy by means of an 'increase of devotion'. This involved a *renovatio* of traditional religion through liturgical innovations in the form of new feasts and greater elaboration in ritual performance, also in a fresh emphasis on the exercise of private devotion. The enhancement of feasts like that of St George, promoted to a Greater Double (the second highest category of liturgical festivals) in 1415, is likely to have had an impact on image production.[20]

An inventory made of St Stephen Walbrook half a century after St Kerrian's reveals just how image-rich London churches had become:

> Also, ther bene viij Imagis stondyng In the quer that is Sent Stevyn, peyntyd, and the fot is platyd wt Sylvvir.
> Also, a nothir Image of Sent Stevyn, un peyntyd.
> Also, an Image of Sent Anne, and owre lady stondyng by her.
> Another of sent laurens, and a nother of Sent vinsent.
> Another of Sent petir, and a nother of Sent poule.

In the Lady Chapel were

> vij Imagis of tre [tree, i.e. of wood], ij of hem bene peynted that is owre lady, and sent John baptist, and the other v bene un peyntyd that is to sey sent John baptist, sent John Evangelist, sent Elysabeth, sent George, and Sent Anneys.

The Chapel of SS Nicholas and Katherine housed

> vij Imagis of tre, one of hem is peyntyd, that is Sent kateryn and the other vj bene un peyntyd, that is to Sey Sent Nicolas, sent kateryn, sent Myschel, Sent Margret, and sent Jame and Mary Maudelyn.

Surprisingly, an alabaster St Christopher placed adjacent to the font is the only nave image listed; another alabaster, of Our Lady of Pity, stood in the 'Cloister', together with two images of the Virgin and Child, one of stone, the other of wood. The numbers of duplicate images is worthy of note.[21]

Probate and parish records confirm that most churches had acquired their principal stock of images by the late fifteenth century. With a few exceptions, the subsequent story is one of piecemeal rather than wholesale addition, replacement and embellishment.[22] This was not universally so. Not all churches accumulated images; poorer or smaller parishes often had to make do with just the obligatory chancel images. Proliferation also meant diversification. While some images would have been replacements for worn-out or damaged old images, there was also a whole host of representations of new cults. The process was more or less continuous. Long-established favourites such as Katherine, Margaret, Christopher, John the Baptist and Lawrence were joined by contemporary holy models like Sitha, Roche and Brigitte of Sweden.[23] The venerable figures of Anthony, Eligius, Erasmus, Sebastian and Ursula, not to mention the less respectable Uncumber, were reconditioned and pressed into service to meet new demands.[24] The vast majority of saints were of continental origin, but their images could be found in the company of the indigenous Edmund, Edward the Confessor, Becket and a very few more recent holy men like John of Bridlington. A passer-by from Normandy or Northumberland entering Eaton Bray church in *c.* 1500 would have recognized immediately most of the images as belonging to the same 'holie companie of Heven' as those in their own parish churches.[25] In a Catholic world and in a country as regionally diverse as England, the images of the saints provided a common cultural denominator. Yet the saints represented by these images also bore site-specific meanings for the individuals in each community.

Saints were socialized: they were an essential feature of everyday life and in a sense their existence (and to an extent, the form they took) was contingent on the everyday experiences of their clients. This is not to claim that the provision and sustenance of images were exclusively politically, geographically, economically or socially determined; that spiritual factors were important imperatives must be acknowledged, even if by their very interiorized and personal nature they were rarely made explicit. None the less, distribution patterns can indicate the significance of non-religious factors in image-choice.

This was a world in which more and more of the laity invested in the visual topography of their parish church and possessed the means in cash or kind to do so. Bequests to lights and images show that large numbers of laity were claiming for themselves the kind of individual personal relationships with the fabric and fittings of the parish church which hitherto had been the preserve of the clerical and lay elites in the community. The *patronus loci* and the chancel Virgin acted as the guardian saints of the parish as an entity. This sense of *communitas*, of *genius loci*, was an important symbol of tradition, continuity and permanence in a rural society whose demography tended to be one of constant movement, of emigration and immigration. Yet in late medieval England the addition of numerous other saintly images suggests that the patronal saint's powers were considered too general and that more specific helpers were required. For individuals and groups, whether familial units or collectivities bound by social, occupational or devotional ties, the image of the saint who was their personal, household or patronal protector or protectress may have been the prime concern, regardless of that saint's official status in the heavenly hierarchy as manifested in liturgical commemoration. In this process the saints were brought closer to their viewers not just literally but also metaphorically. As with Christ, and the Virgin, their lives and representations were constructed or reconstructed to approximate to the needs and daily experiences of their clients. They became highly visible and potent vehicles for the expression of selfhood.

One of the six reasons given in the *Golden Legend* for venerating the saints was that 'we be called to ensue and follow them. So that by the example of them we despise all earthly things, and desire celestial things.'[26] Yet for the ordinary parishioner in late medieval Christendom the majority of the saints were inimitable. Images of male saints predominated, mostly dressed in the robes and trappings of high office in Church and State. Their role was not so much exemplary as that of helpers and intercessors in daily life.[27] The saints might be 'dukes and leaders', but they were also friends of God and their advocacy was to be enlisted 'for the augmentation of our surety', to alleviate the pains of Purgatory and plead for eternal salvation. The *Golden Legend* also advocates the veneration of the saints in order:

> to have aid in our infirmity, for by ourselves we may have none health, therefore have we need of the prayers of saints, and therefore we ought to honour them, that we may deserve that they aid and help us.

A lost alabaster depicted a cleric kneeling at the feet of St William of York and addressing to him this text: 'St William you procure us help without reward.'[28] The festival Collects in the Sarum Missal are full of entreaties for the help and intercession of the saints. The light keepers at Morebath (Devon) prefaced their annual accounts with an 'ora pro nobis' addressed to their saint, a bidding prayer used repeatedly on owner scrolls in illuminated manuscripts and by donors in stained glass.[29]

Mâle observed that the saints were never closer to people, and more loved, than in the fifteenth and sixteenth centuries.[30] The adoption of saints as personal patrons by non-elite individuals stemmed from the basis that these celestial beings were once human and therefore could comprehend the needs and concerns of their suppliants. To medieval parishioners there was no great distinction between the divine and the human; instead the saints formed an essential link in the chain which bound their suppliants to God. The individual–saint–God nexus is exemplified pictorially by the relief at Goudhurst (Kent) to the family of Sir Alexander Culpeper (d. 1537), who are kneeling in prayer to St George and Our Lady who occupy the same celestial plane as God the Father (**123**).

The saints acted as household and familial patrons through the generations. Two members of the Copping family, both named Robert, left wax tapers respectively in 1499 and 1520 to the image of St Anthony at Boughton Monchelsea (Kent). At Ringwold in the same county John Upton stipulated in 1530 that his body was to be buried beside that of his mother before Our Lady of Pity. The gentle-born Stathums of Morley (Derbys.) had a devotion to St Christopher which was transmitted from one generation to the next (**62**).[31]

## LOCUS

It was argued in the last chapter that the emergence of the image marked a disassociation of the saint from their cult centre and a relocalization in churches containing their image.[32] If patronal images were transplanted into the *locus*, the choice of the saints whose images acted as a supporting cast was determined by that *locus*, through its physical configuration and by those whose living was dependent upon it. This is not to deny any clerical agency in the process, but the successful implanting of a saint was bound to depend on their relevance to the life-experiences of the members of the community. As a prelude to examining the relationship between late medieval parishioners and images, we should examine how they were absorbed into the *locus* and became appropriated to and identified with it.

A basic question is whether there is a discernible correlation between images and population density and size of parish. **Map 5 (p. 279)** shows the numerical distribution of images in Bedfordshire parish churches in the late fifteenth and early sixteenth centuries.[33] The norm seems to have been between three and five images, regardless of parish size and population. The parish of Holcot in the west of the county comprised only 904 acres and had at least seven images in the

62. Morley (Derbys.), St Matthew's church: brass of Sir Thomas Stathum
(d. 1470) and family

church, whereas Turvey, to the west of Bedford, was four times the size and yet only five images are recorded. Thirty-four men worth more than £5 per annum are listed for Turvey in the *c.* 1538–9 Muster Rolls, which provide some indications of wealth and therefore disposable income. The largest number of images in any church in the county (twenty-two or twenty-three), apart from prosperous and extensive Houghton Regis, occurred in the rural parish of Eversholt, comprising a fairly average 2,145 acres but with a high number of men (forty-four) listed in the Muster Rolls. The village churches with the largest numbers of images are concentrated in the southern half of Bedfordshire and especially in and around the two richest towns in the county, Luton and Dunstable. Neither Eaton Bray nor the neighbouring parish of Totternhoe covered a large area, yet in *c.* 1538–9 they returned quite a number of names for the Muster Rolls (sixty for Eaton Bray, including Lord Bray and his twelve servants, twenty for Totternhoe) (**Map 6, p. 280**). Significantly, the exceptions in this area were the adjoining and remote Chiltern hilltop parishes of Studham and Whipsnade, which between them could supply only seven names.

Ultimately, any attempt to co-relate images with parish size, population or personal wealth is bound to be reductive. The demographic evidence presented by the Muster Rolls and taxation records is problematic and the image figures are extracted from testamentary evidence, so it is not certain that they represent the full complement for each church. The town of Biggleswade is a case in point. Although situated on the Great North Road and in one of the most extensive parishes in the county, there is no direct reference to any images in its parish church. However, at least four can be inferred by assuming their presence at Our Lady's altar and for the Trinity fraternity, plus the obligatory chancel pairing of the patronal saint (Andrew) and Our Lady.

Wills also do not highlight variables such as differing prosperity, fluctuating economic fortunes, occurrences of disease and famine and the histories of individual communities and their members. While it is impossible to ignore a link between prosperity and church-building and furnishing (including image-provision) in late medieval East Anglia, it needed only one wealthy and pious individual to transform a church that was hitherto poorly endowed with images. Morebath in Devon is a salutary lesson in how the enrichment and maintenance of images in a small and remote parish could be driven by the presence of a dynamic and committed personality like Parson Trychay.[34] Studies of twentieth-century southern Mediterranean cultures have shown that communities burdened by disaster and hardship might put as much – if not more – trust in divine helpers than did more affluent settlements.[35]

In the 1960s the villagers in the Nansa valley of northern Spain had a developed sense of proprietorship over their images, particularly those specially revered; they were very much *their* images and only on special occasions such as fiestas did the inhabitants of neighbouring communities have recourse to them (unless they had relatives in the village in question).[36] This exclusivity might in part have been determined by the geographical configuration of this valley, which was such that direct communication between the villages on the slopes was very restricted. At the risk of comparing apples with pears, are similar traits apparent in fifteenth- and early sixteenth-century England? Margery Kempe seems to have roamed freely, not just to recognized places of pilgrimage but also to widely dispersed churches. She venerated a rood in a Leicester church and an image of Our Lady of Pity in a church in Norwich, as well as visiting other churches.[37] Margery's 'life' cannot be read too literally. She also belonged to a select social group and was exceptionally (even excessively) devout, factors which would have given her more freedom than most women of her era enjoyed. A more reliable and typical indicator of the extent to which the devotion of the individual parishioner was focused on the images in their own parish church is the small number of bequests by testators to lights/images in other churches. Of the more than 800 published pre-Reformation wills from the archdeaconry of Bedford, only just over one-fifth specify bequests to churches (excluding monasteries and friaries) other than the testator's parish church. No more than eight make any reference to lights. Some of these bequests convey more than a hint of direction, namely those assigning money or produce to neighbouring churches which seem to have been poor, but this is not a catch-all explanation. Apart from those testators who lived in London and who were of Bedfordshire birth or origin, all places were within a very small radius of the testator's domicile.

Villages were not sealed, self-contained entities. In their study of an Essex village in the sixteenth and seventeenth centuries Wrightson and Levine classified under a series of headings the types of relationship which existed between the inhabitants of Terling and those of neighbouring parishes.[38] One such heading was ownership of property by Terling villagers in neighbouring communities. In Bedfordshire a number of testators had property in the parishes where they made bequests. For example, in addition to gifts to his parish church, Henry Abbot of Husborne Crawley (d. 1511) bequeathed some arable land he owned in Aspley Guise to the upkeep of the light of the Virgin in that church. Membership of a fraternity located outside the parish could be a factor. Edward Dermer (d. 1518) was buried in Caddington church, to which he made some small specific bequests, including one of 12*d* to the light of Our Lady. He also left 6*s* 8*d* for the maintenance of Luton church and the same sum to the fraternity of the Holy Trinity there, to which several members of the family belonged.[39] The urban pattern is not markedly different from the rural picture. Bedford is the only town in the county to have consisted of more than one parish and here some testators made small bequests to the nearby churches and other religious buildings as well as to their own church.[40]

## *PAYS* AND SELFHOOD

The proliferation of specialist saints was a target for the reformers' ridicule:

> With blessynges of Saynt Germyne,
> I wyll me so determyne,
> That neyther foxe nor vermyne,
> Shall do my chuckens harme.
> For your duckes saynte Lenarde,
> For horse take Moses yearde,
> There is no better charme.
> If ye cannot slepe but slumber,
> Geve otes unto saynt Uncumber,
> And beanes in a serten number,
> Unto saynt Blase and Saynt Blythe.
> Geve onyons to saynt Cutlake,
> And garlyke to saynt Cyryake,
> If ye wyll shurne the head ake,
> Ye shall have them at Quene hythe.[41]

*Pace* the wit of the polemicists, the emergence of specialist saintly helpers merits study. Through their images they provided a binding force for communities and smaller units within communities, encompassing occupation, family and the individual. The appearance of these images might be determined by the special needs and identities of their suppliants. Two alabaster images offer very different aspects of St Katherine which suggest they were made for different clients. In one she is portrayed conventionally as a queen; the other bears the same sword of martyrdom but lacks the wheel and is vested as a non-royal widow or even a nun (**63**).[42]

England was not homogeneous in its choice of saints. For example, the religion of Devon and Cornwall, with its hosts of local saints, was self-evidently distinctive and removed from that of Bedfordshire or Kent. In late medieval Bedfordshire, apart from the few patronal images there is no record of any devotional images of the great figures of Anglo-Saxon sainthood like Dunstan, Edmund of East Anglia, Edward the Confessor and Etheldreda. Despite its illustrious past, the same is true of Kent. Absent are Alphege, Dunstan, Eanswith, Ethelburga, Mildred (with one non-patronal exception), Paulinus, Radegunde (one non-patronal exception) and Sexburga; the only older insular saints to feature are Thomas Becket and, much less frequently, St Augustine of Canterbury.[43]

Is it possible to identify the kinds of factors which underlay the introduction and popularity of the plethora of saints venerated by means of their images in the parish churches of England? It is probably more meaningful to avoid a synthetic overview and address this question through the micro-level of the parish. Our old friends at Eaton Bray and their neighbours in the adjoining parish of Totternhoe will introduce us to the saints whose images they endowed (**II, 4–6, 64, 65, 171**); with the aid of their counterparts elsewhere, and particularly in Kent, we will look at the nexus between *pays*, person and piety.

The Eaton Bray cast, excluding as usual the rood and St Sunday and apart from the two Marian images, was entirely male: the Trinity, Anthony, Christopher, Eligius, Erasmus, George, Nicholas and Thomas (presumably Becket).[44] The sexes were more balanced at Totternhoe, with images of Christopher, Giles (the patronal saint) and Roche, in the female company of Agatha, Margaret, Sitha and the two Marian images, one in the chancel and the other probably in the nave north aisle; there was also a Holy Trinity. The communion of saints gathered in the two parishes thus included a giant, female martyrs, hermits, a Greek bishop and a Greek warrior, Early Christian and Gallic bishops, an English martyr, a French plague victim and an Italian servant. Absent were the saints whose shrines were in the vicinity: Frehemund, in Dunstable Priory, which held the advowson of Totternhoe, and the far more illustrious Alban and associated Amphibalus at St Albans. The complementarity of the two parishes is noteworthy: only the Holy Trinity and St Christopher are common to both. One is tempted to see this as deliberate rather than providential, reflecting the close ties which existed between the two communities, manifested *inter alia* by the ownership of land in both parishes by some of the testators and by the sharing of the lordship by the Zouche and then the Bray families.[45]

The landscape and its fertility, its flora and fauna, the beasts which inhabited it and the climate on which the villagers of Eaton Bray and Totternhoe depended, like everyone else in Christendom, were all controlled by means of the power of the divine. What sort of *pays* did the saints represented in the two churches dwell in? The land to the north, west and east of both parishes is flat, with the line of the Chiltern Hills providing a backcloth to the south. Eaton Bray and Totternhoe were typical medieval settlements at the foot of the Chiltern escarpment, with a narrow strip configuration providing mixed agricultural resources (**66; Map 6, p. 280**). The arable open fields were located in the heavy clay soils of the lower ground in which the villages were set,

63. *Alabaster statuettes of St Katherine of Alexandria, fifteenth or early sixteenth century (left, private collection in Portugal; right, Victoria & Albert Museum, inv. no. A148-1946)*

64. *Totternhoe (Beds.), St Giles's church from the south-east; watercolour by Thomas Fisher, c. 1815 (Luton Museum Service)*

together with small closes; sheep were grazed on the chalk open downland slopes and the uplands were wooded and provided pasture for cattle and pigs.[46] Eaton Bray's village layout in late medieval and early modern times has been obscured by the gradual filling-in of the series of greens which characterized it, especially by a rash of new building in recent years. In contrast, Totternhoe's plan was L-shaped, with the houses laid out along two streets meeting at right angles.

Both parishes would have been very different places during the reign of the first two Tudor monarchs than they had been before 1300 when (probably) the first images of the saints were installed. Subsequently England had experienced the horror of the Black Death, which reached Bedfordshire in 1349 and saw the loss of nearly half its parish incumbents, including the vicar of Eaton Bray. Plague was recurrent and together with famine, widespread livestock epidemics and slumps in corn and wool prices, was responsible for the long agricultural depression of the fifteenth century.[47] By the early sixteenth century, when labour services had long been abolished and demesne leasing was widespread, there were opportunities for the more enterprising villagers to prosper. One such was Alys Cooke, an Eaton Bray widow. Alys was not short of a shilling or two. Her will of 1521 mentions sons, a daughter and grandchildren, a servant, a house, meadow and other land, arable produce (wheat, barley and malt), cattle, sheep, a horse and an ox bullock.[48] Alys made comprehensive provision for the well-being of her soul. She bequeathed land for her annual obit in perpetuity and 10 shillings 'To the sowle prest or brotherhed prest if the parrish have oon'. Every light received a small offering, ranging from 1*d* to 12*d*, including the rood and Sepulchre lights. The only image lights specified were those of St Nicholas and the Trinity. Cuthbert Cutlat and John Rudde also named Nicholas, among the other images, some of which were singled out by their fellow-parishioners.[49]

65. Totternhoe (Beds.), St Giles's church: interior looking east

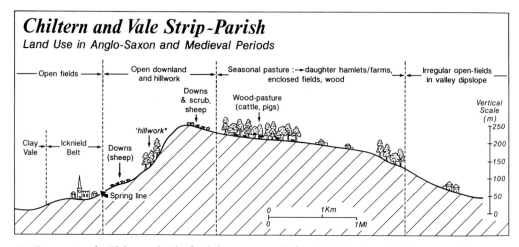

*66. Cross-section of a Chiltern and Vale of Aylesbury scarp-parish (from L.W. Hepple and A.M. Doggett,* The Chilterns, *Chichester, 2nd edn, 1994, fig. 44)*

Alys Cooke and her fellow-testators were well-to-do, but illness, hardship and early death were never absent from late medieval England. It is within this context that the saintly helpers of Eaton Bray and Totternhoe should be seen. Not all the saints present at Eaton Bray and Totternhoe had specific powers. Giles, the latter's patron saint, falls into this category, as does Thomas Becket. For obvious reasons the latter's popularity was eclipsed in Bedfordshire by the number of his images to be found in Kent, especially in the eastern part of the county. The majority of the non-Marian images in the two parishes, however, between them offered a range of specialisms.

## DEATH AND DISEASE: SS CHRISTOPHER AND ROCHE

The light of St Christopher at Eaton Bray received a bequest of 8*d* from John Rudde.[50] The standard iconography is a giant figure of the saint carrying the Christ-Child on his shoulders across a river (**XI**; **68**). His universality stemmed from his powers 'to put away sickness and sores from them that remember his passion and figure'. He was also efficacious against sudden death. An inscription in the wall-painting at Wood Eaton (Oxon.) reads 'who sees this image shall not die an ill death this day' ('Ki cest image verra le jur de male mort ne murra').[51] An ill death meant both an untimely end and death without benefit of the sacraments. The image is frequently painted on the wall opposite the principal lay entrance to the church to facilitate viewing (**III**; **8**). Images of St Christopher were among the first of the saints to appear on the pages of English illuminated manuscripts. As we saw at the beginning of this chapter, Henry III commissioned a St Christopher in 1240 for the chapel of St Peter ad Vincula; within a decade or so the saint had entered the repertoire of the mural painters of the Buckinghamshire Chilterns.[52] His appeal for the common man and woman is underlined by the presence in murals of landscapes with windmills and houses, fishermen and boats (**67**). A lost inscription at Pakefield (Suff.) referred to St Christopher as a sustainer against fatigue in daily toil.[53]

If venerating the image of St Christopher in his parish church was part of John Rudde's daily routine, he could be assured of the saint's protection and succour in his work in the fields or when setting out to visit his lands in Houghton Regis. St Christopher was much invoked by travellers and was frequently represented in the archdeaconry of Bedford. He features even more prominently in Kent wills, for this was a county of transit with many ports and centres of commerce. Whereas Bedfordshire testators mention only lights, in Kent there are requests for burial before the image of St Christopher, for furbishing the image by means of new tabernacles, for painting and gilding and candleholders and for endowing lights. At Lympne there was a fraternity of St Christopher. Although by the late fifteenth century Becket's shrine had lost much of its former popularity, it was still a powerful magnet for pilgrims and this, as well as Canterbury's position as the leading urban centre in the county, would explain the prominence accorded to St Christopher in its numerous parish churches. At Faversham, which like Canterbury lay on the principal road from London to the coast, the saint had a dedicated chapel in the parish church. Given his hazardous occupation, it is not surprising

*67. Horley (Oxon.), St Etheldreda's church: detail of fisherman in St Christopher mural, c. 1500*

that a fisherman like John Rykeman left a taper of 1lb of wax to the image of St Christopher in his parish church at Milton Regis near Sittingbourne.[54] For mariners, merchants and pilgrims embarking at Bristol for the shrine of St James at Compostella a primer was placed at the foot of the image of St Christopher in the church of All Saints.[55] The significance of this saint in such locations is exemplified by the gigantic late fourteenth-century sandstone image at Norton Priory (Ches.), a focal point for anyone crossing the Mersey (**XI**).[56] The clerical donor at the feet of an alabaster image, the Stathum brass at Morley (Derbys.) and the Lovell monument at Minster Lovell (Oxon.) all show that St Christopher appealed to every level of society (**62, 68, 122**).

In 1533 the small sums left by Thomas Bottisford, the parish priest of Totternhoe, to the lights in his church included 8*d* to a saint who was introduced for protection against the ever-present threat of plague:

> Then let us reverently with devotion pray unto this glorious saint S. Rocke, that by his intercession and prayer we may be delivered from the hard death of pestilence and epidemic, and that we may so live in this life and be penitent for our sins. . . .[57]

St Roche was a noble-born native of Montpellier in the south of France. In the second half of the fourteenth century he went on pilgrimage to Italy where he cured many victims of the plague. In the following century his cult expanded all over Europe. It had reached England by the 1480s, when his feast-day (16 August) entered the Calendar of the Sarum Breviary and Caxton included

*68. Alabaster St Christopher, c. 1400–50 (London, Victoria & Albert Museum, inv. no. A18-1921)*

a lengthy section on him in his first edition of the *Golden Legend*. St Roche appears on a number of East Anglian screen-paintings and twice among the internal statuary of Henry VII's Chapel, Westminster Abbey. He is usually depicted in pilgrimage garb, and either he or the angel who announced that he had contracted the disease, points to the plague spot on his leg; the dog which brought him food miraculously is also a standard feature. Apart from the Henry VII's Chapel representations, fewer than half a dozen carved English images are known, all alabaster (**69**); however, the fact that five are recorded in Bedfordshire alone (**Map 7, p. 280**) indicates that St Roche was of more significance at parish level than is apparent today.[58] Roche was considered especially efficacious because of his dying prayer that anyone who prayed to him would be delivered from plague; an early sixteenth-century woodcut is accompanied by a text promising the brethren, sisters and benefactors of St Roche's Hospital in Exeter that the day they recited the *Paternoster, Ave* and Creed they would be protected from pestilence.[59]

## *LABOR*: ANTHONY, SITHA, ELIGIUS AND ERASMUS

It was not just people who were vulnerable to disease. Alys Cooke and her peers could call upon divine assistance with the help of a fourth-century Egyptian desert father for the preservation of their livestock. In the surviving English images of St Anthony he is accompanied by a pig, a reference to his sole companion in the wilderness (**14, 15**).[60] The saint was held to be efficacious in the curing of swine-fever and cattle ailments. For a cleric like Thomas Bloxham, a chaplain of Great Addington in Northamptonshire, who requested interment before his image, St Anthony's exemplary eremitical life was likely to have been more relevant (**70**). For the sick and physically afflicted, his bodily torments were a source of solace and comfort and sometimes were stressed pictorially.[61]

Of all the saints found at Eaton Bray and Totternhoe, there was only one whose life-experience could be considered exemplary by her lay clientele. Displayed in a side-chapel of the church of S. Frediano in Lucca is the dessicated body of St Zita. Although officially canonized only in 1696, she was venerated in this city from shortly after her death in 1272. Zita (or Sitha, to use the English appellation) spent her working life in service and was famed for her piety, chastity and charity. It is a long way, in every sense, from a glass coffin in an affluent Tuscan city to an image in a south Bedfordshire church.[62] By the middle of the fourteenth century Sitha had made this metaphorical journey, in the process of which her identity was adjusted to meet the exigencies of a differently structured society. Initially the cult was promoted in Lucca by the Fatinelli family who had employed her. It was then taken up by the city patriciate (to whom the Fatinelli belonged) and disseminated throughout Italy by the mendicants. By 1355 the cult had found its way to London, probably via the Lucchese merchant community; during the course of the next half-century or so it spread to Norwich, York and eventually to every part of the country. A relic of St Sitha was brought to the Knights Hospitaller's commandery at Eagle (Lincs.) in 1446.[63] In addition to Totternhoe, in south Bedfordshire St Sitha was a focus of devotion at Houghton Regis and Luton; slightly further north, her image occurred at Eversholt (**Map 7, p. 280**).[64]

*69. Alabaster statuette of St Roche,* c. *1500 (Basque Museum, Bilbao, Spain)*

Why was St Sitha so popular and with whom? Her life made her a role-model for female servants; indeed her cult was arguably promoted by the Lucca commune in order to control a potentially disruptive underclass.[65] In England service was not confined to the lowest orders, nor was it invariably lifelong, as in Sitha's case. In late medieval England young people of both sexes and spanning the social spectrum spent time in service away from home, in rural as well as urban contexts. For them Sitha provided a model of moral rectitude, diligence and good works. For the daughters of better-off families, her chastity, charity and piety were also exemplary. The socially diverse nature of service in England would explain her presence in word and image on the pages of devotional books as well as pictorially in churches.[66] In 1402 Sir Thomas de Boynton made a

*70. Great Addington (Northants.), All Saints' church: brass of chaplain Thomas Bloxham (d. 1518)*

bequest to the light of St Sitha at Acklam (N. Yorks.) and she is depicted in high-quality illuminated manuscripts made for John Duke of Bedford (d. 1435) and William, Lord Hastings (d. 1483).[67] St Sitha was sufficiently venerated by the Fitzherbert family to be accorded the place of honour in the centre light of a window they donated to their parish church at Norbury (Derbys.). She is also one of the saints represented on the brass of Maud, Lady Willoughby (d. 1487) at Tattershall (Lincs.).

In the so-called *Bolton Hours*, probably of *c.* 1415–40, Sitha is depicted as a well-dressed maiden with rose-petals in her lap, a reference to the miraculous concealment of bread which she was giving to the poor (**71**). No keys are shown, but like her rosary beads (symbolizing her piety) they are a common attribute on the fifty or so screen-paintings and stained-glass representations – also on the handful of extant murals and alabaster carvings which would have functioned as devotional images (**72**).[68] The keys signified Sitha's efficaciousness as a retriever of lost property and also associate her with housekeeping: 'For los of good by casuel negligence/In al such caas do thy dilligence.'[69] This was not merely servanthood but referred to women's work in general. A small mural at Horley (Oxon.) depicts her surrounded by kitchen utensils (**73**). In common with other late representations, she is shown as a well-dressed woman of mature years, indicating an appeal to wives and widows as well as to daughters and servants. Although the female suppliant in the *Bolton Hours* and the location of the Horley image on the inner face of the westernmost pillar in the nave north arcade (**III**), a part of the church often assigned to women, underline the saint's relevance to women's lives, devotion to her was not exclusive to the gender. Sir Thomas de Boynton of Acklam was far from being the only male testator to endow an image of St Sitha; as usual, the majority of testamentary references were from men, including clergy. A fraternity of St Sitha was in existence at All Hallows London Wall by 1529–30 and several male testators in Kent requested burial before her image. At Boughton Monchelsea devotion to her spanned three generations of the Copping family.[70]

Less obviously than St Sitha, two saintly prelates present at Eaton Bray became associated with particular occupations.

St Eligius (or Loye, as he was usually known in late medieval England) lived in seventh-century Gaul. As a boy he was apprenticed to a goldsmith and later became master of the mint to the Frankish kings. In 641 he was consecrated bishop of Noyon, in which office he performed many miracles and lived a very holy life. As a saintly cleric St Eligius was a moral exemplar to anyone in holy orders. He also had a special relationship with the poor: 'S. Loye loved well poor people. . . . The poor people also loved him, that where he went they followed him, and they that would speak with him must ask and enquire of the poor people where he was.'[71]

His cult was widely diffused from the fourteenth century. Pictorially two miracles performed by him are highlighted, both concerning his metalworking skills but neither is recounted in the *Golden Legend*. Eligius's goldsmithing is emphasized in an initial in the *Carmelite Missal* of *c.* 1393 and associated with the London Whitefriars, but also containing lay donors/owners; here the bishop presents the golden saddle to Clothair (**74**). In 1492 the goldsmiths, locksmiths and bladesmiths were gathered under St Eligius's banner in the Ipswich Corpus Christi procession.[72] The tinworking industry of early sixteenth-century Chagford (Devon) would explain the existence of a guild dedicated to St Eligius. For other clients it was his powers with horses which were the most valued and determined his representation. 'The horse ys fayer, God save hym and Send Loye . . .' wrote the wool merchant Richard Cely in 1479 during his attempts to sell the animal.[73] Unsurprisingly St Eligius found especial favour with farriers, as he still does in parts of

71. *St Sitha in the* Bolton Hours, *c. 1415–40 (York Minster Library, MS Add. 2, f. 40v)*

Europe. The farriers of Derby were responsible for the maintenance of his light in All Saints' church there and in 1539 blacksmiths and farriers in the archdeaconry of Exeter refused to work on St Eligius's day.[74] Possibly the association of the Anglo-Saxon St Dunstan with goldsmithing was initially a factor in channelling Eligius towards farriers. A mural at Slapton (Northants.) has been dated to the fourteenth century and an alabaster at Freckenham (**75**) might have been executed in the early fifteenth century. All the other known monumental representations are no earlier than the second half of the fifteenth century.

The Freckenham panel is typical of the English carved representations in depicting the miraculous shoeing and re-attachment. According to this legend, St Eligius was shoeing a horse possessed by the devil; the horse was rearing and kicking violently, so the saint cut off one of its legs, shod and then replaced the leg. Unlike some of the continental renderings, all the English versions show St Eligius as a bishop, not a layman.[75] He thus signals the ability of a saintly bishop to become concerned in, and affect, the daily concerns of the laity. The Freckenham alabaster panel might be classified as a narrative subject, but in this instance it is one that acted as the saint's attribute.[76] The singling out of this episode enabled the beholder to identify with the saint in a way that was not offered by textual representations.

St Eligius was to hand at Eaton Bray if Cuthbert Cutlat or the blacksmith who shod his horse had need of recourse to him. Only at Houghton Regis is his image recorded elsewhere in Bedfordshire (**Map 7, p. 280**), whereas he appears in more than a score of Kent churches.[77] In both counties his association with masculine occupations is confirmed by the fact that no female testators mention bequests to his image and/or light.

72. *Alabaster image of St Sitha, late fifteenth century (Glasgow, Burrell Collection, inv. no. 1/44)*

Cuthbert Cutlat was the only one of the Eaton Bray testators to endow St Eligius and he also endowed another foreign bishop whose cult enjoyed a renaissance in the later Middle Ages.[78]

73. Horley (Oxon.), St Etheldreda's church: mural of St Sitha on a nave north-west pier, c. 1500

74. *St Eligius presenting the golden saddle to King Clothair in the* Carmelite Missal, *c. 1393 (London, British Library, MS Add. 29704–5, 44892, f. 164r)*

Probate and parish records show that St Erasmus had arrived in England sooner than is indicated by his tardy appearance in the Sarum Missal and his omission from the first edition of Caxton's *Golden Legend*.[79] The *tabula* of 1417 in St Kerrian's, Exeter, cited above, may be the first recorded representation of St Erasmus in England while St Crux church in York possessed an image by 1442.[80] The popularity of St Erasmus overshadowed that of St Eligius and by the Reformation images were distributed widely. He did not, however, find favour with everyone. A late fifteenth-century Lollard was enraged by devotion to the saint at Newbury (Berks.): 'when devote Cristen people be offering their candel to the ymage of seint Erasme I have wold I had a hatchet in my hand And wer behynde theim to knoke theim on their heddis'.[81] While references occur throughout East Anglia and the West Country, only two have been documented in Buckinghamshire, only one each in Northamptonshire and Surrey and a handful in Sussex. In Bedfordshire there was a concentration in five churches in the south of the county, including Eaton Bray, plus the screen-painting at Roxton, east of Bedford (**Map 7**, p. **280**; **7**). Devotion to St Erasmus was strong in Kent, but not everywhere. Most images were found in the Weald, with

75. *Freckenham (Suff.), St Andrew's church: alabaster panel of St Eligius and the miraculous shoeing and re-attachment, early fifteenth century*

76. Painted panel depicting the martyrdom of St Erasmus, dated 1474 (London, Society of Antiquaries)

a secondary distribution among settlements on or near the coast (**Maps 8, 9, p. 281**). Erasmus was one of the saints before whose images special offerings were made on their feast-days at Canterbury Cathedral in the fifteenth and sixteenth centuries.[82]

Is there an explanation for the distribution pattern? One late medieval English account promised a comprehensive range of corporeal and spiritual boons to those who said prayers, offered candles during the liturgy or performed an act of charity in the name of St Erasmus.[83] The writer also described more than fifty different tortures inflicted on the saint's body during his martyrdom under the Emperor Diocletian, but only one of these is represented pictorially. The panel commissioned from a Netherlandish painter in 1474 by John Holynbourne, a monk of Christ Church, Canterbury, depicts the disembowelment of the bishop with a nautical windlass (**76**).[84] The same emblem is used for iconic images (**7, 77**), but the quantity of panels depicting this particular torment is remarkable. It is another instance, like St Eligius's representations, of a narrative scene performing the function of an attribute. The choice of this torture, or the windlass attribute, is also common on the continent and must have been dictated either by a pre-existing receptive clientele or by the desire to create one – or both. In the *Miracles of Henry VI* is an account of a seaman named Henry Walter who had visions both of the king and of St Erasmus sharing his sufferings with his own. As the windlass indicates, St Erasmus (as St Elmo) had special significance for sailors like Walter and he protected them in storms.[85] The saint's maritime clientele is underlined in the background of Holynbourne's panel with its rendering of shipping.

*77. Alabaster panel of SS Faith and Erasmus, c. 1500 (Glasgow, Burrell Collection, inv. no. 1/3)*

Flocks of sheep are also depicted, showing that St Erasmus's clientele extended to those engaged in spinning and weaving. For the former, his windlass performed the same function as a distaff. A weaver named William Hill in 1493–4 bequeathed a taper to burn before St Erasmus in his parish church of Milton-by-Sittingbourne (Kent).[86] The concentration of images of St Erasmus in the Weald is thus doubly significant. It was both a centre of the cloth industry and a provider of timber for ship-building; Milton-by-Sittingbourne and Faversham were both ports.[87] St Erasmus also occurred in other areas where spinning and weaving were practised, including Bedfordshire. Eaton Bray's sheep provided the raw material for the industry. In 1505 Giles Hebulwhete, a Shillington weaver, left half a pound of wax to the light of St Erasmus in his parish church; for Richard Swift, a fellow-weaver, the image of the saint with his windlass on the screen of Roxton church may not have been without significance (**7**).[88] Mariners and wool- and clothworkers were not the only occupational groups which looked to this saint. He was considered efficacious for stomach diseases, hence his presence in the murals of the Commandery at Worcester (a former hospital) and the occurrence of a surgeon among the numerous testators who mentioned his light. Others were a baker and a fletcher, while Holynbourne was a monk. In common with Eligius, very few women were numbered among those who posthumously endowed his image. However, he seems to have enjoyed more favour among the social elites than Eligius. Queen Elizabeth Woodville founded a chapel dedicated to Erasmus in Westminster Abbey, in gratitude for Edward IV's preservation from a storm through his intercession. St Erasmus is one of the saints depicted on the alabaster tombchest of Sir Thomas Rodney (d. 1471) at Rodney Stoke (Som.).

## MORE HELPERS: NICHOLAS AND GEORGE

The image of St Nicholas which stood in Eaton Bray church is one of a score recorded in Bedfordshire. His episcopal figure was even more frequent in Kent, where the extensive coastline ensured the enduring popularity of a saint whose protection, like that of St Erasmus, extended particularly to those whose livelihood depended on water. There his importance is signified by his occurrence as patronal saint in a number of locations on or adjacent to the sea (**Maps 8, 9, p. 281**).[89] The sequence in the Sarum Missal on St Nicholas's feast-day (6 December) contains nautical metaphors emanating from his miraculous rescue of sailors in a storm. It also refers to his fasting while an infant and learning as a youth.[90] St Nicholas's cult was of considerable antiquity in Eaton Bray, for the manorial chapel already bore this dedication in 1210.[91] Judging by the number of bequests to this saint's light in the parish church, devotion to him was still very much alive in the early sixteenth century: together with the Trinity, St Nicholas's light is mentioned by more testators than any other. Perhaps it was his patronage of children which appealed to Alys Cooke with her numerous progeny in landlocked Bedfordshire. Alternatively, she may have looked to St Nicholas to preserve her substantial worldly goods. The efficacy of the image would have been reinforced by the tale recounted in the *Golden Legend* whereby a Jew who had been robbed vented his anger by whipping an image of St Nicholas which he had used to protect his house; the saint appeared to the thieves, bearing the marks of the beating inflicted on the image, as a result of which they returned the Jew's goods and he became a Christian.[92] The widespread custom of the boy-bishop, associated with St Nicholas, was observed at this time in nearby Wing; in the parishes the ceremony involved the vesting and processing of a child as bishop, soliciting contributions which were passed to the churchwardens.[93]

John Rudde and Walter Swanson were numbered among the benefactors of St Nicholas's light; these two were also the only Eaton Bray testators to leave small sums to the light of St George, who enjoyed great popularity in late medieval England. 'This blessed and holy martyr S. George is patron of this realm of England and the cry of men of war' says the *Golden Legend*.[94]

The cult of this archetypal warrior-saint became widespread in western Christendom as a result of the Crusades. Royal support was at the root of its burgeoning in England. Edward III adopted George as patron saint of his new Order of the Garter and of England. In 1388 the English army was instructed to wear the red cross of St George on its surcoats. Under Henry V the cult was boosted still further. As was observed earlier, shortly after Agincourt the feast of St George ('the special patron and protector of the English nation') was raised to the highest rank of a Greater Double. With the presentation of the saint's heart to Windsor by the Emperor Sigismund, England came into possession of a major relic. Later monarchs continued to promote the cult of the 'parfit knight'. Edward IV demonstrated continuity with the past by breathing new life into the Order of the Garter and embarking on the lavish rebuilding of the Windsor chapel. Henry VII bore a standard of St George at Bosworth and at his coronation 6 yards of velvet cloth were ordered for the making of a hanging with the cross of St George. His son matched his devotion and during his reign the first coins bearing the saint's image were minted.[95]

As the *Golden Legend* states, St George was particularly associated with the military caste. Books of Hours owned by nobles and knights often portray them kneeling before him. Images of George can still be seen in windows at Cranbrook and Lullingstone (Kent), paid for in the early sixteenth century by Sir Richard Guilford and Sir John Peche respectively. He is depicted on the Culpeper tomb relief at Goudhurst (**123**). Less exalted fighting men also identified with his martial attributes. Peter Horney, another Kentish man, instructed his executors to sell his armour and crossbow in order to purchase an image of St George for his parish church of Cobham.[96] In Eaton Bray there were those who had good cause to invoke the saint. Walter Swanson was one of forty-seven men of the parish listed in the Muster Roll to serve under Lord Bray. Some indeed fought in France, including another Cuthbert Cutlat, who made his will at Guisnes in September 1544 and probably died there soon afterwards. John Lord Bray himself was to die of wounds received during the battle of St Quentin in Queen Mary's reign.[97]

The fifteenth and early sixteenth centuries saw the burgeoning of St George's cult in the parishes of England and he came to enjoy the prolonged affection of the people at large. George is quite a common Christian name among testators and their witnesses in pre-Reformation Bedfordshire. In this county the number of images (in stained glass and murals as well as in three-dimensional form) and altars dedicated to him was at least fourteen. No fewer than seventy-six churches in Kent are known to have possessed devotional images of St George; there is no reason to think that either of these counties was exceptional. References to the acquisition of St George images occur more frequently in wills and churchwardens' accounts from the late fifteenth century onwards than for any other saint. It is little wonder that Henry VIII's government treated this potent national symbol with circumspection when it embarked on its campaign of church reform. St George's day was one of the very few exempted from the abolition of holy day observance in the decrees of 1536 and 1541.[98]

A handful of carved George images have survived, clad in the armour of their time. The first extant fourteenth-century representations in illumination, glass and mural painting depict the saint as a knight without either horse or dragon. This model continued into the following century (**78**), when the equestrian image known as a 'rydyng George' began to come into

vogue.[99] These were elaborate tableaux, with
the saint mounted and engaging in combat
with the dragon in the presence of the
princess and sometimes her parents. Some
were mechanical, like the George made in
1473 for the London church of St Botolph by
Billingsgate, which by means of a series of
ropes and pulleys enabled the saint to slay the
dragon and rescue the princess.[100] An early
example of a 'rydyng George' is the
freestanding image in Washington, one of the
finest English alabasters (**79**). It dates from the
early fifteenth century and the violence of the
combat between the equestrian saint and the
dragon is subordinated to elegance of
composition. The reverse is fully carved, a rare
feature of English alabasters, albeit in a
flattened profile, indicating that the image was
to be viewed from both sides; possibly it was
placed in an open tabernacle or on an altar.
The multi-media George belonging to the
Worshipful Company of Armourers and
Brasiers was created about a century later than
the Washington image (**XIII**).[101] Dendro-
chronology has established that the dating is
compatible with the 'George of compleate
Armor on horseback' presented to the
Armourers Company in 1528 by the Master,
William Vynard. The group is principally of
polychromed oak, with iron used for the body
and horse armour and leather with gilt-metal
rosettes for the reins; Vynard almost certainly
made the armour for the group. It provides
some indication of the monumental and
elaborate 'rydyng Georges' which involved
parishes and individuals in heavy expenditure.

*78. St Albans Cathedral (Herts.): freestone image of St
George, c. 1400*

George images were set up in a number of
different locations within churches and served a variety of functions. The George commissioned
in 1518 by John Ratcliffe was to be housed in a specially built private chapel or oratory within
Ripon Minster; it comprised an enclosed space with a loft. Georges were similarly elevated at
Reading, Southwark (Surrey) and Kendal (Cumbria).[102] The well-preserved polychromed
George at Coventry was the patronal image of the chapel at Gosford Bridge (**80**).[103] St George
images played a central role in the devotional life of the numerous guilds dedicated to him which
were established in late medieval England. The patronal image of the St George guild at
Nottingham was set up in the south aisle of St Peter's church and that of the powerful fraternity

79. *Polychromed alabaster St George, early fifteenth century (Washington DC, National Gallery of Art, Kress Collection, inv. no. K1377)*

*80. Polychromed oak St George, late fifteenth century (Coventry, Herbert Art Gallery)*

at Norwich (whose leading officials were effectively the city corporation) was located in the guild chapel near the high altar.[104]

Such locations were not fixed. Processions featuring St George were common in late medieval England. The members of the Nottingham guild took special measures to protect the armour of their George when they paraded with it in the Corpus Christi processions. On St George's day the patronal image of St George's church, Canterbury, was removed from its place on the north side of the high altar and carried in procession. After the Reformation a second, rather battered, George at Coventry served as 'Peeping Tom' in Godiva processions and it is possible that previously it had been used in St George's day rituals.[105] The two heads with different helmets and three arms supplied for Ratcliffe's George provided a variety of gestures, probably associated with public rituals.[106] The processional George was not invariably the same one which was set up in the church. At Norwich individuals paraded as St George, the dragon and the princess (or 'Maid' or 'Margaret') and acted out the drama on the saint's day. A painted and carved dragon's head in Norwich Castle Museum perhaps dates from this period.[107]

Many of the 'riding' Georges, like the Coventry 'Peeping Tom' image, were life-size or even larger and this was reflected in the costs. The £20 price of the Ripon George was not unusual. The total cost of the George which the Exeter freemason and 'Jorge-maker' John Carter made for Croscombe (Som.) between 1506–7 and 1511–12 amounted to £27 11s 8d.[108] For some parishes investment in such monumental groups was a protracted process. The churchwardens of Bassingbourn (Cambs.) started fund-raising for an image of St George by 1511/12, in which year 33s was collected. In 1518 John Hubard, the parish guild priest, bequeathed money for this image as an alternative to a vestment. In 1521–22 Robert Jones of Saffron Walden was paid £10 13s 4d 'for makeng of the seid ymage & the standyng'. Still to be made were the attendant figures of the queen and king, for which Jones received 4d in down-payment or 'ernest'. The churchwardens kept a watching brief on their investment, for they incurred expenses 'att diverse tymes Rydyng to see' their new George at Saffron Walden. The George was delivered in 1521–22, at which point Nicholas Benett undertook to paint it. Part-payment for this amounted to 30s. In the following year Benett received a further 40s 4d. Gold for the gilding cost 5s 4d. Funds were raised from 'devotione mony' and in the same year (1522–23) the king and queen were delivered for 10s 1d, inclusive of carriage. Work was still in progress in 1525–7, when 2d was paid for 'the sewyng of sanct george', although this could be a repair.[109]

Such images were perhaps not dissimilar to the Georges which survive in northern Europe, especially in Scandinavia.[110] Like Bernt Notke of Lübeck's theatrical masterpiece in the Stockholm City Church and the Armourers' George, verisimilitude was provided in some of the English examples by the employment of natural materials. Four calf-skins and four horse-skins were used for the George at St Lawrence's Reading in 1534 and, like Notke's horse, its harness was embellished with bells, which also featured on several London images. The St George belonging to St Peter's church at Nottingham was clad in real armour with copper-gilt spurs, necessitating its maintenance by an armourer.[111] Georges used in processions and incorporating easily damaged materials were fragile items. It was probably as much for this reason as for accessibility that the churchwardens of St Peter's commissioned from John Pekke 'a small image of St George in alabaster newly purchased for offering to be kissed etc.'.[112] Some of the extant smaller alabaster reliefs or figures may have performed a similar surrogate service, functioning in the same way as images of the Christ crucified placed below the main Crucifixion scene in expensive illuminated Missals (**81**).

*81. Alabaster relief of St George slaying the dragon, fifteenth century (Glasgow, Burrell Collection, inv. no. 1/45)*

Whether the St George image at Eaton Bray resembled any of the extant or documented representations is unknown. Equally unknown are the circumstances in which the Eaton Bray images were commissioned and who paid for them. The wills show that the full complement was in place by 1515, with the possible exception of St Eligius, first mentioned in 1521. The devotional histories of this saint, Erasmus and probably Anthony and even George suggest that their representations were acquired during the fifteenth century or at the beginning of the sixteenth. Newer cults were less in evidence at Totternhoe, yet here too SS Sitha and Roche must have been late additions.[114]

There can be little doubt that in many places the acquisition of images was prompted by the clergy. Under Abbot William de Trumpington (1214–35) images were displayed in the north transept of St Albans Abbey 'for the edification and consolation of the laity'. Maurice Hardwicke, the incumbent of All Saints' Bristol, employed the ancient *topos* of images exciting people to devotion when he commissioned a wooden image of St Ursula.[113] Other clergy wills and the presence of clerics on existing images demonstrate that Hardwicke's act was hardly exceptional (**54, 68**). Yet it is one thing to broadcast the worth of the saints, but quite another to have them take root and flourish. More explicitly than any of the Eaton Bray testators, in solely endowing their parish churches with the images of St Sitha and St Erasmus respectively, Elizabeth Wynch of Luton and Giles Hebulwhete, our Shillington weaver, revealed their empathy with their special helpers and protectors.[114]

# CHAPTER SIX

# AN YMAGE FUL NOTABLE LYKE A PYTE: THE PROLIFERATION OF MARIAN IMAGES

Chapter Three examined the introduction of devotional images of Our Lady into parish churches from Anglo-Saxon times. The process of addition, replacement and renewal continued until the Reformation. On the continent the thirteenth and especially the fourteenth centuries saw a massive expansion in Marian images. A study of the département of Seine-et-Marne in France has revealed nearly ninety fourteenth-century statues of the Virgin and Child, almost all from parish churches; most are of stone, and no doubt many more made of less durable wood formerly existed in this region.[1] The argument that this was an exceptionally rich area – and one which enjoyed proximity to the great cathedral *chantiers* – can be countered by reference to the large numbers of existing Marian images of the same period from Scandinavia, the Holy Roman Empire and Spain.[2] It is apparent from visitations and the few surviving examples that images of the Virgin were commonplace in England during the thirteenth and fourteenth centuries. Through her representations the Virgin became familiar and accessible to every English man, woman and child. Communities, fraternities and sufficiently wealthy individuals and families endowed separate chantry chapels and altars, many of which were dedicated to the Virgin as the most efficacious of saintly intercessors. The provision of these new architectural features and fittings was among the most important agents in the transformation of parish church design from the thirteenth century.

Marian images not only multiplied, they also diversified. New kinds of images of Our Lady came into being, endowing her with various identities which brought her closer to the life-experiences of her devotees. The church of St Mary serving the mid-Bedfordshire village of Marston Moreteyne demonstrates the wide choice of Marian images available for veneration in the later Middle Ages (**82**). Like nearby Elstow Abbey, this handsome church is distinguished by its detached bell-tower. The fourteenth-century chancel was re-fenestrated in the following century. The heraldry on the external label stops of the east window indicates that the work was carried out at the expense of Sir Thomas Reynes (d. 1451), the manorial lord, who with his wife is commemorated by a brass in the place of honour to the north of the high altar. The remodelling of the chancel was followed by a new and spacious nave with its aisles, one of which extends alongside the south side of the chancel; the presence of Reynes heraldry on the south porch stonework shows that Sir Thomas's descendants were also involved in funding the work. Decoration and embellishment were still in progress in the early sixteenth century. In 1505 a

82. *Marston Moreteyne (Beds.), St Mary's church: interior looking east*

bequest was made to the painting of the still-existing Doom over the chancel arch and the style of the surviving figures painted on the rood screen dado suggests a similar date for their execution.[3]

By this time Marston Moreteyne church housed one of the largest assemblages of devotional images in the Bedford archdeaconry (**Map 5, p. 279**). Apart from the rood, St Sunday and the Jesus altar, wills mention representations of All Souls, the Trinity (in the Trinity Chapel), St Anthony, St Christopher (probably the mural image of this saint which exists under the whitewash of the nave north aisle wall east of the porch), St James, St John the Baptist, St Katherine, St Margaret, St Nicholas and St Thomas Becket (the last being located in the chancel). An outlying chapel at Roxhill, west of the village, had an image of St Lawrence, its titular saint. This heavenly company was dominated by the Virgin, who was represented by more than half a dozen images. There was the titular image at the high altar; another must have stood at Our Lady altar (presumably at the east end of either the nave north chapel or the chancel south chapel). A third image, known as Our Lady in the Pillar, was in the nave. Also present were images of Our Lady in Gesyn, Our Lady of Pity, or *Pietà*, the Assumption and the Virgin as a child or young woman with St Anne, her mother.[4] None of these representations has survived and it is impossible to assign any of them to the eight niches and brackets or corbels in the nave, or to the ninth at the east end of the south chapel. The only possible exception is the recess in the north aisle, which from its shape might have housed either the *Pietà* or the Gesyn. This formerly bore a painted inscription referring to a year (erased) in Henry VII's reign. Even when an event like the Assumption or Nativity was represented, it functioned as a specific Marian attribute. By the early sixteenth century it was possible for the parishioners not only to venerate each image individually, but also, were they so minded, to construct a pictorial narrative of the Virgin's life.

The various iconographical types represented at Marston Moreteyne provide a helpful starting point for a study of the diffusion and expansion of Marian imagery in parish churches during the later Middle Ages. The types will be examined in conjunction with surviving images and written sources from elsewhere. Those about which most is known will be discussed first.

## AN YMAGE FUL NOTABLE LYKE A PYTE

Only one Marston Moreteyne parishioner referred to the image known as either Our Lady of Pity or the *Pietà*. Nevertheless, this Marian iconography was universally popular throughout late medieval Europe. It was a powerful and moving representation which epitomized the late medieval shift towards a more self-focused and affective piety.

Our Lady of Pity emerged from a South German cultural ambience in which mystics like Henry Suso (*c.* 1295–1366) also flourished. The earliest extant images from this region date from *c.* 1320. The iconography combined the narrative of the Lamentation at the foot of the Cross with the symbolic promise of salvation for humanity through Christ's sacrifice. Simultaneously it fused the belief in Our Lady as grieving mother, who nevertheless remained steadfast in her conviction of the coming Resurrection, with her role as *mediatrix* for mankind. The result was a potent emotive cocktail.[5]

The iconography was known in Italy by the middle of the fourteenth century; by the late 1380s it was circulating among the elites in France and had found its way to the Netherlands. Despite the enormous scale of destruction, it is reasonably certain that the *Pietà* became a familiar item in the repertoire of painters and carvers in England at about the same time as in France and the Netherlands.[6] Our Lady of Pity appears in at least one English late fourteenth-century book of hours, on some folios added towards the end of the century (Oxford, Keble College MS 47, f. 10v) (**83**). The manuscript may have belonged to the high-status Bohun family.[7]

Imagery in books of hours may only have reached an elite audience, but by the same date the *Pietà* in monumental form had made its way into the public space of the church. A chapel and altar of the Pity existed in Cromer church (Norf.) by 1388 and three years later an image of the *Pietà* in Norwich Cathedral was attracting substantial oblations. Thame and Hornton churches in Oxfordshire both preserve wall-paintings of Our Lady of Pity (**84, 85, 87**).[8] The former has a canopy which is comparable with those in the glazing of New College Chapel in Oxford, of *c.* 1380–6, and is unlikely to be far removed in date; stylistically, the same applies to the Hornton figure.[9] That the image was present in a rural church like Hornton suggests that Our Lady of Pity was widely known in England well before 1400. Documentary evidence shows that by the early fifteenth century the *Pietà* could be found in churches from Devon to Yorkshire and was as ubiquitous as anywhere in Europe. Apart from Marston Moreteyne, pre-Reformation wills mention twenty other Bedfordshire churches with this image; this represents a lower total than once existed, for neither of the two surviving images at Blunham and Tilsworth is documented. The figures for Kent are sixty-two in east and twenty-seven in west Kent. In other words, between one in four and one in six of the parish churches and parish chapels in Bedfordshire and Kent are known to have had an image of Our Lady of Pity. Devotion to the Virgin was very strong in England, so the true figure is likely to have been considerably higher; Waterton's assessment that there was no church in England without a *Pietà* may not have been too wide of the mark.[10]

We also know the power of the image to move its viewers. A *Pietà* in a Norwich church is the only instance of a specific image in England to which a response is singled out in Margery Kempe's spiritual 'autobiography'. The sight of the image reduced Margery to her usual lachrymose state: she was impelled to 'cryyn ful lowde & wepyn ful sor'.[11] The image is unique among devotional images (apart from the rood) in spawning vernacular poetry. For example, one poet claimed to have been inspired by a *Pietà* which spoke to him:

> In a chirche as I gan knele,
> This enders daye to here a masse,
> I sawe a sighte me liked wele,
> I shal tell you what it was.
> I saw a pite in a place,
> Owre lady and her sone in feere;
> ofte she wepte and sayde, 'Alas.
> Now lith here dede my dere sone dere!'[12]

A score or so of monumental *Pietàs* of English workmanship have survived, mostly carved from alabaster. Several found their way to the continent, exported either before or after the Reformation. The iconography of some of those now outside England may have been dictated by foreign clients, but since much alabaster carving was on an industrial scale they are treated here as an insular cultural phenomenon. Other images of Our Lady of Pity, like those at Blunham and Tilsworth, were discovered during church restorations. The Oxfordshire mural *Pietàs* were concealed by whitewash. The representations are as diverse as their continental counterparts.

83. Pietà *in a book of hours, end of fourteenth century (Oxford, Keble College, MS 47, f. 10v)*

84. *Hornton (Oxon.), St John the Baptist's church: chancel arch showing murals of* Pietà *(left) and St George (right),*
c. *1380–90*

*85. Hornton (Oxon.), St John the Baptist's church:* Pietà *mural, c. 1380–90*

*86. Battlefield (Salop), the former collegiate church of St Mary Magdalen: oak* Pietà, *fifteenth century*

Apart from the variety of materials (freestone, alabaster, wood, textile, painted panel, mural and miniature painting), the sizes range from the monumental to the diminutive; some of the alabasters are in the form of relief panels, others are free-standing. The largest of the extant carved images are just over a metre high (at Battlefield in Shropshire, the Musée national du Moyen Age in Paris and the chapel of St André-de-Cubzac, Gironde, France) (**86**, **88**). If, as seems likely, a bracket in the Bauchun Chapel of Norwich Cathedral was made for a *Pietà*, its width indicates that the height of the image must have been at least 2.5m, rivalling the size of some of the more substantial continental examples. The complete Thame mural would have been of similar height while that at Hornton is just over 1.5m. At the other end of the spectrum is the miniscule alabaster at Wood Ditton (Cambs.), which when entire cannot have been much taller than 30cm, a size more appropriate to a personal image associated with a tomb, or even the designated seat of a parishioner. Alabasters at Blunham, Breadsall (Derbys.) and in the Victoria & Albert Museum probably represent the norm of between 70 and 80cm in height (**VII**, **89**, **90**).

*87. Thame (Oxon.), St Mary's church:* Pietà *mural (detail), c. 1380–90*

Painting and gilding gave different emphases to the image. The Virgin's garments are painted with ermine on an alabaster at Burghley House (Cambs.), stressing her role as Queen of Heaven. Most of the surface of the Blunham Pity is left unpainted, and the red lining of the Virgin's robe evokes the splashes of Christ's bleeding wounds. The total of 33 shillings left by three members of the Caryngton family to the painting of the *Pietà* at Dunton (Beds.) suggest that it was much more elaborately polychromed than the Blunham image.[13] For an impression of the appearance of the Dunton and Battlefield images (the latter retains traces of pigmentation) recourse has to be had to well-preserved examples like a Swabian *Pietà* in the Cloisters Museum, New York (**VI**). On this, the Virgin's regal status is expressed by her gilded mantle.[14]

A mood of emotional restraint is evoked by the majority of the alabasters. The fine Cluny Museum alabaster has iconographical features found on many of the English *Pietà*s (**88**).[15] The image is not a simple compression of the Lamentation scene. The Virgin is enthroned and the body of her son is turned outwards, displaying His wounds to the spectator. Despite the wounds, His body does not reflect the agony of the Passion, but lies in repose. Nor is it clasped in an expression of lamentation by His mother. The Virgin, whose size is magnified, does not look at Christ but gazes into the distance with an expression of contemplation. Her pensiveness lacks the

*88. Alabaster* Pietà, *early fifteenth century (Musée national du Moyen Age, Paris, inv. no. Cl.11906)*

*89. Alabaster* Pietà, *early fifteenth century (Victoria & Albert Museum, inv. no. A197-1946)*

*90. Breadsall (Derbys.), All Saints' church: alabaster* Pietà, *early fifteenth century*

*91. Drawing of a* Pietà *prefacing a poem by John Lydgate, late fifteenth century (Cambridge, Trinity College, MS R. 3. 21, f. 238r)*

joyfulness of some of the German images, which stress belief in redemption through Christ's sacrifice rather than her maternal grief. Our Lady's participation in both the Incarnation and the Redemption is emphasized by holding her veil in her left hand. As expounded in the *Meditationes Vitae Christi*, at His birth the Virgin took Christ in her arms and 'so wrapped hym in the keuerchiefes of hir heued and leide hym in the cracche'. The action is repeated at the Passion: the Virgin, distressed by her son's nakedness before He was nailed to the Cross, 'wente in haste to her dere sone and clipped hym and girt hym aboute the lendes [loins] with the keuerchief of her heued'.[16] On the Cloisters *Pietà*, the Virgin's veil and Christ's loincloth are both white and have identical fringes. The interweaving of biblical episodes on the Cluny alabaster is continued on the hillock representing Golgotha, on which Our Lady is enthroned.

The veil-touching gesture evidently was much favoured in England; it is a feature of the majority of the surviving carved images, including the Battlefield *Pietà* (**86**), and not only those, like the Cluny image, which date from the early fifteenth century. It appears on a late fifteenth-century *Pietà* in Lisbon and on a drawing of similar date prefacing a poem by the monk John Lydgate (**91**).[17]

The Cluny Museum image is not a type followed by all English representations of Our Lady of Pity. The veil gesture was widespread but not universal. It is not depicted in the Keble College Hours (**83**) and is also absent from examples in other media, including some of the carved and mural versions and the embroidered image on the London Vintners' Company funerary pall. In some versions, such as a stained-glass panel at East Harling (Norf.), Christ's body is closer in scale to the Virgin than in others. In the Keble miniature Christ's head and upper body are supported by the Virgin's left arm, rather than her right, a feature shared with the battered remains of the

92. *Long Melford (Suff.), Holy Trinity church: stained-glass image of the* Pietà *and donor, late fifteenth century*

freestone image at Tilsworth and the stained-glass panel at Long Melford (Suff.); in the latter Christ has His eyes open and looks at His mother (**92**). Several alabasters have a cast of supporting characters. On a panel at Thorning in Denmark the *Pietà* is placed between God the Father in Heaven and the descent into Hell. The temporal context within the scriptural account is sometimes underlined by the presence of Joseph of Arimathea and St Mary Magdalen and/or the cross in the background (**89**). Our Lady is represented as an elderly woman on an image in Lisbon. In a rare case where the support for a carved Our Lady of Pity can be identified, the iconographic enrichment is continued. The bracket at the south-east angle of the nave south aisle at Dunton, adjacent to an altar, is embellished with carved roses (**93**). The rose had been connected allegorically with the Virgin since at least the twelfth century in hymns and prayers and became the subject of English vernacular poetry:

> There is no rose of swych vertu
> As is the rose that bar Jesu.[18]

During the fourteenth century roses began to be linked pictorially with Our Lady and not just on the *Pietà*. Several German Pities also have roses on their base (**94**).[19]

The English *Pietà* thus exhibited considerable variation. One application of the image seems to have been peculiar to England and represents a moralizing tale about personal conduct. Early fifteenth-century murals at Broughton (Bucks.) and Corby Glen (Lincs.) depict Our Lady of Pity surrounded by fashionably attired young men, who by swearing by parts of Christ's body in effect had caused His Passion and symbolically had dismembered Him, thereby condemning themselves to Hell. The Broughton version shows this literally, with the men holding various bodily parts and Christ's body lacking a foot (**95**). At Corby there are seven youths, each attended by a devil, an allusion to the seven deadly sins.[20]

93. Dunton (Beds.), St Mary
Magdalen's church: image-bracket at east
end of nave south aisle, late fourteenth or
fifteenth century

94. Polychromed wooden Pietà with its
base, c. 1360 (Rheinisches
Landesmuseum, Bonn, inv. no. 12983)

*95. Broughton (Bucks.), St Lawrence's church: mural of the Pietà surrounded by blasphemers, early fifteenth century*

Conversely, there are continental versions which do not occur on this side of the Channel, although this may be attributable to lack of survival. For example, no English image of Our Lady of Pity exhibits the graphic horror of the earliest German images. Neither has any image survived which is absorbed into the patron's familiar landscape in the manner of the panel at Grand-Vabre (Rodez, France), where the locally venerated Ste Foy (Faith) is one of the ancillary figures.[21] The tiny fraction of the former vast numbers of English *Pietàs* to have come down to us makes it impossible to construct a formalist taxonomy of the image. Whether or not there was a pattern of distinctive regional types, as has been argued for the Rhineland and France by Krönig and Forsyth, the majority of extant examples are products of the Midlands alabaster trade which at least by the early fifteenth century operated through itinerant agents and a diffused series of urban retail outlets.[22]

In what ways might an image like the Cluny Museum *Pietà* have functioned? How was it viewed and received? Unlike the images in books of hours, most of the carved images were in the public domain and therefore were available to all strata of society. Researching the reception of the *Pietà* too has obvious limitations. The Cluny and the other English Pities are not just separated temporally from their medieval devotional contexts; with the exception of the mural images they have also been divorced from their original locations. Only in a few instances are the precise emplacements verifiable. The bulk of the evidence relating to Our Lady of Pity is documentary, chiefly late medieval wills. But collectively the various kinds of evidence, including the artefacts themselves, shed considerable light on the various meanings attached to the image.

Our Lady of Pity at Thame is painted on the south-east crossing pier, facing the congregation (**87**). The Hornton mural also faces west, in this case from the north side of the chancel arch (**84**). Both are adjacent to the site of the chancel screen, above which was the rood, the image of Christ on the Cross, flanked by the Virgin and St John. At Hornton a mural of the Doom, with Christ enthroned in Heaven as judge and attended by Our Lady and St John as intercessors, survives on the wall above the chancel arch. The *Pietà* may be an iconic image, but its proximity at Thame and Hornton to the rood permitted the viewer to construct a narrative of the Passion. In describing the image as depicting the Virgin at her son's Passion and burial, a Kent vicar seems to have been accustomed to performing that very act of building a narrative around it.[23] The Thame image certainly stood above an altar and the height and position of the Hornton Pity suggest that it too may have been placed over an altar. The physical association of the *Pietà* with an altar underlined its role as a Eucharistic image, especially during Mass, when the symbolic Real Presence could be echoed graphically by Christ's broken body in the arms of His grieving yet meditative mother. The lower section of the Thame mural is lost and the Hornton image is severely damaged, but both are likely to have followed the usual pattern of showing Christ's body turned towards the viewer, exhibiting the wounds of His sacrifice for humanity and offering the promise of redemption through that sacrifice. At Thame the Virgin's role goes beyond that of *mediatrix*. The tears of blood she sheds manifest her share in Christ's redeeming Passion, demonstrating the interchangeability of their blood and thereby presenting her as co-Redemptrix. The centrality of the Virgin in the process of salvation is also made explicit by her position in the mural, between her son's body and the Cross, and by the scale of her representation which makes her the dominant element.[24]

Altars dedicated to the *Pietà*, like other altars of Our Lady, were used for Masses of the Virgin, especially on her major festivals. At Thame, Our Lady Mass was celebrated every morning either at this or the high altar. The image would have had particular resonance at the performance of the Lady Mass every Saturday, a day dedicated to the Virgin in commemoration of her steadfastness between Good Friday and Easter Sunday.[25] A fifteenth-century incised slab at Corfe

*96. Corfe (Dorset), St Edward's church: incised Purbeck marble slab requesting prayers and a lamp before the* Pietà
*altar, fifteenth century (rubbing by F.A. Greenhill from* Monumental Brass Society Transactions, *15, pts (1997))*

(Dorset) invites prayers for the souls of a husband and wife who are also recorded as having given
a lamp to burn before the altar of the *Pietà* and a cow for five Masses for their brothers and sisters
on the vigils before five feasts of the Virgin (i.e. in the order of the festive year, the Purification,
Annunciation, Assumption, Nativity and Conception) (**96**).[26]

   Images of Our Lady of Pity did not have to have a dedicated altar to be in receipt of special
honour during liturgical celebrations. Indeed, the majority of references to the image do not
mention an altar. A parishioner of Sutton-at-Hone (Kent) bequeathed five substantial wax tapers
to burn before the image, which were to be renewed on the feasts of the Nativity of Our Lord,
the Resurrection and the Assumption of the Virgin. Our Lady of Pity was much honoured on
feast-days of the Virgin. The fraternity of St Peter at Bardwell (Suff.) was charged with providing
five lights for the image at every principal feast of Our Lady, which were also to be lit at every
antiphon sung in her honour.[27] The laity were encouraged to use antiphons and other familiar
prayers in their private devotional exercises. The text of the *Salve regina* in books of hours is
sometimes accompanied by an image of the *Pietà*. Readers of the aforementioned Lydgate poem,
which opens with a description of an image seen by the narrator in a manuscript, were requested
to recite the *Pater noster* and *Ave Maria*, prayers commonly said before images (**91**).[28] In the early
fifteenth century a South Creake (Norf.) man ordered to recite these prayers as penance before
Our Lady of Pity refused, saying that he would only do so before God at the high altar; this is an
early instance of Lollard hostility to the image, a hostility that was grounded in its lack of
scriptural authority and was to be echoed by sixteenth-century reformers.[29]

Although Our Lady of Pity was venerated by both sexes, she had obvious appeal for women, as
the emotional reaction of Margery Kempe makes clear. The verses quoted towards the beginning
of this section on the *Pietà* come from a poem which is addressed specifically to women:

> Therfore, wemen, by town and strete,
> Youre childer handes when ye beholde,
> Ther breste, ther body, and ther fete,
> God were on my sone to thinke, and ye wolde,
> How care hath made my hert full colde,
> To see my sone with naile and spere,
> With scourge and thornes manifolde,
> Wounded and dedd my dere sone, dere.[30]

Quite a number of bequests to the image were made by widows. In 1484 Margaret Lemans bequeathed her best girdle to Our Lady of Pity in her parish church at Bromley (Kent).[31] Girdles were items of considerable value. If her intention was for her gift to adorn the Virgin, rather than for sale, Margaret Lemans was enhancing the image for the benefit of the parish as a whole as well as honouring the prototype. Through the same act, she was providing a posthumous mnemonic souvenir of her personal devotion to that image.[32]

The *Pietà* was placed in the chancel or a chancel chapel in some churches, but more often the nave was the favoured emplacement. As foci of devotion, images of Pity needed to be accessible to large numbers of people. The south aisle, as at Dunton, was a location for the image in a number of churches from different areas. It was not merely for the purposes of veneration that space was required by the image, but also because it was a favoured burial site. As already suggested, the image of the Pity was closely associated with Our Lady's power as *mediatrix*. The initial in the Keble manuscript containing the *Pietà* image accompanies the text for the Hours of the Compassion of the Virgin, the saying of which carried an indulgence of three hundred years (**83**). In many books of hours Our Lady of Pity is associated with the bidding prayer which begins with *Obsecro te domina mater dei*. This moving prayer, which combines supplication with meditation, extols the Virgin's multiple virtues, recites her role in the Incarnation and grief during Christ's Passion and asks for her intercession and help. The ending of the prayer assigns to the Virgin a special importance at the death of the suppliant:

> And at the end of my life show me your face, and reveal to me the day and hour of my death.
> Please hear and receive this humble prayer and grant me eternal life. Listen and hear me,
> Mary, sweetest virgin, Mother of God and of mercy. Amen.[33]

In some texts of the Hours a rubric is attached promising that the Virgin will indeed appear and bestowing spiritual benefits on the dying:

> To all them that be in the state of grace that daily say devoutly this prayer before our blessyd
> lady of pitie, she wyll shewe them her blessyd vysage and warne them the daye et the owre
> of dethe, et in theyr laste ende the aungelles of God shall yelde theyr sowles to heven, & he
> shall obteyne v. hundred yeres & soo many lentes of pardon graunted by v. holy fathers
> popes of Rome.[34]

In the London church of St-Christopher-le-Stocks, the 'dyvers good prayers of Oure Lady and the sauter of charite' inscribed on a tablet below the *Pietà* presumably included this or similar texts.[35] On the continent the image often occurs in a sepulchral context, as a tomb relief and on the exterior of churches, facing into or placed in burial grounds. In England the image was depicted on funerary palls and in at least one instance it was set up in the cemetery.[36] Burial before images of the Pity inside churches became desirable from at least the beginning of the fifteenth century among all classes of society who were of sufficient means and status to be accorded internal interment. Wills from priests, gentry, widows, craftsmen, merchants, yeomen and husbandmen all express the wish that their bodies should be interred before the *Pietà*. In Kent Our Lady of Pity was more in demand for this purpose than any image other than the rood. At Faversham the *Pietà* was placed against the south aisle wall and was the site of several graves. The first recorded request for burial here is in the 1502 will of Henry Sayer, Mayor of Faversham and a Yeoman of the Crown. Subsequently his mortal remains were joined by those of Thomas Malpas and his wife. Edmund Andrewe had to make do with a grave in the churchyard, but was anxious to ensure that it was in proximity to the image, stipulating that his body was interred 'on the back side of Our Lady of Pity'.[37] A rare instance of a sepulchral monument almost certainly *in situ* is that of a cloth merchant named Thomas Sheffe (d. 1520) at Cranbrook, also in Kent. In his will he requested burial before Our Lady of Pity in St Thomas's aisle, identifiable as the chancel south chapel, where his brass remains in its original slab; there is no trace of the image's emplacement (**97**).[38]

The existing structure and documented history of the Bauchun Chapel in Norwich Cathedral reveals how the *Pietà* could bear several layers of meaning.[39] The chapel takes its name from William Bauchun, who made a major contribution to its erection in the late 1320s on the south side of the cathedral presbytery. Bauchun was a lay official of the cathedral priory and his tomb formerly existed in the chapel, which seems to have served as his chantry. Although today it is known as the Chapel of Our Lady of Pity, a lost inscription on the exterior wall recorded the original dedication as the Virgin and All Saints. The elaborate Perpendicular tabernacle in the position of honour on the north side of the former altar would have housed the titular image. It is unlikely at this early date that this image would have been a *Pietà*. In 1391 an image of unknown location within the cathedral but described as 'sancta maria de compassione' attracted offerings of more than £5; in the remaining years of the century offerings to this image exceeded £2 annually. The first unequivocal reference to a *Pietà* in the Bauchun Chapel is in 1460–1, when William Sekyngton requested his executors to bury his body in the Chapel of the Blessed Mary of Pity in Norwich Cathedral. There can be no doubt that this is the Bauchun Chapel. By the early sixteenth century there were two *Pietà*s in the cathedral, one in the nave and the other in the Bauchun Chapel, where it probably stood on the long bracket on the east wall. In 1516 the former attracted much larger receipts than the latter (6s 7d compared with 4d), perhaps suggesting that the image mentioned in 1391 was that in the nave.

William Sekyngton left his mark on the Bauchun Chapel. If no trace of his tomb remains, his transformations of the upper sections of the building are intact. Sekyngton raised the walls and added a stone-vaulted ceiling richly embellished with numerous carved bosses. Two of the corbels from which the vaults spring have angels bearing his arms. A third corbel, located in the east wall above the altar, shows Our Lady of Pity. On the opposite corbel is a half-length male figure, a mimetic representation of Sekyngton, clad in legal costume, in prayer and facing towards the image (**98**). Sekyngton was a lawyer or proctor who served the Consistory Court which sat in this chapel and also held the office of Corrector of Crimes in the diocese of Norwich.[40] The Marian theme is explored further on the roof bosses, which include the

*97. Cranbrook (Kent), St Dunstan's church: monumental brass of Thomas Sheffe (d. 1520)*

*98. Norwich Cathedral, Bauchun Chapel: stone corbels depicting (left) the* Pietà *and (right) William Sekyngton, mid-fifteenth century*

Coronation and Assumption of Our Lady. The principal subject-matter is the legend of the empress wrongfully accused first of seeking an adulterous relationship and then of infanticide; she was saved by the miraculous intervention of the Virgin. The bosses feature a number of scenes apposite to the business of the Consistory Court transacted under Sekyngton's stone canopy, including the marriage of the emperor and empress performed by a bishop, the empress's trial and her reconciliation with her husband. Only one other pictorial rendering of this particular legend has been noted in England, in the slightly later wall-paintings of Eton College Chapel. However, as its frequent occurrence in medieval literature includes Chaucer's *Man of Lawe's Tale*, there can be no doubt of its relevance for the legal profession. Sekyngton did not appropriate Bauchun's chapel, but amplified its imagery to provide references to its legal function. The carvings combined biblical and present time, personal piety and commemoration. To those summoned to appear before the Consistory Court the bosses provided a moral exemplar and evocation of the powers of Our Lady, in whose dedicated space the court was held. The presence of a large image of the *Pietà*, or Our Lady of Compassion, at the side of the chapel altar was a potent reminder to the judge and lawyers that justice should be tempered with mercy. The mortal remains of both Bauchun and Sekyngton were watched over by representations of Our Lady, through whose intercession their eternal salvation could be secured and to whom the prayers of those entering the chapel were offered. The corbel carvings memorialized both Sekyngton's 'good works' in enriching the fabric and his personal devotion to the *Pietà*, as well as acknowledging his earthly status.

Our Lady of Pity was a subject whose primary appeal lay in emotional responses evoked by sight. The capacity of this particular image to embody a subtle range of meanings could be conveyed with greater effect visually than by means of the written word. It is not surprising therefore that literary texts like the first poem quoted in this section claimed to have found their inspiration in the viewing of a pictorial representation. The second verse of Lydgate's poem on the Fifteen Joys and Sorrows of the Virgin also refers to an image:

> Tofor which was sett out in picture
> Of Marie an ymage ful notable,
> Lyke a pyte depeynt was the figure
> With weepyng eyen, and cheer most lamentable:
> Thouh the proporcioun by crafft was agreable,
> Hir look doun cast with teerys al bereyned –
> Of hertly sorwe so soore she was constreyned.[41]

Particularly with the *Pietà*, form and function elided. The emotive power of an image might depend as much on the painter or carver's 'crafft' (presumably a reference to the way the image was fashioned) as on the subject-matter. The carvers of the English alabasters did not produce a standard image of Our Lady of Pity, but offered variations on the theme. The displacement of almost all of the insular *Pietà* makes it impossible to establish whether there was any correlation between particular variants and function or context. Only the bloody tears of the Thame mural are suggestive of its function as an altar image. Agency belonged to the craftsmen in focusing the viewer's response, but it also belonged to viewers like Sekyngton. The conjunction of a contemporary document and the survival of a favoured image (if not the principal one) still in its original space is rare in England. Even this gives no insight into the factors which led Sekyngton to choose burial in and enhancement of the Bauchun Chapel. It is only the poetry and Margery Kempe's narrative which provide glimpses of the emotional intensity generated by images of Our Lady of Pity in the urban centres and villages of late medieval England.

## OUR LADY IN GESYN

Between 1505 and 1533 the wills of six Marston parishioners mention a devotional image designated variously as Our Lady 'in Jhesum', Our Lady of Joseph, Our Lady of Bedlam (Bethlehem), Our Lady in Childbed and the Nativity. Elsewhere it is described as Our Lady 'in Gesyn'. Despite the multiplicity of labels, they all refer to one and the same image, which, in common with so many other representations of the Virgin, retained its popularity to the Reformation. The Nativity is the subject, but a particular aspect is signalled by several of the titles. The word 'Gesyn' is derived from the Norman-French *gesin* = to lie, hence lying-in, and thus refers specifically to the Virgin in her post-natal state; 'Jhesum' is probably a corruption of this word. An informative description of the salient features of this image-type exists from the early fourteenth century. Roger of Waltham, a royal clerk and influential canon of St Paul's Cathedral, in 1325 founded a chantry dedicated to Our Lady, St Lawrence and All Saints on the south side of the choir, in which he was to be buried:

. . . in the south wall, opposite to the said oratory, [he] erected a glorious tabernacle, which contained the image of the said blessed Virgin, sitting as it were in child-bed; as also of our Saviour in swaddling clothes, lying between the ox and the ass; and St Joseph at her feet.[42]

This description could apply to an accomplished late thirteenth-century freestone relief in the parish church of Bolsover (Derbys.) (**99**). It depicts all the features mentioned: the Virgin sitting up in bed, holding Christ upright on her thighs (not quite as described at St Paul's) and separated from Joseph on the far right by the ox and ass. There is also a midwife in attendance and a small angel below the beasts. The size and rectangular shape of the panel suggest that it was an altarpiece – likewise the fragmentary but similar Gesyn in Newark St Mary's (Notts.).[43] The prominent scene filling the centre of the mid-fourteenth-century high altar retable of Christchurch Priory (Hants.) has the same iconography. The latter, St Paul's and Bolsover all might easily be described as the Nativity and the terms are interchangeable. None the less, the label 'child-bed' is applied to the St Paul's version. The iconic nature of the image and its isolation from pictorial narratives of the early life of Christ distinguish it for example from the Nativity and Adoration of the Magi scenes which occur as parts of English alabaster altarpieces.

What is the origin and significance of the image of Our Lady in Gesyn? As was observed in Chapter Three, the Nativity had been established as a feast-day since the early Middle Ages. A particular impetus may have come about through Franciscan spirituality, occasioned by such events as St Francis's mimetic experience at Grecchio on Christmas night 1223. On this occasion Francis made a Nativity crib and during Mass, as a result of his prayers, the image of the Christ-child came to life when he took it in his arms.[44] The Gesyn is not unique to England and examples are found in France, Germany and the Low Countries.[45] The French images, unsurprisingly, bear the 'Gesine' label and the German images are known as 'Maria im Wochenbett', which has the same meaning. In all three countries, as in England, there is a marked longitudinal axis imparted by the emphasis on the bed (**100**). Devotion to the Nativity enjoyed a long vogue in German regular and mendicant nunneries.[46] By the middle of the fourteenth century the Nativity began to appear in English vernacular verse, perhaps under the influence of the mystery plays in which, like the Gesyn image, the Nativity enjoyed an autonomous existence.[47]

In contrast with the strong German link with nunneries, only one of the admittedly patchily recorded and surviving single images of the Gesyn/Nativity in England has a female monastic connection and none has as yet been traced in a female mendicant house. The sole nunnery is the Benedictine house at Elstow (Beds.), where the image of Our Lady of Jheysou was the designated recipient of Katherine Vincent's (a laywoman) best rosary beads and best gold ring, the latter after the death of one of the nuns.[48] Marston Moreteyne is the only other church in the county known to have possessed this image and its presence here may be connected with the proximity of the village to Elstow. On the other hand the Nativity was of particular significance for the parish as from 1324 an annual fair was held on the vigil, feast and morrow of that festival.[49] The distribution pattern of the Gesyn in wills and odd survivals is one of concentration in the southern half of the country. Kent and Northamptonshire have the largest numbers, with respectively nine and six. Two per county are known from Norfolk (including some surviving alabaster fragments at East Rudham), Berkshire, Buckinghamshire, Cornwall (one an alabaster in Treslothan church) and London; Cambridgeshire, Devon, Essex, Hampshire, Oxfordshire, Somerset, Suffolk, Surrey (an alabaster at Chessington) and Wiltshire each produce a grand total of one.

*99. Bolsover (Derbys.), St Mary's church: freestone relief of Our Lady in Gesyn, late thirteenth century*

*100. Polychromed wooden* Maria im Wochenbett, *fourteenth century (Bayerisches Nationalmuseum, Munich, inv. no. MA 1088)*

*101. Long Melford (Suff.), Holy Trinity church: alabaster relief of Our Lady in Gesyn, late fourteenth century*

The east Kent examples are dispersed widely but the west Kent locations are clustered around Rochester and in the neighbourhood of the nunnery at Malling. No wills refer to a Gesyn in the latter, although the parish church there possessed this image.[50] Four of the six Northamptonshire images lay between Daventry and the county town, an area containing both regular and mendicant nunneries.[51] From points further north there are only the Bolsover and Newark survivors. Although the documentary evidence is sparser for the north of England, it is perhaps significant that none is known from the comparatively well-recorded York churches.

In addition to St Paul's, the cathedrals of Rochester, Salisbury and Wells (and possibly Winchester) possessed a Gesyn.[52] An elaborate tabernacle which included an image of 'gesina Beate Marie cum ymagine Joseph' is listed in 1384 at the collegiate foundation of St George's, Windsor.[53] The majority of locations are parish churches, several of them in towns. Apart from the Bolsover and Newark examples, the score or so extant Gesyns are all of alabaster and appear to date from the late fourteenth century.[54] They bear a strong family resemblance. The oblong Gesyn at Long Melford in Suffolk is a typical example. Unlike the earlier panels at Bolsover and Newark, the *dramatis personae* include the Magi presenting their gifts to the child who has achieved a remarkably swift growth; strictly speaking, therefore, this image is a fusion of the Nativity and the Adoration (**101**). The panel in St Lawrence's church, Reading, was almost certainly associated with the altar of the Nativity which stood at the east end of the nave to the south of the chancel arch. The Eucharistic connotations there and at Long Melford are underscored by the reception of the cup by the Christ-child. As nearly half of the surviving examples of English alabaster Gesyn images are found in north Germany and present-day Poland, it looks as if there was a demand for them in the Baltic region.[55] Given the vogue for this image in Germany, this might be a case of coals to Newcastle and illustrates the complexities of the international exchanges in such artefacts: it should not be assumed that England was always merely the recipient.[56]

The majority of English testamentary bequests to the Gesyn came from men. Of the half-dozen Marston Moreteyne testators mentioning this image, only one was female. At Faversham (Kent) three of the nine will-makers endowing this image were women.[57] As the latter comprised only a small minority of testators in this period, the preponderance of men is not surprising. Clerics too venerated the image. Apart from Canon Roger of Waltham, the eminent humanist John Gunthorpe, dean of Wells, in 1498 requested burial in his cathedral church under 'imaginem beate Marie le Gesian'.[58]

If the cult was not gender-specific, it had strong resonances for women (like the *Pietà*). As Gibson has observed, the Gesyn carried a dual significance both as a representation of a sacred act and through its relevance to life-cycle.[59] Our Lady was not only the Queen of Heaven and an ideal role-model – her experience of childbirth and nursing was one which must have had particular appeal. The Gysine image in Salisbury Cathedral attracted offerings from pregnant women from at least the second quarter of the fourteenth century.[60] The most informative glimpse of the centrality of this image for a devout laywoman is provided by *The Book of Margery Kempe*. The Gesyn chapel in St Margaret's church in King's Lynn was located on the north side of the church (probably in the north transept) and was in existence by 1365. The image from this chapel was sufficiently important in the fifteenth century to be accorded a place in the Corpus Christi procession.[61] There are two references to the Gesyn in Margery's narrative. On the first occasion her confessor finds her praying in this chapel and subsequently it is revealed that he was custodian of the chapel. Neither reference alludes directly to an image, but the text is suffused with visions of the Nativity. In a particularly striking passage, redolent of the Long Melford panel, Margery takes on the midwife's role:

> And than went ye creatur [Margery] forth wyth owyr Lady to Bedlem [Bethlehem] & purchasyd hir herborwe [lodgings] every nyght wyth gret reverens, & owyr Lady was receyved wyth glad cher. Also sche beggyd owyr Lady fayr whyte clothys & kerchys for to swathyn [swathe] in hir Sone whan he wer born, and whan Ihesu was born, sche ordeyned beddyng for owyr Lady to lyg in [lie in] wyth hir blyssed Sone. . . . And aftyr on ye XII Day, whan iij kyngys comyn wyth her gyftys & worschepyd owyr Lord Ihesu Crist being in hys Moderys lappe, yis creatur [Margery], owyr Ladys hand-mayden, beheldyng al ye processe in contemplacyon, wept wondyr sor.[62]

Margery Kempe was devoted to this theme, as is also evidenced by her pilgrimages to centres with Nativity relics, including Assisi and Aachen, where she venerated the smock worn by the Virgin at the birth of Christ and his swaddling clothes. Margery's own severe sufferings during pregnancy and the birth of her son had much to do with her identification with the Gesyn. In this she would not have been unusual. For many women, resort to the image in St Margaret's and other parish churches would have been most fitting, whether praying or giving thanks for a safe birth or seeking solace after a stillbirth or an infant death.

There is less to say about the other types of Marian imagery which existed at Marston Moreteyne. In the two Marian images considered so far, for all the prominence given to Our Lady, it is Christ as redeemer who remains a central focus. In at least one, and probably two, of the other Marston representations Mary featured without her son.

## THE ASSUMPTION OF THE VIRGIN

Although most wills give the dedication of Marston Moreteyne as Our Lady, two rectors requested burial in the chancel of the Assumption. No testators who left bequests to Our Lady in the chancel mention the Assumption and vice versa.[63] Possibly the Assumption image was paired with the titular image on the other side of the high altar. The feast (15 August) was introduced into England before the Norman Conquest. Its latter-day vogue may have been boosted by the Lancastrian monarchs. Henry V's victory at the battle of the Seine (1416) occurred on the feast of the Assumption and his son's great foundation of Eton not only took over this dedication from its parochial predecessor but also promoted the patronal image itself as possessing miraculous powers (**153 (b)**).[64]

Almost all the extant carved representations of the subject are as usual of alabaster and most of those belonged to altarpieces; all date from after 1400. The larger dimensions and elongated

shape of a few suggest that they functioned as iconic devotional images.[65] There are some variations on the standard iconography, which shows the Virgin standing in a glory borne heavenwards by angels towards a bust of God the Father. The freestone panel at Sandford-on-Thames (Oxon.) depicts the crowned Virgin. An unusual, if not unique, feature at the base is the pair of angels holding what looks like a ciborium (**102**). Sometimes the Assumption iconography is combined with that of the Coronation, with the Virgin crowned by the Trinity. A high-quality relief in the Cluny Museum, Paris, shows this imagery. In the lower left of the panel is St Thomas holding the end of Our Lady's girdle and below her feet is an angel (**103**).[66]

## ST ANNE TEACHING THE VIRGIN TO READ

Three Marston wills refer to an image of St Anne. Although strictly speaking St Anne was venerated in her own right, in English medieval art she is depicted in her capacity as the Virgin's mother and in particular teaching her daughter to read. This remained a popular devotional image in English churches to the Reformation. In 1381 her festival was made a feast of obligation.[67] St Anne's cult does not

*102. Sandford-on-Thames (Oxon.), St Andrew's church: freestone relief of the Assumption of the Virgin, fifteenth or early sixteenth century*

appear to have been prominent in Bedfordshire; only one St Anne fraternity seems to have existed, at Potton, and even that dedication is uncertain. St Anne images are known in eight of the Bedford archdeaconry's churches, of which the most important was Northill, where her chapel occupied the room over the porch.

The cult of St Anne first appears in English books of hours in the late thirteenth century. The episode of her teaching the Virgin to read, however, is not included in the apocryphal gospels; it is mentioned in a ninth-century Byzantine text, but this is most unlikely to have been widely known in England. The pictorial representation, therefore, has no textual authority in the west. The first references in parish churches occur from the end of the thirteenth century, when images of St Anne were recorded in the churches of Kirby-le-Soken (Essex) and Drayton (Middlesex).[68] The image has been linked to the role of aristocratic women in educating their daughters by following St Anne's example. The image thus marked a stage on from childbirth in the life-cycle. Visual evidence attests to St Anne's popularity with the social elites. Miniatures of St Anne appear in illuminated manuscripts, sometimes with an alphabet on the pages held by the Virgin. The Pembrugge chantry chapel in Cleohanger church (Herefs.) is dedicated to her and she is also represented on funerary monuments of high-status individuals (**62**). The presence of the image in carvings, on the walls and in the windows of parish churches suggests that from the outset the subject had wider social appeal. St Anne as represented in the fourteenth-century paintings on the nave walls at Chalfont St Giles (Bucks.) and Croughton (Northants.) would have been accessible to a predominantly illiterate audience comprised of both sexes. For these

103. Alabaster relief of the Assumption and Coronation of the Virgin, c. 1500 (Musée national du Moyen Age, Paris, inv. no. Cl.19341)

viewers the image is likely to have been intended to stress the importance of teaching children to pray, especially to Our Lady. For village and townswomen as well as elite ladies, the Virgin's mother provided an exemplary and imitative model for the raising of their children.

The images themselves are far from rigidly formulaic. The variations indicate a responsiveness to evolving demands – presumably related to social changes. Only two carved images of the

*104. Kersey (Suff.), St Mary's church: polychromed and gilded alabaster St Anne, mid-fourteenth century*

subject dating from before 1400 have been noted, both alabaster and both mutilated. The version at Montpezat near Montauban (France) dates from the middle of the fourteenth century. In common with most of the pictorial examples of the period, St Anne enfolds her daughter within her cloak. The image at Kersey in Suffolk is unlikely to be very different in date; unusually for this period she is seated (**104, 105**).[69] The richly gilded attire of the Kersey image contrasts with the modest garments worn by St Anne in the later alabaster images, which depict a less obviously aristocratic image; often St Anne is portrayed as a widow of mature years (**106**). Perhaps this change of emphasis was designed to produce an image less remote from the experience of the ordinary parishioner. In one of the later representations St Anne appears with an adult Virgin holding the child Christ (**107**).[70] St Anne's didactic role is still evident from the book and pointer she holds; her status as chaste grandmother to Christ as well as mother to the Virgin is also underlined. This panel is more akin to the contemporary German *Anna Selbdritt* images in which the human, corporeal aspect of Christ is shown as derived through the female line. The alabaster panel bears additional meanings, centred on the nuclear family and lineage. St Anne's role is expanded from that of a mother educating her daughter in the tenets of faith to encompass her matriarchal role in the family. Her gaze is directed towards Christ, not her daughter, but the portrayal of warm relationships across three generations provided an ideal model for emulation.[71]

The original provenance of the last panel is lost. We will never know whether the St Anne image at Marston Moreteyne resembled it, or what the responses of the parishioners were. The image might have had a strong appeal for women, but St Anne's fraternity at Faversham (Kent) was evidently open to both sexes, and men as well as women endowed the lights before the image. Indeed, if the relief of St Anne with the Virgin and Child stressed female familial relationships, the privileges of a patriarchal society on earth were exercised at Faversham through seating and burial. In 1512 John Brode instructed that his body was to be buried under his pew in front of the image of St Anne.[72]

*105. Montpezat church (France): alabaster St Anne teaching the Virgin to read, mid-fourteenth century*

106. *Upper section of an alabaster St Anne teaching the Virgin to read, late fifteenth or early sixteenth century (Fitzwilliam Museum, Cambridge, inv. no. M4-1923)*

*107. Alabaster relief of St Anne, the Virgin and the Christ-Child, fifteenth century (Victoria & Albert Museum, inv. no. A 99-1946)*

## MARIA LACTANS

The foregoing are the only Marian images at Marston Moretaine to be given distinctive labels. The precise attributes of the others – the patronal image, Our Lady in the Pillar and the image associated with the altar of the Virgin – are lost. The generic label of Our Lady concealed several iconographical types which varied according to the meanings they were intended to convey.

One of two alabasters at Broughton-in-Craven (W. Yorks.), probably dating from the middle of the fourteenth century, shows Our Lady crowned as Queen of Heaven and suckling her child (**108**). This is an example of the Virgin *lactans*, an image of Byzantine origin. It had already appeared a century before in English monumental art, as the Great Canfield (Essex) mural attests (**29**). The lactating Virgin was a polysemic image, bearing complex and overlapping layers of meaning.[73] Context as ever was an important factor. Images like Great Canfield's, placed above or close to an altar, were linked with the sacrifice of the Mass. They were agencies by which the doctrine of transubstantiation, in which the consecrated host was accepted as Christ's real body, was explained to the laity. The Virgin's breast is the source of Christ's nurturing milk and therefore of His blood which itself nurtures mankind through its shedding at the Crucifixion. With the adoption of this doctrine at the 1215 Lateran Council, Our Lady was perceived to be the source of that body and hence was intimately connected with the consecration of the Eucharist during the Mass. The Virgin also shares in Christ's redeeming sacrifice by virtue of the fact that the blood shed by the Saviour is also her blood. This convergence between the corporeal bodies of Christ and His mother endowed the latter with eucharistic associations in her own right and thus enhanced her centrality in the Christian faith. An image's proximity to an altar was not a *sine qua non* for such readings.

The alabaster statue at Flawford (Notts.) fuses the themes of Christ's sacrifice for humanity with the Virgin's role as intercessor and her status as Queen of Heaven (**54**). The image links the Incarnation and the Passion by Our Lady touching her veil in the gesture mentioned in connection with the *Pietà*. The veil is both metaphor (the Virgin as *tunica humanitatis*) and symbol of her purity. This action occurs on French and English images from at least the early fourteenth century.[74] The bared breast may also refer to the Virgin interceding with Christ on behalf of humanity. The Virgin is shown baring her breast to her son at the Last Judgement in English late thirteenth-century illumination; the alabaster imagery perhaps echoes this appeal by reference to her nurturing the God made man, whose purpose was the salvation of humankind.[75] She is reminding her son of her compassion to Him, so that He too should be merciful. Her queenly attributes are manifested not only by the crown but also in her regal gaze.

## ALBA MARIA

All the Marian images considered so far have been identified by iconographical labels. One representation of Our Lady, however, was designated by its physical appearance. An image which stood in the south chapel of Shillington (Beds.) was termed the *alba Maria*; another 'white Virgin' was at Newenham Priory, just outside Bedford, and there were more images so described in Kent and Lincolnshire.[76] A famous image in Toledo Cathedral, Spain, known as *La Virgen Blanca*, is one of several French statues dating from the late thirteenth and first half of the fourteenth centuries which bear this label (**VIII**). All have a prestigious provenance and must have been highly prized in their day.[77] Only the lining and hems of garments are painted and

*108. Broughton-in-Craven (W. Yorks), All Saints' church: alabaster* Maria lactans, *mid-fourteenth century*

gilded, leaving exposed the marble or alabaster (the heads of the Toledo Virgin and Child have been re-polychromed). The surface of the fine mid fourteenth-century alabaster standing Virgin at Blunham (Beds.) is treated in similar fashion to the Toledo image and so may give some idea of the appearance of the white Virgins at Shillington and Newenham (**IX**).[78]

White or non-polychromed sculpture and painting enjoyed quite a vogue during the fourteenth century, but what lay behind it remains obscure. The Toledo and Blunham images recall the exquisite contemporary Marian ivory statuettes. Metaphors based on the *Song of Songs*, such as the tower of ivory (*turris eburnea*), which were applied to the Virgin in the twelfth century by St Bernard of Clairvaux and others, imparted symbolic significance to these artefacts (**41**).[79] The unpainted appearance of the 'white Virgins' may be connected with the fact that white (a signifier of the Virgin's purity) is the liturgical colour used for the feasts of Our Lady as well as in the Lenten rituals. This cannot be the only explanation, as the use of white or monochrome was not confined to either liturgical or Marian imagery. There could have been a more utilitarian factor: images like the Toledo *Virgen Blanca* make a dramatic contrast with the standard fully polychromed statues and their appeal to the viewer may have lain in their apparent stark simplicity.[80]

Marston Moreteyne was selected as a starting-point for the study of late medieval Marian devotional imagery in the parish church because it possessed a range of different types – more than any other church in the Bedford archdeaconry. However, the Virgin was represented in every one, either as the patronal image or as its companion. Many had several images of Our Lady, and as we have seen the *Pietà* was very common. Only the battered stone remnants at Tilsworth and the mutilated alabasters at Blunham remain today as testaments to the centrality of the Virgin in parish worship and devotion.

CHAPTER SEVEN

# RITUAL AND DEVOTION

In the Middle Ages images were the pivot around which revolved a series of activities. In the course of the preceding chapters, reference has been made to various practices associated with veneration of images, some collective, some individual. This chapter will draw these strands together in order to examine the relationships which existed between images and their users. What were these relationships? How were they structured and enacted? How did personal devotion of images interact with their role in the liturgy?

The activities associated with images will be analysed principally with the help of the fabric and images of what was the largest parish church in the archdeaconry of Bedford. The nature of the evidence dictates that the enquiry is principally confined to the fifteenth and early sixteenth centuries. St Mary's church in Luton served what was the most prosperous town in the county in the later Middle Ages. The parish itself was extensive and encompassed (as it still does) a good deal of the surrounding agricultural hinterland. A good number of wills of its parishioners exist, ranging from the manorial lords to the wealthier artisans and merchants and including the clergy. There were a number of large and smaller estates within the parish. In the fifteenth and early sixteenth centuries the lordship of the manor of Luton was held by some prominent individuals, notably Sir John Wenlock (killed in the battle of Tewkesbury in 1471) and his successor Thomas Rotherham, Bishop of Lincoln and subsequently Archbishop of York and Lord Chancellor to Edward IV. The manor remained in the Rotherham family's hands after the archbishop's death in 1500. Other important landholders in late medieval Luton were the Acworth, Hoo and Hay families and St Albans Abbey, which held the lucrative advowson to St Mary's church.[1]

Many of these estate owners left their mark on the fabric of the parish church. Parts of the existing building, with its west tower, aisled nave, transepts with eastern chapels, sacristy and short chancel, date back to the twelfth and thirteenth centuries. For the most part, however, the church presents a Perpendicular appearance (**109**, **110**, **111**). The elaborate chancel sedilia bear the arms and motto of Abbot Wheathampstead of St Albans (abbot 1420–40 and 1451–65); adjacent is the small but elaborate chantry rebuilt by or to commemorate Richard Barnard (d. 1492), one of a number of well-connected incumbents. Barnard also glazed a nave south aisle window. A prominent lay benefactor to the fabric was John Hay (d. 1465), whose funerary brass recorded that he had repaired Luton church. East of the north transept and adjoining the chancel is the impressive Wenlock Chapel, rebuilt by Sir John Wenlock in 1461 and containing the tombs of the manorial lords of Luton. There is some evidence from the glazing that this served as the Lady Chapel. Wenlock heraldry was formerly painted on the walls in other parts of the church, suggesting that the family's contribution to the fabric was not confined to the chapel. In the south transept or its east chapel was the site of the chapel of the important Fraternity of the Holy and Undivided Trinity and Blessed Virgin Mary, founded in 1474 by Bishop Rotherham, his brother John, Sir John Acworth, the vicar of Luton and nine of the more prominent residents of the town and its hamlets.[2]

*109. Luton (Beds.), St Mary's church: exterior from the south-east*

*110. Luton (Beds.), St Mary's church: interior looking east*

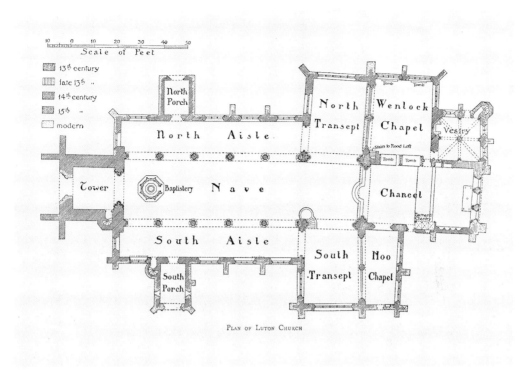

*111. Ground plan of St Mary's church, Luton (Beds.) (from VCH Bedfordshire)*

By the early sixteenth century the patronal image of Our Lady had numerous sacred companions. In addition to the main rood, there was a green rood (a green-painted cross). The image of the Trinity must have stood in the Fraternity chapel. Another chapel contained an altar dedicated to St Nicholas and one will refers to a Marian image there; a representation of St Nicholas must also have been present. The only other image which can be placed is that of St Thomas Becket, which stood in the Wenlock Chapel. The other images consisted of Our Lady of Pity, St Anne, St Armel, St Blaise, St Christopher, St Clement, St Erasmus, St George, St James, St John the Baptist, St Katherine (with her own altar), St Margaret, St Roche and St Sitha (the last with her own altar).[3] This was a selective 'holie companie of Heven'. Rubbing shoulders with the Virgin and other senior and long-established figures like John the Baptist, Anne, Katherine and Margaret were specialist saintly helpers who had emerged as foci for parochial devotion much later and were more closely attuned to life as experienced by the ordinary layman and woman. As already discussed in Chapter Five, St Roche's powers were needed to guard against plague in a closely packed town while those involved with wool and cloth were watched over by St Blaise and St Erasmus. For merchants and traders St Christopher was at hand to protect them on their travels. Sheep-farming and commerce were important elements of the economy of late-medieval Luton.

## IMAGES AND THE LITURGY

Like altarpieces, images were not a prerequisite for liturgical performance; on the contrary, the text and structure of the Mass and canonical hours were established long before devotional images began to proliferate in churches, so ritual involving images does not feature prominently in the rubrics of medieval service-books.[4] These books present a problem in this respect. In the later Middle Ages the Use of Sarum was the prescribed form in the Lincoln diocese, to which Luton belonged, but the paucity of surviving missals and breviaries from identifiable parish churches makes it difficult to establish whether the Use was modified to meet specific local requirements; rubrics added in the few that have been examined show that modifications were indeed made, although the rationale behind them is elusive.[5] Once images had been introduced, they constituted a presence during collective worship. Their presence and participation was signalled by various means. In broad terms the relationship between devotional images and the liturgy in St Mary's church at Luton can be reconstructed with the aid of the wills and the various service books.

**Table III** sets out those saints represented by images in Luton church, arranged according to the Sarum Calendar. Some major movable festivals such as Corpus Christi and Trinity Sunday,

---

TABLE III: IMAGES AND THE RITUAL YEAR IN ST MARY'S CHURCH, LUTON (INCLUDING MAJOR FEASTS)

| | |
|---|---|
| 2 February | PURIFICATION OF THE VIRGIN (Candlemas) (Greater Double) |
| 3 February | Blaise |
| March/April | EASTER DAY (Principal Double) |
| 23 April | George (Inferior, elevated to Greater Double) |
| 27 April | Sitha |
| 2 June | Erasmus |
| 24 June | Nativity of St John the Baptist (Lesser Double) |
| 2 July | VISITATION OF THE VIRGIN (Greater Double) |
| 7 July | Translation of Thomas Becket (9 lessons) |
| 9 July | Octave of Visitation of Virgin |
| 20 July | Margaret (9 lessons) |
| 22 July | Mary Magdalen (Triple Invitation; 9 lessons) |
| 25 July | James (if the Greater; if Lesser, then 1 May) |
| 26 July | Christopher (Mem.) |
| 15 August | ASSUMPTION OF THE VIRGIN (Principal Double) |
| 16 August | Armel |
| | Roche |
| 22 August | Octave of Assumption of Virgin |
| 29 August | Decollation of St John the Baptist (Triple Invit.; 9 lessons) |
| 8 September | NATIVITY OF THE VIRGIN (Greater Double) |
| 15 September | Octave of Nativity of the Virgin (Triple Invit.) |
| 1 November | ALL SAINTS (Principal Double and Octave) |
| 2 November | All Souls (Inferior Double) |
| 23 November | Clement (9 lessons) |
| 25 November | Katherine (9 lessons) |
| 6 December | Nicholas (9 lessons) |
| 8 December | Conception of the Virgin (Lesser Double) |
| 25 December | CHRISTMAS DAY (Principal Double) |
| 29 December | Thomas Becket (Inferior Double) |

*112. Blessing an image of the Virgin and Child on an altar, early fifteenth century (Cambridge, Corpus Christi College, MS 79, f. 216r)*

both of which were graded as Greater Doubles, are omitted. However, the table includes other important celebrations in the year.[6]

The saints' days and other festivals within the annual cycle created 'an ordered structure of relationships with the sacred, encompassing persons, places, times and things', neatly summed up in the phrase an 'economy of the sacred'.[7] This world was regulated by the Calendar. Liturgical celebration ordered human relations with the divine. Relationships between individuals were structured through shared responses to the sacred, i.e. piety. Piety itself is 'the expression of gratitude in one way or another for a faith that is held by the believer as a gift from the one in whom one believes'.[8]

These relationships were expressed through a range of externalized acts, all of which involved getting physically close to the holy.[9] Apart from the rituals of blessing and censing performed by the clergy (**112**), the range of gestures or acts an individual might perform before a devotional image were summarized by Pecock:

Wherfore bi lijke skile it is leeful ynous [is lawful in us] forto knele and preie and bere light [bear lights] and sette up candelis bifore an ymage, whilis these deedis ben not doon to the

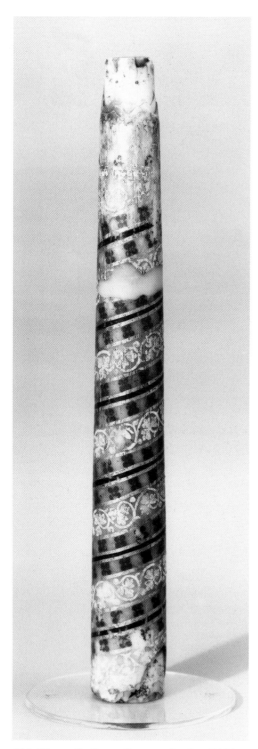

113. *Wax candle, fourteenth century (London, British Museum, Dept of Prehistory and Europe, reg. no. MLA 1965, 4-3, 1)*

ymage but to God or to a Seint. . . . Tho lightis men mowe take and use bi sight of hem [by sight of them] as rememoratijf signes and mynding signes that greet cleernes of wisdom, greet solace is and schal be in heven bifore God and among Seintis.[10]

Lights were central to all the liturgical celebrations and signalled an active participation in the collective rituals by the celestial protectors and helpers whose images stood in the churches.[11] Lights were associated with each of the images in Luton church and, as everywhere, comprised the most common category of testamentary bequest. Lights of wax were in demand for their sweet smell and purity of the flame and accordingly they had a particular symbolic value (**113**). Usually lights were in the form of tapers or lamps. The former might be set on a candlestick or a stand designed for multiple lights, hence the name 'braunche' (**114**). In 1531 John Master bequeathed a latten candlestick with three branches for the patronal image of St Giles in Upper Gravenhurst church (Beds.).[12] Alternatively, ranks of lights were arranged on the kinds of racks still in use in Catholic and High Anglican churches; these were known as 'beams' (**3**). A widow left two gold rings for the making of a bar of iron called a beam to be placed from a pillar to the wall next to St Katherine's altar at Fordwich in Kent.[13] Provision for lights might be a permanent fixture. A fourteenth-century niche probably for an image of the Virgin in the north transept of the former church of the Order of Bonhommes at Edington (Wilts.) incorporates a shelf either for lights to burn underneath the image or perhaps for offerings (**115**). More makeshift are the arrangements at Edlesborough (Bucks.), where lead plugs to hold a light-stand are inserted below an image-niche (**116**).

The major images may always have had lights burning permanently before them. John

Rotherham of Someries, esquire, lord of the manor of Luton, in 1492 left 6*s* 8*d* for the maintenance of the continuous light of the Virgin (the patronal saint) in the chancel of Luton church.[14] The number of lights signalled the relative importance of the image and of the festival itself. On Principal and Greater Doubles the high altar of Salisbury Cathedral displayed eight candles and two more before the Virgin; on all Lesser Feasts and Inferior Doubles there were to be four candles and two before Our Lady's image.[15] Parish churches did not match the liturgical elaboration of cathedrals and monasteries, but at this level the saint's day or other festival was still honoured by the burning of additional lights before the relevant images. It was common practice for the lights before images to be lit for Mass. Richard Bower of Sharnbrook (Beds.) left a candle to burn in perpetuity before the image of Our Lady at the chancel door at service times.[16] Testators paid for the lights to be lit on feast-days. The widow of Thomas Knevett of Elstow (Beds.) was to supply a taper for Our Lady's image in service time on holy days for one year following her husband's death.[17]

Censing of images ranked second only to the burning of lamps and tapers in externalized acts of collective devotion: 'thurificacioun may be doon only for steryngge to devocioun and for tokenyngge'. Censing of the image of Our Lady at the high

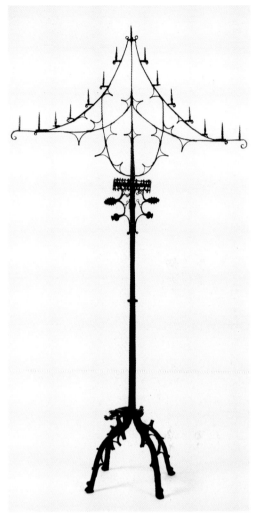

114. Fribourg Cathedral (Switzerland): latten paschal candlestick, fourteenth century

altar and the 'ymaginem de sancto de quo est ecclesia' on feast-days is specified in the Use of Sarum.[18] In addition, those sacred images which had dedicated altars were censed by the priest after first vespers on the vigil of their feast-day, followed by the saying of the bidding prayer, *Ora pro nobis, beate/beata* ——. At Luton this rubric applied to the images of the Virgin, the Trinity, St Nicholas, St Katherine and St Sitha.[19]

The lighting of candles and tapers and thurification are the only actions explicitly mentioned in connection with images during the celebration of the liturgy. During the festival Mass prayers were offered to the commemorated saint. On 25 November the Luton parishioners would have heard their priest invoke St Katherine:

Grant, we beseech Thee, O Lord, unto Thy people health of mind and body by this holy Sacrament which we have received; and at the intercession of S. Katherine, Thy Virgin-

*115. Edington (Wilts.), former priory church of the Bonhommes: fourteenth-century image niche in north transept with a space below for lights or offerings*

Martyr, in whose honour we rejoice, fill the hearts of Thy faithful with everlasting consolations, that they being upheld by Divine protection may both please Thee with holy devotion, and ever obtain a part in the benefits which Thou bestowest.[20]

The liturgical phrases might be supplemented by a sermon or homily recounting the saint's story. A set was compiled by John Mirk for the use of parish priests. An image is only invoked specifically in the homily for St Margaret's day:

Herfor Margret ys payntyd over coruen [painted with her crown] wher scho ys wyth a dragon undyr her fete [dragon under her feet] and a cros yn her hond, schowyng how by vertu of ye cros scho gate ye victory of ye fynde [fiend].[21]

Neither prayers nor homilies are dependent on a visual image. None the less, the highly descriptive language of many of the homilies, some of which end with an exhortation to kneel and pray to the saint commemorated, would have gained effect from having a representation of that saint as a focus. Thus in Mirk's homily for the feast of St Katherine the instruments of her torture and martyrdom, which served as the attributes of her image, are described (**63 (right)**).[22]

The feasts of saints were celebrated with the degree of solemnity laid down in the Calendar or by custom. A highlight of the ritual year, and a reaffirmation of communal identity, was the celebration of the patronal feast, which ranked as a Principal Double, the highest category in the Sarum Rite.[23] At Luton this fell on the major Marian feasts, of which the most important was the Assumption (15 August). Everywhere the great feasts of Our Lady were celebrated with pomp. The feast of the Purification of the Virgin or Presentation of Christ in the Temple, commonly known as Candlemas (2 February), was a major point in the seasonal cycle, marking the passing of winter (darkness) and the advent of spring (light). Each parishioner took part in a procession, bearing a candle which was blessed by the parish priest; this practice is reflected in the tapers carried by Joseph and the midwife in manuscript illuminations of the Presentation (**117**). Mirk's *Festial* includes the tale of an immoral woman who was restored to life by the Virgin because she had maintained a candle before her image at Candlemas; this suggests that it was not uncommon for the candles offered at this festival to be set before Marian representations in parish churches.[24]

To this day, on Mayday and 19 September in St Mary's church in the Oxfordshire village of Charlton-on-Otmoor, a large wooden cross already covered with box leaves is taken down from the roodscreen, dressed with flowers and then replaced. The cross is known as the Garland and until 1857 a garland-cross used to be taken to the nearby village of Studley, where there was formerly a priory. Before this date the embellishment of the garland-cross was done by a woman, who spoke of it as 'my Lady' and referred to her dress. This may be the relic of a pre-Reformation ceremony involving the dressing of the patronal image of the Virgin by women and its carriage in procession.[25] If so, the practice would not have been unusual. Images of Our Lady often had a rich and varied wardrobe, which was changed regularly according to her various feasts and the major points in the church Calendar. Inventories of the London churches compiled in Edward VI's reign list a staggering array of rich garments and other accoutrements which formerly adorned the images.[26] Much-venerated images (especially cult images) on

116. Edlesborough (Bucks.), St Mary's church: plug-holes for a light-stand below an image-niche in the nave north aisle

the continent today are frequently clad in splendid robes (**XXII**; **150**). Rural churches also sometimes had vestments for images. A Virgin and Child at St Nicholas at Wade in the Isle of Thanet (Kent) was provided with a frontlet and a 'bonett for her Son'.[27] For the literate elites, embellishment of images may have been linked with devotional texts which described the making of garments through prayer. The practice of dressing images was reviled by the reformers: 'As little girls play with little puppets, so be these decked images great puppets for old fools to play with.'[28]

Lent, and Easter, was the most solemn and protracted event in the ritual year. First, the images were cleaned. In 1490 the churchwardens of St Dunstan's in Canterbury paid for the 'makyng clene of the Sayntis'.[29] A possible echo of this ceremony survived in the parish church of SS Peter and Paul at Glentham (Lincs.), where until 1832 it was the custom for seven maidens to wash a fourteenth-century recumbent tomb effigy of a woman. The effigy was known as 'Molly Grimes', possibly a derivation from the Old Norse 'Grimr', meaning a mask of evil or covering of darkness or dirt. The substitution of a sepulchral effigy for an image might have been an acceptable post-Reformation practice and one which recognized the affinity between seigneurial families and the chancel images.[30] During Lent the images were covered (**XIV**):

. . . in tokene of mornyng [mourning], nought only for Adamis synne but also for oure owene synne. Also they been hydde in partye of pennaunce and in tokene that meen [men] in Lentoun shuldyn wtdrawyn hem from lykynnge of eye [sight] as they doon from the lykyng

*117. Presentation of Christ in the Temple in the* Bray Hours, *c. 1490 (Stonyhurst College Library, Lancs., MS 60, f. 26v)*

of the ere [ear = sound] and as they wytdrawyn here tastyngge and smellynge fro mete and drynke be fastyngge and here felyyngge from lust of the flesh be contynence and chastete.[31]

The Lenten or veil cloths for the images are listed in several inventories and exhibited considerable variation. Two veils at St Albans Abbey were dyed and portrayed with the five wounds of Christ. Like those covering the images in the miniature depicted in Plate XIV, the patronal images of SS Peter and Paul in West Cheap, London, had 'ij clothes wt rede crosses' and the others bore the attributes of their respective saints, such as the rosary beads for St Sitha. In another London church, St-Christopher-le-Stocks, the patronal saint was depicted on his image cloth. The stained cloths bequeathed by Margaret Bate to cover the images of the Trinity and St John the Baptist in Houghton Conquest church (Beds.) may also have had representations of the holy personages. It was important, therefore, that in some places the identity of the saint continued to be revealed, despite the shrouding.[32] No lights burned before images during this period. The end-process is revealed at Bethersden (Kent), where a taper which had been set up before the Easter Sepulchre from Good Friday 'and there to bren [burn] at all Divyne servyce all the Easter holidayes' afterwards was placed before the image of Our Lady in the chancel.[33] At Matins on Easter Sunday the images were exposed to public gaze again and their lights rekindled. The Resurrection was one of the feasts at which a parishioner of Sutton-at-Hone (Kent) required that the five wax tapers he had endowed before Our Lady of Pity were to be renewed.[34]

The Luton parishioners had their own spiritual priorities which did not altogether coincide with the official hierarchy as enunciated through the grading of feasts. Saints like Erasmus, Blaise and Sitha had their representations, but absent were the apostles (with the exception of St James), evangelists and four Latin doctors of the Church (apart from Clement), all of whom ranked higher than the saints represented. An indication of a local pecking-order is signalled by the reference to the maintenance of lights before every saint 'that continually have light yerely renuyd [renewed] afore them by old custome'; these were the standing lights mentioned in several other wills; elsewhere the other lights are called small lights, as at Eaton Bray.[35]

Several Luton testators were selective in their image bequests. John Norrys was one of the very few to name only a single image, that of St Erasmus, but several endowed only two or three out of the large stock in the church.[36] Although the possibility cannot be discounted that this reflected communal or clerical directives to ensure that provision was made for every image, it is likely that it indicated a special personal relationship between individual and saint. We have already seen that clergy often expressed a bond with the patronal saint. Edward Sheffield, vicar of Luton (d. 1525), had his tomb with its brass made before his death and placed below the patronal image (118).[37] The emplacement of St Thomas Becket's image in the manorial Wenlock Chapel and John Rotherham's desire for burial before it were manifestations of familial devotion; his wife's maiden name was Becket.[38] Birth on the festival of a saint might be considered to bring their special protection. In the fifteenth-century Bokenham's *Legends of Holy Women* St Faith is exhorted to grant the author her special favour on his deathbed 'for he on your day to live did first begin'.[39]

For the individual parishioner, their own personal saintly protector may have been their prime devotional focus, irrespective of their saint's liturgical ranking or whether the image was framed or had been designated as 'principal'. The varying amounts bequeathed by John Rudde to the image lights of Eaton Bray church may well be a measure of the respective values he personally attached to them. Only he and Walter Swanson among this parish's testators mentioned

118. *Luton (Beds.), St Mary's church: brass of vicar Edward Sheffield (d. 1525); from Thomas Fisher,*
Monumental Remains and Antiquities in Bedfordshire *(London, 1828), no. 35*

St George.[40] The personalized nature of veneration to a saint meant that the status of its image was neither guaranteed nor indissoluble. An anthropological study of religion in a northern Spanish valley revealed that, apart from the patronal images, images in the churches were added and removed as devotion to a particular saint waxed and waned.[41] If they were not taken away, the images retained their potential but lacked the activating force of prayer. Conversely, any image, whether carved, painted on a wall or in a window, free-standing or part of a decorative scheme, contained within itself the latent power to be elevated to a cult image by becoming miracle-working, if the power of grace was perceived to work through its agency.

## COMMUNAL DEVOTIONAL PRACTICES

A will from Ivychurch (Kent) refers to every light which was kept at the cost of the parish.[42] By the later Middle Ages the proliferation of images meant that not all lights and their images were supported by communal funds and evidently some lights were maintained by sub-groups or even individuals within parishes. Membership of fraternities brought spiritual and temporal benefits; the brethren were placed under the special protection of the guild's patronal saint, whose image therefore took on added significance for the members. The rules governing the Luton Trinity fraternity have not survived. In like institutions in other parishes, each member usually paid a small subscription to maintain the light and sometimes contributed to the repair of their titular image itself. The brothers and sisters of the guild of the patronal saint in St James's church at King's Lynn (Norf.) paid a half-penny at his festival towards the cost of the light which was lit during the liturgy on feast-days.[43] The annual renewal of the image light might be marked by a special procession. Members of the fraternity dedicated to St Thomas Becket at Heacham (Norf.) who lived within a 5-mile radius had to meet at a designated spot and process with the lights to the church. Their Suffolk counterparts at Lawshall did so barefoot.[44]

From at least the thirteenth century it was customary in the larger parishes for responsibility for the upkeep of designated images and their lights to be apportioned among the laity, with elected keepers or wardens, who were in turn accountable to the churchwardens. There is no record of this at Luton, although specified light-keepers are mentioned in the locality at Totternhoe and Wing. At Bethersden (Kent) the list of seventy-seven brothers and sisters associated with St Katherine's light reveals how many parishioners might pledge themselves to the support of a single image.[45]

Along with the burgeoning importance of images in the religious life of the later Middle Ages, their influence was also felt in the more 'secular' aspects of town and country life. The annual feast-days of the saints might be the occasion for communal veneration and honour by means of their images, yet they were also used for more profane celebrations, often associated (like Candlemas) with the passing of the seasons. The purpose of a holyday, in the words of John Mirk, was

> To here goddes serves and ye mas,
> And spene that day in holynes.[46]

Not everybody could be relied upon to devote the day to 'holynes'. An occasion to use the temporary release from manual labour to indulge in the more hedonistic pleasures offered by sporting activities and the alehouse might end in excess. This was a cause of concern to the ecclesiastical authorities, together with the proliferation of such festivals in the later Middle Ages and certain practices which took place on these occasions.[47] The riotous nature of the *Kermes* or *Kirchweih*, the anniversary of the founding of a particular church and other feast-days, comprised an entire genre in German and Netherlandish sixteenth-century painting and engraving; how these events were received by their intended audiences is the subject of scholarly debate. While images do not feature prominently, nevertheless they are present, borne in the processions which occur among all the merry-making. The religious element is never absent from these scenes.[48]

Business transactions were often concluded on saints' days and the images might be called upon to participate. Two testators from the Bedfordshire parish of Harlington bequeathed property for which account was rendered annually on the festivals of St Katherine and the Annunciation. That these days could have significance for the associated images is suggested by a practice at Tong (Salop). As early as 1200 some lands there were granted in return for a chaplet of roses, to be rendered annually to the grantor or his heirs on the feast of the Nativity of St John the Baptist; if the intended recipients were absent, then the chaplet was to be placed upon the image of Our Lady in Tong church.[49]

## INDIVIDUAL DEVOTION

Structured collective devotional activities were inseparable from private expressions of veneration by the individual. The function of images as 'rememoratijf signes' was reinforced by offerings in cash or kind and/or physical contact with the image. The 1538 Injunctions against image veneration mentioned both kissing and licking; two admittedly hostile witnesses referred to the kissing of the feet of images (major statues sometimes wore silver shoes), followed by the venerator stroking their hands and faces.[50] These actions might take place during the liturgy, but were not exclusive to it. Essentially they were expressions of devotion from the individual to the saint(s). In the later Middle Ages the proliferation of saints and their accessibility in the nave led to increased opportunities for the outward expression of veneration.[51]

### Prayer

Prayer has been defined as 'a discourse, spoken or silent, expressed in the first person (singular or plural), which establishes a relationship with a person or persons believed to have supernatural power'.[52] Images were no more a prerequisite for prayer-activities by the Luton parishioners than they were for ritual performance, but their presence could provide a focus for that relationship between the suppliant and the sacred. A number of prayers featured in collective worship as well as private devotion.

Prayer invoking the saints was not a monolithic activity and falls into several categories.[53] As medieval wills for the most part were made towards the end of the testator's life, they are concerned with salvation and so request actions aimed at reducing their soul's time in purgatory. This might involve the undertaking of 'dedes of pitie', into which category fell the bequests by Elizabeth Wynch of the annual rent of an acre to fund a perpetual light to St Sitha in Luton church and 13s 4d for the repair of the candlesticks at the Trinity fraternity altar.[54] Under the same heading came petitions to the saints to intercede with God for their souls, like that already cited from the Sarum Missal on St Katherine's feast-day. The Luton parishioners would have repeated countless times the plain entreaties, 'pray for me/us' or 'Lord have mercy on me' and the Marian images must have been the recipients of bidding prayers like 'Mother of God remember me'. Richard Brother and other Luton parishioners who bequeathed legacies to the *Pietà* would have been familiar with the spiritual benefits associated with the prayer beginning *Obsecro te*.[55]

Other kinds of prayer were part of the standard devotional equipment of every medieval parishioner. The parochial clergy were instructed to teach the *Ave Maria* and *Pater noster* as part of the catechism. Such prayers were intended to add to the stock of divine grace towards humanity and to be placed in the balance to offset sins committed against God. These might be described as generalized affective prayers, to which no specific response was expected. They might, however, be addressed to favoured images. The *Salve regina* was said or sung before Our Lady, as on the scroll held by the owner of a smart Book of Hours (**XVI**), but the *Ave* and *Pater noster* might be recited before any image considered to be especially efficacious by the devotee. The image sanctified the space in which the prayer was spoken and therefore enhanced the prayer. A Northamptonshire testator instructed his widow to recite the *Ave*, *Pater noster* and Creed every Sunday before St Augustine's image in Daventry parish church.[56]

Instrumental prayers invoked the special powers of a saint or celestial personage to aid the suppliant in his or her everyday crises. They might be addressed either to the patron (perhaps the name-saint), or to a saint considered to have specialist powers in respect of the particular problem. A rare recorded instance of an instrumental prayer to an image was the attribution of the recovery of a man from a wound inflicted by a crossbow bolt through praying before St Leonard in Axminster church (Devon) in 1535–6.[57]

Like instrumental prayers, requests for forgiveness sought a response. At one end of the spectrum this might involve a kind of general protection; at the other it could comprise an act of atonement for a committed sin. Prayers said after confession fell into this category, as did prayers performed as penance before images, like the five *Pater nosters* and the *Ave Maria* said before the image of Our Lady of Pity by William Colyn of North Creake (Norf.).[58]

The distinction between affective prayers like these and petitions for the preservation of the existing order in community and family is a fine one. The latter, however, 'request the perpetuation of what is and the fulfillment of what is to be'.[59] Under this heading might come prayers for a successful harvest or for household prosperity. If Mirk's *Festial* was known to the Luton clergy, on the feast of St Anne (26 July) the parishioners may have been exhorted to pray to her in order that she pray to her daughter the Virgin and she to her son that He keep them healthy in mind and body and that they remain constant in marital vows and beget children.[60]

The individual parishioners through devotion (actions as well as prayers) therefore could construct a special relationship with their personal patron saint, but it was one which could never stand free from collective obligations of one kind or another. This is not to claim that the 'public' and the 'private' spheres are invariably indivisible, rather that they can be seen as overlapping idioms. Just as spaces can be given meaning by the use to which they are put, so devotional images take on different meanings according to the circumstances of usage and the personal involvement of the viewer(s).[61] When the Luton image of St Sitha was censed or a collect said before it during Mass on her feast-day, it shared in a communal act. When Elizabeth Wynch addressed a personal prayer to the same saint, either during the liturgy or as an act of solitary devotion, she was engaging in a direct personal relationship with her. By providing for a perpetual light for this image, Elizabeth was both contributing to the common good and expressing veneration for her favoured saint in the hope of securing her intercession.

## Memorialization

As in life, so in death. In a world where dying was a rite of passage, the relationship between individuals and their heavenly guardian continued to find visual expression beyond the grave. Testators desired that the prayers they had been accustomed to utter before an image would be continued after death, so that the personal would become communal.

We have already noted that the most common religious bequest at Luton, as everywhere else, was to the lights of the saints. An explicit instance of association between image and personal commemoration by means of lights is provided by the 1531 will of Dame Katherine Style of East Greenwich (Kent). She stipulated that her body was to be buried in the chapel of SS George and Anne in the parish church of St Alphege's. She bequeathed a taper to burn during service times before the image of Our Lady in this chapel and 6s 8d to the brotherhood of SS George and Anne for seven years and

> . . . two tapers brennyyng and to stand on my tombe and grave and to be lyght at servyce tymes on the holly daye and at the broderode masse [brotherhood Mass] on the worky day and one personne to be lymyted or assigned to light the said tapers and the taper before our ladye . . .

Some bequests directly linked the activating of lights with obsequies. Jasper Hoggelin of Old Romney (Kent) ordered that a wax taper costing 12d be set before the image of St James; it was to be lit at his burial and burn for the duration of the funeral service.[62]

The mnemonic value of posthumous gifts of goods and lights depended on the powers of recall and inclinations of executors and kith and kin – hence the concern of William Foreste of the parish of All Hallows, Hoo (Kent), that his bequest of a cow in perpetuity to St Christopher's light should be recorded in the parish Missal 'that she never dekey'. Foreste's concern may not have been so much for worldly record – it was too late for that – as to register the performance of a 'good work' and ensure that intercessory prayers would be offered by the living on behalf of his soul. This is stated explicitly by Giles Palmar of Hoo St Mary's, who left the wherewithal for a vestment to match a cope he had already given 'to thentent to have my soull there specially in the bedroll prayd for'. Palmar's fellow-parishioner Richard Salmon's 'good works' combined charity with image-endowment. He bequeathed twenty 'moder schepe' and a cow to the image-light of Our Lady on the south side of the chancel, from the proceeds of which 2s 8d was to be distributed among the parish poor every Good Friday and All Souls' Day.[63]

Devotion to a favoured saint might take a more personal, even intimate form. Agnes Newold's bequest of her best girdle to Our Lady's image in the church of St Peter de Dunstable at Bedford associated her posthumously with that image.[64] Girdles were valuable items of female attire; few have survived, but they are often prominently represented on memorial brasses, such as that of Agnes's contemporary Alice Cobbe of Sharnbrook (Beds.) (**119**).[65] The cumulative effect of generations of gifts and bequests was that favoured images like that of Our Lady in Pilton church (Som.) acquired a wardrobe and jewellery-box rivalling that of the wealthiest and most fashion-conscious of noble ladies. The trappings of this image included a velvet mantle on which were sewn fourteen rings, three scallop-shells of St James the Greater (presumably donated by pilgrims to Compostella), three brooches (i.e. pilgrim badges) of Henry VI, a pair of amber beads with jet 'gaydys' (gaudes) and another pair of jet beads bequeathed by Margaret Martyn. Similar beads given by three other women are also listed, as well as 'kercours' (kerchiefs).[66] Such a multiplicity of trappings did not lessen the impact of each individual gift. On the contrary, it testified to the powers of the saint and the desire of each donor to be associated with it and share in the grace bestowed.

Association with a particular image was often expressed by the choice of burial location. Interment *ad sanctos* had been an aspiration since early Christian times, when the sites of martyrs' tombs became surrounded with graves or cemeteries.[67] The practice spread to those churches which were not sites of shrines. At first the ecclesiastical authorities restricted interment within the walls to clergy, but by the early ninth century the privilege had been extended to *fideles laici*, i.e. founders and patrons. This qualification, at least in England, seems to have held good for many centuries. By the thirteenth century the laity in general were pressing for internal burial. The pronouncement of the 1292 Statutes of Chichester, that only lords of the village, patrons of the church and their wives, and rectors and vicars could be buried in either church or chancel, indicates that already this restriction was proving difficult to enforce. It seems that, following royal precedents in the second half of the thirteenth century, sepulchral monuments of the nobility and gentry began to appear in chancels from at least the early part of the following century.[68] A late and fruitless attempt at control was made in 1342 by the Bishop of Carlisle, but already by this date marked graves (and no doubt unmarked ones too) of people who fell outside the categories had appeared in churches.[69]

119. Sharnbrook (Beds.), St Peter's church: brass of Alice Cobbe (d. 1522); from Thomas Fisher, Monumental Remains and Antiquities in Bedfordshire (London, 1828), no. 21

By the time of the Luton wills church burial was open to those who could afford it – or were of sufficient status. Within and outside the church, there was a hierarchy of burial spaces, the approximate scale of values are set out in Table IV.

Burial before images ranked among the most desirable of sites. No doubt the practice spread from the religious to the laity. Abbots William Long (d. 1264) and Hugh de Dodyngton (d. 1294) of St Augustine's Abbey, Bristol, both specified interment before the image of Our Lady in the north transept, the latter between the graves of two earlier abbots.[71] It is impossible to establish when this privilege was extended to the laity, owing to the paucity of documentation and the displacement of many memorials. Edward Sheffield is the only Luton incumbent known to have been buried before the titular image (**118**). Apart from John Rotherham and the Becket image in

TABLE IV: BURIAL SITES, VALUES AND NUMBERS IN LUTON CHURCH, *c.* 1412–1545[70]

| SITE | GRAVE | VALUE | NUMBERS |
|---|---|---|---|
| Chancel, before patronal image or high altar | Marked/ unmarked | Best | 1 |
| Chancel (general) | Marked/ unmarked | V. desirable | 8 |
| Chantry chapel | Marked/ unmarked | V. desirable | 8 |
| Altar (other than high altar) | Marked/ unmarked | Desirable | 1 |
| Before rood | Marked/ unmarked | Desirable | – |
| Before image | Marked/ unmarked | Desirable | 3 |
| Within transepts | Marked/ unmarked | Desirable | 7 |
| Within nave | Marked/ unmarked | Good | 12 |
| Within church | Marked/ unmarked | Good | 20 |
| Churchyard | Unmarked | Commonplace | 24 |

his chapel, two Luton parishioners stipulated burial before images. John Norrys desired interment 'nere unto the Image and light of St Erasmus' and Richard Spayne wished his body to lie 'in the great space before Our Lady that stands in St Nicholas's chapel'.[72] To have a seat in front of an image was a mark of status. Some testators continued social distinction beyond the grave by burial on the site, under their lifetime holy guardian. A late example is John James of West Malling in Kent, who in 1545 wished to be interred in the Lady Chapel 'whereas I have used to sytt at s'vice tyme right under the foote of the ymage of our lady there'. Two Faversham parishioners requested burial before the images of St Anne and St Anthony, either under or next to their pews.[73]

Two altar-tombs in the Wenlock Chapel at Luton, possibly those of Thomas (d. 1543) and George Rotherham (d. 1545), formerly included brass representations of the Trinity; both were one-time Masters of the Trinity guild.[74] An early example of the inclusion of sacred images in tomb monuments is the mid-thirteenth-century grave-slab at Sutton Mandeville (Wilts.), with relief carvings of the (evidently female) occupant of the tomb kneeling below a much larger figure of the Virgin and Child (**120**). From the fourteenth century monuments might include multiple images of the saints, or of a single saint for whom the deceased had a particular veneration. Alternatively, an image could be specially commissioned to form part of a funerary ensemble. At Chalgrave (Beds.) a bracket for a small image is set in the nave pier at the feet of an early fifteenth-century knight on a tombchest, an arrangement recalling Dame Elizabeth Fitzwilliam's (*c.* 1503) request that an image of the Trinity be placed at the east end of her tomb in the mendicant church at Tickhill (S. Yorks.) (**121**).[75] The role of the saints as personal advocates is made explicit at Goudhurst (Kent), where a small freestone relief shows Sir Alexander Culpeper and his wife with

120. *Sutton Mandeville (Wilts.), All Saints' church: stone coffin lid with the deceased kneeling before the Virgin and Child, mid-thirteenth century*

their children kneeling under St George and the Virgin and Child, who flank the bust of God as judge in heaven over the Culpeper arms; below are the wooden effigies of the couple (**123**).[76] Representations of the familial patron saint might be essentially personal, but that does not preclude the possibility of their triggering a viewer's reflections on their intercessory powers. The choice and emplacement of St Christopher at the west end of the late fifteenth-century alabaster Lovell monument at Minster Lovell (Oxon.) is suggestive in this respect (**122**).[77]

In the *teatrum sacrum* of the parish church the popular and the elite, the private and the public conjoined. The laity as a whole and the seigneurial classes shared a commonality of tradition. Distinctions of rank might be maintained at Luton by seating and burial customs, but the Wenlocks and the Rotherhams participated in the same rites as the humblest of parishioners. This is not to claim that social differentiations were erased in the parish church. The observation that in fifteenth-century Florence it was not possible to 'worship God without worshipping man' is equally applicable to fifteenth-century England.[78]

In the buttressing of difference and of hierarchy, images played an important role. They were inseparable from the society that commissioned, endowed and used them, a statement encapsulated in the phrase 'the social frame'.[79] Inevitably those who could afford to contribute materially to an image were privileged in the eyes of their contemporaries. Donations to, and commissioning of, images are not distinctive features of elite wills. This does not reflect lack of devotion. Nobles and gentry had access to images in their books of hours and private chapels, like that which survives in ruins at the Rotherham residence at Someries, just outside Luton (**XVI**; **13**, **14**, **40**, **117**). Moreover, their wealth meant that 'good works' quite often took the form of reconstructing all or parts of the parish church lying within their domains. Existing and recorded inscriptions and heraldry bear witness to the considerable scale of church-building undertaken by the Bedfordshire elites in the later Middle Ages. Between the middle of the fourteenth and the middle of the sixteenth centuries the churches of Lower Gravenhurst, Wymington, Northill, Toddington, Flitton, Marston Moretaine, Millbrook and Willington were in part or entirely rebuilt at the expense of their seigneurs. Substantial chapels were also added to Biddenham and Cople churches as well as the Wenlock Chapel to Luton.

Commissioning of parochial images by gentry was not unknown. As part of his rebuilding of the chancel at Great Brington (Northants.), Sir John Spencer (d. 1522) included an image of Our Lady with its tabernacle and gilding.[80] The images of the Trinity, St Anne and Our Lady of Pity in Luton church were of sufficient importance to John Rotherham for him to leave large wax candles to them.[81] Images in chantry chapels in cathedral or large monastic churches could benefit by inclusion in liturgical celebration. Among the provisions made in the fourteenth century by Sir John Pulteney for his chapel in St Paul's Cathedral was the requirement that the cathedral choristers daily after Compline should go to his chapel, sing an antiphon (no doubt the *Salve regina*) before the image of the Our Lady, recite the psalm *De Profundis* and the prayer for the dead, terminating with the words 'Anima Johannis de Pultoney fundatoris hujus capellae, et animae omnium fidelium defunctorum per Dei misericordiam requiescant in pace'.[82]

Even (or especially) in the gift of an image for the site of collective worship, the social status of the donor was made manifest. Several surviving images have donor figures in armour, together with smartly attired spouses. While the provenances of the alabaster St John the Baptist in Quimper Cathedral (Brittany, France) and the Boston Museum All Saints are unknown and might have come from a private chapel or monastery, the stone Trinity at Brant Broughton (Lincs.) was found in the parish church; all three have knightly donor figures (**124**, **125**). Transfers from private

*121. Chalgrave (Beds.), All Saints' church: tomb of a knight with image-bracket at feet*

*122. Minster Lovell (Oxon.), St Kenelm's church: alabaster Lovell tomb with St Christopher in relief at the west end*

123. *Goudhurst (Kent), St Mary's church: relief dated 1537 from the monument to Sir Alexander Culpeper and his family*

124. *Alabaster image of All Saints, c. 1400 (Boston Museum of Fine Arts (USA), Decorative Arts Special Fund, inv. no. 27.852)*

125. *Brant Broughton (Lincs.), St Helen's church: stone Trinity with male and female knightly donors, mid-fourteenth century*

to public devotional spaces were not unknown. In 1449 William Bruges, Garter King of Arms, willed that polychromed images of the Virgin, St George and the Trinity were to be removed from his chapel in Kentish Town to the Lady Chapel in St George's church, Stamford (Lincs.).[83]

Yet the smallest of donations in cash or kind meant that many individuals could secure a stake in an image. Moreover, the proliferation of images, as at Luton, offered opportunities for more people to express their devotion to individual saints. None the less, the most potent means of associating images with individuals were those which were visual and thus only available to the better-off. A streamer of stained cloth bearing the representation of St Hildebert and the arms of William Swanne must have been connected with the image of this saint which stood in the south aisle of Swanscombe church (Kent). In the same vein was the velvet canopy given to the patronal image in All Saints, Bristol by vicar Hardwicke, embroidered with his initials.[84] Other kinds of artefacts offered fields for personalization. In 1512 John Barbour, priest of St Clement's in

Ipswich, charged his executors with commissioning a tabernacle for the image of St Thomas, which was to bear a bidding prayer for the souls of Richard and Katherine Barber (presumably his parents).[85] A rare survivor of such practices is the image–niche built into a nave pillar at St Alphege's, Canterbury. Immediately below is a brass plate with the shield of arms of Thomas Prowte (d. 1468) and an inscription recording his donation of the pillar (127).[86] A few stone niches and rather more brackets testify to the importance accorded to heraldry as a means of associating individuals with images (XII; 126).

In no respect was the social frame made more explicit than in those cases where the donor(s) appear with the image itself, like the examples in Boston Museum and Brant Broughton cited above; also the mural at South Newington (Oxon.) (XII). The viewer of these images did not just see the representation of the saint, their gaze also encompassed its provider(s). The latter's diminutive size and kneeling pose reflect the inferior status of the terrestrial being (however exalted) in the company of the sacred; yet their presence in the foreground provided a permanent association with the representations of the saint.[87] The fine alabaster patronal image of St Peter from Flawford (Notts.) with its clerical donor conveyed a series of messages which implicated the viewer in its relationship with

126. Great Horwood (Bucks.), St James's church: image-niche with shields of arms, including the arma Christi and the Basset family, fourteenth century

the clerical patron (54). By providing the image, the donor invited the viewer to honour and share his devotion to St Peter and attested to the saint's efficacy. He was also promoting a special affinity between the clerical estate and the patronal saint, who in this case happened to be the rock on which the Church was founded. His devotion to St Peter was manifested through his own representation and the scroll on which presumably was a bidding prayer. Unlike many images in personal devotional artefacts like books of hours, where they incline their heads towards or look at the suppliant/owner (XVI), St Peter's 'arc of address' was directed into the distance. Indeed, the bidding prayer might have been general (Ora pro nobis), rather than specific to the donor. Nevertheless, the presence of the donor and probably an inscription with his name meant that when the viewer prayed for St Peter's help, he or she was also invited to include him.[88] Equally, the image of St Thomas Becket in Luton had honour conferred on it precisely because of its association with the Rotherham family.[89]

*127. Canterbury (Kent), St Alphege's church: shield and inscription to John Prowte (d. 1468) below an image-niche in a nave pillar*

## IMAGE USE AND GENDER

From 1519 the Luton Trinity fraternity admitted young people under the headings of maidens and bachelors.[90] The organization of social bodies by gender, age and marital status was common in some parishes during the later Middle Ages. Sometimes separate image lights were maintained by the unmarried girls and the young men of parishes. No examples are known in Luton or anywhere else in Bedfordshire, but Bachelors' and Maidens' lights are mentioned in the 1530s at Langley Marish, in the south of the adjoining county of Buckinghamshire.[91]

There were far fewer images of female than of male saints at Luton, apart from the Virgin in her various manifestations. SS Anne, Katherine, Margaret, Sitha and George, often seen as appealing more to one sex than the other, were all represented. Men and women might have been predisposed by life-experience to venerate some saints over others, but the dearth of female testators (only two occur in surviving pre-Reformation wills) makes it impossible to establish whether there was a gender-specific polarity for the Luton images; it was not apparently the case at Eaton Bray and Totternhoe, as we saw in Chapter Five.[92] At Luton male testators contributed to lights burning before the images of Our Lady of Pity and SS Anne, Katherine and Margaret. Elizabeth Wynch clearly had a special attachment to St Sitha, but three male parishioners also endowed her lights. Even Bachelors' and Maidens' lights were not exclusively gendered. Three male testators made bequests to Our Lady's light maintained by the womenfolk at Whitstable (Kent), while Alice Pamplett of Reculver did likewise to the Bachelors' light in her parish church.[93] Quantitative analysis of course is problematic, as more men than women were in a position to make wills; also the imperatives which lay behind a testator's preferences are unknown and allowance has to be made for the possibility of direction from the parish priest.

Did it follow therefore that there was no difference in the relationships of men and women with the devotional images in their parish churches? In the microcosm of the Nansa valley in northern Spain it was observed that the women of the villages were more inclined to have a personal patronal saint than the menfolk and were entrusted with negotiations with the sacred as part of the division of familial responsibilities. The man was the head of the household in matters concerning livelihood and business, while the woman assumed authority over nurturing of children, feeding and health of the family – and also its spiritual well-being. The last was a natural concomitant, for quotidian concerns as often as not were contingent on the benign operation of the sacred.[94] To what extent is a situation which pertained to a corner of a Mediterranean country in the 1960s applicable to English society some four centuries earlier?

Contemporary commentators from as divergent positions as Wycliffe and Thomas More held that women were excessive in their devotions, especially to the Virgin. In 1516 a male parishioner of Wimborne St Giles (Dorset), was reported to have proclaimed that it was 'alewde thyng and amadde condition or use occupyed in his contree or paryshe that wemen will cum and sette their ca[n]dles a fore atree [i.e. a wooden image], the Image of Saynt Gyles'.[95] Underlying such statements was the male view that in devotional matters women were more gullible than men. This accusation was levelled explicitly in the *Homilies* issued in Queen Elizabeth I's reign, where images are criticized because they appealed especially to wives and young maidens.[96]

Sources like these need to be contextualized. An unpublished enquiry into the stereotypical roles assigned to Englishmen and women in the late medieval and early modern periods has been made by Christine Peters.[97] She argues that there was no substantial difference between the sexes in matters devotional, but that some outwardly distinct manifestations stemmed from social practices. Pre-Reformation conduct literature stressed piety as an integral part of female virtue:

'the devotion of holy thynges most agreeable for a woman . . .'.[98] Whereas it was the wife's duty to attend church regularly and use her beads, this was not an expectation of men. There was thus a conjunction of pious virtues and expected female virtues, reinforced by the exercise of male hegemony through their virtual monopoly of the leading offices in the parish church.

There are only three references to gifts of garments or personal adornment to images in the Bedfordshire wills, all from women. Of the few references to similar items in the published Kent wills, almost as many were from men as from women. For example, a widow named Alice Stevyn in 1487 left to the image of Our Lady in St Leonard's chapel, Hythe, her coral prayer beads, gold ring, crucifix and lawn kercher, while her contemporary, Alexander Tanner, likewise endowed the image of St Michael with one of his girdles.[99] However, although men like Tanner had a greater choice of cash and kind to dispose of, such bequests of valued items of adornment and apparel enabled Agnes Newold, with her bequest of her best girdle to the image of Our Lady in the church of St Peter de Dunstable in Bedford, to construct a more intimate relationship with the sacred. Alice Wodill's bequest of her wedding ring to the titular image of the Virgin at Marston Moreteyne might signal a dying woman's metamorphosis as *sponsa Christi*. This desire for identification with the Virgin is made more or less explicit in Jane Chaumerleyn of York's will of 1501:

> my weddyng ringe of gold, a gyrdill the tusheys theroff of gold of vynes hernest [harnessed] with sylver and gylt, and a payr of corell baydes [beads] gaudiett wt sylver unto yt blessed ymage of Saynt Anne in St Mary Abby; and I will that the rynge the day of my buriall be putt on her fynger the gyrdill about her, and the baydes in her hand.[100]

Agnes Newold's donation of her best girdle forged a direct link with the proof of the Virgin's Assumption (the passing down of her girdle to St Thomas as she ascended to heaven, as is often represented) (**103**). Sometimes testators stipulated that such items were to be sold for the image's upkeep, but such accessories could be transformed either temporarily or permanently into the hallowed by means of display on a favoured image of Our Lady.[101] This sharing of bodily apparel with the sacred mirrored the nurturing, caring roles of women.

An interiorized world of private prayer to a revered saint via his or her visual sign may have offered fulfilment and solace to a female parishioner which was largely denied her in communal liturgical worship. In Luton St Mary's Our Lady offered female experiences which were expressed by different kinds of material representation: as instructed child (by St Anne) and grieving mother (*Pietà*).[102] Within the parameters set by contemporary mores and beliefs, potentially fulfilling roles could be found for women in instructing their children in the tenets of faith and worship. If in twenty-first-century eyes rites such as the churching of women after childbirth are seen as humiliating and oppressive, to culturally conditioned contemporary women the ceremony might have reinforced selfhood. The ritual of the purification of women after childbirth occurs in wills from several Kent parishes. In 1503 Margaret Joye of St Werburgh's at Hoo bequeathed a green coverlet 'for to be okupeyd att the churchyng of purificacion of women'. Ten years later a widow named Alice with the same surname and from the same parish left 5 shillings for the purchase of a cloth 'for to laye before women whan they be purified wt the picture of the purificacion of our ladie'.[103] According to the Uses of Sarum and York, the brief ceremony took place outside the church, before the porch. In the Sarum rite the priest recited Psalms CXXIII and CXXVIII (*Ad te levavi oculos meos* and *Beati omnes*), followed by the saying of the *Pater noster*, prayers and a Collect and concluding with the sprinkling of holy water over the woman, who was then led by hand by

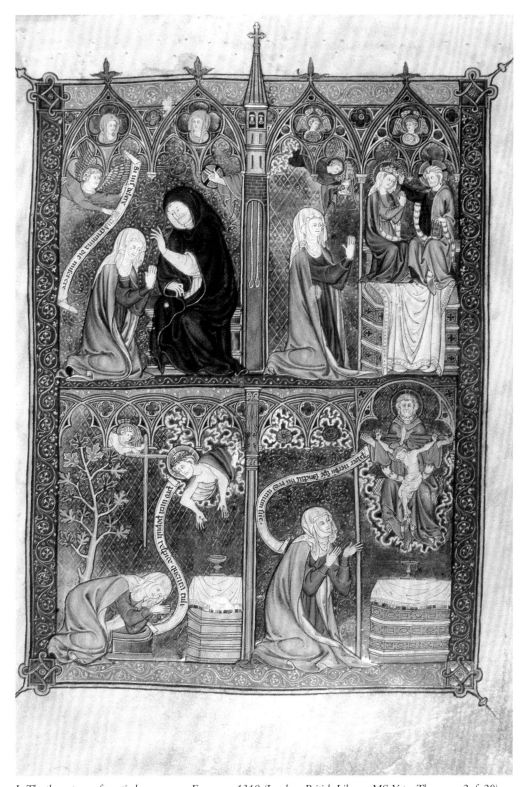

*I. The three stages of mystical appearance, France, c. 1310 (London, British Library, MS Yates Thompson 2, f. 29).*

*II. Eaton Bray (Beds.), St Mary's church: south chapel interior.*

*III. Horley (Oxon.), St Etheldreda's church: murals of St Christopher and St Sitha on the north side of the nave.*

Left: IV. Polychromed oak Virgin and
Child from St Mary's church, Langham
(Essex), c. 1220–30 (London, Victoria
& Albert Museum, inv. no. A79–1925).

Right: V. Winchester Cathedral: limestone
image of the Virgin and Child, c.
1475–90.

VI. *Polychromed and gilded limewood Pietà, Swabia (Germany), c. 1435–40 (The Metropolitan Museum of Art, New York, The Cloisters Collection, inv. no. 64.80).*

VII. *Blunham (Beds.), St Edmund's church: alabaster* Pietà, *late fifteenth century.*

*IX. Blunham (Beds.), St Edmund's church: alabaster Virgin and Child, c. 1350.*

*VIII. Toledo Cathedral (Spain):* La Virgen Blanca, c. *1250–70.*

X. Fingringhoe (Essex), St Andrew's (formerly St Ouen's) church: polychromed limestone St Margaret in niche, c. 1450–1500.

XI. Sandstone St Christopher from Norton Priory (Ches.), c. 1375–1400 (National Museums and Galleries on Merseyside, Liverpool).

*XII. South Newington (Oxon.), St Peter ad Vincula's church: mural of the Virgin and Child and donors, early fourteenth century.*

XIII. St George, polychromed wood, iron, leather and fabric, c. 1528 (The Worshipful Company of Armourers and Brasiers, London).

XIV. *Penance during Lent,*
*Flanders, c. 1500 (London,*
*British Library, MS Add.*
*25698, f. 9).*

XV. *Monk painting a statuette of the Virgin, from the*
Lambeth Apocalypse, c. *1260–7 (London, Lambeth Palace*
*Library, MS 209, f. iiv).*

*XVI. Virgin and Child and patron, c. 1410–20 (Cambridge, Trinity College, MS B. 11. 7, f. 20r).*

*Left: XVII. Anwick (Lincs.), St Edith's church: polychromed stone Virgin and Child, early fourteenth century.*

*Right: XVIII. Twelfth-century German wooden image of the enthroned Virgin with a fourteenth-century head (Schnütgen Museum, Cologne, inv. no. A989).*

*XIX. Cobham (Kent), St Mary Magdalen's church: three carved and polychromed freestone heads, probably c. 1362.*

*XX. Votive crown of Margaret of York, c. 1461–74 (Domschatzkammer, Aachen).*

*XXI. Vièrge ouvrante, German, c. 1400 (Germanisches Nationalmuseum, Nuremberg, inv. no. Pl.2397).*

*XXII. Cologne Cathedral: cult image of Our Lady of Grace, fourteenth century (with later ex-votos).*

*XXIII. Milton Keynes (Bucks.): Chapel of Our Lady of Bradwell from the south-west, early fourteenth century.*

*XXIV. King's Lynn (Norfolk): Chapel of Our Lady of the Mount from the south-west, late fifteenth and early sixteenth centuries.*

*128. Abbotsbury (Dorset), St Katherine's Chapel, fourteenth century*

the priest into the church.[104] Alice Joye's bequest shows that at Hoo the ritual was associated with pictorial imagery of the Purification of the Virgin. It appears from other Kent references that sometimes the ceremony took place within the church and before an image. In about 1543 the parishioners of Chartham complained that their vicar had removed an image of Our Lady to which candles had been offered at the purification of women. At Margate the churching of women was performed in the Lady Chapel, which would have housed an image of the Virgin.[105]

The assigning of specific roles to discrete categories of women in parish festivals provided opportunities for them to experience a sense of pride and distinction. Apart from the exclusively female rituals performed at Charlton-on-Otmoor and Glentham, as mentioned above, on the patronal feast-day at St Margaret's, Westminster, the maidens of the parish processed through the parish dressed in special costumes in honour of the saint's chastity.[106] Another custom involving maidens which was still practised until comparatively recently may also have been a pre-Reformation survival. St Katherine was seen to be particularly efficacious in finding husbands and on her feast-day the young women of Abbotsbury (Dorset) would walk up to the fine fourteenth-century chapel dedicated to this saint and invoke her aid (**128**).[107] The exclusion of women from the exercise of sacerdotal powers could lead to investment in ancillary parochial activities, such as fund-raising by means of 'gatherings' or making, repairing and washing image accoutrements and vestments. Anne Buckmaster of Wing (Bucks.) was unlikely ever to aspire to her husband's office of churchwarden, but perhaps she found fulfilment in making up the curtain before Our Lady in Gesyn.[108]

Principally with the help of the clergy and layfolk of St Mary's church at Luton, some of the complex issues, social and religious, involved in the use of, and meanings attached to, images have been explored. It has not been an attempt to tell the whole story, nor are the aspects which have been raised unique to this small corner of Bedfordshire. Hardest to disinter are the echoes of distinctive local customs and practices, some of which may have been peculiar to the locality, even to the Luton community.

# CHAPTER EIGHT

# CULT IMAGES

One of the pages in Lady Katherine Bray's Book of Hours is adorned with *trompe l'oeil* representations of pilgrim keepsakes from some of the major cult sites of late medieval Christendom (**129**). Several depict the Virgin, including an Annunciation associated with the premier Marian cult-site in England, at Walsingham in Norfolk. Such embellishments are found in several high-quality devotional books produced by Netherlandish illuminators for the elites, so it is doubtful whether the badges were specifically made to reflect Katherine's personal devotional interests.[1] Equally it is unknown whether she went on any pilgrimages herself. If she did, she would have been faced with a plethora of destinations, without even having to quit the shores of England.

Katherine was in the service of Henry VII's spouse, Elizabeth of York. In March 1502 pilgrimage was undertaken by two individuals acting as proxies for the queen:

> Itm delivered to Sr William Barton preest for thofferinges of the Quene to oure lady and Saint George at Wyndesoure and to the Holy Crosse there ijs. vjd. to King Henry ijs. vjd. to oure lady of Eton xxd. to the Childe of grace at Reding ijs. vjd. to oure lady of Caversham ijs. vjd. to our lady of Cokthorp xxd. to the holy blode of Heyles xxd. to prince Edward vs. to oure lady of Worcestre vs. to the Holy Rood of Northampton vs. to oure lady of Grace there ijs. vjd. to oure lady of Walsingham vjs viijd. to oure lady of Sudbury ijs. vjd. to our lady of Wolpitte xxd. to oure lady of Ippeswiche iijs. iiijd. and to oure lady of Stokeclare xxd. . . . Item to Richard Mylner of Bynfeld for money to bee offred for the Quene to our lady of Crowham ijs. vjd. To the roode Grace in Kent [Boxley] xxd. to Saint Thomas of Canterbury, vs. to oure lady of undrecroft there vs. to Sainct Adrean xxd. to Saint Augustyn [Canterbury] xxd. to oure lady of Dover xxd. to the roode of the north dore in Poules [St Paul's Cathedral, London] xxd. to our lady of Grace there xxd. to Saint Ignasi xxd. To Saint Dominik xxd. To Sainct Petre of Melayn [Peter Martyr] xijd. to Saint Fraunces xxd. to Saint Saviour ijs. vjd. to oure lady of Piewe [Our Lady of the Pew, Westminster] ijs. vjd. to oure lady of Berking ijs vjd. and to oure lady of Willesdone ijs. vjd.

Later in the same year the queen made a further offering to Our Lady of Caversham and paid for a garment to be worn by the child of Grace at Reading.[2]

With the exception of Hailes, Northampton, Worcester and some unlocated cults, this list is concerned with sacred sites in the south-east, especially East Anglia and Kent. However, it is far from a *Who's Who* of all English cult centres at the turn of the sixteenth century, even within its self-defined boundaries. The queen's list can be supplemented by two Norfolk wills, which include proxy pilgrimages to Our Lady of Rafham, Our Lady of Ardenbourg at Great Yarmouth, Our Lady of Grace at Cambridge, Our Lady of the Mount at King's Lynn, St Spirit of Elsing, St Petronella of Stratton, St Leonard without Norwich, St Margaret and Our Lady of Pity at Horstead, St John's Head at Trimingham, St Etheldreda of Ely, St Theobald, St Wandred of

Bixley and the holy roods at Beccles, Bromholm and Crostwight. Even within the eastern counties this list is not exhaustive. Margery Kempe made pilgrimages to St Michael's church at Mintlyn, just outside King's Lynn, and to the tomb of the priest Richard of Caister in St Stephen's church, Norwich (**Maps 10, 11, p. 282**).[3]

A similar catalogue, mainly for the north-east of England, was compiled in the will of William Ecopp, rector of West Heslerton (N. Yorks.), in 1472. While Becket, Our Lady of Walsingham and St Etheldreda occur, the principal foci were much nearer his home. He mentioned Our Lady of Lincoln, Our Lady of Doncaster, St Thomas of Lancaster (at Pontefract), St Saviour of Newburgh Priory, Our Lady of Scarborough, St Botolph of Hackness, the rood of Thorpe Basset, Our Lady of Guisborough, St John of Beverley, St John of Bridlington, St William of York, Our Lady of Jesmond, Our Lady of Carlisle and St Ninian of Candidcasa. To these, Dame Katherine Hastings (1506/7) added Our Lady of 'Belcrosse' and Our Lady of Hemingborough, as well as Our Lady of Walsingham and Our Lady of Doncaster (**Maps 13, 14, 15, p. 283–4**).[4]

Some of these sites held relics or miracle-working roods, but the majority were of cult images, especially those of Our Lady. This chapter will examine the emergence of miracle-working images and explore their architectural and visual presentations through some surviving and documented sites. It is not feasible to attempt an overview of what is a vast and still inadequately explored subject. There is also the danger of glossing over distinctive features of individual cult images. The issues, therefore, will be approached by means of a few case-studies. The emphasis will be on those cults whose built environment either survives or is well recorded. These provide a cross-section, ranging from the very popular, with a national constituency, to the lesser known, localized, cults. While the impulses behind pilgrimage, the presentation of the foci of pilgrimage and the externalized nature of devotional practices have not altered substantially over the centuries – indeed, pilgrimage flourishes today in all religions – the circumstances in which cults rise and fall, the cultures in which they exist and the socio-economic structures in which they function are very diverse. Diversity is also characteristic of pilgrimage in medieval England.

Before moving to an examination of the individual sites, it is appropriate first to consider the historiographical and methodological issues concerning pilgrimage in general. An influential study by Victor and Edith Turner applied anthropological perspectives to the phenomenon of past and present pilgrimage. For them, pilgrimage was liminal: it freed participants from their social structures and fostered an idealized spirit of commensality or *communitas*. Their concepts of liminality have been criticized for overlooking the fact that people did not leave behind their social baggage when they went on pilgrimage. *The Canterbury Tales* might be fictional, but its social stereotypes underlined the differences in wealth and status among pilgrims, differences which could be manifested at the pilgrimage site by visual tokens of commemoration and veneration. *The Book of Margery Kempe* also shows that fellow-pilgrims could be as trying as vexatious neighbours. The notion of *communitas* as an attainable ideal has also been challenged; instead of places where consensus was forged, pilgrimage sites offered a stage for the acting out of diverse interpretations and also of conflicts, thereby mirroring life as lived. It has been argued that pilgrimage itself was a cultural phenomenon in its own right; also that the pilgrim's experience of his or her journey through time and space was framed to a greater or lesser extent by the architectural topography and other visual features of the pilgrimage site itself. Through patronage, the buildings which enclosed relics or cult images might also have privileged the great and the good. Another criticism of the Turners' approach is that of insensitivity to historical time and place. The dynamic, ever-evolving nature of pilgrimage and the features peculiar to each site

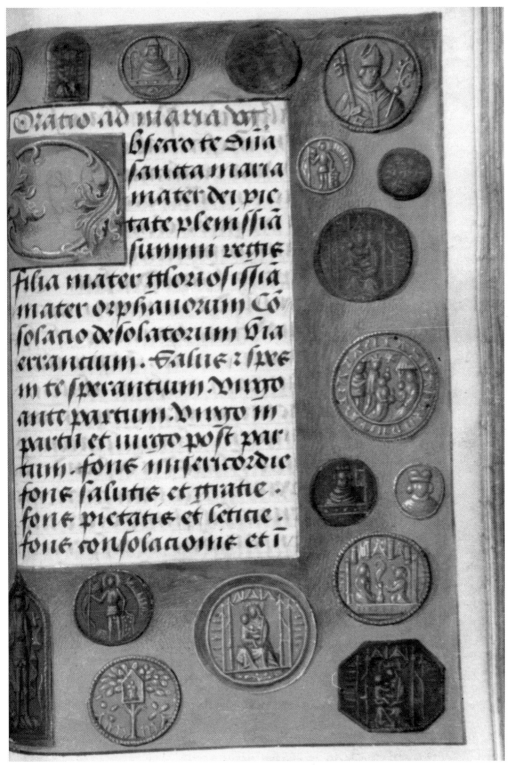

129. *Pilgrim badges in the* Bray Hours, *c. 1490 (Stonyhurst College Library, Lancs., MS 60, f. 61r)*

are ignored.[5] The Turners acknowledged that there was a whole stratum of local Marian cults 'to which pilgrimage may mean hardly more than a walk across a hill. . .'.[6] Their observation was confined to Mexico and they devoted very little attention to the localized nature of pilgrimage. The power of local cults might depend on the known and familiar; nevertheless, the pilgrimage might still represent a journey of the imagination or, more accurately, one of the spirit, thereby distinguishing it from a trip to the local market.

The Turners brought a wider perspective to the study of pilgrimage and their notion of liminality is not incompatible with current thinking that pilgrimage evoked a plurality of responses from participants. For constituent groups on the margins of society, like the sick who occupied a twilight world between the living and the dead, to go on pilgrimage might indeed constitute a transcendent experience.[7] The concepts raised by the Turners and the criticisms they aroused provide useful analytical tools for investigating the sites discussed in this chapter.

Another study from a sociological perspective which prompts questions for medieval pilgrimage is William Christian Jr's work on the Nansa valley in northern Spain. He described the geographical boundary within which a cult was efficacious as a territory of grace, 'an area over which its benevolent power seems especially manifest'.[8] These landscapes could overlap and overlay one another; they were not immutable, but expanded and contracted in accordance with the popularity or decline of a cult. For example, at its height the territory of grace of the Becket cult was international, but by the eve of the Reformation it was confined to England. By contrast, some of the more localized cults might rise up the scale. One measure of popularity is the value of offerings made to a cult object. As late as 1535, according to the incumbent, the image of St Urith at Chittlehampton (Devon) attracted oblations worth £61 15s 10d, even though this figure was subsequently adjusted to £49 5s., it is still an impressive total for what appears to have been a saint with a very limited constituency, especially given that it exceeded the total offerings for the same year (approx. £36) at Becket's shrine.[9] Moreover pilgrimage transcended national boundaries. For very devout (or contrite) and adventurous souls like Margery Kempe, the known world was their oyster. *The Book of Margery Kempe* is a handy guide to the sacred landscape of the late medieval Christian world. The eponymous heroine moved easily through its peaks and troughs, encompassing the great international sites in the Holy Land, Rome and Compostella and taking in the cult centres of northern Europe at Aachen, Wilsnack, the waning Canterbury pilgrimage and the thriving Walsingham site on her doorstep. Her narrative also introduces readers to the lesser-known local cults, like that of Richard of Caister, and even to a substratum occupying the no-man's-land between cult-image proper and popular devotional image. In Margery's text the local cults were supplementary to, not a replacement for, far-flung pilgrimage sites. Before she embarked on a long journey, she enlisted the protection of Our Lady of Ardenbourg at Great Yarmouth as well as the more illustrious Our Lady of Walsingham.[10] The inclusion of pilgrim badges of the Annunciation in Flemish books of hours like that owned by Lady Bray, as well as other documentation, show that the clientele associated with Our Lady of Walsingham included devotees from the Low Countries (**129**).[11]

Finucane was able to trace the shifting boundaries of shrines like St Godric of Finchale and Thomas Cantelupe at Hereford through the geographical distribution of recorded miracles.[12] This kind of data is not available for the image-cults which are the subject of this chapter. Instead, representations of the saint in glass, mural and screen-paintings and pilgrim badges (plus occasional testamentary references) are the best guides to the boundaries of their territories.[13] The fifteenth- and early sixteenth-century topography of St Urith can be defined roughly by a hymn or sequence in her honour copied by a Glastonbury monk, the presence of her feast-day in two prayer-books and several pictorial representations, all within a small area in north Devon and south-west Somerset (**136**).[14]

Pilgrimage remained popular throughout society until the Henrician proscriptions. It offered a diversion, with attached spiritual benefits, from workaday concerns. The picture is one of dynamism, not stagnation or decline. Not all the cults were of equal status or retained their power to attract throughout the period; the story is one of fluidity, with individual cults waxing and waning. Some of the local cults may have enjoyed a short shelf-life, although we should be wary of assuming their ephemerality from the silence of written records.

## STRUCTURES OF VENERATION: THE ARCHITECTURE OF PILGRIMAGE

The architectural setting provided the theatre for the ritual of viewing.[15] It channelled movement and also enhanced the object of veneration by the splendour of its fabric and fittings. The layout of the structural frame might orchestrate the pilgrim's experience until the climax was reached with the viewing and veneration of the image itself. Whether the 'territory of grace' of a cult image was local or national, the experience of the supplicant or pilgrim was essentially personal and included elements common to every site to a greater or lesser extent. Their experience was enriched further by collective witnessing of masses and litanies, especially those performed on major feast-days, and by the saying of individual prayers and antiphons.

The sites examined below are not the great relic-shrines of the post-Conquest cathedrals and monasteries, which were sited behind the high altar; cult images had more random locations.[16]

### Monastic Sites

*Our Lady of the Undercroft, Canterbury*
Among the most generous of Queen Elizabeth's offerings was the 5s to be given to 'oure lady of undrecroft'. This image, as its name suggests, was located in the crypt beneath the choir of England's foremost cathedral, which was also a Benedictine abbey (**130**, **131**).[17] Little or nothing is known about the form of the image. A pilgrim badge identified as possibly showing Our Lady of the Undercroft depicts a seated Virgin (**153 (c)**), but another badge of the same group with a flanking figure labelled St Thomas Becket shows a standing Virgin.[18] As we shall see, the cult image was housed in a tabernacle whose size proves that it could have been no more than 1.5m high.

The crypt itself is late Romanesque in date and Robertson noted paintings of an angelic choir in the apse vault, which he dated to the twelfth century.[19] The chapel, however, is first mentioned in Henry III's reign, when there are references to the altar. It is not certain at what date miraculous powers were first attributed to the image, but it benefited from royal favour in the reign of Edward I. He presented it with a gold brooch every year and paid for musicians to perform before it. The cult enjoyed its heyday during the second half of the fourteenth century, when the chapel was lavishly fitted-out, principally by Joan, Lady Mohun, and received rich benefactions from Edward III and the Black Prince. Between 1262 and 1279 annual offerings averaged £2; by 1350 they had jumped to £50 and between 1371 and 1383 they totalled on average more than £40. The Treasurer's accounts are missing after this date, but the account book of Thomas Anselm, warden of the altar of Our Lady of the Undercroft for 1510–11, shows

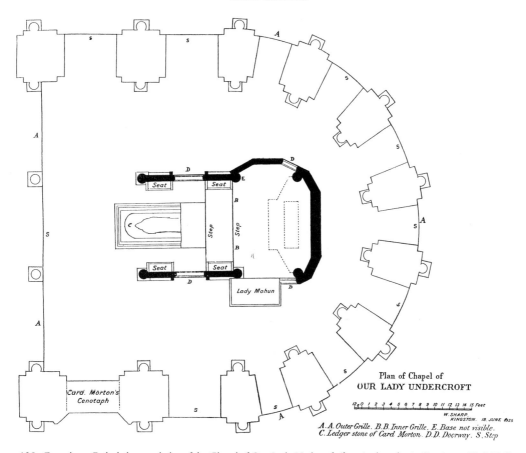

*130. Canterbury Cathedral: ground plan of the Chapel of Our Lady Undercroft (from* Archaeologia Cantiana, 38 (1926))

oblations at Our Lady of the Undercroft amounting to only half this total. In 1467–8 the Prior's rolls recorded no offerings at all from the chapel (or indeed from Becket's shrine), although on average 6s 6d per year was received in oblations during this century. This might indicate a relatively short shelf-life for the image as a major cult-figure. However, the rich mural decoration dates in part from the fifteenth century and in the middle of that century a great crowd is reported as resorting to the chapel for the springs that flowed into it; even in 1510–11 it attracted visitors daily and Erasmus was impressed by the richness of the spectacle.[20]

Given the importance of Canterbury as a national pilgrimage centre, it follows that Our Lady of the Undercroft would have received visitors from all over the country.[21] It is possible, however, that its appeal may have changed over time. The first endowments in the thirteenth century were all made by ordinary citizens of Canterbury. Later decorations and burials suggest that after Edward I bestowed royal approval it found favour with the court and aristocracy.[22]

Canterbury Cathedral represented a sequence of cultic sites, of which the relics of Thomas Becket took primacy of place. Erasmus may well have been typical in viewing Our Lady of the Undercroft after visiting Becket's shrine and the site of his first shrine in the crypt beneath the Trinity Chapel.[23] For local devotees, however, the image would have been a focus in its own right.

*131. Canterbury Cathedral: interior of the Chapel of Our Lady Undercroft, looking east*

The chapel occupies a defined space within the main area of the crypt and was itself formed of three zones. The outer was bounded by the twelfth-century piers of the hemicycle. These piers are linked by a raised step which separates the inner space from the outer ambulatory. There are traces of enclosures between the piers and the west end was enclosed by the massive iron grille erected in 1377–9, fixed to timber beams. These screens formed a second ambulatory from which the image could be glimpsed. The second zone is enclosed by an elaborate stone screen dating almost certainly from the early 1360s.[24] This delineated the chapel proper. However the image was housed in a yet more sacred space. The altar at the east end, surmounted by a painted and gilded stone reredos with six stepped openwork niches flanking the larger and more elaborately canopied central tabernacle, which framed the image of Our Lady, was divided off from the body of the chapel by an iron grille erected on the step across the eastern bay. Presumably this inner sanctum comprised the third zone.

The two sections of the chapel vaulting are also distinguished by their painted decoration. The vaulting throughout is embellished with suns and stars. Around the altar are added heraldic shields bearing the royal arms (including those of the Black Prince), and those of Archbishops Arundel and Chichele and some of the leading nobility of late fourteenth- and fifteenth-century England. The astronomical iconography also occurs in hymns in the Sarum Hours of the Virgin. Originally each sun and star seems to have had a silvery surface, which simultaneously added to the illumination of the chapel by reflecting the lights burning in the silver candelabrum and bowl placed before the altar and image, and distributed the grace of the reflected image to the pilgrims crowding into the constricted space.[25]

Thomas Anselm's accounts provide a snapshot of the ritual year in the chapel as performed in 1510–11. His duties included the saying of Mass at the altar every day; the chapel was also used for a sort of trial-run for monks saying Mass for the first time. On the major Marian feast-days High Mass was celebrated in the chapel by the subprior assisted by an Epistoler and Gospeller and a third monk, all wearing full vestments. In addition, votive Masses were said, notably the daily one for Lady Mohun, and her obit was kept annually.[26]

The chapel was a favoured burial site for the great and the good, both lay and clerical. In 1395 Joan, Lady Mohun desired to be laid to rest in the chapel, in the tomb which she had prepared some two decades previously. The tomb's construction necessitated the replacement of the screenwork on the south side of the east bay of the chapel and reveals the steps which were permitted to be taken to accede to the wishes of powerful benefactors, even in such hallowed places. In this case, Lady Mohun's contribution to the chapel's reconstruction would have given her a strong bargaining position. The Black Prince, under whom Lady Mohun's brother Bartholomew, Lord Burghersh had served in France, shared her devotion to Our Lady of the Undercroft. He requested that his body be buried in the middle space no more than 10ft from the altar, to which he bequeathed costly plate and fabrics. In the event he was interred in a more prestigious site adjacent to Becket's shrine, although it seems that the original preparations advanced as far as digging the grave. In 1500 Lady Mohun's tomb was joined by that of Cardinal Morton. He had requested his body to be buried 'coram Imagine Beatissime Virginis Mariae, vulgariter nuncupatae, *Our Lady of Undercroft*, et quod co-operiatur cum uno plano lapide marmoreo basso absque aliis voluptuosis expensis'. The large floor-slab with the indent of the archbishop in the western bay of the outer chapel was considered too self-effacing by the Canterbury monks, who replaced it posthumously by a very lavish monument, complete with an effigy in the round and an elaborate canopied frame adorned with symbols of the cardinal's political associations with the Tudor dynasty.[27] These burials added to the sense that the chapel of Our Lady of the Undercroft was an elite space.

*Our Lady of Walsingham*

The largest single sum (6s 8d) bestowed by Queen Elizabeth in her list of pilgrimages was on Our Lady of Walsingham. The image belonged to an Augustinian priory, founded to curate the chapel in which it stood, situated on the north side of the nave of the priory church (**132**, **133**). Although destroyed at the Reformation, the chapel of Our Lady of Walsingham is well recorded in contemporary descriptions and the site has been excavated.[28]

The complex had at its heart the 'Holy House at Nazareth', a small chapel built probably in *c.* 1130–1 by Richelde of Fervaques, founder of the priory. This was a replica of the house in which the Annunciation occurred and where Jesus had grown up, revealed to Richelde in a dream. The miracle-working image of the Virgin did not feature in the original legend. The reverse of the priory seal depicts the Virgin enthroned with 'Ave Maria Gracia Plena Dominus Tecum' forming the inscription and thus linking the image with the Annunciation. The inclusion of veils or curtains drawn back to reveal the Virgin suggests that it represented the image itself (**134** (left)).[29] The seal dates from the thirteenth century, but the Virgin is shown enthroned, crowned and full-frontal in the manner of Romanesque *sedes sapientiae* images, indicating that the prototype cult image was of twelfth-century date. The Holy House was an apt location for an image of Our Lady, whose presence in turn legitimated the architectural setting.

The pilgrimage was popularized by Henry III, who contributed 20 marks towards her gold crown.[30] A visit to the site was *de rigueur* for every subsequent English monarch and it became the

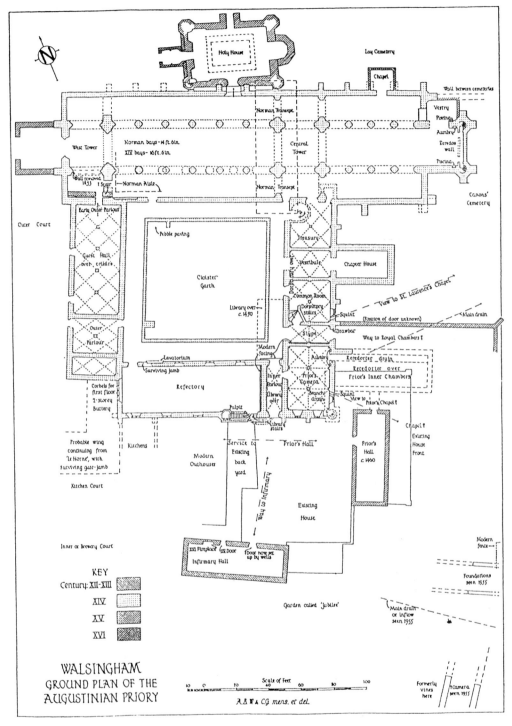

132. *Walsingham Priory (Norf.): ground plan of the priory with the chapel of Our Lady of Walsingham adjoining the nave north aisle (from* Norfolk Archaeology, *125 (1968))*

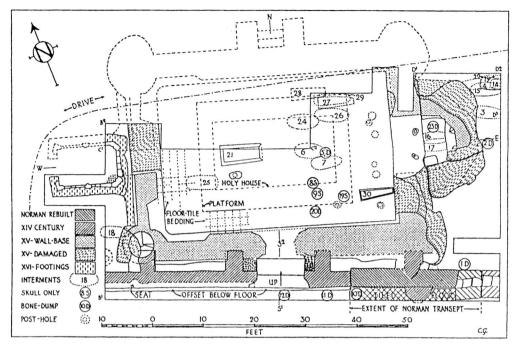

*133. Walsingham Priory (Norf.): ground plan of the chapel of Our Lady of Walsingham (from* Norfolk Archaeology, *125 (1968))*

country's most famous late medieval cult.[31] Embellishment both of the image and of its setting continued throughout the Middle Ages and the site described here is as it was in its final form.

From the start the place was marked out as especially holy. On arriving at Walsingham (perhaps barefoot or on their knees) the pilgrims would first have encountered a brass plate fixed to a gate in the precinct wall commemorating a miracle associated with a knight seeking sanctuary.[32] There were also holy wells, possessed of thaumaturgical qualities. It has to be assumed that the priory church was visited next. A few of its attractions are listed by a Northamptonshire testator in 1531: '. . . to our Ladye mylke jd, to our Ladye of Pite jd, at the chapell of Seint Laurens jd'.[33] The phial containing the Virgin's Milk, together with its indulgence value, was sufficiently meritorious to warrant display on the high altar.[34] The scene was thus set for Marian devotion, specifically focused on her maternal aspect. The devotee then entered the chapel of Our Lady of Walsingham, either from its west end, where a porch was added to the fifteenth-century structure early in the following century, or (less probably) from a door on the south side connecting the chapel with the priory church (**133**).

The chapel was double-skinned. The outer structure was a flint building, described as 'novum opus' in 1478–80 by William Worcester and still unfinished in 1512, when Erasmus commented on the open windows and doors.[35] It was paced out by William Worcester and archaeological investigations confirm the accuracy of his measurements of 14.64 × 9.15m. The glazing was executed and installed at Henry VIII's expense after Erasmus's visit. The work was carried out by Barnard Flower, the King's Glazier, and the windows would have represented the latest Flemish fashion, as exemplified in the contemporary glazing of Fairford (Glos.) and the early windows of King's College Chapel, Cambridge.[36] Presumably the iconography included scenes from the history of the site and of the image.

*134. (left) Thirteenth-century seal of Walsingham Priory (Norf.) (London, British Library Seal LXIX. 32); (right) Our Lady of Walsingham pilgrim badge, c. 1400 (King's Lynn Museum, acc. no. PB11-13)*

The outer wall created an ambulatory, whose inner boundary comprised the walls of the Holy House itself. This was a rectangular wooden building, measuring approximately 7.11 × 3.91m. It was raised on a platform covered with Purbeck marble tiles and may have resembled the wooden Anglo-Saxon church at Greensted in Essex. The processional path could be perambulated both at ground level and via a wall-passage at window-sill level, accessed from turrets at the angles, perhaps for the purpose of providing a better view of the Holy House. Subsequently a polygonal apse was added at the east end, probably to avoid interrupting the narrow ambulatory by an altar.

The final stage of the pilgrimage was reached with the entering of the House through the two small doors in the side walls, described by Erasmus. In his day the image of Our Lady stood to the right of the altar at the east end, adjacent to a gold altarpiece, with a representation of the Virgin in the centre, flanked by images of two angels, St Edward, St Katherine, St Edmund and St Margaret.[37] The image was enhanced by adornment and presentation. As well as her gold crown, Our Lady was festooned with jewels and was presented with a gold chain and a circlet by Henry VIII. Erasmus's description of the whole chapel as glittering with jewels, gold and silver is borne out by the records of rich gifts of jewellery and garments.[38] The image was surrounded by material testaments to Our Lady's efficacy in the form of *ex-votos* and was lit by banks of candles, for almost no natural light would have entered this inner zone. In 1242 Henry III gave 100lb of wax and 500 tapers to Our Lady of Walsingham and Henry VIII maintained a great candle known as the King's Candle burning there permanently. The multicoloured translucency of the windows lighting the Perpendicular outer structure must thus have contrasted with the flickering and mysterious brilliance of the inner core.

One of the priory canons was constantly in attendance as *custos* to receive oblations, to watch over the rich treasures and extol their value, and to give details of their donors and those sufficiently illustrious to be accorded burial in proximity to the image to pilgrims.[39] Apart from chantry Masses sung in the chapel for royal and lesser individuals, details of the liturgy are not recorded and it does not seem likely that its liturgical function was central to its meaning.

## *Our Lady of Bradwell*

Like Our Lady of the Undercroft, the image known as Our Lady of Bradwell was maintained by a Benedictine monastery. However, unlike the Becket cult at Canterbury or the relics of St Alban or those of St Cuthbert at Durham, it did not take pride of place in the ritual of that community. On the contrary, its location in a purpose-built chapel abutting the west end of the priory church indicates that, in common with Walsingham, it was situated to cause minimal interference to the monks in their daily worship (**XXIII**).[40]

Nothing is known of the appearance or history of the image itself, though from the size of its niche it can have been no more than 1–1.5m high and the shape indicates a standing figure (**135**). The chapel appears stylistically to date from the second half of the fourteenth century, but there is no documentary evidence for it before the sixteenth century.

The chapel is a simple rectangle, measuring 4.88 × 2.745m, with no evidence of internal divisions. It is lit by a window in the façade and a pair of smaller windows in the side walls. The

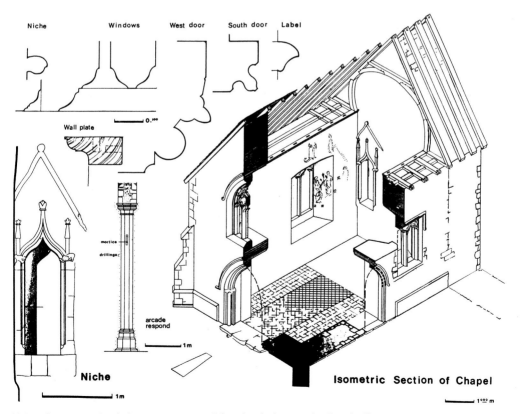

*135. Milton Keynes (Bucks.): isometric section of the Chapel of Our Lady of Bradwell*

structure is therefore much smaller than the Walsingham chapel. The situation of the chapel at the west end of the church suggests that it was the first point of call for pilgrims. They presumably entered the building through the door below the west window. A circulation route is indicated by a door in the south wall, through which pilgrims could have exited and then perhaps have entered the monastic church through the adjacent portal. Alternatively, this door could have been used by the clergy processing from the church in order to asperge the chapel altar.

The interior retains a considerable amount of decoration. The floor at the west end has an elaborate pavement of stamped tiles, acting as a 'carpet of honour' for the image. As pilgrims moved towards Our Lady of Bradwell, they were reminded that they were in a space dedicated to the Virgin by the letter M painted on the walls and by the scenes of her early life depicted on the north wall. The efficacy of the image is demonstrated by the representations on the south wall of kneeling layfolk holding *ex-votos*. The paintings have been dated to the late fourteenth century, shortly after the chapel's construction.[41] Unlike Our Lady of the Undercroft and Our Lady of Walsingham, the image did not form the centrepiece of a retable above the altar, but was placed in a canopied niche in an elevated position to increase reverence at the north end of the east wall. Its positioning recalls the place of honour accorded to the patronal saint in churches. The structural stone frame suggests that the image was always exposed, apart from during Lent. Her permanent accessibility would have been desirable for a predominantly local clientele.

The presence of an altar, whose piscina was formerly in the south wall, shows that services took place in the chapel and, as we have seen, the twin door arrangement would have facilitated processions. Other than this, nothing is known of the liturgical life of the image. Nor was it honoured by burials; the small size of the chapel would have precluded many interments.

*Our Lady of Boulton*
The image known as Our Lady of Boulton was located in the main body of the Benedictine cathedral priory at Durham. From the description in the *Rites of Durham*, we know that it was a *Vièrge ouvrante*, examples of which from the late thirteenth and fourteenth centuries survive in Germany, Portugal (of French origin), Sweden and Switzerland.[42] As the appellation indicates, these comprise an enthroned image of the Virgin which opens usually to reveal the Trinity, with paintings on the interior of the wings. These images aroused the ire of the eminent theologian Jean Gerson (d. 1429), on the grounds that it was heretical to depict the Trinity as the fruit of the Virgin's womb.[43] Most of the extant *Vièrges ouvrantes* are quite small and the Durham version probably approximated in size to the larger ones, like the image in Nuremberg (**XXI**).

The date and history of the Durham image are unknown, though it seems probable that it was of the fourteenth century. It acted as a supplement to the main pilgrimage goals of the shrine of St Cuthbert and the relics of the Venerable Bede, but was an object of veneration in its own right, at least for men. Women were not allowed to progress further than the west end of the nave, where there was a Lady Chapel they could use. Although this would have had its own image and also housed a *Pietà* (and the relics of the Venerable Bede), there is no evidence that either of these Marian images was accorded cultic properties.[44]

Our Lady of Boulton was placed in a south transept chapel dedicated to the image. This chapel was appropriately decorated, the image being repeated in the centre light glazing of the window above the altar.[45] The bracket on which Our Lady of Boulton stood is still *in situ*, with its arms of the Neville family as recorded in the *Rites*. The latter also provides rare evidence for the liturgical use of the image. The compiler recalled:

a mrveylous lyvelye and bewtifull Image of the picture of our Ladie socalled the Lady of boultone, whiche picture was maide to open wth gym' [wings] from her breaste downdward. And wth in ye said image was wrowghte and pictured the Image of our saviour, marveylouse fynlie gilted houldinge uppe his handes, and holding betwixt his handes a fair & large crucifix of christ all of gold, the whiche Crucifix was to be taiken fourthe every good fridaie, and every man did crepe unto it that was in the churche as that Daye . . . and every principall Daie the said immage was opened that every man might se pictured within her, the father, the sonne and the holy ghost, moste curiouslye and fynely gilted.[46]

A heightened sense of reverence was therefore imparted to Our Lady of Boulton on feast-days; the process of exposure on these occasions of the inner scenes must have appeared miraculous in itself. Its role in the Easter ritual, when the crucifix was to be taken as it were from the Virgin's womb, also shows how the experience of the cult image was orchestrated by liturgy.

## Parochial Images

### St Urith of Chittlehampton

Chittlehampton, in rural Devon, was the place of martyrdom of St Urith, a Christian maiden mown down by the local heathens. Her relics were housed in the parish church and formed the basis of a pilgrimage, albeit principally of regional importance. Despite the presence of bodily relics, however, the cult centred on an image of the saint and it was to this that oblations were made.[47]

The appearance of the image is unknown, although it would probably have been shown with a scythe, as in the much-restored representation in the stained glass of Nettlecombe church (Som.) (**136**). The history of the cult is equally vague, but it was evidently popular in the late Middle Ages, when Chittlehampton church was rebuilt on an appropriately imposing scale and in a form designed to accommodate pilgrims. It has been suggested that the latter entered the building through a now-blocked door in the north transept.[48] Certainly the space of the transept would have provided a convenient place for pilgrims to congregate. St Urith's relics were housed in an unusual tall and narrow structure at the angle of the transept and the chancel (**137**). Its location appears to

*136. Nettlecombe (Som.), St Mary's church: (restored) stained-glass panel of St Urith, early sixteenth century*

137. *Chittlehampton (Devon), St Urith's church: site of St Urith's relics and image niche, fifteenth/early sixteenth century*

reflect St Urith's status as Chittlehampton's patron saint. The titular image, as it were, has been brought forward from its standard position against the chancel east wall. The chapel accommodated the relics, but the main focus of devotion was the image, framed by the elaborate niche at the entrance.

The church was heavily restored in the 1870s and no internal decoration now remains, although the niche was doubtless originally painted and gilded. It is visible from both nave and transept and there would have been plenty of space for pilgrims to pray or prostrate themselves before the image.

Absence of other parochial structures makes it impossible to assess how typical (or unusual) was the Chittlehampton scheme. It is probable, however, that late medieval devotion was so image-focused that even relics would have had an associated image, as in the cases of Henry VI in St George's Chapel, Windsor and John Schorn at North Marston (Bucks.) (before the latter's relics were translated to Windsor).[49]

## Our Lady of Long Melford

The image of Our Lady at Long Melford (Suff.) occupied the twilight zone between a miraculous image and an especially venerated one. No miracles are recorded, nor does it feature in the usual lists of East Anglian pilgrimage sites mentioned in wills. Nevertheless, the architectural setting and records of offerings and adornments indicate that it had greater significance than most images of the Virgin in parish churches.[50]

Nothing is known of the appearance of the Long Melford image or its history. From 1459 there are wills referring to the repair or amending of a Lady Chapel, but it was not until 1495 that the decision was taken to build a new chapel, probably on the same site. In this year £6 13s 4d was left to the building.[51] The chief benefactor was the rich local clothier John Clopton. In a codicil to his will added in 1497 he bequeathed the substantial sum of £66 13s 4d to the 'garnysshying of oure Lady Chapell, and of the cloister ther aboute that he said John Clopton hath done new made in Melford churcheyard'.[52] It is not certain what 'garnysshying' meant here. The crenellations to the building bear inscriptions to Clopton, John Hyll (mentioned in the codicil and with whose executors Clopton had concluded a business transaction from which his benefaction had come) and his butler. These inscriptions point to a close association between Clopton and his circle and the image housed in the chapel. It may therefore have been an intensely personal cult; alternatively there is a possibility that it was intended to have a wider appeal which never caught on. At most it must have been thought to bear witness to the operation of Our Lady's special grace in Long Melford.

*138. Long Melford (Suff.), Holy Trinity church: the Lady Chapel at the east end*

The 'cloister' mentioned by Clopton refers to the double-skinned form of the chapel, which resembles and may have been intended to recall the final structure at Walsingham (**138–140**). At 15.64 × 11.56m it is slightly larger than its possible prototype. The exterior, with its three pitched roofs, is as lavishly embellished with flint flushwork as the rest of the church. The principal entrance for the laity is likely to have been the door at the south-west end of the chapel, leading from the churchyard. This brought the visitor into the ambulatory, well lit by five windows in the side walls and four at the east end. The richly carved roofs are of the same design as those in the Clopton Chantry in the church; the latter still retain their rich polychromy and scrolls bearing verses by John Lydgate. The aisle encircles an inner core, accessed via a large doorway at the west end and pierced by a triple arcade on each side. The elevation of the inner space is articulated by blank cusped arches above the arcades and projecting niches carried on shafts. Today the interior of the Lady Chapel, with its cream-washed walls and largely clear glass, is a monochrome shadow of its former splendour. Above all it lacks its intended focus, the image of Our Lady. It stood against the blank wall at the east end, above a large shallow arched recess which would have held the altar. The image was presumably placed centrally and surrounded by wall-paintings, hangings or other signals of her prestige. An inventory of 1529 lists the jewels, buckles, beads, rings and girdles which had been donated to it. Some were placed in an apron worn by the image itself. There were also three garments, changeable on major feasts:

First, one coat for the good days of cloath of tissue, borderd with white; and for her son another of the same, in like case.
Item, a coat of crimson velvet, and another for her son, in like case.
Item a coat of white damask, and another for her son in like case, bordered about with green velvet.[53]

139. Long Melford church: interior of the Lady Chapel, looking west

140. Long Melford church: the west ambulatory of the Lady Chapel

The recorded changing of the garments provides an insight into the interplay between the image and the liturgy. No doubt the ambulatory was used for processions, to which it was admirably suited, having an exit door on the north side opposite the south entrance. There was also a separate access for the clergy from the vestry behind the high altar of the church. The Lady Chapel evidently had a special place in the affections of at least one member of the officiating clergy, for in 1497 a chaplain requested burial there.

## Capellae Extra Muros

### Our Lady of the Mount

Although usually described as marking a station on the route to Walsingham, the evidence of Norfolk testators shows that the image known as Our Lady of the Mount at King's Lynn formed a cult in its own right. It was housed in a chapel outside the town ramparts which still survives (**XXIV; 141**). A modest receipt of £1 13s 10¾d is recorded in 1481–2 but income increased enormously after a mason named Robert Curraunt began to construct the chapel in 1485. In that year over £20 was received and similar totals were frequently achieved throughout Henry VII's reign; in 1497–8 receipts rose to £34 13s 4d. Income declined under Henry VIII, but in 1531–2 still totalled £11.[54] Its Walsingham link and the status of King's Lynn as a regional centre and active port must have given the cult a wide territory of grace.

The building consists of a brick octagon raised on a tunnel-vaulted basement. In 1505–6 this structure was altered and enhanced by the insertion of a cruciform stone chapel on the upper level at a cost of £21 18s 4d. The principal door is in the west wall above the basement and was entered via a raised platform. From this the pilgrim would have accessed a staircase to the space between the outer wall of the chapel and the inner octagon. This passageway pre-dated the upper stone chapel, for the altar is raised to accommodate the passage beneath, suggesting that the image was always located at an upper level. Having climbed the dark and narrow staircase, the pilgrim entered the small but magnificent chapel. It is crowned by an elaborate fan-vault in the centre and panelled tunnel-vaults over the arms, whose ambition is clear from their affinities with the work of John Wastell at King's College Chapel, Cambridge and Peterborough Cathedral.[55] The splendour of the surroundings is provided by masonry rather than light, for this upper chapel is lit only by four quatrefoil oculi. Presumably the image of Our Lady was placed on or above the elevated altar.

Because the Mount chapel does not resemble any of the other known English pilgrim structures, it is necessary to look abroad for parallels. In mentality, if not closely in design, the site has affinities with the Jerusalem church in Bruges, constructed by the Adornes family in the fifteenth century.[56] This structure embodied a Passion narrative and it is possible that something of the kind existed at King's Lynn. Calvary is evoked by the location of the building on a mount outside the town walls, an allusion which would have been reinforced if the chapel were capped by a crucifix. In this context the large recess in the basement is suggestive of the Holy Sepulchre. If indeed a Passion narrative loomed large here, one might speculate that the image of Our Lady in the space between the crucifix and the tomb was a *Pietà*. The sequence of devotional stations could have been explained and orchestrated by the resident clergy, for whom a separate access, cell and circulation passage were provided.

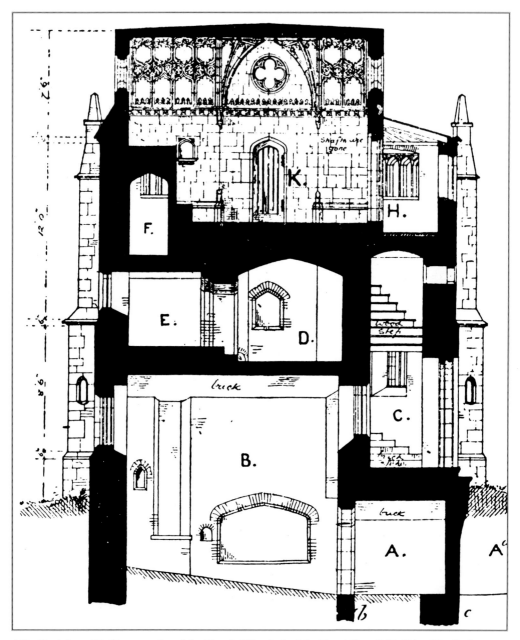

*141. King's Lynn (Norf.), cross-section of the Chapel of Our Lady of the Mount (from E.M. Beloe,* The Red Mount King's Lynn with the Chapels thereon, *King's Lynn, 1925)*

## Sacred Wells

### St Winifred's Well

Many of the pilgrim sites of Our Lady were associated with wells or streams (for example, Walsingham, Woolpit in Suffolk). Although in Wales and therefore strictly speaking beyond the pale of this study, the holy well associated with St Winifred of Shrewsbury at Holywell

(Flints.) is included because of its well-preserved architectural structure.[57] Like Chittlehampton, Holywell was a site where an image was an essential part of the devotional experience.

The legend of St Winifred purports to date from the seventh century and the well at Holywell played a prominent role in her hagiography (**144** (right)). The saint was restored to life there after decapitation by a would-be seducer; a spring gushed on the spot where her head fell. In 1138 her body was translated to Shrewsbury Abbey. It appears that her cult only gathered momentum in the following century, when Shrewsbury became of major importance. In 1398 St Winifred's feast was ordered to be kept with particular solemnity throughout the Canterbury province and a few years later Archbishop Chichele raised it to the status of a double-feast. The cult was fostered by the Lancastrian dynasty, perhaps in thanksgiving for the victory at Shrewsbury and from which Holywell benefited.[58] In 1427 the Pope granted indulgences to the monks of Basingwerk, who owned the site, for sale to pilgrims. In 1439 Isabella Beauchamp, Countess of Warwick, bequeathed a gown to the image of St Winifred there.[59] The present building replaced the structure which existed at this time. Like other major pilgrimage sites, Holywell enjoyed royal favour which uniquely extended beyond the Reformation. Successive sovereigns from Henry V to Henry VII visited it; Richard III gave an annuity of 10 marks for a priest to celebrate there. In 1683 Mary of Modena, queen of James II, restored the chapel.

The design of the building was dictated by its hillside location and the well (**142, 143**). It is in two storeys. The upper chapel has a four-bay clerestoried nave with a north aisle of three bays and a chancel with three-sided apse. This structure is raised over the well-chamber, which is a display of small-scale Perpendicular at its most appealing and inventive. The well-chamber is on a different axis to the chapel. An open narthex, placed directly underneath the north aisle of the upper chapel, gives access to a vaulted ambulatory around the well-basin. This has triangular projections on three sides, providing a stellar pattern; on the fourth side, facing the entrance, are steps for bathers to enter the well. Between the enclosing pillars is a delicate screen, now lacking its transoms. There is a plethora of carved heraldry and decoration, including a pendant boss over the basin depicting episodes from St Winifred's life. A prominent feature is the large niche set in the narthex north wall which contains the nineteenth-century replacement statue of St Winifred, a tangible sign of her presence at the site (**144** (left)).

Both the well-chamber and the upper chapel were begun during Henry VII's reign. Their traditional attribution to the patronage of the king's mother, Lady Margaret Beaufort, has been challenged on the grounds that the devices on the roof bosses are associated not with her but with her third husband's family, the Stanleys. They were local and it has been claimed that the chief mover was the king's chamberlain, Sir William Stanley, with some help from Lady Margaret's spouse, Lord Thomas. Sir William's role may well have been played down after his execution in 1495.[60] None the less, the presence of the Beaufort portcullis suggests that Lady Margaret had some involvement here.

The design of the well-chamber permitted easy circulation of pilgrims and of processions around the basin. The management of modern pilgrimage to the well may be not so far removed from how Holywell functioned as a ritual site in the late Middle Ages. The devout are enjoined to cross themselves as they enter and venerate the image of St Winifred. They then proceed to the front of the basin where they state the purpose of their supplication and say the Creed. Finally they perambulate the well while reciting one decade of the rosary.[61]

*142. Holywell (Flints.): exterior of St Winifred's Well*

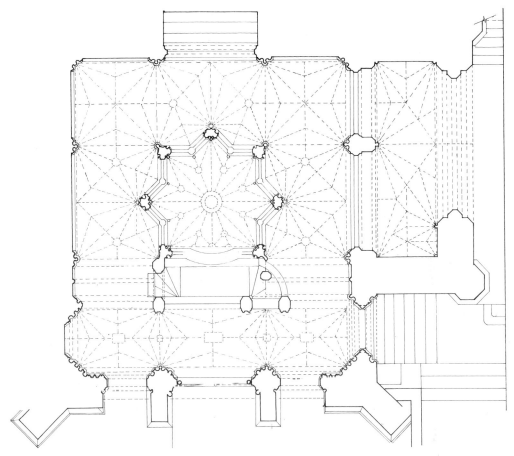

*143. Holywell, St Winifred's Well: ground plan of the well-chamber*

## EVALUATION

### History

The spiritual landscape with its miraculous roods and Marian cult images, as mapped by Elizabeth of York and contemporary testators, was transformed from that which existed in the twelfth century. Although in essence they were different from relics, functionally cult images operated in similar ways and over the course of time, they came to supplement the earlier shrine-based sacred topography. The representation of the sacred in human form was also essential at locations associated with a saint whose relics lay elsewhere. It appears that after the translation of John Schorn's body to Windsor an image of the good pastor formed an effective surrogate for the corporeal relics at North Marston (Bucks.). It was considered to have absorbed the virtues of Schorn's body by becoming a source of miraculous cures in its own right and so was marked out for destruction by Henry VIII's commissioners (**170**).[62]

Leaving aside those images which served as relic-receptacles, the status of an image of a saint might be enhanced by association with relics of other saints.[63] The guardian of the chapel

*144. (left) Holywell, St Winifred's Well: the original niche with a nineteenth-century image of St Winifred; (right) Warwick, St Mary's church: St Winifred in the east window of the Beauchamp Chapel, 1447–c. 1449*

containing the celebrated image of Our Lady at Caversham showed pilgrims a whole host of relics, among which were the weapons used to slay St Edward the Confessor and Henry VI. With Our Lady of the Undercroft at Canterbury were exhibited relics on a piece of red silk on the image's robe.[64] The fact that at these sites relics played second fiddle to a cult image sheds light on the relationship between the two.

Images containing relics had existed since the middle of the tenth century, but by the late eleventh or twelfth century, representations in carved form began to be associated with the workings of divine grace without the presence of relics (**163**). Both miracle-working images and images that exhibited signs of animation by moving, bleeding, speaking or weeping were present in northern Europe. Unlike a container in the form of a casket or shrine structure, 'lifelike' images gave the sacred personage a human identity and therefore had the potential to appear animate; if they were indeed deemed to have exhibited 'lifelike' signs, and prayers or petitions addressed to the signified through them were answered, the image became associated with the miraculous.[65]

The universality of the cult of the Virgin stemmed from her corporeal assumption into Heaven; because no single location could lay claim to possess her bodily relics, her presence could manifest itself anywhere. Bishop Pecock saw the apparently random occurrence of miraculous images of the Virgin as an expression of the will of God:

> And ferthermore it is so, that God takith upon him forto make such now seid pointing and chesing. Forwhi he hath wrought myraclis in summe placis in whiche ben ymagis of Marie, and in manye othere mo placis in whiche ben ymagis of Marie he hath not so wrought . . . and wherfore he chesith this place and this ymage bifore othere, we han noon evidence withinne doom of resoun.[66]

God's grace manifested itself in various ways. One model is provided by the still much-revered image of Our Lady of Guadalupe in Mexico. Following the Virgin's apparition to two poor men in 1531, she 'gave people her image, which no earthly human artist made or coloured. It was she herself who made her own copy, because she lovingly saw fit to make her residence there.'[67] The Guadalupe image therefore was of the type known in Greek as *Acheiropoietos*, i.e. not made with human hands. In such instances the image itself becomes the relic. Images like this were 'miraculous to begin with, so why should they not continue to work miracles?'[68] Unfortunately there is no information on the origins of most of the English images whose settings are known. The finding underground of the image of Our Lady of Ipswich, at which site 'divers great miracles have been wrought', replicates the origins of miracle-working images like Our Lady of Montserrat in Spain, by which the Virgin signalled the location of the shrine through her apparition or the discovery of her image at that spot.[69] The miraculous did not occur through supplication but because Our Lady had taken the initiative and bestowed grace on a particular local community. Similarly at Walsingham the Virgin revealed in a dream to Richelde the form of the house where the Annunciation had occurred and told her to replicate it. Unlike the Spanish legends, however, it was not to the poor and humble that the Virgin showed herself at Walsingham.[70]

A protracted row in the East Riding of Yorkshire sheds light on the origins of a lesser-known cult image.[71] The story began in the late thirteenth century with the purchase in Scotland of an image of the Virgin by one Thomas de Poynton, who placed it in his local chapel at Fraisthorpe, where it became an object of veneration. Fraisthorpe lay in the parish of Carnaby, which was appropriated to Bridlington Priory. The latter and the vicar of Carnaby disputed the receipts from oblations to the image and eventually a 2:1 division was agreed, with the larger portion going to the prior and convent. De Poynton retained ownership of the image and after his death in 1299 his widow sold it to the rector of Foston-on-the-Wolds, who removed it from Fraisthorpe and set it up in his church (**145**). Incensed by the loss of this moneyspinner, in 1313 the prior and a band assaulted the rector, seized the image and placed it in the priory. The rector brought a suit against Bridlington and Archbishop Greenfield forbade veneration of the image until he had carried out an inquiry. That his sympathies perhaps lay with the canons is hinted at in the wording of his edict, where he referred to the throngs of simple folk attracted by the image at Foston and thereby risking idolatry: 'as if there was more holiness in it than in other similar images'.[72] Subsequently the priory petitioned for the ban on veneration to be lifted, indicating that it retained the image.

145. *Foston-on-the Wolds (Yorks., East Riding), St Andrew's church from the south-east*

Pecock emphasized God's agency as the key factor; he was careful not to say that the Marian images themselves possessed miraculous powers, i.e. that the Virgin was herself present in the image. Images associated with the miraculous did not manifest their powers automatically. Medieval miracle legends contain many instances of unanswered supplications and those desirous of divine assistance did not expect it to happen on demand; it was the very singularity and randomness of its occurrence which made the event so memorable. Even the normal non-miraculous parochial images exhibited a dualism. Alongside their internal (i.e. not relating to divine will) properties (empathy, capacity to suffer and be offended), they possessed the potential to become active agents in the working of the divine will through miracles.[73] The Fraisthorpe image of Our Lady began life as a normal devotional image and it was only subsequently that 'God worked for the said image'. Generations might elapse before this latent power was released. The famous image of Our Lady of Sablon became miraculous only after her repair and repainting and removal from Antwerp to Brussels.[74]

The occurrence of the miraculous at a particular site determined the *locus* of the cult. To the inhabitants of Ipswich, Woolpit, Northampton, Lincoln and the many other places which possessed an image of Our Lady through whom God's grace was believed to have worked, especially by the performance of miracles, that image was *theirs*, hence the appellation Our Lady of Doncaster, etc. – and hence the disapproval of certain prelates and dissenters alike (**153 (a)**). The presence of the miraculous on the doorstep might coexist with, or even supplant, the role of the patronal image as *genius loci*, although with a wider constituency than the parish.

Our Lady could be all-embracing in terms of the protection she offered. Pilgrims visited the shrine of the Virgin at Walsingham as penance, for succour, or to give thanks for deliverance from a host of manmade and natural afflictions, including escape from enemies, success in battle, preservation from sudden death or injury and cures for ailments. Other images acted as specialists. Badges associated with the image of St Margaret at Ketsby (Lincs.) seem to have been made as amulets to be worn by local women in labour.[75]

As we have seen at Walsingham, the prototype cult image was probably already a focus of veneration in the twelfth century (**134**). However, it was not until the thirteenth century that this and other Marian images appear to have attracted widespread pilgrimage. Walsingham, Our Lady of Woolpit, Our Lady of the Undercroft at Canterbury and Our Lady of the Pew in the Palace of Westminster emerged as pilgrimage sites in or shortly before Henry III's reign. Our Lady of Ipswich is first mentioned in 1297.[76] Royal patronage was a major factor in their popularity and Henry was the prime mover, but this was the effect rather than the cause of the new importance accorded to the sacred image. Pecock's explanation of the cult image might provide a valid theological justification, but the timing of its appearance as a major feature of pilgrimage in England should not be overlooked. The loss of the Holy Land, which made access to the great Christian sites difficult, must have been a factor in the emergence of new sites nearer home.[77] The popularity of pilgrimage may have bred a desire to find evidence for the working of the miraculous everywhere and not just at sites possessing the corporeal remains of a saint, hence the centrality of Christ and the Virgin. The burgeoning interest in Christ's Passion is manifested in the miraculous roods found at many locations. The famous rood at Bromholm (Norf.) was a relic of the True Cross itself, but this was not invariably the case. In England the dearth of relics of the Virgin in the form of her apparel may have facilitated rather than hindered the emergence of cult images, although Walsingham possessed a relic of the Virgin's milk as well as the Holy House. Between the middle of the thirteenth and the middle of the fourteenth century the pace of image-cult creation quickened. In every known case the cult was not created through the erection of buildings but proceeded from the perceived miraculous relic of a pre-existing image of the Virgin or other holy person, although veneration of the latter might be enhanced subsequently by the elaboration of the setting.

## Mapping the Sacred

Margery Kempe and Queen Elizabeth of York shared a wide knowledge of pilgrimage sites. Like Our Lady of Ipswich, many Marian cult images were in urban centres. The Virgin at Ipswich was located in an extramural chapel outside the walls; others were placed in cathedrals (Canterbury, Durham, Lincoln, Salisbury and Worcester) or the principal parish church (Cambridge); the mendicants also possessed several important cult images of Our Lady (e.g., the Carmelites at Doncaster and Northampton) (**153 (a)**). Places of transit were also a favoured site for a cult image. Our Lady of Ardenbourg at Great Yarmouth and Our Lady of the Mount at King's Lynn occur on the Norfolk lists. The parish church at Poulton near Dover possessed an image of the Virgin which was the focus of pilgrimage. Cult status was also accorded to sacred figures other than the Virgin. For example, as at Holywell, Bristolians were accustomed to resort to the well and image of St Anne at Brislington. In addition to demonstrating the presence of God's benign grace in the sites, these cult images also offered pilgrims and travellers alike a series of stations of the sacred on routes to other attractions, both here and abroad. Cult images provided practical indications of God's favour to their custodians. For the most part the territory of grace of miraculous images, like those which William Christian studied in the Nansa valley of northern Spain, would have been very circumscribed and confined to their immediate locality and predominantly local populace. As such, they performed a valuable function for those who could not afford, or were too elderly or infirm, or otherwise unable, to undertake arduous pilgrimages to distant shrines. Recourse could readily be had to them for cures and in times of personal difficulties.[78] This may have been the case for a site such as Long Melford. Through her images Our Lady was present and attuned to local needs and to the supplications of the inhabitants of their respective territories of grace, for whom the miracle-working images were special friends, neighbours and protectors. Pilgrimage was thus a socially diverse activity and although the possession of worldly goods meant that the wealthier elements of society were more likely to visit major sites at a distance from their home, Margery Kempe's peregrinations show that a clear distinction cannot be made between lesser and greater cults by the status of the devout.

William Christian's territories of grace can be mapped socially as well as geographically. Records of oblations and bequests mostly relate to the great and the good. Yet wills also testify to the riches offered in kind by laypeople below gentry rank. Two Northamptonshire testators, William Nevell and Elizabeth Halley, bequeathed respectively a gold chain and 'a payr of beads of moder of pearl gawded with sylver & gylt, & on every syde of the gawdys a bead of corall' to Our Lady of Walsingham; a Bedfordshire woman from Goldington gave her best girdle to the same image.[79] The status of the donor as well as the value of their gift (and, as we shall see, the imagery of the enclosing structure) may well have afforded them privileged status at the shrine. Nevertheless, that pilgrimage was open to all is attested by reforming narratives as well as by the survival of quantities of cheap as well as more expensive pilgrim souvenirs. While the intricately framed fourteenth-century images of an enthroned Virgin and Child (possibly associated with Our Lady of the Undercroft in Canterbury) must have been intended for an elite clientele (**153 (c)**), the latter did not refrain from buying at the Woolworths end of the market. In 1481 John Lord Howard's wife purchased badges and amulets at Walsingham for 1½d (**134 (right)**).[80] The gentility of Lady Bray and her peers may have dissuaded them from wearing such commonplace devices, but they could and did sew them into their books of hours or represent them fictively (**129**). At some sites, like the chapel of Our Lady of Ardenbourg at Great Yarmouth and St Anne's well at Brislington, fraternity membership might confer on ordinary layfolk a privileged relationship with the cult image.[81]

The less well-off may not have been able to offer costly jewellery and rich raiments, but were as much consumers of the wax, wooden, stone and base-metal *ex-votos* with which shrines and images were enclosed as their more materially endowed co-devotees. These were as ubiquitous in England as in any of today's active Catholic shrines, as is evidenced by contemporary representations and this brief description of the interior of the chapel enclosing the image of Our Lady of Caversham just outside Reading: 'the place she stood in with the lights, shrouds, crutches, images of wax about the chapel' (**146**).[82] Many continental sites retain pictorial testaments to the efficacy of the cult image, in painted, cast and moulded form. These and the remarkable survival of *ex-votos* associated with Bishop Lacy's tomb at Exeter expressed either the

*146. York Minster: panel from the St William window depicting pilgrims with* ex-votos *at St William's shrine, c. 1414*

hope or gratitude of pilgrims for cures for loved ones, for diseased or injured limbs, livestock and beasts of burden (**147**).[83] Such offerings might reflect the particular concerns of a cult's local constituency. William Worcester observed the model ships offered to the St Anne image at Brislington by Bristol seamen, a practice which until recently was as common in Orthodox and Protestant churches as in Catholic Christianity.[84]

Pecock defended *ex-votos* against Lollard criticisms:

. . . wherfore a ful good and a resonable cause it is to ech pilgrime . . . that he bere openli an ymage of wex or of tree [wood] or of metal or of stoon in his hond, that alle men whiche schulen se him go or meete him, be remembrid therbi that he gooth in pilgrimage and that thei bi thilk ensaumpling be stirid for to at sumwhile make her pilgrimage. . . . If thilk ymage be offrid up in the place into which the pilgrimage is mad, and be hangid up into open sight forto there abide, undir this entent that who ever schal aftirward come into the same place he schal weel se bi thilk ymage that sum man . . . hadde devocioun forto visite thilk place bi pilgrimage, and mai therbi be stirid forto do pilgrimage into the same place, (and the mo suche ymagis up offrid hange there, the more ech comer thidir and biholder of hem mai be stirid forto visite thilk place bi pilgrimage).[85]

147. *Exeter Cathedral: wax ex-votos from the tomb of Bishop Lacy, fifteenth – early sixteenth century*

*Ex-votos* thus boosted the cult image or relics and they encouraged others to undertake the same pilgrimage as the bearer and donor of the *ex-voto*. They have been classified under four headings, two of which (the representations of the saint or cult image and the inscription giving the condition, event or supplication) have left no traces in medieval England. The third type (the event or condition which was the reason for the supplication) has survived in the form of the Exeter waxes and the Bradwell murals. The latter also include representations of the suppliants, which form the fourth category. Such records enable us to view pilgrims not as an intangible group, classed by geographical or social origin, but as real people with a real relationship with the sacred.[86] When John Paston fell ill in 1443 his mother-in-law paid for his image in wax of his weight to be set up at Walsingham.[87] It was widespread practice for elites to offer costly images of themselves to well-known shrines. In 1381 William of Ufford, Earl of Suffolk, bequeathed the

*148. London, church of All-Hallows-by-the-Tower: altarpiece panels given by Robert Tate to the adjacent Chapel of Our Lady of Barking, c. 1500*

silver figures of a horse and a man bearing his heraldic device to be offered at the altar of Our Lady of Walsingham. His munificence was far exceeded by Richard Beauchamp, Earl of Warwick (d. 1439), who instructed his executors to have gold images of himself offered to the shrines of Alban, Becket, St John of Bridlington and St Winifred of Shrewsbury. Henry VII willed a silver-gilt kneeling image of himself to Our Lady of Walsingham.[88] Pecock argued that costly gifts of this kind by men of high status had added value in attracting pilgrimage:

> if a notable ymage be offrid up there, it schal move the seers for to enquere who offrid thilk ymage; and if it be answerid, that a bischop or an other notable man it offrid there and it brought thidir bi pilgrimage, the seer and heerer hereof schal thinke that the offrer therof hadde sum notable cause forto so bringe thilk ymage thidir and so offre it, and therbi be the more stirid into devocioun toward God or the Seint in thilk place.[89]

Social diversity did not mean equality, at least in this world. Rank could secure privileged viewing. Erasmus observed that the image of Our Lady of the Undercroft was only shown to men of high status or special friends.[90] The reconstruction of the architectural setting or fittings associated with a cult image offered opportunities for display by the well-to-do. As we have seen, Walsingham was always associated with royalty and nobility. In about 1500 Alderman Robert Tate commissioned an altarpiece from a Netherlandish painter for the chapel of St Mary of Barking adjacent to All-Hallows-by-the-Tower, London, which housed the celebrated cult image of Our Lady mentioned on Queen Elizabeth's list. His generosity is memorialized on the wings by his own image and arms and is associated with sacred gift-giving by the depiction of the Adoration of the Magi (**148**).[91]

In 1448 William Mynot requested that the figures of his grandfather and parents be placed in the east window glazing of the chapel of Our Lady of Ipswich, with himself and his wife depicted in the west window. He bequeathed 40s towards the construction of a porch 'for pour pepil to sit in', which suggests that distinctions of rank were maintained here, and desired that his body be interred in front of the chapel door.[92] As the Chapel of Our Lady of the Undercroft has shown, burial in close proximity to a cult image or relics was highly desirable and had been so since early Christian times, replicating practice – and some of the tensions – between the private and the communal spheres.[93]

Endowments by the great and the good (or not so good) might be inspired by worldly as well as spiritual motives. John Clopton's inscription on the Long Melford Lady Chapel reveals how *vanitas* and self-promotion were barely concealed by a thin veil of self-denial: 'Let Christ be my witness that I have not exhibited these things in order that I may win praise, but in order that the Spirit may be remembered.'[94]

## The Experience

Although the pilgrim's experience could be affected by his or her geographical relationship to the image and social position, certain features common to all the sites examined in this chapter aimed to maximize the impact of the image on all visitors. All the architectural frameworks set the scene for the culmination of the pilgrimage journey. The built environments for these cult images are very varied structures, the products of individual circumstances and designed to meet diverse needs. Their visual distinctiveness might serve to preserve the memory of each site in the minds of pilgrims. What they have in common is provision for votive and communal Masses and microcosm of scale. They did not attempt to replicate the size of the perambulatory structures at the east ends of the great twelfth-century shrine-churches; most are free-standing structures or adjuncts to a main church (or discrete spaces within it). Yet they represented architecture as theatre as much as their monumental predecessors. The encasing structures, whether architectural or delineated by screens, were designed to bring the devotee into intimate contact with the object of the pilgrimage. They prepared pilgrims for the experience of viewing and orchestrated their expectations. Once inside the built enclosure, visitors were shepherded into the presence of the sacred. The outer zones or ambulatories at Canterbury, Walsingham and Long Melford (also Holywell) enabled pilgrims to circulate without disrupting services at the altar adjacent to the image. However, the smaller scale and restricted space of the majority of cult image sites described here presumably meant that circulation had to be more controlled, at least on major feast-days.[95] Pilgrim access might have been managed, but this does not mean that everyone's response was the same. Each individual, whether on their own or in a crowd, conducted their own dialogue with the source of solace and succour, sharing their own histories and concerns.

The fixed decorations of the structures in which cult images were presented enhanced their claims to be agents of the miraculous and reflected their status and varying ability to attract benefactions. Even in their present stripped state, the contrast is marked between the two monastic cult image sites of Bradwell and Our Lady of the Undercroft. The simple canopied Decorated niche which housed the Bradwell image does not even approximate to the contemporary Decorated frames found in some churches in the neighbourhood (**135, 57**), let alone aspire to the intricate magnificence of the screenwork above the altar of Our Lady of the Undercroft (**131**). In the latter, this played an important role in the presentation of the image.

*149. Eton College (Berks.): chapel mural showing the miracle of the woman who took the Christ-child, c. 1477–87*

Like the gold altarpiece of Walsingham, Our Lady was appropriately framed and the flanking niches would have housed a supporting cast of sacred figures. Far more impressive than the Bradwell *ex-voto* paintings are the late fifteenth-century murals of the Miracles of the Virgin in the great collegiate foundation of Eton; although not primarily a dedicated pilgrimage church, the Eton paintings could only have served to heighten expectation of the powers of its cult image of the Assumption (**149**, **153 (b)**).[96]

The experience of viewing the image was essential. The destruction of every English cult image makes it impossible to assess whether any were of outstanding quality or beauty. In a sense, this question is irrelevant, for the image's power had nothing to do with either its size or its beauty *per se*, in terms of twenty-first-century value-judgements.[97] To what extent did the aesthetic qualities of an image influence the devotional responses of pilgrims? Not at all, according to the caustic tongue of Erasmus (hardly a paradigm for a late medieval pilgrim). He dismissed Our Lady of Walsingham as 'a small image . . . unimpressive in size, material, and workmanship'.[98] We have already observed that most likely this image was a standard Romanesque *sedes sapientiae* (**134** (left)). Erasmus's dismissive comments on the small size of the Walsingham image could have been applied to the Bradwell image and our Lady of the Undercroft. However, the appearance of an image was bound to colour the beholder's perception of the sacred prototype, whether as the enthroned Queen of Heaven (Walsingham) or as a more maternal representation. This, of course, might be problematic in that images were only meant to be signs, not the signified itself.[99]

Freedberg observes that presentation and embellishment are frequently more distinctive than the form and size of the cult image itself.[100] Aesthetic sensibilities are aroused as much by the setting and surrounds and the garnishing of the image as by the image itself. In the case of Our Lady of Walsingham, venerability may have enhanced veneration. It was not always thus. *The Myracles of Oure Lady*, published by Wynkyn de Worde in 1496, includes the tale of an Oxford clerk who went on pilgrimage to Rome to see the image of the Virgin painted by St Luke. His reaction was one of disappointment and rejection evidently because of its smoke-blackened state.[101]

Something of the appearance of the Walsingham and other English cult images can be obtained from that of Our Lady of Aachen. This too has an English royal connection. On certain major feast-days it wears the elaborate crown given by Margaret of York, sister to Edward IV and wife of Charles the Bold, Duke of Burgundy, possibly on the occasion of her visit to Aachen in 1474. Of silver-gilt, this crown is embellished with precious stones, pearls and enamels and Margaret's association with the image is signalled for posterity by her name, her initials (and those of her husband) and the enamelled white roses (also a metaphor for the Virgin) (**XX**; **150**). Other major adornments of Our Lady of Aachen include an equally costly collar and pendant, also of fifteenth-century date. A series of rich mantles dating from the early seventeenth century to the present were also made for and presented to this image; like those of Our Lady of Long Melford, these were changed during the liturgical year. Divested of her robes and accoutrements, Our Lady of Aachen is no more than a run-of-the-mill piece of fourteenth-century statuary.[102] As we have seen, such embellishments were applied to non-miraculous devotional images, but the practice was intensified with cult images.

Vesting and adorning thus enhanced the visual value of the image, just as the discarded crutches and *ex-votos* offered the material proofs of the site's efficacy. The spectacle provided for the pilgrim was illuminated literally by the hundreds of candles constantly burning around the image to which he or she could contribute. Lighting was enhanced on major feast-days. On the feast of the Assumption in 1241 Henry III gave no fewer than 3,000 tapers to the Holy House at Walsingham. Pilgrimage to sites on special festivals carried the promise of enhanced indulgences and the additional numbers resulted in increased oblations. At Canterbury the offerings in 1510–11 at Our Lady of the Undercroft on the principal feast-days of the Virgin and the Becket feasts totalled just over £4, compared with the weekly average of 3 or 4 shillings.

*150. Votive crown of Margaret of York on the cult image of Our Lady of Aachen*

For St Cuthberga's day the church of Wimborne (Dorset) was cleaned specially, the lights in the Lady Chapel were lit and special collections were made at her image.[103]

Viewing the image was only part of the experience; if possible it should be touched, though some sites positioned the image to make such a close relationship impossible. Mention of pilgrims kissing and licking the alabaster image of the Virgin behind the high altar in St George's Chapel, Windsor shows that transmission of grace through physical contact was a vital part of pilgrimage. Cranmer too listed the kissing of the feet of cult images (and devotional images in general) as an externalized expression of devotion, along with offering 'candles, and ymages of wax, rynges, beades, gold and sylver aboundantly'.[104]

The experience of touching was probably not the norm, except perhaps on special occasions. The iron grilles at the chapel entrance and in front of the altar and image of Our Lady of the Undercroft were designed to safeguard the image itself as much as the accumulated offerings.[105] On major feast-days even seeing the object of the pilgrimage here must have been difficult, hence the silvered suns and stars in the vault of the chapel, enabling pilgrims to absorb the reflected grace of the image. Small mirrors and badges incorporating mirrors were made for pilgrims at very popular sites. Pilgrim badges and ampullae were deemed to have absorbed elements of the grace of the holy site if they had been in physical contact with the relics or holy image and they could act as agents of transfer.[106] They were brought back and given by their purchasers as votive offerings to an important image in their local church, or for retention and use at home. The image of the Virgin in Pilton church (Som.), whose mantle had three scallop shells of St James and three pilgrim 'brochys' (badges) of Henry VI sewn on it, was perceived to have possessed some of the apotropaic potency of these famous cults. Their donors hoped for spiritual rewards not only for themselves, but also for their fellow-parishioners, who could all partake of the divine grace thus bestowed on the communal image.[107] Such devices were not necessarily acquired on pilgrimage. In 1501, on the eve of departing for the famous shrine of St James the Greater at Santiago, John Bawde of Woolpit (Suff.) made a will. His devotion to St James had already been made manifest by his gift of a tabernacle to house the saint's image in his parish church. Now he decided to do it further honour:

> the tabernacle of Seynt Jamys weche I ded make in the north yle, and the troues of the auter ther by, be well and suffyciently peyntyd and a cloth bought to save the sayd tabernacle fro[m] soyle; also the stooll [stall] weche I ded make, coloord and garnyschyd wt scalepps and othyr sygyns of Seynt Jamys.[108]

What Bawde was doing is analogous to the *trompe l'oeil* depictions of pilgrim badges painted in the borders of Lady Bray's Book of Hours. His stall or pew at Woolpit was a means of encouraging his fellow-parishioners to undertake the pilgrimage to Compostella as well as honouring himself.

## SIMULACRUM/REPLICATION

'. . . the replica was a witness of the original and aroused the same hopes as the latter . . . By the duplicate one honored the unique original.'[109] Replicas of images came in two forms: devotional images set up in the public spaces of churches which purported to be copies of the cult images venerated elsewhere and small-scale pilgrim souvenirs purchased as personal keepsakes. The texts of well-known prayers and antiphons were inscribed on some badges of Our Lady and would have served both as devotional aids in their own right and as mnemonic associations with the cult image (**153 (d)**).[110] Copies of Our Lady of Walsingham are recorded in two parish churches in the early sixteenth century, in St Denys Walmgate in York and Newington next Sittingbourne in Kent.[111] As they were at opposite ends of the country, such copies may not have been uncommon. Were they endowed with some of the miraculous powers of the original, or could their function be either mnemonic or exhortatory (or both)? What defined them as images of Our Lady of Walsingham? How closely did they replicate the original? The first of these questions raises the problem of sacred *locus*: if Walsingham was first and foremost a site made sacred by Our Lady's bestowal of grace, how did the images at York and Newington function when divorced from that site? Like the pilgrim badges, they may have been perceived to have extended the grace of Our Lady at Walsingham towards the places where they were set up.[112] Among the cult images mentioned by a Norfolk testator at the beginning of this chapter was that of Our Lady of Ardenbourg at Great Yarmouth.[113] The image took its name from a miraculous image known as 'Notre-Dame d'Aardenburg' near Damme in the Netherlands, before which Edward III had given thanks after the nearby battle of Sluys (**151**). Miracles performed by means of the Aardenburg image are first recorded in the late thirteenth century and it remained an important pilgrimage site until the end of the sixteenth century.[114] Many men from Yarmouth participated in the Sluys seafight and on their return they established their own image bearing the same name. The image was in existence by 1349. William Worcester noted that a chapel to house it had been founded in 1380.[115] It attracted devotion from non-residents, including Margery Kempe, who venerated it before embarking for her pilgrimage to the Holy Land. Probably Our Lady of Ardenbourg was considered to have extended the Virgin's protection over those travelling by sea.[116] It is also likely that by answering the prayers of the Yarmouth men at Sluys, something of the efficacy of the prototype image was transferred to the new image in their town. Unlike the Yarmouth version of Our Lady of Ardenbourg, there is no evidence to indicate that the York and Newington copies of Our Lady of Walsingham attracted any more veneration than the other images in their respective churches. The presence of such representations might promote pilgrimage to the cult site itself. A panel in the St William window at York depicts the episode when Edward I, just before the translation of St William's body, attributed his preservation from injury after a fall in Wales to the saint, and this caused him to hasten to York for the ceremony. This scene is translated pictorially into the king praying before St William's image on a pedestal, although there is no mention in the text of an image (**152**).[117]

Some light may be shed on the visual relationship of copy to archetype by pilgrim badges. Souvenirs of Our Lady of Walsingham survive in numbers from the fourteenth and fifteenth centuries. Those relating to the Virgin image proper consistently depict an enthroned figure with the Child on her left arm and touching her sceptre. They are not reproductions in the modern sense, yet although betraying their date by the drapery and framing the enthroned Virgin bears some resemblance to the thirteenth-century priory seal which, as has already been suggested, probably represented the cult image itself (**134**).[118] Several exceptionally high-quality fourteenth-century badges depicting another enthroned Virgin and Child and enframed in an elaborate tabernacle are related stylistically to some Becket badges and so have been associated with Our Lady of the Undercroft (**153 (c)**).[119] If the tabernacle was meant to replicate the reredos in which the Canterbury image was placed, then it mattered that a reproduction incorporated features by which the original could be distinguished. Some badges of cult images bear labels in the form of place-names or letters, occasionally incorporating rebuses (**153 (a), (b)**).[120]

151. *Pilgrim badge of Notre-Dame d'Aardenburg, fifteenth century (Catharijneconvent Museum, Utrecht, acc. no. RMCC mooo32)*

*152. York Minster: panel from the St William window depicting Edward I praying before an image of St William of York, c. 1414*

Apart from the stylistic connection with the Becket badges, there is no evidence to relate the so-called Our Lady of the Undercroft badges with the Canterbury image. The Museum of Lynn in King's Lynn contains an incomplete fourteenth-century pilgrim badge of a standing Virgin and Child (**153 (d)**), which is ascribed to the same workshop as the Undercroft images. Our Lady is placed on an angel-corbel, and it has been suggested that this and another type with the Child standing on the Virgin's right arm were variants of this image.[121] The badges may however have represented different cult images. An alternative explanation is also possible. Studies of continental cult images and their copies suggest the relationship was defined by three models.[122] There are replicas of the celebrated image of Our Lady at Altötting (Bavaria) which are close imitations of the original. By contrast, a version of the venerated Italian panel-painting known as *Notre-Dame de Grâce* in Cambrai Cathedral is what Belting terms an 'interpretation': it is not an

153. Four pilgrim badges: (a) Our Lady of Doncaster (King's Lynn Museum, acc. no. PB26), fifteenth or early sixteenth century; (b) Our Lady of Eton, c. 1450 (Museum of London, acc. no. MoL 84.134); (c) Badge associated with Our Lady of the Undercroft, Canterbury, fourteenth century (Museum of London, acc. no. MoL 84.394); (d) Our Lady with Latin antiphon [MAT]ER: CELI REG[INA], fourteenth century (King's Lynn Museum, acc. no. PB28)

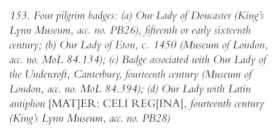

exact copy of the original, but is recognizably a derivative executed by a Flemish artist. The third variant is one where the relationship between copy and archetype is not defined by resemblance but by a label or contact with the miraculous prototype. It may be that the so-called Canterbury badges approximate to the last category, with the 'label' function performed by the enframing tabernacle in place of an inscription. There are no known English instances of a replica being empowered by touching the original; however, the practice is recorded on the continent.[123] These variants suggest a plurality of readings of 'copies' of cult images, ranging from a situation where more or less faithful replication mattered, to one where this was not critical.

## FALSE IDOLS: TRANSGRESSIVE IMAGES

The proliferation of cult-sites claiming miracles was problematic for the ecclesiastical authorities, who made efforts to police the phenomenon. Archbishop Greenfield's invoking of idolatry in the Foston affair was not an isolated occurrence and official sanction for miraculous images was far from automatic.[124] At the beginning of the fourteenth century multitudes flocked to Ashingdon church in Essex, attracted by miracles allegedly emanating from certain images (**154**). These claims were challenged and Ralph Baldok, Bishop of London, appointed a commission of inquiry.[125] In this climate it is little wonder that a tract enjoined parish clergy to instruct their flocks not to venerate or visit places and relics which did not have ecclesiastical approval. In a sermon preached in Oxfordshire in 1356 Archbishop Fitzralph of Armagh launched an attack on cult sites of the Virgin which had proliferated as though each and every one was Our Lady herself and therefore was in receipt of her grace. He reminded his audience that the Virgin could be found in no other location than Heaven.[126] Bishop Pecock followed a similar line, expanding it to embrace miraculous images in general:

> thei mowe not be multiplied so wijde that at ech chirche, at ech chapel, at ech stretis eende, or at ech heggis [hedge's] eende in a cuntre be sett such an ymage, for certis thanne tho ymagis schulden be as foule or of litil reputacioun and schulde be vndeinteose [?] for the grete plente of hem, that bi hem no solempne and fereunt remembraunce schulde be maad . . . plente is no deinte, and ouermyche homelines with a thing gendrith dispising toward the same thing.[127]

An affair with major political repercussions involved the miracle-working image of Our Lady in the chapel at Court-at-Street in Kent, the ruins of which still remain. This cult enjoyed a vogue in the early sixteenth century and was made famous by the visions of Elizabeth Barton, the 'Holy Maid of Kent'.[128] Elizabeth claimed that she had been preserved from death through praying before the image in the chapel. During her illness in 1525 she began to make prophecies based on visions in which the Virgin spoke to her and through her. Pilgrims began to flock to Court-at-Street; women who were unable to suckle their children in particular came to seek the help of the image. Elizabeth, who had become a nun, continued to frequent the chapel and pray before the image, but now her visions trod on very dangerous ground indeed. From 1528 she spoke against the king's attempts to put aside Katherine of Aragon and she became a major weapon in the armoury of those opposed to Anne Boleyn. Her fate – and that of her supporters – was sealed after Anne became queen. Following interrogation by Cranmer, Cromwell and Latimer she recanted and was executed as a traitor in 1534. Attention has rightly focused on the Maid and how the affair was caught up with the breach with Rome. However, the role of the image of

*154. Ashingdon (Essex), St Andrew's church, from the south*

Our Lady at Court-at-Street has perhaps been downplayed. This image was the agent, even the *deus ex machina*, through which the business arose. Secondly, by condemning Elizabeth Barton, cult images of Our Lady were called into question. Within a few years they were all abolished and destroyed. In this, the episode was a harbinger of what was to follow.[129]

Episcopal efforts to control the diffusion of cult images were dictated at least partly by local circumstances. Official censure was not founded on the premise that veneration of images through which the divine was manifested was wrong, but on the abuse of the practice: either that the working of grace through the images and sites in question had not been established, or by confusing sign and signified through worshipping, as opposed to venerating, the cult image. On a totally different scale were the attacks of those who attacked pilgrimage and the veneration of images with thaumaturgic powers as inherently idolatrous and blasphemous. In England the most sustained assault on cult images came first from the Lollards and ultimately from the mid-sixteenth-century reformers. The basis of the heretical attack on pilgrimages has already been well rehearsed, so here the focus is on those aspects of the attack which bear on cult images rather than relics and, in particular, on their material form.[130]

Although Lollard views on pilgrimage, as on other aspects of religous practice, were not uniform, their criticisms centred principally on the same charge of idolatry that they levelled at images in general and in particular on the enrichment of the clergy who served the cult centres from the offerings of the faithful. Here are the opinions attributed to Hawise Moone of Loddon in Norfolk (1430):

> And that no pilgrimage oweth to be do ne be made, for all pilgrimage goyng servyth of nothing but oonly to yeve prestes good that be to riche and to make gay tapsters and proude ostelers.

226

Also that no worship ne reverence oweth be to do to ony ymages of the crucifix, of Our Lady ne of noon other seyntes, for all suche ymages be but ydols and maade be werkyng of mannys hand, but worship and reverence shuld be do to the ymage of God, whiche oonly is man.[131]

Another text of about the same date adds the charge that pilgrimage encouraged lechery, gluttony, drunkenness and worldly pride. The Lollards were especially hostile to 'place images', echoing the concerns expressed by Archbishop Fitzralph:

And therfore they seyn 'the swete rode of Bromholme', 'the swete rode of Grace', 'the swete rode at the northe dore' [at St Paul's Cathedral, London], 'oure dere Lauedy of Walsyngham', but noust 'oure Lauedy of hevene', ny 'oure lord Iesu Crist of hevene', but cleven sadly strokeande kyssand these olde stones and stokkis, layying doun hore grete offryngis, and maken avowis right there to thes dede ymagis to come the nexst yeer agayn, as sif thei weren Crist and oure Lauedy and Ion Baptist and Thomas of Caunterbery and siche other.

The Lollards referred with contemptuous alliteration to cult images of the Virgin and relics of the saints in terms which anticipated the invective of the sixteenth-century reformers: 'the Lefdy of Falsyngham, the Lefdy of Foulpette and to Thomme of Cankerbury'.[132] Elizabeth Sampson, accused of heresy in 1509, was highly disrespectful to Our Lady of Willesden, describing it as 'a burnt arse elf and a burnt arse stock'.[133]

Destruction by fire is precisely what the Henrician government was to prescribe. In July 1538, in an action which mimicked the ritual of pilgrimage journey and procession, the most revered of the cult images, including Our Lady of Walsingham and Our Lady of Ipswich, were brought to London and consigned to the flames before the people. The event was intended to be a public demonstration that these images, after all, possessed no latent powers and were no more than idols made by human agency.[134]

Such was the thorough-going efficiency of the Henrician government and its agents that not one of the major and lesser cult image sites retains any trace of its images. Thus was a spiritual topography erased so utterly that in this as well as in other aspects of devotion the affinities of pre-Reformation religious practices with Catholic Europe as a whole have been forgotten. It was not until the appearance of the Anglo-Catholic movement and the revival of Roman Catholicism that a serious interest began to be taken once more in the pilgrimage centres of the pre-Reformation church. In the 1850s sites like Our Lady of Walsingham were opened up, but more than a century was to pass before the Chapel of Our Lady at Bradwell was identified and studied. In the memories of the compiler of the *Rites of Durham*, Nicholas Roscarrock and a few others who shared their beliefs in the old ways, the sacred landscapes retained some meaning. One or two centres enjoyed afterlives following the Reformation, even in the absence of the image of the saint associated with that place. St Urith was known to seventeenth- and eighteenth-century antiquaries and in 1764 the niche in which her image was placed at Chittlehampton was painted with an inscription referring to her (**137**). Urith also persisted as a Christian name in north Devon villages in the second half of the sixteenth century.[135] At North Marston the connection between John Schorn and his well was preserved in local folklore into the nineteenth century. This seems to have been due to the continuing curative properties of the waters, rather than to the saintly qualities of the good parson. More remarkably, St Winifred's well at Holywell has remained a centre of Catholic pilgrimage in what appears to have been an unbroken tradition since before the Reformation.[136]

# CHAPTER NINE

# *MAAD BI MENNYS HONDIS:* THE PRODUCTION OF IMAGES

The exemplary churches used in the preceding chapters have furnished information on quantities, iconography, location (sometimes) and use of images, largely predicated on documentary evidence. Wherever possible, surviving images have been cited. The present chapter examines the process of production of such images. Although large numbers of what I have defined as devotional images were murals, the focus here is on sculpture in the round and in relief. As with the other questions posed in this book, in terms of production the written sources (especially in the last three decades before the Reformation) partly compensate for the dearth of carved devotional images. However, the scattered nature of documentation and surviving images requires that this chapter be based on a wider pool of evidence than the case-studies used elsewhere.

The production process of carved devotional images was essentially collaborative: in addition to the carver and painter, image-making might involve the services of a smith, a metal-worker, an embroiderer and a wax chandler. It was often both incremental and infinite. For many – perhaps even the majority – of images there was no fixed moment at which their manufacture can be said to have finished. Their very *raison d'être* required that they were frequently repaired, renewed and (re)framed – in other words, that they were remade. Through such means images might take on a contemporary identity and thereby impart a sense of proprietorship to those contributing to the refurbishment.

## *STOK OR STOON:* MATERIALS

The late fifteenth-century inventory for the London church of St Stephen Walbrook includes the materials most commonly used by image-carvers.[1] The seven images in the Lady Chapel were all of 'tre', i.e., wood, and only two of them were painted. Another seven wooden images were in the chapel of SS Nicholas and Katherine, six unpainted and one painted. An alabaster St Christopher stood in the nave and another alabaster, of Our Lady of Pity, was placed in the 'Cloister', together with two images of the Virgin and Child, one of stone and the other of wood.

So ubiquitous were wooden images that it is only rarely that the material was mentioned in contemporary documents. 'Stok', 'tre' and 'tymbre' are catch-alls, but what kinds of wood were used by English carvers? Of the indigenous species, only oak and lime were suitable for carving. Oak was the staple material for wood-carvers in the Netherlands, north Germany and Scandinavia (in Norway it supplanted other materials like willow); there is no reason to doubt that in England too it was much in demand. Most of the surviving wooden images are of oak and it was used in the later Middle Ages for benches and roofs with figural and ornamental embellishments (**I**; **11**, **80**, **86**). The stipulation by Bishop Cornish in 1513 that the high altar images of St Cuthbert's church in Wells were to be either of freestone or of oak demonstrated his concern that inferior materials should not be used.[2] The high cost of oak in the fifteenth century led to an increase of timber imports from the Baltic. Scandinavian fir was also shipped to England.[3]

The two St Stephen's Walbrook alabaster images represent a medium much in demand for images. During the Middle Ages the chief quarries were located at Hanbury in Staffordshire and, 10 miles distant, at Chellaston in Derbyshire.[4] Early distribution and patronage patterns suggest that initially alabaster carvings were artefacts executed by the leading carvers for elite commissions only. Carved alabaster images on tombs of the highest status are first documented in the 1330s and 1340s; by the middle of the century devotional images were being produced. In 1348 an alabaster Virgin was bequeathed to the new Trinity altar over the treasury in York Minster.[5] Alabaster images also appeared in parish churches around the middle of the century. The elegant drapery dispositions on the figures of St Anne and the Trinity respectively at Kersey (Suff.) and Upton near Slough (Berks.) are comparable with the freestone Coronation of the Virgin group from the tomb of Peter, Lord Grandisson at Hereford (d. 1352) and therefore should be dated to the middle of the century (**104**, **155**). In 1371 three alabaster images were bequeathed to Bridgwater church in Somerset.[6] By the 1390s images in alabaster were to be found in parish churches and private chapels or oratories from Somerset and Sussex to north Yorkshire (**IX**; **54**). In the 1417 inventory of St Kerrian's church in Exeter four of the images listed were of alabaster.[7]

Only one of the St Stephen's Walbrook images was of stone. Stone images are less well documented than alabaster and systematic geological analysis needs to be done before a full list of stones used for carving devotional images can be compiled. Limestone with its easily worked surface was much in demand where it was available.[8] The truncated fragments of images of Our Lady and Our Lady of Pity at Tilsworth (Beds.), were carved from the soft clunch quarried a few miles away at Totternhoe. Several fourteenth-century images in Lincolnshire were fashioned from the excellent limestones found in the county (**XVII**). In other areas less malleable stones had to be employed for figurative work. A Midlands workshop produced altarpieces and/or images at North Wingfield (Derbys.) and Tuxford (Notts.) from the local gritty sandstone. The imposing St Christopher from Norton Priory (Ches.) is also of sandstone (**XI**). In Northumberland the figures of St Sebastian and Henry VI at Alnwick were hewn from a local stone (**156**). An image of St Anthony at Tresillian (Cornwall) shows that in the late fifteenth century carvers made use of the unyielding local catacleuse stone.[9] Judging from the freestone image of the Virgin and Child at Sennen, near Land's End, the scarcity of easily worked stone in areas like Cornwall occasioned the importation of images from outside the area in the fourteenth century. By the following century the alabaster carvers had made inroads into the county.[10]

Not all three-dimensional devotional images were of wood, alabaster or freestone. The 1550 Act for the abolition of 'divers books and images' included 'earthe', a term applicable to all fired clays.[11] From around 1520 terracotta was employed for some highly prestigious commissions. Outside royal and metropolitan circles there was a vogue for terracotta tombs and architectural embellishments in East Anglia during the 1530s.[12] A head of St John the Baptist found at

155. *Upton near Slough (Berks.), St Lawrence's church: polychromed alabaster Trinity, mid-fourteenth century*

156. *Alnwick (Northumb.), St Michael's church: sandstone reliefs of Henry VI and St Sebastian (heads modern), early sixteenth century*

*157. Terracotta St John's head from Fulmodeston (Norf.), fifteenth or early sixteenth century (Norwich Castle Museum & Art Gallery)*

Fulmodeston in Norfolk and now in the Norwich Castle Museum shows that devotional images in this medium were made (**157**).[13] During the fifteenth and early sixteenth centuries the Lower Rhineland and Utrecht, Liège, Antwerp and other Netherlandish towns were centres of a flourishing trade in pipe-clay altarpieces and small devotional images (also in terracotta), the latter mass-produced cheaply from moulds. These artefacts were imported into England for use as domestic or personal devotional images (**158**).[14]

Small-scale devotional images were also executed in more costly materials. Between the tenth and the early fifteenth centuries, ivory was much in demand: it was rare and exotic, it could be worked in minute detail and it possessed symbolic values.[15] At first English ivory products were usually fashioned from walrus tusks imported from Scandinavia. From

*158. (left) metal mould for pipeclay images of the Virgin and Child, Netherlandish or North German, early sixteenth century (British Museum, Dept of Prehistory and Europe, reg. no. MLA 1905, 12–29, 1); (right) pipeclay figurine of the Virgin and Child found in London; Netherlandish or North German, late fifteenth or early sixteenth century, Netherlandish or North German (Museum of London, acc. no. MoL 4970)*

about the second quarter of the thirteenth century elephant ivory became available and it is in this medium that the masterpieces of Gothic miniature sculpture were produced.[16] Ivory images feature in documents from the middle of the thirteenth and the early fourteenth centuries. In 1299–1300 Edward I possessed two ivory tabernacles with various images and an ivory Virgin and Child in a tabernacle. Similar references occur in aristocratic inventories of the early fourteenth century.[17] Surviving examples have wings with scenes in low relief, which enclosed a central figure of a seated or standing Virgin and Child (**159**). Paris was a major production centre for ivory figurines of the Virgin and Child and some are likely to have been imported into England. Pieces which have affinities with English monumental sculpture suggest that English elephant ivory carving was already flourishing before 1250 and continued for about one hundred years (**41**).[18] A Bury St Edmunds will of 1463 mentioning small ivory tables engraved with 'ymages wiche were the pryour hooly John of Bredlyngtone' indicates that some kind of ivory carving was still taking place in England during the fifteenth century.[19]

Although most of these small-scale ivories seem to have been used as private devotional objects, they also occurred in churches. An ivory image allegedly owned and donated by Thomas Becket stood near the shrine of St Edward the Confessor in Westminster Abbey. A will of 1324 refers to an ivory image of the Virgin in a tabernacle standing on an altar dedicated to her in the parish church of Holy Trinity Goodramgate, York.[20]

At the end of the period low-relief mother-of-pearl carvings seem to have been imported from south Germany. One bearing an image of the Virgin and worth 4*d* was in the counting house of John Porth, who was buried in 1525 in the church of St Mary at Hill in the City of London; a large number of these objects framed as pendants survive (**160**).[21]

159. Ivory wing from a tabernacle with reliefs of the Annunciation, Nativity and Adoration of the Magi, English, c. 1240–60 (Victoria & Albert Museum, inv. no. A 9-1933)

*160. Pendant with mother-of-pearl relief carving of the Pietà, South German, early sixteenth century (Victoria & Albert Museum, inv. no. A 59-1929)*

## THE PROCESS OF PRODUCTION

The churchwardens' accounts for Morebath in Devon provide a well-documented record of the stages by which images were commissioned and executed on the eve of the Reformation. The initiative came from Christopher Trychay, the long-serving vicar. As soon as he arrived in the parish in 1520 he gave an image of St Sidwell at a cost of 33s 4d, including the carving and gilding; her 'tabyllments' were purchased for a further 13s 4d, raised by Trychay and the parishioners. Donations to gild the image, towards her silver shoes and for a latten candlestick were made at the end of the decade, by which time the parish had embarked on a wholesale revamping of its stock of images. In 1529–30 new images of St George, the patronal saint, and of 'ye nativete of our Laydy' (presumably a Gesyn) were commissioned from the carver Thomas Glasse; the sum agreed for the latter was £5, including all 'stoffe', and Glasse received a down-payment of 40s. The image was to be finished and installed by Lammas 1531, when he received the balance. The George was a more complicated affair. Glasse had an initial payment of 1d as 'ernyste' (a deposit), followed in 1530 by part-payments of 40s and 20s (and possibly another 20s). In 1531 a revised agreement was made, by which Glasse was to make a new horse and George, but would reuse the dragon belonging to the existing image. He was to have the old George as part-payment (presumably for renovation and resale) and a cash payment of 13s 4d 'and yff he doo well hys p(ar)te he schall have of us xvs when hyt ys done & sett up'. It was not until 1534 that Glasse received a final payment of 16s 4d for 'chawngyn of ye iorge'. In the meantime he made a tabernacle for Our Lady; this and the George image and its tabernacle were gilded by John Creche. Creche's work on the Virgin image and tabernacle came to more than £4 6s 4d, paid in instalments; for gilding the George he was paid 16s 4d and for its tabernacle and its 'sylyng' he received an interim sum of £4 16s 8d, plus 39s on completion. This was not the end of expenditure on these two images. Creche was also paid for a streamer and altar cloth for the George, and iron spikes to hold the candles were purchased. For Our Lady a five-light candlestick costing 8s 5d was obtained and 3s 1d was expended on the purchase of 7 yards of linen cloth and the making of the suspension rings and the lace trimmings for the Lenten veil to hang before the image. Nor were the other images neglected. In 1530 a new tabernacle for St Sunday was installed and in the following year this image's vestments were repaired and another set of spikes for its candles bought. Then in 1531 the painter of Treborough received 20d for gilding the image of St Eligius and two years later Creche gilded Our Lady of Pity. In 1537 the base below the image of St Anne received attention and finally, between 1537 and 1539, a new rood with attendant figures was made by a carver named William Popyll for £7 and gilded by Creche.[22]

The Morebath arrangements did not differ in essence from other late medieval European commercial agreements, such as those made between the limewood retable sculptors of south Germany and their patrons. They combined the deposit or 'ernest' by the commissioner to the craftsman, the acceptance of which bound the latter to complete within an agreed time, and the obligation of the patron in turn to pay the balance. In addition, a bonus might be paid on completion, as was written into the agreement for Glasse's St George. In England contracts on these terms likewise governed stained-glass production.[23]

The Morebath accounts can be fleshed out by comparing them with two image-contracts between patron and carver. Happily, they both also concern a new George, albeit in different contexts, and both are virtually contemporary with Morebath.[24] The first of these was concluded in 1518, when a Yorkshire gentleman named John Ratcliffe made an agreement with William Brownflet, carver of Ripon:

That the said Willam Broneflett schall make a George Apon horsebak and a dragon Accordyng to a georg at Crystall [Kirkstall] Abbay and a lofte betwyxe the pelowrs [pillars] off ix fowte wyde in the Colleg Kyrche off ripon next adioinyning unto Sanct Wilfrids closet and abowne off the said lofte A parcloys wall of brest heght wt a Howyfftree and ownder [under] that A Conterfette of Barres of hyryn [iron] off temer of Temer [timber] and be twyx every Barre fyve Inche and onder the flower [floor] syled wt wanschot [wainscot] and a greye [horse] to Ryde upon wt a counterpaye And a Alter off temer wt on Allmare [almary or cupboard] in the sede lofte and a selor of Wanschot a bown the said Georg for cortyns [curtains] to hange by. And the said Willam schall pante [paint] ye said Georg And the dragon wt silver burnet [burnished] and vernesched [varnished] abowne And at the Bordare of Burnet gold And the Georg to hayff towo heds and thre Armes and on the tone hed a Sallet and of the other hede a Schaplet Also the said parties es Agreed that the said John Ratclyffe esqwyer schall delyver to the said Will'm Mone [money] to bye temer for makyng off the saym And the said Willam to alowe to the said Johan for the said temer and the said Willam Broneflett schal fynde Wanschotte hewyng and sawyng at his costs and charge, and the said Johan Ratclyffe schal fynde hyrne [iron] to hyng ye selowr with yt, and ye said Willam schall make ye cost of makyng off the said hyrne and ye said Willam schall make a stole [stool], with on Almere in hyt for ye said Johan to sytt att in ye said loft and also ye said Willam shall make ye Armes of ye said Johan at iiij places in ye loft and ouer [other] scripts of remembrance And ye said Johan Ratcliffe Esqwyer schall content to ye said Willam Bronflet or to his Assngan [assignee] xx li. of lawfull money for the makyng of ye saym at thre [three] convenant tymes. Also the said parties ar commanded and agreit yt incontent efter that he hays said Willam fenyschyt his warke at Byrdlington that then ye said Willam schalbe gyn wt the said warke and to make all ye hast yt he can possabille of the said wark, and to thes comandez well and trowly to be performed and kepyt either partie to othur hathe bonde them selff in tow oblygacions and either them of a xl li. in witnes her of eider partie to other hays sette ther sell [seal].[25]

Both the Morebath and Ripon images were specially commissioned, not purchased off the shelf. Payments to the craftsmen were made by instalments and both Glasse and Brownflet supplied the principal materials. Unlike Morebath, no mention is made of an 'ernest' at Ripon, although Ratcliffe was to advance Brownflet the cost of the timber. The ambitious nature of the Ripon commission may account for the large bond entered into by both parties. Brownflet was responsible for providing the entire setting of the George, including the enclosure with its ceiling, and even the stool on which Ratcliffe was to sit. Although the Ripon indenture only stood at the end of a process of negotiation, it reveals both the extent of patronal control and its limitations. Ratcliffe set out exactly what he required in terms of material and size. The George was also to be modelled on an image of the saint at Kirkstall Abbey.

Ratcliffe was not dealing with a journeyman craftsman. William Brownflet was a well-established carver whose work was in demand. His career began in York, where he took up the freedom of the city in 1482–3. In 1518, as the contract shows, he was employed in Bridlington; by this time he had been resident in Ripon for some years and was mayor there in 1511. He carried out further commissions in the Minster in 1520–3, including work on the feretory for St Wilfrid's shrine and behind the high altar. The elaborate choir-stalls and misericords which grace Ripon and several other northern churches have been attributed to Brownflet, although none is specifically associated with him in the documents and other carvers are recorded in the area.[26] Aspects of the agreement suggest that Brownflet was in a strong position when it came to negotiating terms with his client. Ratcliffe had to wait until the carver had completed his current task. Even then he was not prepared to sign up to a deadline and Ratcliffe had to be content with his undertaking to 'make all ye hast yt he can possabille'. Brownflet's eminence may also account for his retention over every aspect of the production, from supply of the timber to the painting and embellishment of the George with burnished silver and gold. At Morebath the gilding was entrusted not to Glasse the carver but to Creche.

Lack of documentation precludes examining the extent to which, by Brownflet's day, image-provision and conditions of trade differed from what they had been in the twelfth and thirteenth centuries – possibly even in the fifteenth. We can at least test whether Brownflet's status and the circumstances of image-provision in the north meant that the Ripon agreement was atypical in its time by reference to the second of the 'rydyng George' contracts. Two years after the Ripon agreement an indenture was made between a guild at Wymondham (Norf.) and Thomas Sterlyng and William Bale, 'Gravors' of the same town. The agreement was for

. . . the Tymber Warkmanschep and makyng of oon [one] ymage of Seint George callyd a rydyng George with ye horse to ye same ymage of xv hande hye and a dragon with a beme vowted [vaulted beam] to sett ye seyd image horse and dragon upon Provydyd that the seyd Thomas and William Bale schall warke & make or do to be wrowte and made ye seyd ymage horse dragon & beme vowted of good & sufficient seasoned Tymber warkmanly and in dewe proporcyon accordyng to ther patron whyche is the rydyng George of Leystofft except the lyeng of the Dragon schall vary from ther seyd patron for thys Dragon schall lye rampyng on the seyd beme befor the ymage and horse . . . [to be] wrowte [wrought] made and sett up in ye Body of ye paryshe churche of Wymondham . . . by the Feste of the Nativite of Seint John Baptyste next . . .

Sterlyng and Bale were to receive £13, of which £7 was paid in advance. The costs of the ironwork and trappers for the horse were to be met by the guild.[27] As at Ripon, the material was specified and also the 'patron' to be followed, as well as those features in which it was to deviate from the model. The use of 'patrons', in this case an existing image, or design drawings was established in building and associated crafts (including stained glass) from at least the early fifteenth century in England.[28] Unlike Ripon, there was an agreed time-limit in which the Wymondham image was to be set up and installed. Painting and gilding is not mentioned in connection with the latter, so this was to be carried out at a future date, presumably by another craftsman, as at Morebath.

The two contracts show that within the confines of a legal document a range of patron–craftsman relationships was possible. In contemporary south Germany the mercantile patriciate applied their normal commercial practices to the commissioning of altarpieces in exerting as much control as possible over the products they were acquiring.[29] Similar values can be seen operating with the Georges at Morebath, Ripon and Wymondham. All three were executed for a fixed price and not on an open-ended piecework or daywork basis. On the other hand, the respective clients do not appear to have shared their German counterparts' desire to retain control over the supply of materials. This was left to the carver, although at Wymondham the patrons took care to stipulate that the wood had to be of good quality and properly seasoned. English patrons did not always cede control of the materials to carvers. In the 1490s a London gentleman bought for his new chapel at Pott Shrigley (Ches.) 'a tre of Aynysworth . . . for to gete it karied to sum sae [saw] pytt and than I trust to god that shal both sett up my ymages and desk the chaunsel to'.[30]

The use of existing artefacts as a cornerstone of contractual agreements was as widespread in image-making as in other late medieval artistic production. The dimensions of a new image might be determined by an existing one. In 1417 the Chancellor of Wells Cathedral willed that an image of St Mary Magdalen was to be made in wood of the length and width of the image of St Katherine standing in the chancel of Bruton, next to which it was to be placed. A parishioner of Brettenham (Suff.) stipulated that a new tabernacle was to be made after the pattern of one in St Peter's church, Sudbury.[31] Another Suffolk testator, from Walberswick, instructed that his executors 'do peynte and gylde the tabernakyll of our Lady of Pity at my cost, according to the forme of the image of Seynt Mary of Pity of Southwold'.[32]

Neither the Ripon nor Wymondham agreements made provision for a third party to assess the value of the work, as the images were to be done for a predetermined price. This was not always the case. In 1516 the churchwardens of St Lawrence's church, Reading, paid the King's Painter 6s 8d to inspect a new tabernacle. Someone must have advised the Morebath churchwardens whether or not Glasse did 'doo well hys p(ar)te' and thus would earn his bonus for his George. In south Germany the selection of the moderator could have considerable bearing as to whether the outcome of the assessment favoured client or carver.[33]

The Ripon and Wymondham contracts were concerned with size, materials, iconographical detail and time. The role of the patron was far from passive. The carefully described aspects of the Wymondham George which were to differ from the Lowestoft model were presumably requested by the guild. Image-commissioning and image-making made up a far more complex business than a simple binary between patrons formulating and practitioners fabricating. The act of fabrication was also an act of formulation, in that the manner in which an image was fashioned determined to a greater or lesser extent the viewer's perceptions and therefore response. It was one thing for theologians to promote the concept of affective piety, but it was expounded and instilled in the mass of the laity through the visual medium of images. The relationship between form and function was symbiotic. The origination of an image in a patron's mind might be governed by iconographical conventions, as was how it was fashioned by the carver. However in complaining that laypeople and clerics alike chose on aesthetic grounds to venerate one image more than another, the French theologian Jean Gerson (d. 1429) recognized that qualitative differentials existed.[34] The rendering of facial expression and of the body, especially the enveloping (and hence concealing), drapery configurations, might be read in terms of abstract theological concepts, yet the means of expression was a matter for the creator of the image.[35] Carvers could innovate and express individuality. The images of Our Lady produced in the later Middle Ages were very different in treatment of form from the *sedes sapientiae* of the eleventh and twelfth centuries (**IV**, **IX**; **25, 26, 54, 55**). Agency, therefore, has to be allowed to the carver as well as to the patron and the beholder. Quality mattered, evident as much in the Cobham (Kent) heads, almost certainly executed for a family which looked to the best in all forms of artistic endeavour, as in the encomium applied to Master Walter of Colchester, sacrist of St Albans Abbey 'pictor et sculptor incomparabilis' (**XIX**).[36] Few today – and, one suspects, few in the medieval past – would dispute the aesthetic superiority of the alabaster St George in Washington over another in the same medium (**79, 81**).[37]

In neither the Ripon nor the Wymondham agreement does skill or artistic individuality feature.[38] Yet at Morebath Glasse was to receive a bonus payment for his George 'yff he doo well'. How was 'doo well' defined and what criteria were applied? The absence of a contemporary vocabulary of critical judgement, as well as the objects themselves, precludes much of an answer to this question. The standard late medieval descriptive word for physical appearance was 'fair'. Margery Kempe used it for the *Pietà* image at Norwich. The epithet was applied to another Pity at Lenham in Kent, where in 1542 the parishioners complained that their parson had smashed the image, although it was 'the fairest image in the church and never abused'.[39] The term 'proporcioun' employed in the Wymondham contract and also in the Lydgate poem on Our Lady of Pity is as vague as the adjectives 'decent and beautiful' employed by the vicar of Stoke-by-Nayland (Suff.) for a tabernacle he wished to have made. The last was to cost the high sum of £20 and the terminology may have related more to value for money than aesthetic criteria, although the two are not mutually exclusive.[40] Precisely what such labels meant is unclear; however, their use underlines that the reception of images was not solely framed by what was represented but by how it was represented. What made an image 'fair' to Margery and to the people of Lenham? Were their Pities larger or more dramatic, or more lavishly polychromed and embellished than the other images? Painted and gilded finishes ranked high in patronal satisfaction; in the case of the ivory images the costliness of the material and exquisite craftsmanship gave them an appeal to the senses as well as to the spirit.

Form mattered, although what drove changes in the rendering of bodies is hard to fathom as the rationale is never specifically articulated. Whether or not a Marian image was standing or seated affected the way in which it was viewed. The former was more distanced from the gaze of the suppliant; the latter brought the sacred physically closer (**IX, XVII**). A common thread transcends the supplanting of the hieratic formalism of the Romanesque *sedes sapientiae* by the elegance and refinement of the High Gothic Virgins and in its turn by the volume of the *Schönen Madonnen* (Beautiful Madonnas) of the Holy Roman Empire (**26, 54, 55**). In every phase the representation is idealized: the medieval viewer might have empathized more with the more human expressions and gestures of a thirteenth-century image of Our Lady than with its twelfth-century regal equivalent, but it was still far from a mirror image of his or her fellow-parishioners. The elision of image with prototype could be challenged through size. Extant images and their supports indicate that most were less than life-size, yet in relation to their donor figures they appeared gigantic (**54**). The enhancement of the image through framing, polychromy and not least skill could affect fundamentally the powers of the image. It was by means of the material object, and hence through the artifice of craftsmen as much if not more than through the abstract formulations of theologians, that changes in the role of Marian (and other) images were brought about.[41] The recurrence of bequests for the repainting of images may reflect a desire to maintain their visual appeal as much as to express veneration for the signified. Devotion (or the absence of it) might also be affected by the way in which an image was presented and where it was located. Devotional hierarchies could be expressed through differing degrees of adornment and numbers of lights. The inclination of the head of an image of Our Lady and the delineation of her eyes affected the gaze of the viewer. The differing expressions imparted by carver and painter to the two fourteenth-century limestone heads of the Virgin at Cobham in Kent may well have been dictated by their respective locations and functions (**XIX**).[42] It has been argued that the advent of the painted devotional panel in Flanders and Italy in the 1430s marked the moment when the cult of the medieval image began to be replaced by the cult of the work of art. However, the threshold between devotion and art had been crossed in north European sculpture long before Netherlandish and Italian devotional panel-paintings made their appearance.[43]

The price-range of devotional images is like the proverbial piece of string. Apart from the familiar handicap of the lack of a corpus of documentation prior to the late fifteenth century, there are also variables of materials and size. The open-ended nature of production also means that it is hard to determine a final total: did it comprise merely the cost of carving and painting the image itself, or should it include all additions and accoutrements, like a framing tabernacle, the stand for lights – even any garments in which the image might be robed and items like Lenten veils? Both the Ripon and Wymondham Georges were at the upper end of the market in their time (respectively £20 and £13, the latter exclusive of painting and gilding). But even these figures might be doubled, as in the bequest of £40 at Reading in 1514 for an image of the Visitation to stand in the north part of St Lawrence's church, Reading.[44]

The middle range is represented by Glasse's Our Lady image for Morebath, the basic price for which was £5, plus the cost of the tabernacle. The gilding of both image and tabernacle came to over £4, i.e. not far short of the cost of carving the image. On top of that were candlesticks and Lenten cloths. The costs involved in gilding and painting might easily outstrip the price of carving. In 1503–7 the carver's fee for an image of St Margaret at Bassingbourn (Cambs.) was 10s; the bill for painting the image and its associated wings and frame came to £4 6s 8d.[45]

The Bassingbourn figure was at the lower end of the spectrum. One posthumous donor at this level even specified the carver:

> That Thomas Church shall make for me one Image of St John the Baptist like that made and painted at Bilsington, which Image I give to the Chapel of St Leonard of Hythe, and the same Thomas for carving that Image have 12s when it is made.

A testator gave the Bedford Franciscans an image of Our Lady costing 20s as his burial fee.[46]

Additional costs were incurred in transporting the image from workshop to church. This might be only a few pence, like the 2d for carting the new image of Our Lady to Sutterton (Lincs.), plus another penny for bread and drink for the labourers. Artefacts which had to travel a greater distance involved considerably heavier outlay. The price of sending tabernacles to Reading by barge (presumably from London) was 6s in 1518–19.[47] In 1449 William Bruges,

Garter King of Arms, left very precise instructions for the transfer of the images of the Virgin, St George and the Trinity he was bequeathing to St George's church, Stamford. They were to go from his chapel in Kentish Town, London, each in '. . . a gret cofyn of elmyn borde the seyd ymages to be nayled in fast stuffed with hey . . .'.[48]

## EMBELLISHMENT

The carving of the Morebath images by Glasse thus represented only the beginning of the production process. Subsequently these and other images at Morebath were framed and enriched with lavish colouring and gilding. The saintly 'dukes and leaders' of the parish were displayed in a manner which 'betokenyst the blisse that they been now inne, nought the aray that they haddyn upon erthe'.[49]

### Ryaly tabernaclid

The Morebath tabernacles represented a very common means of image-enhancement. Monumental sculpture and *Kleinkunst* indicate that framing by means of canopies of at least the principal images was commonplace from the twelfth century, although there are only isolated survivals from before 1300 (**24**, **36**, **161 (a)**).[50] Both Aylesbury and Llantwit have the cusped arches found in contemporary English manuscripts and ivories; they are a flattened version of the projecting tabernacles housing images of the Virgin in Norway which have been linked with England (**35**, **39**, **159**).[51] During the fourteenth century stone niches became common accessories for the chancel and chantry chapels or subsidiary altars of parish churches (**57**, **58**).

The erection of the well-preserved Perpendicular tabernacle occupying the east wall of the nave north aisle at Aldsworth (Glos.) necessitated the filling-in of a window; this, together with its location at the focal point of the aisle, its size and its elaboration, all point to its housing an important image. Unusually for stone niches, it bears identifying labels in the form of a Katherine wheel on the base and the letters SK on shields on the vaulted canopy, confirming that the image was that of St Katherine of Alexandria (**161 (c)**). The attribute and the letters served to dissolve the boundaries between the frame and the framed.[52]

Not all images were displayed so elaborately. Many were mounted on corbels or brackets, termed either 'basys' or 'stondyngs' (**6**, **34**, **40**, **46**, **52**, **93**, **171**, **176**). In 1469–72 William Mason's brother was paid 40d 'for makyng the stondyng under seynt Johns fote and the other syde' in Bodmin church (Cornwall).[53] Brackets could be more than mere slabs and some have moulded corbels carved with faces, angels or shields of arms. In 1502–3 a new image of St Katherine at Yatton (Som.) was set on an angel corbel costing 8d.[54]

The material and structure of the freestone image niches and brackets preserved many of them from destruction at the Reformation, although sometimes their canopywork was chipped off or defaced (**115**). It is possible, therefore, to study the taxonomy of stone image frames from the thirteenth century to the middle of the sixteenth century (**36**, **57**, **161**).

The costs of wooden tabernacles ranged as widely as for the images themselves. The bottom end of the market is represented by the basic painted wooden boxes for small alabasters, which at the end of the Middle Ages might cost a few pence, inclusive of painting (**162**). At the middle end of the scale was the new tabernacle of Our Lady, purchased for 20s from the bequest of John More of Wing (Bucks.) in 1537–8. A Sittingbourne testator in 1448–9 requested one tabernacle

161. Stone image frames:
(a) Aylesbury (Bucks.), St
Mary's church: niche in north
transept, thirteenth century;
(b) Great Ellingham (Norf.),
St James's church: polychromed
image tabernacle in nave south
aisle, fourteenth century;
(c) Aldsworth (Glos.),
St Bartholomew's church: image
tabernacle in the nave north aisle
east wall, fifteenth or early
sixteenth century

162. Alabaster St John's head in its polychromed wooden casing, fifteenth century (Glasgow, Burrell Collection, inv. no. 1/34)

for four images, the cost of which was not to exceed £10.[55] The more elaborate frames were much more expensive. The £16 left in 1512 by John Barbour, vicar of St Clement's in Ipswich, for St Thomas's tabernacle in memory of his parents included the gilding as well as the carving. The carving alone of the tabernacles for the patronal image and St Katherine at St Margaret's, Westminster amounted to £30 apiece in 1525–8.[56] As with the images, the application of colour and gold-leaf could exceed the cost of carving. In 1487–8 the churchwardens of St Mary at Hill in London spent Agnes Breten's gift of £27 on the decoration of the tabernacle housing the patronal image.[57]

As at St Mary at Hill, the costliest tabernacles were reserved for the most revered images in the church, often but not exclusively the patronal saint and the Virgin. Of the fourteen Bedfordshire parish churches for which tabernacles were made, painted and gilded or repaired from testamentary bequests, only at Oakley, Sandy and Shillington is any mention made of framed images other than the titular saint or Our lady; a similar picture emerges from Buckinghamshire and Kent.[58]

The appearance of the richest and most sumptuous wooden tabernacles can only be guessed at. The tabernacle over the patronal image of St Margaret's, Westminster, erected in 1525–6, included three 'stories' of St Margaret in relief as well as a dozen smaller figures, all painted and gilded.[59] Martin's descriptions of the tabernacles of the patronal and Virgin images at the high altar of Long Melford (Suff.) give an impression of how elevated they could be:

And at the north end of the same altar, there was a goodly gilt tabernacle, reaching up to the roofe of the chancell, in the which there was one fair large gilt image of the Holy Trinity, being patron of the church, besides other fair images. The like tabernacle was at the south end.[60]

Doors or shutters no doubt were common. On Palm Sunday 1471 Edward IV venerated an image of St Anne in a church at Daventry, Northamptonshire:

in a pillar . . . was a lytle ymage of Seint Anne, made of alleblaster . . . closed and clasped togethars with four bordes, small, paytyd [painted], and gowynge round about the image, in manar of a compas . . . And this ymage was thus shett, closed, and clasped accordynge to the rulles that in all the churchis of England be observyed, all ymages to be hid from Ashe Wednesday to Easter in the morninge.[61]

A reference in the York Minster accounts for 1518 suggests that, as on the continent, the doors/shutters might be painted with scenes from the life of the saint depicted: 'Paid to two painters for painting two images of the Blessed Mary, with their tabernacles and histories.'[62]

Tabernacle-making was perhaps the most collective of all the activities involved in the creation of images and their accessories. A new tabernacle for St Mary at Hill was commissioned in 1495–6 from the carver who had created the (unidentified) image which it housed. The base below the tabernacle was entrusted to a carpenter and bricks were laid to support it. A smith was paid 4d for adjusting the rod for the Lenten cloth above the tabernacle and a further 6d for the drawstrings of the cloth.[63] The degree of elaboration involved in the forming of tracery patterns and minor figures on tabernacles ensured that, as at Morebath, it was the sculptor and the painter and/or gilder who were the key figures. In 1522 a parishioner of Yalding in Kent willed that 'ther shal be a tabernacle made to the ymage of Seynt Petir standing in the chaunsell at Yaldyng acordng to the bargyn that I have made with Thomas Thorngate of Goutherst, carver'. A few years later we have the record of Roger Weston, carver of St Albans, and his tabernacles for St Margaret's Westminster. It was to carvers that churchwardens turned to repair image frames. Grace, carver of Stoke-by-Nayland, Suffolk, was employed in 1533–4 to mend tabernacles in Boxford church in the same county.[64]

The ostentation and costliness of the various frames used for images attracted opprobium from certain quarters. A Lollard text criticized the embellishment of images as much by elaborate framing ('ryaly tabernaclid') as by gilding and the application of jewels.[65] At the Reformation they were rendered redundant by the destruction of the images they framed. Unlike their stone counterparts, wooden tabernacles could be removed without damage to the fabric and also had a value, albeit only a fraction of the original expenditure. In 1547–8 one Bishop's Stortford parishioner purchased a tabernacle for 6s 8d and another went for a shilling. Shortly after, a deposit of a shilling was paid for the tabernacle of the patronal saint (Lawrence) from Hawkhurst (Kent), the gold-leaf from which was sold separately for 23d. Three other inferior tabernacles here fetched 2d, 4d and 1s.[66] Either through burning or breaking-up, wooden tabernacles have vanished even more completely than the images they once enclosed.

### Graved and ourned with gold and othere gay peinturis

A very considerable proportion of Morebath's investment in images was disbursed to Creche for gilding. Ratcliffe was also very precise about the painting and gilding of his St George at Ripon. The application of paint and gold-leaf to images, whether in wood, stone, alabaster or ivory, acted as a code and thereby affected the status of that image and how it was interpreted.[67] The chromatic cipher was flexible. A fifteenth-century Florentine churchman invested colour with symbolic overtones: white=purity; red=charity; yellow/gold=dignity; black=humility.[68] An English sermon-writer shared the same reading of red, but to him white represented prayer and black fasting and abstinence. In considering that images were only empowered through the application of polychromy he was subscribing to the orthodox view:

> it is nececarie that thou be-have ye as a peyntur behawyth hym in ys peyntynge an ymage. A peyntur penteth now is ymage with white colours, now with blake, now with red colours, now with mydle colour aftur that it be-commes ye ymage.[69]

Such beliefs found pictorial expression in two illuminations in the *Smithfield Decretals*, which relate how a devil's attempt to prevent a painter from colouring an image of the Virgin was thwarted by the image (**163**). How painting rendered images more 'lifelike' is suggested by the way the statuette of the Virgin and Child inclines towards the monk-painter in a well-known miniature in the *Lambeth Apocalypse* (**XV**).[70]

How might these colour codes have worked? Together with location and framing, they enabled hierarchical distinctions to be drawn. When found at Flawford (Notts.) in 1779, a fine trio of alabaster images retained most of their original pigmentation (**54**). Two of the figures are of prelates, and it is the smaller, not the taller, which functioned as the patronal image of St Peter. It may be a question of survival, but it is perhaps significant that the accounts of the discovery mention only the rich colouring of St Peter and the third figure, of the Virgin. Together with the latter, which can be assumed to have been the accompanying chancel image, St Peter retains traces of gilding applied to the vestments, mitre and attributes. The use of gold, the symbol of divine splendour, even more than polychromy helped to elevate this image above its fellow-prelate.[71] A better-preserved example of hierarchical enhancement by paint is at Brent Eleigh (Suff.), where the patronal image of the Virgin was enclosed by censing angels and stars (**164**).

Written and pictorial assertions of the efficacy of the brush did not go uncontested by Lollards and sixteenth-century reformers:

> But so it is, that ech lyvyng man is verier and perfiter and fuller and better representing ymage of Crist and of ech Seint, than is eny unquyk stok or stoon graved and ourned with gold and othere gay peinturis. Wherfore it is vein [vain] and waast forto make such labour and cost into the making and havyng of suche unquyke gay ymagis.[72]

As usual, there were shades of Lollard opinions on such matters. For some, the 'lifelike' properties imparted by painting rendered images more idolatrous: 'Ye peyntour makith an ymage forgid wth diverse colours til it seme in foolis izen [eyes] as a lyveli creature.' Others were prepared to countenance modest images, but not those whose embellishment invited offerings:

*163. Miracle of the Virgin in the* Smithfield Decretals, *c. 1330–40 (London, British Library, MS Royal 10. E. IV, f. 209v)*

For to ye gayest and most rychely arayed ymage ratheest wil ye puple ofur [people offer], and noust to no pore ymage stondyng in a symple kirk or chapel, but zif it stonde ryaly tabernaclid with kervyng and peyntid with gold and precious iewelis . . . Dere Lord! what almes is it to peynte gayly dede stones and rotun stokkis with such almes that is pore mennus good and lyfelode [livelihood] . . . ?[73]

A prime candidate for this kind of criticism might have been the patronal image at the high altar of York Minster, which, together with its tabernacle, was gilded at vast expense in 1482. The total payments to the painter Francis Foster and his assistants, for his labour and materials, including old and new gold-leaf, amounted to £27 11s 8½d.[74]

The application of gold to images was a matter of concern within ecclesiastical circles in the fifteenth and sixteenth centuries and it has been suggested that the emergence of the unpolychromed carved wooden retable in late fifteenth-century Germany reflected a sensitivity to such criticisms. Does the preponderance of unpainted wooden images listed at St Stephen's Walbrook suggest a similar concern in late fifteenth-century England? In both countries monochromatic treatment of images in various media had been known since the fourteenth century (**IX**). Secondly, with the exception of commissions from leading craftsmen, it seems to have been standard practice for images and their enclosing tabernacles to have been painted and gilded after delivery, as funds permitted. The unpainted images at St Stephen's Walbrook were installed in the church and there is no reason to suppose that they were not fulfilling their purpose; however, whether their unpolychromed stage represented deliberate choice or an interim stage is unclear. In 1521 John Paynter was paid 20d for painting St Leonard's image in St Lawrence's church, Reading, 'left by the wyffs onpaynted'.[75] Creche embellished the Morebath images very soon after Glasse delivered them. The process could be much more protracted. In the populous and prosperous south Bedfordshire parish of Houghton Regis the fund-raising required for the making, painting and gilding of a new tabernacle for the patronal image extended over at least sixteen years.[76] Such a time-lapse puts into perspective the dozen years that passed between Tilman Riemenschneider's completion of a new altarpiece for the parish church of Münnerstadt (Franconia) and its painting by Veit Stoss.[77] Documentary sources

*164. Brent Eleigh (Suff.), St Mary's church: wall-painting enclosing the former emplacement of the Marian patronal image, fourteenth century*

show that images the length and breadth of the land were being painted and gilded until the beginnings of the Henrician Reformation.

Through polychromy, differences of expression could be emphasized. The three fourteenth-century freestone female heads at Cobham (Kent) are the work of the same carver. Two are of the Virgin, but it is principally the painted facial features that impart *gravitas* to one and a more empathetic, smiling expression to the other (**XIX**).[78] The polychromy is applied sparingly to the very fine statue of the Virgin and Child at Blunham (Beds.), thereby playing a subordinate role to the bare alabaster. Formal as well as iconographical issues are involved here. The tactile nature of the medium and the careful delineation of drapery folds underline the fact that the alabaster carver had more to offer than merely providing a field for painting. The Blunham Virgin's monochromatic finish presented to the viewer a humbler representation than the regality of the richly painted freestone image at Anwick (Lincs.) (**IX**, **XVII**). In churches like Shillington (Beds.), which had multiple images of Our Lady, including an *alba Maria*, the contrast must have been striking.[79]

### Arayid so gay

Pigment and gold-leaf were far from the only means by which images were honoured and made memorable. The Morebath image of St Sidwell was provided with silver shoes. Unsurprisingly, such embellishments were attacked by the Lollards, prompting an orthodox response. *Dives and Pauper*'s justification for the use of footwear in precious metal was that it protected the feet of the image from damage through the kisses of the faithful. The dialogue extended beyond the use of silver shoes to encompass a wider range of image-embellishment:

> DIVES: I suppose that the seyntys in herthe [earth] weryn nought arayid so gay, wyt shoon of sylver and clothys of gold, of baudekyn, of velvet, ful of brochis and rynggys and precious stonys, as here [their] ymagis been to qheche the peple offryst, for they shuldyn an had mechil cold on here feet and sone a been robbyd of here clothis.
> PAUPER: Soth it is they they wentyn nought in sueche aray. Nevereles, al this may be doon for devocioun that meen han to the seyntys and to shewyn mannys devocioun.[80]

The most venerated images of all – the miracle-working cult images – were frequently covered with precious metals, not just in the form of *ex-votos* but also their entire surfaces. Descriptions of images like Our Lady of Caversham 'plated with silver' evoke such renowned survivors as Sainte-Foy at

Conques.[81] The richness of such objects can be gauged by the costs of the alterations made in 1418 by the London goldsmith Cornis Melver to the image of Our Lady at the high altar of Windsor Chapel. The amendments amounted to £30 and new silver came to £30 6s 8d; in 1552 this image (which may have been that given by Henry III in 1240–1) weighed no less than 126lb ½oz.[82]

As the *Dives and Pauper* debate shows, fabrics also enhanced the splendour and dignity of images (**XXII**; **150**). As we saw in the last chapter, the most lavishly robed were those images deemed to have been endowed with miraculous powers, but vestments could also be found adorning favoured parish church images. Many London churches in Edward VI's reign still retained at least some of the garments in which their images used to be clad. All Hallows in Bread Street had several robes for the Virgin and Child of green satin and gold. The Marian image at St Stephen's Coleman Street possessed no fewer than four such garments and elsewhere others were worn by St Ursula, St Katherine and the Holy Trinity. A Virgin image at St Michael's, Queenhithe, had a silver-gilt crown and another at St Sepulchre wore a 'chaplet . . . with a sapher with dyverse other stones & perles'.[84] Painted imitations of cloths of honour like those donated by the vicar of All Saints', Bristol, to the patronal image occur in image-niches at Elsfield (Oxon.) and Great Ellingham (Norf.) (**161 (b)**).[85]

## Fresshing

In 1519–20 the churchwardens of St Mary at Hill disbursed the considerable sum of £5 to a painter named John Wolf for cleaning and 'fresshing', i.e. refurbishment, of the tabernacle enclosing the image of the Assumption of the Virgin.[85] Images were kept in damp environments and their surfaces were vulnerable to damage from touching and kissing and to general wear and tear and discoloration through candlesmoke and grease. The complaint that an image was 'male depicta' is heard in visitations and officials were keen to direct parishioners to fulfil their obligations to maintain their devotional images in good order. In the Salisbury diocese Dean Chandler imposed fines on parishes if they did not carry out the work within a prescribed period. If the inadequately painted patronal image at Wantage (Berks.) had not been attended to by the following Michaelmas, a fine of 6s 8d was to be levied on the parishioners.[86]

Continental examples of repainting abound. An enthroned Virgin of the late twelfth century in the Schnütgen Museum, Cologne, had paint applied on three occasions during the Middle Ages: its original colouring, another probably in the thirteenth century and finally a third in about 1350.[87] The last phase was associated with a more drastic 'makeover' involving the carving of a new head (**XVIII**). The Schnütgen Virgin lacks her hands as well as the entire figure of the Christ-Child; similar defects are documented in England. For example, in 1342 images of Our Lady at Dean-Prior and of the patronal saint of Beaworthy in Devon had lost their hands; in 1519 the face of the image of the Virgin in the north aisle of Wormshill (Kent) needed mending.[88]

In orthodox eyes the process of renewal gave fresh life and therefore efficacy to the image and did honour to the prototype. However, renovation could expose the use of images to Lollard and sixteenth-century evangelical charges of idolatry. While the replacement of an old by a new image might be seen as preserving that distinction between signifier and signified, the act of large-scale repairs to ancient images eroded it dangerously: renovation implied that the representation itself possessed virtue.[89] The German images also reveal that 'fresshing' did not mean replicating the original carved style or polychromy of the image. This may have been more than just a question of ability: medieval craftsmen were capable of imitation when required, but the desire to update the appearance of an ancient image could have been a factor.[90] The image itself retained the accumulated reverence of previous generations, but giving the head and the polychromy the same appearance as new images increased, or indeed 'refreshed', the appeal to contemporary users.

## LEWED WRIGHTES OF STOKKES

### Kervers

For all craftsmen, of whatever ability, image-making was a sacred task, a simulacrum of God's creation of the physical universe and mankind. The fourteenth-century writer Thomas Usk observed that the value of property and artefacts did not reside with the owner or user but with their creator: 'if they be good or faire, the mater of the workeman that hem made is to prayse'.[91] Before starting work, Glasse, Brownflet, Sterlyng and Bale and Creche should have gone to a priest to be shriven, do penance, make a vow to fast, pray or undertake a pilgrimage and ask him to pray that they 'have grace to make a faier and a devoute ymage'. The craftsman who carved a crucifix for Meaux Abbey (Yorks., East Riding) in the fourteenth century worked only on Fridays, when he fasted.[92]

The demands for imagery from the thirteenth century must have led to a vast expansion in the numbers of craftsmen engaged in the craft of carving in stone and wood. Prior to this period there is insufficient evidence to discern any pattern of production, even in the great churches. It has been argued that in the twelfth century the production of architectural sculpture like capitals and tympana was in the hands of masons, with the specialist carver only emerging in the following century.[93] The latter, however, may have come to the fore earlier. From the middle of the twelfth century large-scale stone statuary began to be produced and the wooden *sedes sapientiae* images started to proliferate. In the 1140s Ralph the sacrist of Ramsey Abbey made an image of the Virgin and Child in silver and gold; nearly a century later Walter of Colchester, sacrist of St Albans Abbey, carved a new and splendid image of Our Lady for his monastic church.[94] Even though both Ralph and Walter were monks, the latter at least had probably learned his skills outside the cloister. There seems little doubt that during the thirteenth century the carving of images became almost exclusively the preserve of paid lay craftsmen. The purchase of a small image of Our Lady at Winchester in 1227 for the royal residence of Guildford Castle points to the presence of urban carving workshops at this date.[95] In the thirteenth and fourteenth centuries 'imaginator' was a common term, replaced subsequently by 'kerver'; 'graver' occurs from at least the late fourteenth century. A distinction seems to have been made between these terms and 'marbler', which was applied to anyone engaged in tomb sculpture (including monumental brasses), apart from those working in alabaster.[96]

Craftsmen at the top of their profession worked in both stone and wood and were in demand over a wide area. The Massinghams between them exhibited a wide range of skills. John senior in 1438 made an inn-sign in Canterbury and a decade later carved the important patronal image of the Virgin for Eton College Chapel. Eton was a royal undertaking and Massingham was also employed as master-carver at Archbishop Chichele's foundation of All Souls College, Oxford, and by the executors of Richard Beauchamp, Earl of Warwick, on the latter's mausoleum in St Mary's church, Warwick, for which he made the model for the earl's tomb effigy. It is likely that his commissions at All Souls included the stone figures of Chichele and Henry VI, which originally stood above the main gate, and the chapel reredos. He must also have been closely involved with the lavish sculptural embellishment of Henry V's chantry chapel in Westminster

Abbey. Massingham's son John worked with him at All Souls and was subsequently employed at Winchester College, for which he carved the statue of the Virgin and Child over the outer gate, images for the chapel reredos and the crucifix for the new rood loft; he also painted as well as carved the flanking figures of the Virgin and St John.[97]

Glasse at Morebath and Bale and Sterlyng at Wymondham were locally based. Wills and churchwardens' accounts confirm that at least by the early sixteenth century most carvers served their immediate neighbourhood. They were not specialist image-makers but turned their hands to other ecclesiastical fittings and furnishings. An extended programme of work might involve the taking up of temporary accommodation, as Peter Kerver did at Ashburton (Devon) in the 1520s; a decade later Edmund More of Kingston-upon-Thames also retained a property in Ely to enable him to fulfil his contract for the imagery of Bishop West's chantry.[98] Sources for woodcarvers are uneven in geographical coverage; there are large tracts of the country where no traces of image-makers survive in the written records.[99] Apart from London and Westminster, the major concentrations were in East Anglia, followed by Devon and Somerset. This is to be expected, given the scale of work on roofs, screens and seating, let alone image-making, in the churches of these regions in this period. Although Bristol, Exeter, Cambridge, Ipswich and Norwich were centres, many carvers were located in the smaller towns and even villages, like Ashburton, Saffron Walden, Brandon and Tuddenham St Mary's. Whether by accident or not, Suffolk features much more prominently than Norfolk. In the south-east Kent may have been a centre of some activity, although most of the evidence comes from Mary's reign. Carvers occur regularly from the late fourteenth century in the York Register of Freemen and they probably played a dominant role in the region, as did the city's glass-painters.[100] Thomas Drawswerd matched the prominence of Brownflet. He obtained the freedom of York in 1495–6 and three years later executed some carving in association with the paschal candle in the Minster. In 1508 he obtained final settlement from St Mary's church, Newark (Notts.), for a great reredos (presumably for the high altar).

In terms of required skills there was little difference between fashioning a figure for a devotional image and one intended for an East Anglian hammerbeam roof or for a bench-end like those at Wiggenhall St Mary (Norf.). Such commissions meant close interdependence between the crafts of carving, carpentry and joinery. John Fisher of London (occ. 1486–1504) was described as joiner and carver, quite a common combination. His commissions included a rood loft with carved images for Merton College chapel, Oxford, alterations to the roof of the college library and an oratory and cupboards for Magdalen College. Carpenter and carver was another combination.

The explosion of work on church fabrics and furnishings seems to have led in some of the major centres to a demand by the carvers for autonomy. The York carvers had long been members of the carpenters' craft guild, together with sawyers, joiners and cartwrights. The right of the carvers and joiners to have their own ordinances in 1546 no doubt was a formal recognition of a *de facto* shift in power away from the carpenters. It is likely to have been connected with the prominence of the likes of Brownflet and Drawswerd (the latter was mayor in 1515 and 1523). The separation from, indeed elevation of carving above, other woodworking skills at the time is apparent elsewhere. In 1528 the Coventry carvers left the carpenters' craft guild and joined the painters.[101]

As we have seen, however, many carvers operated outside the major urban centres and where the writ of the craft guilds did not run. Indeed, it is uncertain whether such self-regulatory bodies existed even in towns the size of Bury St Edmunds and Sudbury (Suff.). This is a matter of some importance, as the blame for what has been perceived to be the mediocrity and lack of invention of English late medieval sculpture has been laid partly at the door of the craft guilds.[102]

The wills of five Bury St Edmunds carvers between the early fifteenth and early sixteenth centuries survive. In this period the town seems to have been an important centre for the production of stained glass, manuscript illumination, monumental painting, bell-founding and brass-engraving as well as carving.[103] John Myldenhale (1420) possessed silver spoons and John Aleyn (1457) owned two tenements in the town.[104] The latter made generous provision for the well-being of his soul in several religious institutions as well as in his parish church of St James and left 10 marks as dowry to each of his six daughters. His executors included a mercer and a cordwainer as well as Joan, his widow. The tenement where he lived was located in the great market, so he was at the hub of things. It was left to Joan, with reversion to their son Thomas. His other property was disposed of in similar fashion to his other son John. The sale of his tools is not mentioned, so he may have hoped that one or both of his sons would take up his craft, or had already done so. The will of Richard Aleyn, presumably a kinsman of John's, was made eleven years later.[105] Although his occupation is not named, Richard also made his living from working timber. As both of his sons were intended for the priesthood, his yard next to West Street, his tools (a long saw and a 'framyyng sawe', a lathe and three axes) and his planks were to be sold; he also bequeathed to John Wylwys what were evidently two pattern books 'cum exemplaribus'. One of John Myldenhale's executors was a fellow-carver named John Worlynch, while Giles Cosyn's (1479) will was to be administered by two fellow-carvers of Bury, Robert Robynson and William Wuley, or Wolsey. The last seems to have been entrusted with a commission by John Clopton of Long Melford and became a freeman of Norwich in 1484.[106] Robert Stonard (1511) intended his elder son Thomas to continue the family business as he left him 'all myn instruments that longyth to myn occupacion' as well as one of his properties next to one of the abbey gates.[107]

All those who left detailed wills seem to have been comfortably off, with cash in hand and goods and chattels and property to dispose of. Some looked to fellow-practitioners of their craft to administer or oversee their wills, others did not. Only Stonard for certain made provision for a son to carry on his craft; of the others Myldenhale and Cosyn had no living sons and the son of William Belamy (d. c. 1512) was still a child.[108] The Aleyns provide some evidence of the family-centred nature of woodworking. This might account for the occurrence elsewhere of women in the craft. Joan de Mymms (d. 1349) of London was described as an 'ymaginatour' and had an apprentice. A painter's wife was also paid for gilding part of a tabernacle in St Lawrence's, Reading in the early sixteenth century.[109] The Bury wills tell us something about the material comforts and status of provincial carvers, but little more than that. There are no references to the work they carried out and no indications of the size of their establishments. In York the carpenters' ordinances of 1482 did not limit the numbers of craftsmen which a workshop could employ. Generally workshops were small. The aforementioned John Fisher had a son and two or three assistants. His Ipswich contemporary John Sparhawke also had three assistants. David Carver of Bristol's establishment of six seems to have been exceptionally large. In York the categories of craftsmen comprised master, journeyman, 'yongmen' and apprentices. Craftsmen who had been apprenticed outside were not forbidden to set up within the city, although they had to pay a much higher entrance fine.[110]

Generally painting and invariably gilding of freestone and wooden images was in the hands of professional craftsmen. Polychroming might be carried out by carvers; leading craftsmen like the

Massinghams could paint or had painters in their workshops. Thomas Barsham of Great Yarmouth was a provincial carver who in 1416–21 made and painted two images with their tabernacles in the chapel of Mettingham College (Suff.).[111] Usually it was the preserve of specialist painters, as at Morebath.

The painter portrayed in the *Lambeth Apocalypse* is vested in the monastic habit (**XV**). There are other instances of painting undertaken by those outside the craft. For a chantry priest named William God of Wells the task was an act of contrition. In 1513 he was ordered to paint the image of St Michael with its tabernacle as penance for adultery. Walter Blank undertook the polychroming of the patronal image (St Michael again) in Bishop's Stortford church in lieu of rent. In both cases painting took place *in situ*, as was inevitable with stone tabernacles incorporated into the fabric.[112]

### *Alabastermen*[114]

In the later Middle Ages an alternative organizational model of production to the locally based wood and stone carvers was operated by the alabaster carvers, and it was a system which must have provided strong competition with the former. As was observed earlier in this chapter, alabaster had initially been restricted to high-status commissions for tombs, altarpieces and images and ecclesiastical furnishings. By the early fifteenth century it was possible to purchase uncarved alabaster from the quarries. During the course of this century the craft became a diffused and highly commercial mass production. Alabastermen occur in London in the 1420s, Burton-on-Trent from the 1440s, York from the late 1450s and Nottingham from the 1470s. In 1525 they are recorded with painters, gilders and stainers as members of the Lincoln Guild of St Luke. The alabaster carvers operated through retail outlets and agents like William Bott, who worked for the Nottingham carver Nicholas Hill. Hill also sent his products to London, where it is likely that he had a shop. In the 1540s the mother-in-law of the prominent alabaster tombmaker Richard Parker of Burton-on-Trent rented a shop in Bristol. Whether these regional centres were exclusively showrooms, or were places where working of alabaster took place, is uncertain. The image of the Assumption of the Virgin and parts of a St William altarpiece found at Peasholme Green in York are more deeply undercut than most alabasters and also have distinctive stylistic traits (**165**). Between 1457 and 1473 six 'alblastermen' were enrolled as Freemen there; only two names occur subsequently, in 1487 and 1524.[114] Itinerant alabaster salesmen perambulated through the villages taking orders for their products. In 1532–3 'the alablaster man' was paid 4*d* 'in ernyst' over an agreement at Bramley (Hants.).[115] The extent to which the alabaster carvers were able to attract custom from rural churches far from the centre(s) of production is demonstrated by the extant imagery and documentation at Whittlesford (Cambs.). In 1519 Joanne Webbe, a widow of this parish, bequeathed the wherewithal to purchase an alabaster image of the Virgin for the chancel. There is a good chance that the fragmentary *Maria lactans* is identifiable as this image (**166**). This is accompanied by the remains of at least two and probably three altarpieces and of images of Our Lady of Pity, the Gesyn, the Holy Trinity, St Anne teaching the Virgin to read, St Paul, St Sitha and (probably) St Eligius. (**1**). All are of alabaster. The Trinity also occurs in Joanne Webbe's will and another refers to Our Lady of Pity.[116] Toft, on the other side of Cambridge, has images in the same medium of a bishop-saint, Henry VI, St Christopher and St Eligius.[117]

One of the reasons why the alabaster carvers were able to obtain commissions in places like Whittlesford and Toft was the price of their products. Many alabaster images and altarpieces were

*165. Alabaster image of the Assumption of the Virgin,
c. 1500 (York, the Yorkshire Museum)*

cheap and off-the-peg. An image in this medium at the bottom end of the market could cost no more than a few pence. Valuations in 1492–4 of the very popular St John's heads varied between 1 and 5 shillings (**162**); the former price was placed on an image of St David in 1536.[118] For these a comprehensive and speedy package, with the price including the crude framing and painting as well as the carving, was offered. Many of the craftsmen were described as both carver (or image-maker) and painter.[119]

The control exerted by the alabaster carvers extended to maintenance agreements. The porous, water-soluble nature of the medium demanded particular care in cleaning. In 1523 16*d* was paid by the churchwardens of St Lawrence's church in Reading 'to an Alabast' man for makeying clene the table at Saynt John's Awlt' & other ymages'. The 3*d* allocated from offerings in the church box a few years earlier by the Bassingbourn churchwardens 'to the whassing of the ymages off allablaster' was also probably used to employ an alabaster specialist.[120]

Not all post-1400 output was ready-made. Unusual pairings like the SS Faith and Erasmus panel would have been made at the command of a specific client (**77**). The best craftsmen retained the ability to produce work of high quality, whether image, altarpiece or tomb (**79, 103**). Alabaster imagery was also in demand overseas. In 1382 three figures were exported from Southampton by an Italian papal tax collector and shortly afterwards alabasters were being shipped to Spain. The presence of five images of Our Lady in Gesyn in north Germany points to an alabaster trade with the Baltic ports and Cologne which was already established in the third quarter of the fourteenth century.[121] Flourishing markets existed in the fifteenth century from Scandinavia to Spain. Some images and altarpieces were brought out of England after the Reformation, when bargains could be had, but archival evidence testifies to the scale of the trade well before the mid-sixteenth century. In 1414 a Rouen mason travelled to Chellaston on behalf of the abbot of Fécamp to purchase unworked alabaster. Like the domestic market, many (probably the majority) of the exports were finished products. The shops in London and Bristol provided the marketplaces for the wares; no doubt either shops or middlemen functioned in Southampton, Hull, Boston, King's Lynn, Poole and other ports.

### Straungers

Traffic in carved images was far from being one-way. At the time Glasse and Creche were engaged on the Morebath images, voices were being raised against overseas competition. In 1531 Sir Thomas Elyot complained that the English 'be constrayned, if we wyll hawe any thinge well paynted, kerved, or embrawdred, to abandone our owne countremen and resorte unto straungers'.[122] The purchase of imported products and the presence of alien craftsmen in England was hardly a novel phenomenon in the early sixteenth century. In the fourteenth century sculptors like Jean de Liège and possibly even the renowned André Beauneveu executed important commissions

166. Whittlesford (Cambs.), St Mary and St Andrew's church: alabaster head from a Maria lactans image, c. 1520

for leading English patrons. Not all 'foreign' products were well received. In 1305 a German sculptor named Thydemann working in London carved a wooden crucifix which attracted comment because of its unfamiliar (to English eyes) form and was removed from public gaze by the ecclesiastical authorities. Thydemann also had to undertake not to make or sell any similar crucifixes.[123] This suggests not only that he exercised control over form but also that he was not working solely to commission.

From the fifteenth century imports increased dramatically and affected virtually every branch of artistic production. Tapestries, Italian fabrics, dinanderie, goldsmithswork, woodcuts, printed books, illuminated manuscripts, armour and ceramics found a receptive market in England.[124] The scale of this enterprise was what concerned Elyot, but it was not only imported goods which aroused his ire. He witnessed the settlement of numbers of alien craftsmen in London, principally in Southwark, where they were immune from the regulations of the city craft guilds. What was more, they obtained some of the most important commissions from the king and elite circles. Elyot's views were understandably shared by indigenous London craftsmen dismayed at their failure to secure the most prestigious commissions. As early as 1474 the London Glaziers Company petitioned against foreign glaziers and xenophobia directed against aliens was a principal cause of the May Day riots of 1517. A series of statutes enacted in the 1520s, which attempted to restrict foreign craftsmen by various measures, were probably more honoured in the breach than the observance.[125]

How was the production and consumption of devotional images affected by all this? As we have seen, humble pipeclay statuettes were imported from Utrecht and other centres of production (**158**) and from the beginning of the sixteenth century at least the carvers of the great Flemish retables and images also found a market in England. Ships docking in London, Hull and Southampton carried in their cargoes wooden images of varying sizes, including small-scale

167. *Polychromed and gilded walnut Virgin and Child statuette, Malines (Netherlands), c. 1510 (Victoria & Albert Museum, inv. no. A 637-1897)*

gilded devotional statuettes (**167**).[126] The names of immigrant craftsmen reveal the extent to which sculptural production for elite patrons was dominated not so much by Italians like Giovanni da Maiano, Benedetto da Rovezzano and Pietro Torrigiano but by carvers of northern European origins. In 1477–8 Dirick van Grove and Giles van Castel were entrusted with the major commission of new images of St George and St Edward for the new chapel at Windsor; just previously, Walter Nicholl had carved the rood loft and stalls for Eton College chapel. Nicholl was a resident of Southwark and so was almost certainly an alien; his work must have blended nicely with the grisaille wall-paintings at Eton which have such a strongly Flemish appearance (**149**). Figures from the Winchester Cathedral choir screen and possibly free-standing devotional images (**V**) of the 1470s bear a Netherlandish imprint and a high-quality Christ probably from an Entombment executed for the Mercers' Company chapel in London seems to have been made by a craftsman from the same region during the early sixteenth century.[127] Netherlandish carvers did not enjoy a monopoly; the funeral effigy of Queen Elizabeth of York was a collaborative effort between Wechan Kerver and Hans van Hoof, who made the hands, and Lawrence Emler/Ymber, who undertook the head. The first two may have been Flemings but Emler was a native of Swabia. In 1492 he had received £2 for a new statue of St Thomas for London Bridge.[128]

The discussion has of necessity ranged beyond the devotional image, for as we have seen carvers were not restricted to such production. Elyot's blimpish remarks no doubt were provoked by the acquisitive practices of his own class, but hardly applied to artistic production as a whole. Almost all of the alien names were resident in London and either worked in and around the capital or for leading patrons elsewhere. The extent to which the output of the alabaster carvers and producers of wood carvings in the shires, like Glasse, was influenced by the 'straungers' and imported artefacts is impossible to gauge. English late fifteenth-century sculpture assimilated certain Netherlandish drapery traits and continental woodcuts and prints were used by painters and the carvers of misericords in the early sixteenth century; as the latter also probably carved devotional images, some impact can be assumed.

# CHAPTER TEN

# DEFACE AND DESTROY:
# THE END OF IMAGES

*For in these matters of S[ainc]tes, when wee can saye nothing that is good wee should in reason forbeare to write that which is ill, being bound in all doubtfull thinges to think the best.*
    Nicholas Roscarrock, *Lives of the Saints* (N. Orme (ed.), *Nicholas Roscarrock's Lives of the Saints: Devon and Cornwall*, Devon and Cornwall Record Society, ns, 35, 1992, p. 91.

*Cursed is the ma[n] that maketh any carved or molten image, an abominacion to the Lorde, the woorke of the handes of the craftesmanne, and putteth it in a secrete place, to wurship it.*
    The 1549 Book of Common Prayer (*The First and Second Prayer Books of King Edward the Sixth*, Everyman Edition, London, 1910, p. 280).

Apart from a few niches and corbels, the exemplary churches examined in the course of this book have left no traces of their images. Eaton Bray, Luton, Marston Moreteyne, North Crawley and Totternhoe all have bare, whitewashed interiors (**5, 46, 65, 82, 110**). They stand as witnesses to the extent and efficiency with which the outward trappings of traditional worship and belief were excised from religious and social practice during the second third of the sixteenth century. The purpose of this chapter is not to relate the history of the Reformation in this area but to focus on what light the fates of devotional images can shed on attitudes during this process.

When they made their bequests to the lights of the saints during the second and third decades of the century the parishioners of these Bedfordshire and Buckinghamshire churches could not have imagined that, within fifty years, the religion that they and their forebears had practised for centuries would be swept away. Even if word had reached them of the dissenting voices of the Lollard adherents a score or so miles to the south in the Chiltern Hills, the idea that the State itself would lead the attack on 'traditional' religion and bring crashing down a whole edifice of beliefs and practices would have been inconceivable.[1] Whatever the strength or weakness of traditional pious beliefs in these parishes at the time, the shock wrought upon the social fabric of each community by the forced destruction of its familiar helpers and the practices tied to them cannot be underestimated. By removing the images, the whole structure of parish life and custom was undermined.

  Both devotion to images and their destruction have been used to support or undermine the apologists for the pre-Reformation church and their Reformist opponents: they have become the very field of academic battle. I do not subscribe to a determinist reading of sixteenth-century religious history, by which the Reformation is seen as the inevitable culmination of a process which had been in train for centuries. Such a teleological explanation cannot be sustained. We are dealing with microhistories of individuals and communities operating within the boundaries defined by the principal of *cuius regio, eius religio*. Eventually the shape and nature of the Church in England was decided by the Elizabethan Settlement, but the shifts and abrupt reversals in doctrinal matters during the course of the middle years of the sixteenth century show that ultimately all depended on the personal credo of the monarch. This did not mean that everyone subscribed to the same views, but establishing what all bar the extreme Protestants and Catholics actually felt about the religious changes is another matter.

Images and their use or abuse were central to the ideological struggles of the Reformation. They were, however, a disputed area long before the sixteenth century. The strictures of St Bernard and his generation of Cistercians in the twelfth century against all images except for the crucifix would not have sounded antithetical to Wycliffe's loose group of followers. Bernard's ideal of 'imageless devotion' proved ill-suited to the needs of the vast majority of the Christian *communitas* for whom images were crucial.[2] While it was accepted within orthodox circles that images had an important role to play in worship, it was stressed that veneration should be 'correct' and images not abused; in other words, that there should be no confusion between sign and signified. A sermon preached in 1356 by Archbishop Fitzralph on the feast of All Saints' spoke of the danger of such elision arising from the veneration of cult images known by their location, such as Our Lady of Walsingham or Our Lady of Doncaster (**134**, **153 (a)**). This was also the thrust of a succession of texts dating from the end of the fourteenth century and repeated by the likes of Erasmus, Colet and More a century or so later.[3] The arguments were impeccably orthodox and could have been penned by any theologian in the Western Church. Bishop Pecock, the writer of *Dives and Pauper* and others of their ilk shared the concerns of the great early fifteenth-century theologian Jean Gerson. He was not someone who had a need for images, although he accepted that they could be useful as aids to devotion. On the other hand, Gerson had no truck with images such as the *Vièrges ouvrantes* (**XXI**), or with the indulgences tied to Our Lady of Pity and other images. He also objected to the exercise of aesthetic preferences in the veneration of one image rather than another.[4] The English canonist William Lyndewood (*c.* 1375–1446) was opposed to single images of All Saints, which seem to have become common by the fifteenth century.[5] One of the reasons for his disapproval of this image may have been that one version closely resembled representations of the Trinity (**49**, **124**, **168**).

To the worries about the appropriate use of images were added fears regarding their proliferation. '. . . meen doon makyn these dayis ymagys gret plente bothin cherche and out of cherche', observed the author of *Dives and Pauper*.[6] The same concerns were aired in the international forum of the Council of Constance in 1415–17. Leading reformers within European orthodox circles like Pierre d'Ailly and Henry of Langenstein expressed their concern that the multiplication of images in churches both encouraged idolatry and led to a lack of control over their use. It was not that indulgences and excesses of daily devotion were superstitious, but that they overwhelmed the fundamental tenets of the faith.[7]

Fear of the abuse of images therefore was far from being an insular phenomenon in the later Middle Ages. Nevertheless, *Dives and Pauper* and the writings of Pecock had a specifically English context. They were responses to an attack from a heretical sect and should be viewed as part of a concerted campaign by the Lancastrian episcopate under the leadership of Archbishop Chichele, whose purpose was the *renovatio* of orthodox public worship.[8]

The significance of the Lollards is hotly debated. Judicial interrogations with the flavour of the 'When did you stop beating your wife?' kind of question have imparted to those accused of this heresy a homogeneity of belief which does not reflect the various shades of opinion herded together under the Lollard label. None the less, even if Wycliffe himself were not implacably opposed to devotional images, a consistent strand of belief among his followers was an abhorrence of such things.[9] Lollard objections to images centred on their representing the worship of matter, especially the richly ornamented and expensive statues which presented to the people a travesty of the humility and poverty of the apostles. Objects of especial antipathy were the anthropomorphic rendering of the Holy Trinity (on the grounds that God belonged to a different order of being from mortals and therefore was unrepresentable) and cult images. In respect of images of the Trinity the Lollards merely echoed the criticisms voiced by theologians from the middle of the thirteenth century (**168**).[10] The most hostile elements within the movement did not shirk from acts of violence directed against images. The first recorded instance was at Leicester in the late fourteenth century and sporadic incidents occurred thereafter into the sixteenth century. The records are confined to a bare recital of the facts and do not illuminate the extent to which iconoclasm might be affected by local circumstances. In 1427 a Lollard parishioner of Bergh Apton (Norf.) and a companion from Loddon stole the titular saint from the nearby village of Trowse Newton and burnt it at Bergh Apton.[11] Why did they not select the patronal images from their own parish churches? As it happens, the alabaster patronal images of SS Peter and Paul from Bergh Apton survive (**56**); did the perpetrators stay their hands through fear of incurring the wrath of their orthodox fellow-parishioners?

*168. Alabaster Trinity, fifteenth century (London, Victoria & Albert Museum, inv. no. A 53-1946)*

Small in numbers the Lollards might have been, but they were characterized by both tenacity and elusiveness. Moreover, the persistence of Lollardy formed a bridge with the newer movements for reform emanating from the continent in the 1520s and 1530s.[12]

Destruction of images was by no means exclusively a heretical activity; it might be sanctioned by the Church from non-iconoclastic motives. The twelfth-century stone *sedes sapientiae* from York Minster was discovered after the fire of 1829 in the late fourteenth-century east wall of the Lady Chapel (**25**).[13] Its condition betrays signs of deliberate mutilation. Why was it considered necessary to deface it by removing the head of the Virgin and the upper half of Christ's body?

the history of the image might show that it was permissible for damaged or redundant images to be done away with. Or was it perhaps an example of rubble-filling after defacement in the Reformation period? Such utilitarianism perhaps marked an extreme and not all theologians advocated the destruction of discarded images.[14] The singularity of the wooden Langham Virgin and Child may not be solely due to wholesale destruction during the Reformation but because this type of Marian representation had long been considered obsolete (**IV**). As we have seen, wills and churchwardens' accounts abound with references to the repainting or repair of old images. Those which were no longer required might be put into store or passed on to another parish. In 1488 the London church of St Christopher-le-Stocks had a score of 'Olde Ymages' in its storehouse, including one of Our Lady in a tabernacle festooned with angels. A Wakefield (West Yorks.) testator left 3s 4d to the making of a new image of St Nicholas in his parish church and stipulated that the old one should be given to St John's church in the same town.[15]

Such acts were of course motivated by very different reasons from those which inspired Lollard and Tudor iconoclasts. Image-destruction under Henry VIII, Edward VI and Elizabeth I was in general carried out efficiently. It is easy to stigmatize the perpetrators, whether the instigators of the policy or its agents, as a mixture of mindless vandals, philistines and avaricious despoilers. From the art-historical perspective the scale of destruction of things of beauty during the Reformation can only be deplored. The work of centuries of craftsmanship was obliterated. Yet images did not enjoy an autonomous existence, endowed solely with aesthetic values as works of art and divorced from any other functional concern. Some iconoclasm must have resulted from opportunism or sheer pleasure in the act of destruction; in other cases it was no doubt a carefully considered process arising from sincerely held concerns about the use of images in worship. To reformers, they stood in the way of man's relation with God as manifested by the Word. Their effacement was part of the process of opening up this relationship through the use of the Bible and the prayerbook in the vernacular.[16]

The stages by which images were obliterated were far from smooth. The fate of images was sealed by fits and starts and reversals and counter-reversals of policy, the result of differing and sometimes conflicting ideologies. The legislative landmarks are clearly established, but in respect of images it is instructive to examine how the will of the State was translated into action at parish level.[17]

The churchwardens' accounts for the ancient Anglo-Saxon church at Wing (Bucks.) permit the process of religious change and counterchange in the locality to be followed in some detail.[18] The building exhibits more than one layer of imagery in a variety of media (**169**). On the soffits of the nave arches are traces of early thirteenth-century murals, of which only the Coronation of the Virgin is decipherable. Another Coronation exists in the tracery glazing of the south aisle east window, added in about 1300. A figure of St Lawrence was in the same window and the Perpendicular nave clerestory was glazed with the apostles. In proximity to another south aisle window was a mural of St George.[19] This imagery does not feature in the accounts and wills, but those items which were the focus of devotion do. In addition to the ubiquitous rood over the chancel screen, by the sixteenth century there was an unusual preponderance of female sacred personages. Our Lady was represented by several images, including one presumably located in the nave north aisle (dedicated to the Virgin), a *Pietà* and a Gesyn. At the east end of the nave south aisle was St Katherine's Chapel, no doubt the site of her image. Other images mentioned in wills and the churchwardens' accounts were those of SS Margaret, Mary Magdalen, John the Baptist and Thomas. To these can be added the patronal All Saints and chancel Marian image. The brackets and corbels for some of these images survive.

*169. Wing (Bucks.), All Saints' church: interior before the 1892–3 restoration*

The accounts open in 1527, in which year an inventory of the church's sacred vessels, vestments and liturgical paraphernalia was made. There were two designated lightmen for each of the rood, Our Lady, SS Katherine and Margaret and SS Mary Magdalen and Thomas, suggesting that the last two sets of images were paired by location. By the 1530s, therefore, Wing's stock of devotional images was evidently complete. In England as a whole there is no compelling evidence for a flood of image-making between the early sixteenth century and the proscribing of images, even if due allowance has to be made for the argument that wills show only the tip of the benefactory iceberg. Churchwardens' accounts are also an imperfect and incomplete tool for quantitative analysis of this kind, but few refer to the commissioning of new images in this period. That this was not universally the case is shown by the Devonshire parish of Morebath. Among the new images here was one of St George: England's patronal saint is the one saint represented by numerous new images in the 1520s and 1530s (**XIII**).[20] A St George at Olney in 1534 and an Assumption of the Virgin at Chesham (1523) are the only new images mentioned in the archdeaconry of Buckingham wills between 1483 and 1540. In the neighbouring archdeaconry of Bedford for the same period there are also mentions of a mere two, both of the Virgin, for Campton church and the Bedford Franciscan friary.[21] In the much larger county of Kent the figures are healthier, with testamentary references to twenty-one new images between 1510 and 1547. When these statistics are taken into account, the activities at Morebath, where a total of three new images and a new rood were commissioned between 1520 and 1539, appear as the exception rather than the rule.[22] This is not to imply that image-use had run its course by the early sixteenth century – bequests to existing images suggest otherwise. The lack of new commissions might merely reflect the fact that churches were content with their existing complement. New images might be absent from the accounts and wills of Wing, but some of those already in place were embellished after 1527. In 1535–6 ironwork and other adjustments to the rood loft and rood were undertaken; also rings and ribbon for the curtain before Our Lady in Gesyn were purchased and made up by Anne Buckmaster. Two years later, a tabernacle for another image of the Virgin was carved from a bequest of 20s.[23] To use the provision of new images (or the lack of it) as a measure of the strength of lay religious fervour on the eve of the Reformation is problematic. As we have seen, image culture was a complex mixture of diverse elements, in which the devotional is inseparable from Baxandall's secular satisfactions and Duffy's social consensus.[24]

Isolated and unsanctioned attacks on images had already begun by the time the Wing accounts commence and had spread to London within a decade. Urban centres were the principal locations of these activities, but they also occurred in the countryside. An early instance took place in the Lollard stronghold of the Chiltern Hills, in the village of Rickmansworth. Here in 1522 some of the parishioners indulged in image-burning, which resulted in the razing of the chancel of the church.[25] News of the events surrounding Henry VIII's attempts to divorce Katherine of Aragon, which precipitated the crisis between England and Rome, must have filtered through to Wing, as the proceedings were heard at Dunstable in 1533. This too, like the Supremacy Act of the following year, is unlikely to have affected the tenor of religious life in the parish as no doctrinal matters were involved, although already preachers against 'traditional religion' were becoming active. Soon after, the dissolution of the monasteries in the vicinity of Wing was under way. The small Benedictine nunnery at Ivinghoe was the first to go, in 1536, followed by the larger houses at Ashridge, Dunstable and Woburn, the last accompanied by the execution of its abbot. The Wing churchwardens were not slow to profit from the Woburn tragedy, for in 1538–9 they paid £9 for the abbey's organs and other ornaments, plus an entire window and its transportation. Already, however, Henry VIII's government had started the attack on religion as practised in Wing and every other parish. The brief of the visitors appointed to examine the smaller monasteries included their function as pilgrimage sites. Images began to enter the frame in June 1536, when Bishop Latimer preached a sermon before Convocation in which he denounced shrines, relics, the cult of the saints, the proliferation of saints' days and the worship of images. July and August of the same year saw the publication firstly of the Ten Articles and then of what was to be the first of a series of royal Injunctions, which marked the first official pronouncements of the reign on the subject of devotional images. The Articles included this statement on images:

they [images] may be representers of virtue and good example, . . . and make men often remember and lament their sins and offences, especially the images of Christ and our lady and that therefore it is meet that they should stand in the churches, and none otherwise to be esteemed: And as for censing of them, and kneeling and offering unto them, with other like worshippings . . . the people ought to be diligently taught that they in no ways do it, nor think it meet to be done to the same images, but only to be done to God, and in his honour, although it be done before the images, whether it be of Christ, of the cross, or of our lady, or of any other saint beside.[26]

The tone was mild, reiterating the ancient distinction between *latria* and *idolatria*, although it was also observed that the abuse of images, i.e. idolatry, had led to iconoclasm. Other articles permitted praying to the saints, but pilgrimage was omitted entirely, including therefore cult images. This subject was addressed in the Injunctions (the work of Thomas Cromwell) in very hostile terms. The clergy were urged not to 'set forth or extol any images, relics, or miracles . . . nor allure the people by any enticements to the pilgrimage of any saint'. Instead of undertaking pilgrimages and making offerings to shrines and miraculous images, the laity should give alms to the poor and needy.[27] Any Wing parishioners who had a penchant for pilgrimage would have been affected by this, whereas the village community as a whole would have felt the impact of the instruction to the clergy to implement a recent Convocation edict abolishing a number of saints' days, on the grounds that they stemmed from superstition. That the State's disapproval of images was beginning to have an effect in the parishes is suggested by the fact that the making in 1537–8 of the tabernacle of Our Lady at Wing is the last reference to the enhancement of an image in the entire archdeaconry of Buckingham, with the sole exception of a bequest of 12d to the repair of the patronal image of St Cecilia at Adstock. Similarly, after 1538–9 no new images appear to have been

170. Stone mould for pilgrim badge of John Schorn, fifteenth – early sixteenth century (Ashmolean Museum, Oxford)

introduced into any of the sixteen rural and urban parishes with surviving accounts in the diocese of Exeter.[28]

Soon afterwards, words turned to actions and the destruction of pilgrimage sites and cult images began, not only in the monasteries but also in parish churches. The suppression of the greater houses, which boasted the majority of these reviled objects, began in 1537. The spring and summer saw the removal and incineration of such revered cult images as the Rood of Boxley and Our Ladies of Walsingham, Ipswich and Caversham. The last was the nearest major Marian site to Wing; almost on the doorstep was Our Lady of Bradwell, whose fate after the monastery had been suppressed by Wolsey in 1524 is uncertain (**XXIII**; **135**).[29] Equally accessible was the miraculous image of John Schorn at North Marston. This was a parochial image which had been substituted for the relics themselves when they were translated to St George's Chapel, Windsor, in 1478–80, with no apparent decline in popularity of the site where he had served as vicar (**170**). This cult image too went in 1538.[30]

The winds of change were now indeed blowing close to Wing. After the issuing of another set of royal Injunctions in September 1538, they blew directly and with greater force on every parish in the land. These Injunctions were far more radical than anything that had gone before.

Not only was the acquisition and emplacement in the church of a Bible in English by Easter 1539 made compulsory, but all 'feigned' images in parish churches which were the object of pilgrimage were to be removed. More significant for Wing, which housed no image like that of Master Schorn, was the instruction that, from now onwards, 'no candles, tapers, or images of wax [were] to be set afore any image or picture but only the light . . . by the rood-loft, the light before the sacrament of the altar, and the light about the sepulchre'.[31] Images in general were attacked as lacking scriptural authority, but the position adopted was akin to (and influenced by) that of the Lutherans, for it was only abused images which were to be removed. Even here there was ambiguity, for the Injunctions did not stipulate their destruction.[32] In Wing the images of Our Lady and of the saints evidently were suffered to remain, but from this time the keepers of their lights and the receipts vanish from the accounts. Nor were the churchwardens tardy when it came to acquiring an English Bible, purchased in 1539–40. The first Wing will after the publication of these Injunctions, that of Thomas Adam in April 1540, makes no mention of any lights at all. In 1535–6 Nicholas Buckmaster, yeoman, had been one of the churchwardens under whose supervision the rood had been enriched; his wife had provided board and lodging to the workmen and with her own hand she had made up the curtain hanging before the image of Our Lady in Gesyn. What were Nicholas's thoughts when he came to compose his will on 1 March 1544–5, a will which, in conformity with the new order, referred to no image lights and only to the sacrament light?[33]

The speed with which Wing complied with the new Injunctions is echoed within the archdeaconry of Buckingham as a whole. Here bequests to lights before all images save the rood, the sacrament of the altar and the Sepulchre cease from 1539. Nor was this out of line with the rest of the country. In the Salisbury diocese too, bequests to lights dropped steeply after 1539. Between then and 1541 only 13 per cent of wills outside Salisbury mentioned lights, compared with 35 per cent between 1500 and 1538. In Salisbury itself the change was even more dramatic, with the percentage falling from 50 per cent to nil – no doubt a consequence of the presence of the reforming Bishop Shaxton.[34]

Almost as soon as the tide of radical reform flowed into the parishes of England, it began to ebb. Fear of sparking social discontent and encouraging even more extreme opinions in matters religious led to a more temperate policy, possibly connected with Cromwell's fall and execution in 1540. While the destruction of cult images and pilgrimage sites continued until all had gone, the more conservative official agenda manifested itself in the issuing in 1543 of what became known as the *King's Book*, a revision of the 1537 *Bishop's Book*. Idolatry was still condemned, yet by omission it allowed that images might be venerated through gestures like kneeling, bowing and kissing. This shift seems to have been the king's personal will and represented a retreat from the Lutheran position on images. The *King's Book*, together with the Six Articles of 1539, set the tone for the rest of the reign. It is impossible to measure from the ledgers of income and expenditure for these years whether the redrawn official line had any practical effect in Wing. The new policy was far from turning back the clock completely, for the lighting of candles and tapers before all images save the rood (also the sacrament and Sepulchre) was still forbidden. There is no evidence of any transgression in this matter in Wing. An indication that images had been partly restored to favour in some parishes in the locality is suggested by William Ashwell's will of February 1544–5, in which he stipulated burial before the image of Our Lady in Totternhoe (Beds.) church. The image probably stood on one of the two brackets near the respond at the east end on the nave north aisle which is carved with an angel bearing a shield with the Ashwell rebus (**171**).[35] Ashwell belonged to a leading family in the parish which had been responsible for the rebuilding of the nave north aisle, so he can be considered to have had a stake in the building. None the less, it is significant that, although an isolated instance, it marked the first image-burial in the Bedford archdeaconry since 1539–40. In the diocese of Norwich Stephen Bolte was very aware of the uncertain times in which he lived. In 1546 he requested burial before Our Lady of Pity in his parish church of Sco

*171. Totternhoe (Beds.), St Giles's church: image brackets and Ashwell family rebus at the east end of the nave north aisle*

Ruston and made provision for a quarter of wax to burn at service-time in his chantry, adding the prudent caveat 'as long as the Kyngs lawes wyll suffer'.[36] And well he might, because the dissolution of the chantries was already in hand.

The accession of Edward VI marked the beginnings of the most radical religious policy yet seen. Not only was the position adopted in the last years of his father's reign reversed, but the new line went far beyond anything seen in the 1530s and even surpassed reformist zeal in Zürich and Strasbourg, where donors of images and altarpieces and their descendants were permitted to claim them when the churches in which they stood were cleansed.[37] From the outset images were a focus of attack. A country-wide visitation took place almost immediately, with its brief defined by a set of Injunctions based on those of 1536 and 1538, but with some highly significant amendments. The clauses dealing with images and relics were given greater prominence by being placed first. Among these was an order to the parochial clergy not only to remove but explicitly to destroy abused images. This was a step further than Henry VIII had ever gone, for it sanctioned organized iconoclasm at parish level and encompassed murals and stained glass – and even ordered the clergy to urge their flocks to do likewise within the privacy of their houses. Non-abused images were still to be tolerated, no longer by reason of the Gregorian didactic formulation but solely 'to be a remembrance, whereby men may be admonished of the holy lives and conversation of them that that the said images do represent'. Thus all externalized gestures of devotion like kissing, kneeling and embellishing of images, as well as lights, were proscribed. Furthermore, lights before the rood, sacrament and Sepulchre were now forbidden.[38]

The visitors also put two questions about images to the parish clergy. One asked if any 'misused' images still remained in their churches; the second enquired as to whether they had instructed their parishioners in the commemorative function of images 'and have taught that if the said people use the images for any other purpose, they commit idolatry, to the great danger of their souls'.[39]

The application of these questions and the Injunctions resulted in the widespread destruction of imagery in all media, but there remained a problem with the definition of what constituted a 'misused' image. Unequivocally, it encompassed cult images, but the second question could also be interpreted as giving *carte blanche* to the removal and destruction of images which were wrongly used by the laity. Both opponents and defenders of images cited the instructions in support of their respective positions. The confusion was clarified before the end of 1547, with the official order to remove all images in London; the instruction was extended to the rest of the country in February of the following year by Archbishop Cranmer. Shrewdly, the moment selected for compliance was Lent, when images were concealed from sight by shrouds, 'in partye of pennaunce and in tokene that meen in Lentoun shuldyn wytdrawyn hem from lykyngge of eye. . .'.[40] The contentiousness of the issue is demonstrated by the fact that only removal, not destruction, was mentioned; also that 'the same may be quietly done with as good satisfaction of the people as may be'.[41]

The State campaign against images continued after the introduction of the Book of Common Prayer, with its excision of any reference to the intercessory powers of the few saints permitted to remain in the Calendar. In January 1550 Parliament ordered that individuals who possessed 'anye Images of Stone Tymbre Alleblaster or Earthe graven carved or paynted, which heretofore have bene taken out of anye Churche or Chappell, or yet stande in any Churche or Chappell, and doe not before the laste daye of June next ensuynge deface and destroye or cause to be defaced and distroyed the same Images' would first be fined and subsequently imprisoned. The sole exclusions were images on sepulchral monuments, although in practice they did not always escape removal or mutilation (**172**).[42]

The Wing accounts reveal the impact of these dramatic events. The last entries for the receipts of the rood and Sepulchre lights appear in 1546–7. In the following year the churchwardens attended the visitation at Aylesbury and two meetings of the chapter court. Among their costs was that of 'our byll makyng' – presumably the successive government orders which were to be implemented. The Book of Common Prayer (the 'churche boke') was purchased at a cost of 4*s* 2*d*. A possible reference to the effacing of the imagery in wall-painting is contained in the payment for 'whyt lymyng of the churche'. This certainly occurred in 1550–1, when 16*d* was paid for 'wasshyng out of ye dome in ye rode loft'. In the same year the high altar and the altars of Our Lady and St Katherine were taken down in compliance with an order of November 1550 and replaced by a Communion table, made for the modest outlay of 4*d*. A copy of the prescribed *Homilies*, a series of sermons to be read on Sundays by the clergy, was also obtained. These had been composed variously by Cranmer and some of the more conservative bishops in the early 1540s, which explains why, although preaching the reformed doctrine of justification by faith alone, they had little to say about images.[43] The costs of these acquisitions and the alterations to the fabric were defrayed from the proceeds of the sale of church goods in 1548–9, which had realized £16 2*s*, and the more modest, but for our purposes more significant, 4*s* from the disposal of the gilding from the images in the following year. This entry shows that part of the process of removing, defacing and ultimately destroying the images involved the careful stripping of whatever was recyclable. This was not an unusual practice. The last explicit entries concerning the religious changes of this phase of the Reformation occur in 1552–3, when the new and more radical Book of Common Prayer was obtained.[44] This omitted all references to the saints that had appeared in the 1549 Communion service, although even in the earlier text they were not invoked, only acknowledged for the example of their holy lives. Moreover, in the 1552 version the Decalogue was introduced into the Communion service, led by the commandment against graven images.[45]

Wing demonstrates the problems of trying to read the Reformation from churchwardens' accounts. These do not suggest any foot-dragging by the parish officials in the adoption of the outward signs of the new dispensation. However, this is one of the few parishes where the apparently smooth process of change and acceptance of that change can be tested by additional evidence. Notwithstanding the conformist phraseology of the will of Sir Robert Dormer (d. 1552), lord of Wing, it is clear that he was opposed to the religious changes. His granddaughter Lady Jane Dormer, who married into a Spanish noble family, recalled her upbringing as a member of the village's seigneurial family:

> I was born in such a time when Holy Mass was in great reverence, and brought up in the same Faith. In King Edward's time this reverence was neglected and reproved by such as governed. In Queen Mary's it was restored with much applause.[46]

Nor could the incumbent to be relied upon by the authorities. John Holyman, who had entered the living in 1546 as the appointee of Sir Robert Dormer, was a former monk of Reading Abbey and had opposed Henry VIII's divorce from Katherine of Aragon. Soon after Mary's accession he became Bishop of Bristol.[47]

To what extent the views of the Dormers and Holyman were shared by the ordinary parishioners of Wing is impossible to gauge. The two surviving villagers' wills for Edward VI's reign give no indications of resistance to

172. Dean (Beds.), All Saints' church: brass of rector Thomas Parker (d. 1501) (note indent for missing image of the Virgin and Child)

the new order. Richard Holden left his soul to Almighty God, his maker and redeemer, and the only pious bequests were to Lincoln Cathedral and the high altar of Wing church for tithes negligently forgotten. John Fountain's testament merely left his soul to Almighty God and made no bequests to Wing church.[48] Yet in the country as a whole, the Dormers and John Holyman were far from isolated in their views. Buckinghamshire was one of the counties where riots against the 1549 Prayer Book occurred. Holyman's Yorkshire counterpart Robert Parkyn deplored the dismantling of traditional religious practices, including the use of images and lights, and excoriated the Edwardian reformers as 'vilanus persons'.[49] The Chichester diocese was noted for its conservatism, so it is no surprise to find that in 1549–50 Richard Awdeby made his sympathies clear when he desired to be interred 'dyrectly under the defacyde Image of the Assumpcyon of Our Lady, at theste end of Our Lady Chapel' in Chichester Cathedral. Five years later the vicar of Yapton in similar fashion directed his body to be buried in the chancel of his parish church 'afore the place wher the image of Our Ladye dyd stand'.[50]

The accession of Mary I in July 1553 marked an abrupt reversal in matters religious. Far from being a short-lived blip in the inevitable progress of the Reformation, historians for the most part now accept that the restoration of the Catholic faith in Mary's reign had extensive support; it was not reactionary and might well have endured, had the queen not died so soon.[51] The Repeal Acts of 1553 and 1554 successively annulled the Edwardian legislation *inter alia* on images and turned the ecclesiastical clock back to 1529.[52] An important element in the Marian *renovatio* was the reintroduction of images. Many parishes did not wait for official legislation to re-establish the Mass and the trappings of traditional worship. Wing bought a missal and had a chalice and corporal (cloth used during Mass) hallowed in the first year of the reign. The rebuilding initially of the high altar and then of the secondary altars was followed by the erection of the Sepulchre. Making good and replacing the losses of the previous reign was a slow process, however, and in respect of images priority had to be given to installing the basics. The rood was set up in its loft at Wing in 1556–7, at a cost of 29s 1d.[53] In many dioceses (including Lincoln, to which Wing belonged), it was also a requirement to reinstate the patronal image. In the diocese of Gloucester the rood was to be 5ft high and the patronal image to be of proportionate size. All the images were to be of wood or stone and not merely painted on cloth or board. This was not a universal requirement – or proved difficult to enforce, as Archdeacon Harpsfield's Kent visitations showed.[54] There is no reference to the patronal image of All Saints at Wing in either the accounts or wills, although this omission is not necessarily conclusive.

The frequent annotations in Harpsfield's visitation records indicate that much of the obligatory work had not been done, showing that precept was one thing, practice another. Even where images were reinstalled, it was not always easy to enforce the stipulations regarding size and materials.[55] The costs of the new images in Kent reveal the modest scale of the enterprise. Peter of Appledore was paid 33s 4d for the four images (three for the rood and the patronal saint) he carved for Newendon. The rood group at Strood cost 29s 6d, excluding the timber, and the mitre and crozier of the patronal saint came to 4s. The Smarden expenditure was similar: 27s 8d for the rood figures and 20s for the patronal saint; Gyllam's four figures for Bethersden amounted to 53s 4d, with a further 18d for carriage.[56] These figures were pretty standard outside London, for Martyn the carver was paid 40s for the rood and its 'appurtenaunces' at Ashburton (Devon) in 1555–6. The rood group at Thame (Oxon.) came to 18s, with a further 3s 4d paid to the painter in part-payment; 2s was also disbursed for painting the image of Our Lady.[57] Costs could be higher in the capital: the churchwardens of St Mary at Hill had to pay £7 for the rood images and 26s 8d for the patronal image, with a further 5s for the latter's tabernacle. The price of the first was the same as that laid out by the churchwardens of Morebath in 1539 on a new rood, exclusive of gilding. It is small beer compared with the £27 given by Agnes Breten for painting and gilding the patronal tabernacle alone nearly seventy years previously.[58]

It has been argued that the restoration of patronal images was consistent with current continental counter-reforming attitudes to religious imagery and was not simply a restoration of the old order.[59] The focus on the rood and the absence of any mention of the plethora of saints whose images previously filled Wing and countless other churches could indeed support this suggestion; it is also true that the Marian primers placed less emphasis on the role of the saints.[60] But is a representation of the titular saint a sign of the Counter-Reformation? The status of this image in the later Middle Ages might have varied from parish to parish, but it was embedded in the customs and social fabric of each community; in these circumstances Marian insistence on its reintroduction may be more of a deliberate *renovatio*, indicating a desire to forge a link of continuity with what was still familiar to many, rather than a self-conscious attempt to promote a new kind of Catholicism.

As in the case of the two testators of Edward's reign, it is impossible to measure the attitudes of the Wing parishioners from the nine or ten wills made in the time of his successor. Only three testators reverted to the ancient medieval preamble, leaving their soul to Almighty God, their only maker and redeemer, the blessed Virgin Mary and the holy company of heaven.[61] One of them (Thomas Wells) bequeathed 20*d* to the rood light. Too much significance cannot be placed on this, for Richard Daulton, one of the parishioners who merely bequeathed their souls to Almighty God, left a similar sum to purchase a candlestick for the high altar. Several other testators left sums of money to the church for unspecified purposes.[62]

Whether the Marian Injunctions represented merely an expedient first stage and were intended to be followed by the reinstatement of the full complement of pre-Edwardian images will never be known, for the accession of the queen's half-sister Elizabeth in November 1558 brought to an end the attempt to reestablish the Roman Catholic faith as the official religion in England. The Elizabethan Injunctions and Articles of 1559 signified a tempering of the later Edwardian instructions in respect of images, with a return to an earlier emphasis on abuse. Moreover, although destruction of images in glass and wall-painting as well as sculpture was once again exhorted, churchwardens were also instructed to make good any consequent damage to the fabric of their churches. In 1559–60, the year which saw the acquisition of the new Book of Common Prayer, 7*d* was spent by the Wing churchwardens on 'takynge down of the rode'. In other respects, however, the parish was slow to comply with the new Injunctions. The churchwardens were in trouble in 1561–2 for 'slacknes of our auters'. The same year the south altar was removed and a Communion table purchased. It seems, however, that the high altar stone was not displaced until the following year, when the rood loft was also taken down.[63] This reluctance to dispense with the old order is not surprising. Holyman's successor as incumbent lasted less than a year and he was followed by George Cotton, who held the living until 1562; both were presented by Sir Robert Dormer's widow and so were likely to have shared Holyman's opinions and supported the Marian restoration of traditional religion. The last reference to the effects of the Reformation on the fabric of Wing church is in 1564, when Harry Ward was paid for 'wytyng the cherche'.[64]

The new queen showed herself to be less extreme than Edward in the matter of images and continued to use a crucifix in the chapel royal. Her inclinations had consequences in the country at large for the retention of the rood. While many roods, like Wing's, had been destroyed immediately after Elizabeth came to the throne, others evidently remained. The position was resolved in October 1561, when a Royal Order instructed that rood lofts, and by implication the roods themselves, were to be taken down. None the less, in some areas this instruction was only slowly implemented: some Lincolnshire parishes only destroyed their roods in 1566 and others survived even longer. In the remote Holderness district in the East Riding of Yorkshire a visitation in 1567–8 revealed that many of the parishes were clinging to the old ways, including retention of images.[65]

Destruction extended beyond altars and images to the tabernacles and the corbels and bases on which the latter had stood. This was a simple matter for the wooden supports and frames, which have disappeared virtually without trace from England's churches. Some bishops even insisted on the removal of stone corbels and supports. In the words of Bishop Guest of Rochester, there should be 'no place or case where any images did stand which be not made smooth as though no such image had ever been there'.[66] The dearth of surviving supports in the Rochester diocese and in others where such a policy was enunciated shows that it could be prosecuted with zeal. At South Newington (Oxon.) in 1563 a mason received 5d 'for pollynge stones in the churche where images dyd stand'.[67] The tabernacle of Our Lady carved for Wing in 1537–8 was destroyed, but the several stone brackets still in this and many other churches in the Lincoln diocese suggest that this policy was not always applied so ruthlessly; as so often, much depended on the prevailing opinion within each parish.

The Reformation had devastating consequences for everyone engaged in production for the Church: carvers, painters, glass-painters, embroiderers, goldsmiths and masons alike. Just at the moment when imports and products of the domiciled foreign carvers had brought new kinds of imagery into England and, in some of the major centres, their English peers had achieved a new status, their craft was brought to ruin. The results can be seen in the statistics for admission of Freemen at York: in the years between 1513 and 1542 twenty-six carvers and one alabasterman became Freemen, but none in the following thirty years; a similar picture of abrupt cessation of work can be traced in glass-painting.[68] Although there is evidence that craftsmen in Kent under Queen Mary re-established themselves on the old late medieval pattern in towns servicing their hinterland, even here there were problems in finding sufficient artisans to fulfil commissions. The parish of Goudhurst had to turn to the Ashford carver after the craftsman with whom it had originally made an agreement had fled abroad.[69] The Marian restoration of the old order was too short-lived to restore the popularity of religious imagery, and therefore the fortunes of its creators. A satirical tale in a book of jests published in 1590 reveals the straits in which image-makers found themselves after the removal and wholesale destruction of Elizabeth's reign:

> Whereupon, the painters that lived with such trash, as trimming of shrines and roods, altars and saints, and the carvers, that made such images, were fain . . . to cry out against Paul and his doctrine; having so little work, that they almost forgot their occupation.[70]

The impact on carving in England was catastrophic. Lawrence Stone has observed that the history of medieval sculpture in England was 'cut off sharp'. More than this, it removed the craft of carving from the forefront of visual production and, except for sepulchral monuments, reduced it to the status of architectural ornamentation. Arguably, it was not until the eighteenth century that English sculpture would reclaim its former eminence.[71]

Despite the presence of the recusant Dormer overlords and their appointed incumbents, there is nothing in the written sources to suggest that efforts were made to retain the Wing images, nor do any survive.[72] Two of Wing's adjacent parishes preserve images. At Newton Longville a stone female saint, almost certainly the patronal St Faith, was placed on a corbel on the exterior east wall, close to the original internal emplacement. The alabaster images of Our Lady and St James the Greater were found in 1862 concealed in the base of the window over the chancel arch in the Norman church at Stewkley (**55**). None of the three images has suffered any noticeable defacement, suggestive of deliberate preservation for more sympathetic times, although the precise circumstances of such actions are irrecoverable. Perhaps the removal of St Faith at Newton Longville was considered a sufficient means of disempowerment.[73] Here were artefacts which in the eyes of the concealer might have remained active. The only known instance of the retention of a rood in the Bedfordshire/Buckinghamshire area is at Cranfield (Beds.), where the 18ft-high upright of the cross survived as late as the early eighteenth century, although the motives behind the preservation of only this part are unclear.[74] Elsewhere the material and written evidence is sufficiently numerous and widely scattered around the country to suggest that in rural areas at least images were only removed with the greatest reluctance. The churchwardens' accounts of Morebath (Devon) are explicit about this. Various parishioners 'lyke good catholyke men' hid the rood figures and appendages of the patronal St George from Edward VI's commissioners, only to return them to the church after Mary's accession. Instances of concealment also occurred well into the reign of her successor. At Scaldwell, a Northamptonshire parish, in 1581

> were founde sartayne images and other monuments of poperye, that ys to say ye pycture of Chryst callyd ye roode, ye picture of Saynt Peter [joint patron saint with St Paul], both of wood undefaced, the pycture of ye Trinitye and ye pycture of saynt Mudwyn [Modwen] wt hyr cowe standyng by her both of alabaster undefaced. . . .

The images were not in the church, but the 'towne howse'.[75] Resistance to the new order in the diocese of Chichester led Archbishop Parker's commissioners to complain that: 'They have yet in this diocese in many places images hidden up and other popish ornaments, ready to be sett up for mass again within 24 hours' warning; as in the town of Battell and in the parish of Lindfield.'[76] The discovery of alabaster images other than St John's heads, which were commonly used in domestic contexts, in private dwellings also points to attempts to hold on to what was proscribed by the legislation of Edward VI and treated more leniently under Elizabeth.[77] The concealment of the patronal images of SS Peter and Paul in a cottage fireplace at Bergh Apton (Norf.) was an ironic reversal of events a century before, when the patronal image from a neighbouring church was burned by Lollards in the village (**56**).[78] The three Flawford (Notts.) alabaster images were preserved intact below the chancel floor (**54**). The find location of the freestone enthroned Virgin at Waltham Abbey (Essex) is equally significant. Although headless and with the Christ-Child entirely effaced, it was laid out in a medieval cemetery with every indication of a formal and reverential interment. The image was laid facing upwards on the standard east–west axis and was enclosed by carefully laid rubble.[79]

Other images have survived because they served utilitarian purposes, like the stone Assumption relief pressed into use as paving for the porch at Sandford-on-Thames (Oxon.) (**102**). In such instances there can be no doubt that their preservation was unconnected with any religious attachments to them. The very battered Totternhoe stone images of the Virgin and Our Lady of Pity at Tilsworth, near Wing, were mutilated by the removal of the heads and upper body parts of the Virgin. Many other images which emerged during the Victorian vogue for church restoration are also defaced. Such damage cannot be attributed solely to post-

Reformation vicissitudes. The three fine fourteenth-century polychromed heads at Cobham in Kent show unmistakable signs of systematic damage (**XIX**). Noses and chins are chipped and the heads have been severed from the lost torsos by a clean break, either by a stonesaw or by a blow, although there are no marks of a heavy blunt instrument. The evidence suggests that defacement of the more durable images was as ritualistic as the burning of the celebrated wooden cult images and was designed to deprive them of their lifelike attributes. Indeed, the 1550 Act specified that images were to be defaced and destroyed.[80]

More ambiguous are the alabaster figures of the Virgin and the *Pietà* at Blunham (Beds.) and the Trinity at Upton (Berks.) (**IX, VII; 155**); all had been decapitated but were discovered in their respective churches during Victorian restorations. During the 1960s stone images of the Trinity and St Margaret were discovered walled up respectively in a piscina and niche at Fingringhoe (Essex). The former had been decapitated but the head was still with the body. St Margaret had lost the upper part of its head and the body had been broken. However, it had been reassembled and replaced carefully in its niche, but reversed, all of which is suggestive of a desire for preservation (**X**).[81] Is the concentration of surviving alabaster images in several Cambridgeshire churches purely fortuitous, or does it indicate a concerted attempt at deliberate concealment and preservation after the obligatory mutilation?[82] Alabaster is not as durable as freestone for wall- or floor-packing. These and some of the other examples cited here represent both ends of the sixteenth-century spectrum, signifying simultaneously the efficiency of the Tudor State in ensuring that images were deprived of their meaning (by displacement and mutilation) and, through their preservation, popular resistance to the religious ideology of that State. For those who preserved these images, even if their animate features had been destroyed, the representations retained their *virtu*. The Blunham, Upton and Fingringhoe images were perhaps saved from total destruction in the hope that one day they would be re-empowered through renovation, reinstatement, reconsecration and veneration.

A sense of proportion has to be retained with the *membra disjecta*. Leaving aside the considerable numbers of images painted on walls and piers which have been uncovered from below whitewash or layers of plaster, the total number of carved devotional images which have been recovered would scarcely have matched the complement of a handful of late medieval parish churches. Less than a dozen carved devotional images have survived from the Bedford and Buckingham archdeaconries, of either freestone or alabaster – there are none of wood, the most common but also the most destructible of materials. This is but a minute fraction of the more than five hundred images mentioned in the early Tudor wills from these counties, which themselves are far from constituting a complete inventory. In the enormous scale of destruction England distanced itself from the more tolerant Lutheran attitude to images, which resulted in their preservation in many churches in Germany and Scandinavia.[83]

The passage of time and the transformations of ritual practice have removed the visual traces of the progress of the Reformation (or Reformations) at Wing. The new dispensation might have removed and destroyed the images and other trappings of the old ways, but it shared with traditional religion an acknowledgement of the power of the visual. We saw that Wing church was whitewashed at the outset of Edward VI's reign and again in 1564. The application of whitewash erased not only the painted images but also the memory of them. This did not mean *all* imagery, only that which was offensive through attracting devotion. The St George mural and much of the nave glazing of Wing survived until at least the early eighteenth century.[84]

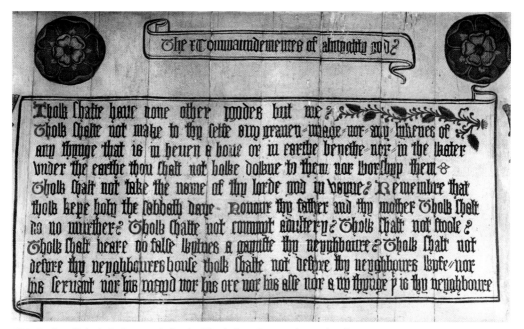

173. Ludlow (Salop), St Lawrence's church: Elizabethan Commandments board

Elsewhere in Buckinghamshire and Bedfordshire painted images on the dados of roodscreens remain to this day – including North Crawley (**60**) and Marston Moreteyne, two of the churches examined in this book – although in far fewer numbers than in East Anglia and Devon. In some places, word quite literally supplanted the pictorial in the form of admonitory biblical texts. As early as 1547 the phrase 'Thou shalt make no graven images, lest thou worship them' was inscribed on the walls of a London church. In Elizabeth's reign it was mandatory for churches to display tables of the Ten Commandments, in which the second – against images – featured prominently (**173**). These were to be erected at the east end of the chancel, in the places formerly occupied by the patronal saint and image of Our Lady. A set dating from about 1570 can still be seen painted on the wall replacing the former medieval high altar reredos in St John the Baptist's church, Bristol, and a few more recent examples have also survived Tractarian zeal and remain in this location (**174**).[85]

In 1559 Robert Norton of Streatley, near Luton, left 20 shillings to newly paint his parish church 'with texts of scripture in English, if it by the laws of England may be suffered'.[86] Wing retains no traces of such texts. In the late sixteenth century a bright spark at Marsworth (Bucks.) decided to exploit the text/location relationship by painting on a redundant image niche the vernacular verses of Psalm 43, which included verse 3: 'O send out thy light and thy truth; let them lead me; let them bring me unto thy holy hill, and to thy tabernacles.'[87] Further to the south-west the parish church of St Mary at Radnage, set in a remote and beautiful valley in the Buckinghamshire Chilterns, is a rare instance where the archaeology of the Reformation survives.[88] Apart from the Annunciation and other wall-paintings on the chancel east wall (**33**), executed shortly after the building of the church in the early thirteenth century, the major emphasis of the surviving mural decoration is textual. As visitors enter the church they are confronted immediately by the traces of a monumental fifteenth-century St Christopher in its

*174. Stragglethorpe (Lincs.), St Michael's church: chancel east end with nineteenth-century Commandments boards*

usual position on the north wall. Most of the image is overpainted by framed texts of the Lord's Prayer, Creed and Ten Commandments (**175**). These date from the eighteenth century and are accompanied by several layers of other texts executed variously between the mid-sixteenth and seventeenth centuries. Over the chancel arch, where the rood formerly stood, are fragments of another set of Commandments, and among others in the earliest layer, probably dating from either Edward VI's reign or the first years of the Elizabethan settlement, are biblical texts justifying the new order:

> I exhort, therefore, that, first of all, supplications, prayers, intercessions, and giving of thanks be made for all men;
>
> For kings and for all that are in authority; that we may lead a quiet and peaceable life in all godliness and honesty.
>
> For this is good and acceptable in the sight of God our Saviour;
>
> Who will have all men to be saved, and to come unto the knowledge of the truth.
>
> For there is one God, and one mediator between God and men, the man Jesus Christ (I Timothy, II, vv. 1–5).

Here at Radnage the saintly intercessors were not just denied, they were physically erased by the words of the Bible. The imageless new order was spelt out further by the well-known texts from Exodus XX ('Thou shalt not make unto thee any graven image', etc. – painted over St Christopher and the rood) and Habbakuk, II, vv. 18–20:

*175. Radnage (Bucks.), St Mary's church: nave north wall with St Christopher mural partly overpainted by post-Reformation texts*

What profiteth the graven image that the maker thereof hath graven it; the molten image, and a teacher of lies, that the maker of his work trusteth therein, to make dumb idols?
Woe unto him that saith to the wood, Awake; to the dumb stone: Arise, it shall teach!
Behold it is laid over with gold and silver, and there is no breath at all in the midst of it.
But the Lord is in his holy temple: let all the earth keep silence before him.

The nave walls of Radnage bear witness to the supplanting of medieval image by reformist word. For the illiterate parishioners the texts could be committed to memory from the words of the

*176. Hillesden (Bucks.), All Saints' church: Denton arms painted on the site of the patronal image*

parson and underlined by the *Homilies* (reissued with additions, including a new text on Idolatry, in Elizabeth's reign) and admonitions in the Book of Common Prayer.

The reference to kings and authority in the Pauline epistle to Timothy is a recurrent element in church mural texts. This emphasis on secular power is connected with the monarch's role as Supreme Head or Governor of the Church of England, but it also buttressed by means of biblical authority those who ruled at parish level, i.e. the manorial lords and the clergy. 'Obey them that have ye rule over you' exhorts the text painted on the chancel east wall, on the site formerly occupied by the image of Our Lady, at Thornage (Norf.). Was the choice of location fortuitous, or did it signify that the spiritual domain formerly ruled by the saintly 'dukes and leaders' was now unequivocally that of the secular lords? In the magnificent Perpendicular parish church at Hillesden in north Buckinghamshire the arms of the Dentons are painted on the wall above the bracket for the patronal saint (**176**).

After the upheavals of the mid-sixteenth century the parishes of England, whether reluctantly, enthusiastically or indifferently (or all three), gradually came to accept the new order. In Wing memories of the old ways would have faded until they vanished. To adapt Bishop Latimer's hard-headed logic, just as the presence of images argued that the saints were efficacious, so their removal argued them not to be.[89] The Reformation broke the ties that bound the saint to *locus* and *locus* to saint and also the relationship between the individual and their special protector. Our Lady, SS Katherine, Margaret, Mary Magdalen, John the Baptist and all the other sacred helpers and friends who watched over Anne Buckmaster and her husband Nicholas, churchwarden of Wing in 1535–6, and their kith and kin, and whose presence in the landscape of the parish was made manifest by their representations in the parish church, were displaced and destroyed. Almost all the names of the saints were erased from the Calendar of the Book of Common Prayer. Until the Reformation the feast of St Nicholas (6 December) at Wing was celebrated by a Mass in which his life and powers were invoked. The churchwardens' accounts in 1535–6 mention the painting of St Nicholas's mitre and crozier, suggesting that the custom of the boy-bishop was practised in the parish.[90] The Book of Common Prayer treated his day like any other, merely designating lessons from Isaiah and the Acts of the Apostles II for Matins, with no reference to the saint. New collects were written for every saint's day, replacing those of times past which invoked their aid. Apart from the Virgin, only St George survived the cut, which perhaps explains why his mural image remained uncovered into the eighteenth century.

However, his day too (23 April) would have been celebrated by Robert Grave, who served as vicar from 1562 until 1591, with no more ceremony than that of the effaced St Nicholas, with a Collect and lessons from I Kings, II, v. 30 and Acts XX. The *Aves* and *Salves*, the lights and offerings which were part of the natural order of things to Anne and Nicholas Buckmaster, disappeared with their images. Their children, who would have known a world of images in their youth, had to adjust to an imageless world, one in which through the repetition of the second Commandment in the Communion service and the ringing condemnation of idolators in the Commination prayers they were exhorted to revile what for Anne and Nicholas and generations before them had been a part of their daily lives:

> Thou shalt not make to thy selfe any graven ymage nor the likeness of any thyng that is in heaven above, or in the yearthe beneath, nor in the water under the yearth. Thou shalt not bowe down to them, nor worshyppe them: for I the lord thy God am a gelous God, and visite the sinne of the fathers upon the children, unto the thyrde and fourthe generacion of them that hate me, and shewe mercye unto thousandes in them that love me and kepe my commaundments (Exodus, XX, vv. 4–6).

> Cursed is the man that maketh any carved or molten Image, an abhominacion to the Lorde, the worke of the handes of the craftes manne, and putteth it in a secrete place to worshyp it (Deuteronomy, XXVII, v. 15).[91]

By the 1570s only the elderly Wing parishioners could have recalled childhood memories of the rood placed above the chancel screen and the saints who once occupied the empty brackets as well as the collective and private rituals which centred on them.

Elsewhere in England there were those who continued to express their regret for the old days and the old ways – men like the compiler of the *Rites of Durham*, who recalled the host of images and rituals in the cathedral, including the 'mrveylous lyvelye and bewtifull' cult image of Our Lady of Boulton, and the Cornish-born recusant gentleman Nicholas Roscarrock, with his compilation of the lives and legends of the saints. At parish level there was Roger Martin of Long Melford and old Christopher Trychay at Morebath, who had lived through it all, from the time of Henry VIII to the latter part of Elizabeth's reign.[92] Unlike these educated voices, the attitudes of the Wing parishioners to their images and their effacement have left no trace. Perhaps for them the changes were more piecemeal and sufficient remained of other ceremonies and activities to make them seem less dramatic.[93] Whether the doctrines and religious practices which emerged from the religious upheavals of the middle of the sixteenth century made the people of Wing, or any of the other parishes examined in this study, a more godly folk than their forebears, we shall never know.

> *Memento etiam, Domine, animarum famulorum famularumque tuarum qui nos praeccesserunt cum signo fidei et dormiunt in somno pacis; ipsis, Domine, et omnibus in Christo quiescentibus locum refrigerii, lucis et pacis ut indulgeas deprecamur Per eundem Christum Dominum nostrum. Amen.*
> (Dickinson (ed.), *Missale*, col. 619)

> 'Remember not, Lorde, our offences, nor the offences of oure forefathers'.
> (*The First and Second Prayer-Books of Edward VI*, p. 361)

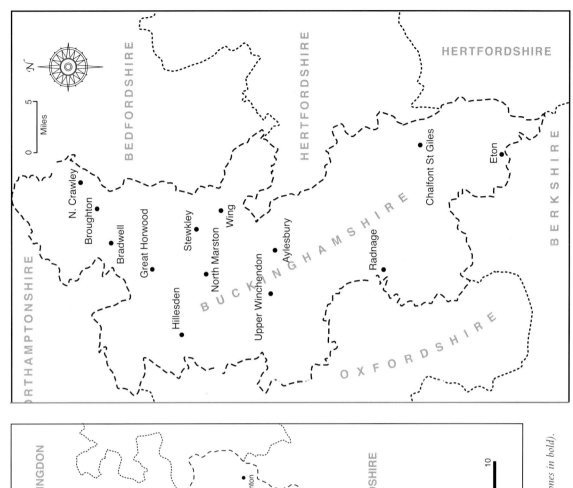

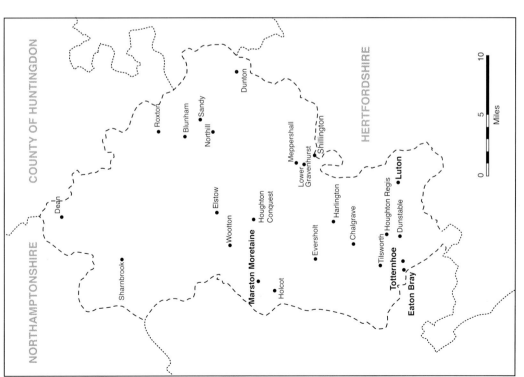

*Left:* 1. *Churches in Bedfordshire mentioned in this book (principal ones in bold).*
*Right:* 2. *Churches in Buckinghamshire mentioned in this book*

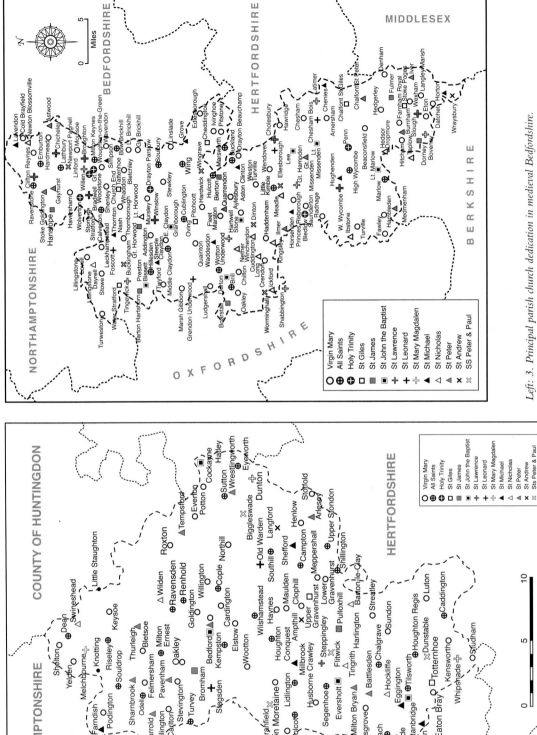

*Left: 3. Principal parish church dedication in medieval Bedfordshire.*
*Right: 4. Principal parish church dedication in medieval Buckinghamshire.*

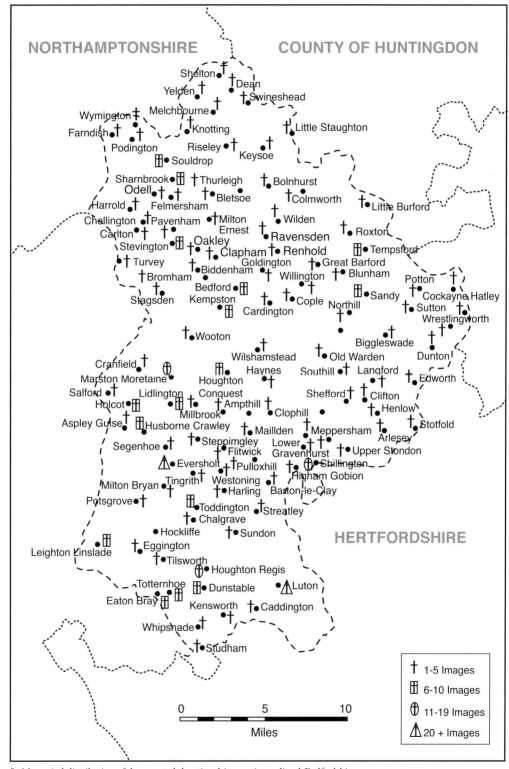

NORTHAMPTONSHIRE     COUNTY OF HUNTINGDON

Shelton
Dean
Yelden
Swineshead
Wymington
Melchbourne
Farndish
Knotting
Podington
Little Staughton
Riseley
Keysoe
Souldrop
Sharnbrook
Thurleigh
Bolnhurst
Odell
Bletsoe
Colmworth
Harrold
Felmersham
Little Burford
Chellington
Pavenham
Milton
Wilden
Carlton
Ernest
Roxton
Stevington
Oakley
Ravensden
Turvey
Clapham
Renhold
Tempsford
Goldington
Great Barford
Bromham
Biddenham
Willington
Blunham
Potton
Bedford
Sandy
Cockayne Hatley
Stagsden
Kempston
Cople
Sutton
Cardington
Northill
Wrestlingworth
Wooton
Biggleswade
Cranfield
Wilshamstead
Old Warden
Dunton
Marston Moretaine
Haynes
Southill
Langford
Edworth
Salford
Houghton
Salford
Lidlington
Conquest
Shefford
Clifton
Holcot
Ampthill
Henlow
Millbrook
Clophill
Aspley Guise
Husborne Crawley
Mailden
Meppersham
Stotfold
Segenhoe
Steppimgley
Lower
Arlesey
Flitwick
Gravenhurst
Upper Stondon
Eversholt
Pulloxhill
Shillington
Milton Bryan
Tingrith
Higham Gobion
Potsgrove
Westoning
Harling
Barton-le-Clay
Toddington
Streatley
Chalgrave
Hockliffe
HERTFORDSHIRE
Sundon
Leighton Linslade
Eggington
Tilsworth
Houghton Regis
Totternhoe
Dunstable
Luton
Eaton Bray
Kensworth
Caddington
Whipsnade
Studham

|  |  |
|--------|--------|
| † | 1-5 Images |
| ⊞ | 6-10 Images |
| ⊕ | 11-19 Images |
| ⚠ | 20 + Images |

0      5      10
Miles

*5. Numerical distribution of documented devotional images in medieval Bedfordshire.*

279

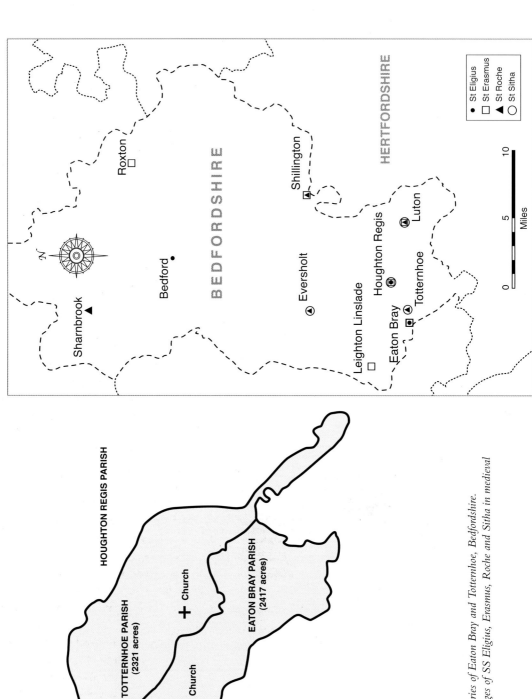

*Left: 6. The parish boundaries of Eaton Bray and Totternhoe, Bedfordshire.*
*Right: 7. Documented images of SS Eligius, Erasmus, Roche and Sitha in medieval Bedfordshire.*

8. *Documented images of St Nicholas and St Erasmus in West Kent and the Weald in the Middle Ages.*

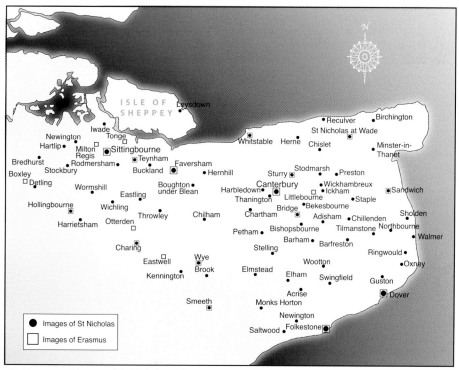

9. *Documented images of St Nicholas and St Erasmus in north-east and east Kent in the Middle Ages.*

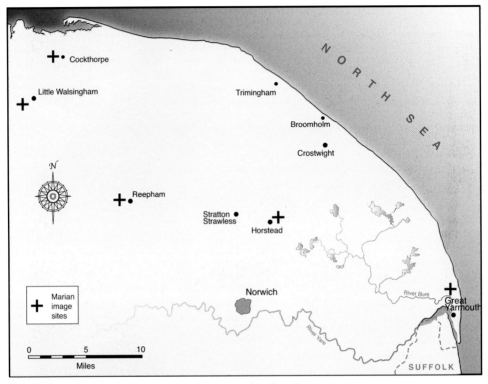

*10. Late medieval pilgrimage sites in East Anglia: Norwich and north-east.*

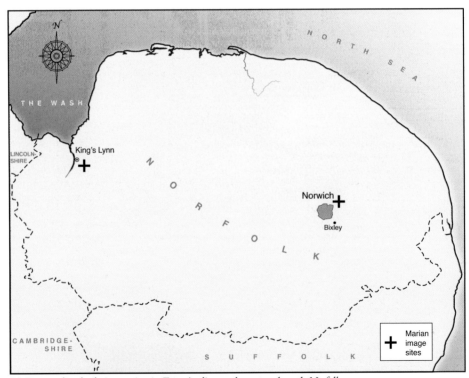

*11. Late medieval pilgrimage sites in East Anglia: north-west and south Norfolk.*

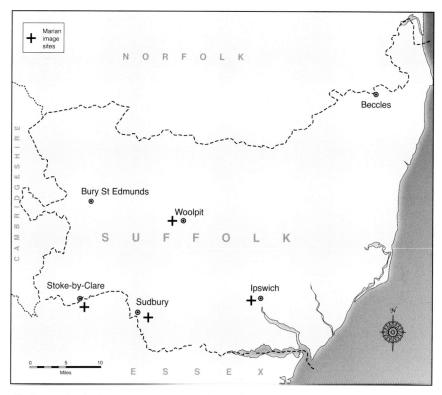

12. *Late medieval pilgrimage sites in East Anglia: Suffolk.*

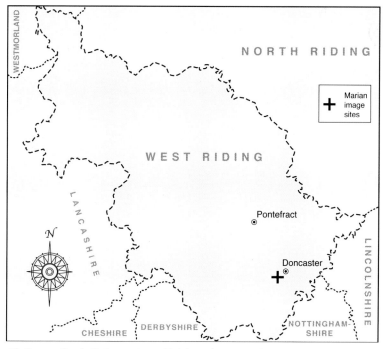

13. *Late medieval pilgrimage sites in Yorkshire: the West Riding.*

*14. Late medieval pilgrimage sites in Yorkshire: the East Riding.*

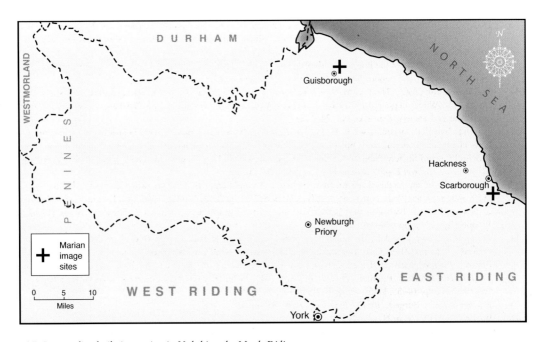

*15. Late medieval pilgrimage sites in Yorkshire: the North Riding.*

# NOTES

## CHAPTER ONE

1   P.H. Barnum (ed.), *Dives and Pauper,* vol. I, pt I, EETS, original series, 275, 1976, p. 82.

2   See Chapter Two for the defining of the devotional image.

3   C. Babington (ed.), *The Repressor of Over Much Blaming of the Clergy by Reginald Pecock D.D.*, Rolls Series, London, 1860, 1, pp. 169, 148; J.P.H. Clark and C. Taylor (eds), *Walter Hilton's Latin Writings*, Analecta Cartusiana, 124, 1987.

4   A. Rapoport, *The Meaning of the Built Environment. A Nonverbal Communication Approach*, Tucson, 1990, p. 178.

5   H. van Os, *The Art of Devotion in the Late Middle Ages in Europe 1300–1500*, London, 1994; *Spiegel der Seligkeit. Privates Bild und Frömmigkeit im Spätmittelaltar* (Nuremberg, Germanisches Nationalmuseum exhibition catalogue, 2000); *Iconoclasme. Vie et mort de l'image médiévale* (Berne, Musée d'histoire/Strasbourg, Musée de l'Oeuvre Notre-Dame exhibition catalogue, 2001).

6   For a helpful study of cultural shifts in viewing sculpture and other artefacts translated from their original settings, see M. Baker, 'De l'église au musée: les monuments du XVIIIe siècle (fonctions, significations, et histoire)', in *Sculptures hors contexte, actes du colloque international organisé au musée du Louvre par le service culturel le 29 Avril, 1994,* Paris Documentation Française, Louvre conférences et colloques, Paris, *c.* 1996, pp. 73–92; N. Netzer, 'Collecting, Re/Collecting, Contextualizing and Recontextualizing: Devotion to Fragments of the Middle Ages', in N. Netzer and V. Reinburg (eds), *Fragmented Devotion. Medieval Objects from the Schnütgen Museum Cologne* (McMullen Museum of Art, Boston College, USA, exhibition catalogue, 2000), pp. 17–30. The commodification of ancient religious art is commented upon by Roland Barthes, 'Le *Guide bleu*', in idem, *Mythologies (Oeuvres complètes, I, 1942–1965)*, ed. E. Marty, Paris, 1993, pp. 637–9, esp. p. 638.

7   M.R. Miles, *Image as Insight: Visual Understanding in Western Christianity and Secular Culture*, Boston (Mass.), 1985, p. 6.

8   H. Michell Whitley, 'Visitations of Devonshire Churches', *Reports and Transactions of the Devonshire Association*, 42 (1910), 446–74; G.G. Coulton, 'A Visitation of the Archdeaconry of Totnes in 1342', *English Historical Review*, 26 (1918), 108–24.

9   E. Mason, 'The Role of the English Parishioner, 1100–1500', *Journal of Ecclesiastical History*, 27 (1976), 17–29.

10   VCH, *Bedfordshire*, 2, London, 1908, p. 297; ibid., 3, London, 1912, p. 170.

11   T.C.B. Timmins (ed.), *The Register of John Chandler, Dean of Salisbury, 1404–17*, Wiltshire Record Society, 39, 1984; K.L. Wood-Legh (ed.), *Kentish Visitations of Archbishop Warham and his Deputies, 1511–1512*, Kent Archaeological Society, Kent Records, 24, 1984.

12   For churchwardens' accounts see E. Duffy, *The Voices of Morebath. Reformation and Rebellion in an English Village*, New Haven and London, 2001, pp. 19–24; C. Burgess (ed.), *The Pre-Reformation Records of All Saints' Bristol: Part I*, Bristol Record Society Publications, 46, 1995, pp. xiv–xxxvii; K.L. French, *The People of the Parish. Community Life in a Late Medieval English Diocese*, Philadelphia, 2001, ch. 2.

13   The quantity of late medieval testamentary material is exemplified by Suffolk, for which in excess of 23,000 pre-1550 wills survive; see P. Northeast, 'Suffolk Churches in the Later Middle Ages: The Evidence of Wills', in C. Harper-Bill, C. Rawcliffe and R. Wilson (eds), *East Anglia's History: Studies in Honour of Norman Scarfe*, Woodbridge, 2002, pp. 93–106.

14   On wills, see especially A.D. Brown, *Popular Piety in Late Medieval England. The Diocese of Salisbury 1250–1550*, Oxford, 1995, pp. 21–5; C.R. Burgess, '"By Quick and by Dead": wills and pious provision in late medieval Bristol', *English Historical Review*, 305 (1987), 837–58; idem, 'Late Medieval Wills and Pious Convention: Testamentary Evidence Reconsidered', in M. Hicks (ed.), *Profit, Piety and the Professions in Later Medieval England*, Stroud, 1990, pp. 14–33; Duffy, *Stripping*, pp. 355–7, 504–23.

15   A point made by Burgess, 'By Quick and by Dead', 837–58.

16   Brown, *Popular Piety*, p. 21.

17   E. Miller and J. Hatcher, *Medieval England. Rural Society and Economic Change 1086–1348*, London and New York, 1978, p. 110.

18     P. Northeast (ed.), *Wills of the Archdeaconry of Sudbury 1439–1474: wills from the register 'Baldewyne' Pt. I 1439–1461*, Suffolk Records Society, 44, 2001. I am indebted to Peter Northeast for kindly allowing me to consult the transcript of Part 2. The Bedfordshire wills are cited *in extenso* throughout this study.

19     J. Middleton-Stewart, *Inward Purity and Outward Splendour. Death and Remembrance in the Deanery of Dunwich, Suffolk, 1370–1547*, Woodbridge, 2001, p. 223.

20     Middleton-Stewart, *Inward Purity*, p. 223.

21     Christopher Baker, in *Art History*, 18, no. 4 (December 1995), 602.

22     For St 'Sunday', see A. Reiss, *The Sunday Christ. Sabbatarianism in English medieval wall-painting*, British Archaeological Reports, British Series, 292, Oxford, 2000.

23     R.W. Scribner, *For the Sake of Simple Folk. Popular Propaganda for the German Reformation*, Oxford, 2nd edn, 1994, p. 251.

# CHAPTER TWO

1     The chief sources for Eaton Bray church are VCH, *Bedfordshire*, 3, pp. 373–4; N. Pevsner, *The Buildings of England. Bedfordshire and the County of Huntingdon and Peterborough*, Harmondsworth, 1968, pp. 81–2; C. Pickford (ed.), *Bedfordshire Churches in the Nineteenth Century. Part I: Parishes A to G*, BHRS, 73, 1994, pp. 242–50.

2     A.F. Cirket (ed.), *English Wills, 1498–1526*, BHRS, 37, 1957, pp. 53–4 , nos 170, 195 (Rudde), pp. 77–8, no. 246 (Cutlat); another version of the last is in P. Bell (ed.), *Bedfordshire Wills 1484–1533*, BHRS, 76, 1997, pp. 64–5, no. 104. For St 'Sunday', or the Sabbath Christ, see Chapter One.

3     R. Chartier, *Cultural History. Between Practices and Representations*, trans. L.G. Cochrane, Cambridge, 1988, pp. 40–1.

4     Much of David Freedberg's book, *The Power of Images. Studies in the History and Theory of Response*, Chicago and London, 1989, is concerned with cult images.

5     S. Ringbom, *Icon to Narrative. The Rise of the Dramatic Close-Up in Fifteenth-Century Devotional Painting*, Abo, 1965, pp. 52–8. For a review of the historiography of the devotional image (albeit omitting Ringbom's contribution), see J.-C. Schmitt, *Le corps des images. Essais sur la culture visuelle au Moyen Age*, Paris, 2002, pp. 35–62.

6     Dehio, quoted in Ringbom, *Icon to Narrative*, p. 53.

7     E. Panofsky, '*Imago Pietatis*: Ein Betrag zur Typengeschichte des "Schmerzensmanns" und der "Maria Mediatrix"', *Festschrift für Max J. Friedländer zum 60. Geburtstag*, Leipzig, 1927, pp. 261–308.

8     Ringbom, *Icon to Narrative*, p. 57.

9     Ibid., p. 53. Nevertheless, 'official church decoration' might include statues or murals of the apostles around the walls of chancels or choirs which were not devotional in his terminology.

10     H. Belting, *Likeness and Presence. A History of the Image before the Era of Art*, trans. E. Jephcott, Chicago and London, 1994, p. 409.

11     Ibid., p. 410.

12     Van Os, *Art of Devotion*. A wider range of objects, including cheap, mass-produced items in non-precious materials, was shown alongside luxury pieces, in *Spiegel der Seligkeit* (Germanisches Nationalmuseum exhibition catalogue, 2000).

13     Ringbom, *Icon to Narrative*, p. 53.

14     The dual function of images as foci for both private devotion and formal organized prayer is recognized by Belting (H. Belting, *The Image and Its Public in the Middle Ages. Form and Function of Early Paintings of the Passion*, trans. M. Bartusis and R. Meyer, New York, 1990, p. 15).

15     Hamburger criticizes Panofsky and Belting for not distinguishing sufficiently between Italian panel paintings and northern devotional images (J.F. Hamburger, 'The Visual and the Visionary: The Image in Late Medieval Monastic Devotions', in idem, *The Visual and the Visionary. Art and Female Spirituality in Late Medieval Germany*, New York, 1998, pp. 111–48, n. 3 on p. 502). Scribner overemphasizes the extent to which painting superseded sculpture in fifteenth-century northern altarpieces (Scribner, *Simple Folk*, pp. xxvi–xxvii). Even in the Netherlands the extent to which carved images were supplanted by paintings has been exaggerated, as the numerous Malines statuettes demonstrate.

16     Babington, *Repressor*, p. 167. The text was written in *c*. 1449. On pp. 162–6 he uses the term 'seable rememoratijf signes'.

17     Barnum, *Dives and Pauper*, 1, p. 82.

18     W. Lyndewood, *Provinciale seu constitutiones Anglie Provinciale* (early sixteenth-century copy in the Society of Antiquaries of London) , f. clxxxii(v), note m.

19     Clark and Taylor, *Hilton's Latin Writings, vol. 1*. The traditional attribution to Hilton is questioned by N. Watson, '*Et que est huius ydoli materia? Tuipse*: Idols and Images in Walter Hilton', in J. Dimmick, J. Simpson and N. Zeeman (eds), *Images, Idolatry and Iconoclasm in Late Medieval England: Textuality and the Visual Image*, Oxford, 2002, p. 97, n. 10. For other studies of this text, see G.R. Owst, *Literature and the Pulpit in Medieval England*,

Oxford, 2nd edn, 1961, pp. 137–9; J.M. Russell-Smith, 'Walter Hilton and a Tract in Defence of the Veneration of Images', *Dominican Studies*, 7 (1954), 180–214; J.P.H. Clark, 'Walter Hilton in Defence of the Religious Life and of the Veneration of Images', *Downside Review*, 103 (1985), 1–25. See also K. Kamerick, *Popular Piety and Art in the Late Middle Ages. Image Worship and Idolatry in England 1350–1500*, New York and Basingstoke, 2002.

20  A. Louth (trans.), *St John of Damascus, Three Treatises on the Divine Images*, New York, 2003, p. 29. For the medieval theology of the image, see especially J. Kollwitz, 'Bild und Bildertheologie im Mittelalter', in *Das Gottesbild im Abendland*, Witten and Berlin, 1959, pp. 109–38; M. Baxandall, *The Limewood Sculptors of Renaissance Germany*, London and New Haven, 1980, pp. 51–4; M. Aston, *England's Iconoclasts, Vol. 1. Laws Against Images*, Oxford, 1988, pp. 20–34, 47–61, 143–54; Freedberg, *Power of Images*, pp. 162–7; L.P. Wandel, *Voracious Idols and Violent Hands. Iconoclasm in Reformation Zurich, Strasbourg and Basel*, Cambridge, 1995, ch. 1; J. Wirth, 'Faut-il adorer les images? La théorie du culte des images jusqu'au concile de Trente', in *Iconoclasme. Vie et mort de l'image médiévale*, pp. 28–37. The last traces succinctly the differing formulations of eastern and western proponents and opponents of images from earliest times to the Council of Trent; see also Schmitt, *Le corps des images*.

21  S.B. Meech and H.E. Allen (eds), *The Book of Margery Kempe*, EETS, original series, 212, 1940 (reprinted 1997). This pre-dates Pecock's text by just over a decade. Scribner adds a third mode of seeing, a variant of the 'bodily eye' by which the sacred is experienced through symbolic acts involving artefacts, especially the Mass and the elevation of the Host (Scribner, *Simple Folk*, p. 4).

22  Louth, *St John of Damascus*, pp. 31, 96.

23  London, British Library, MS Yates Thompson 2, f. 29; this is discussed perceptively in Belting, *Likeness and Presence*, pp. 412–14, and Hamburger, *The Visual and the Visionary*, pp. 131–4; see also M. Camille, *Gothic Art. Vision and Revelations of the Medieval World*, London, 1996, pp. 120–3.

24  Babington, *Repressor*, 1, p. 163. But see especially the comments by A. Vauchez, *Saints, prophètes et visionnaires. Le pouvoir surnatural au Moyen Age*, Paris, 1999, pp. 82–91.

25  *Latria est seruitus debita Deo . . .; Yperdulia vero est seruitus debita humanitati Christi . . . et eadem adoracio debetur eciam beate Virgini Marie . . .; [Dulia]: 'Primo [modo] adorantur adoracione dulie papa, episcopi et ceteri prelati, reges et principes, et alii domini temporales, vice et nomine eius cuius potestatem representant, scilicet Dei. . . . Secundo modo adorantur sancti Dei homines . . .* (Clark and Taylor, *Hilton's Latin Writings*, pp. 211–12); see also Wirth, 'Faut-il adorer', p. 33.

26  Babington, *Repressor*, 1, p. 170,

27  Ibid, 1, pp. 164–5, 168–72. There is a fine analysis of Pecock's text in Aston, *Iconoclasts*, pp. 147–54.

28  Belting, *Image and Its Public*, p. 50.

29  Babington, *Repressor*, 1, pp. 169, 212–13.

30  J. Griffiths (ed.), *Certain Sermons or Homilies Appointed to be Read in Churches in the Time of Queen Elizabeth of Famous Memory*, London, 1864, p. 205.

31  Norfolk Records Service Reg. Spurlyng, ff. 93–9v, will of Nicholas Beaupré, quoted in C. Richmond, *The Paston Family in the Fifteenth Century. Endings*, Manchester, 2000, p. 26.

32  E. Baker, 'The Adoration of the Magi at Shelfanger Church, Norfolk', *Norfolk Archaeology*, 34 (1966–69), 90–1. In addition to Shelfanger, early chancel images painted on walls can be seen at Bramley (Hants.), Stoke Dry (Rutland), Little Wenham (Suff.) and Whitchurch (Bucks.).

33  Cirket, *English Wills*, p. 65, no. 206d.

34  For South Newington, see E.W. Tristram, *English Wall Painting of the Fourteenth Century*, London, 1955, pl. 16b.

35  Beds. & Luton Archives, ABP/R3/103d; L.L. Duncan and A. Hussey (eds), *Testamenta Cantiana: A Series of Extracts from Fifteenth and Sixteenth Century Wills*, Archaeologia Cantiana, Kent Archaeological Society (Kent Records), Extra Volume (1907), (East Kent), p. 203.

36  An observation made by C. Hope, 'Altarpieces and the Requirements of Patrons', in T. Verdon and J. Henderson (eds), *Christianity and the Renaissance. Image and Religious Imagination in the Quattrocento*, New York, 1990, pp. 543–7. The distinction between iconic images and narrative images was criticized by Robert Maniura in his review of Belting, *Likeness and Presence*, in *Burlington Magazine*, 137 (1995), 462–3.

37  J. Alexander and P. Binski (eds), *Age of Chivalry. Art in Plantagenet England 1200–1400* (London, Royal Academy, exhibition catalogue, 1987), no. 698.

38  See M.J. Carruthers, *The Book of Memory. A Study of Memory in Medieval Culture*, Cambridge, 1990, pp. 281–8. esp. p. 284.

39  Baxandall, *Limewood Sculptors*, pp. 90–3 (quotation from p. 93).

40  For the 'Islip' head, see R. Marks and P. Williamson (eds), *Gothic. Art for England 1400–1547* (London, Victoria & Albert Museum exhibition catalogue, 2003), no. 239.

41  R. Marks, 'Altarpiece, Image and Devotion: Fourteenth-Century Sculpture at Cobham', in P. Binski and W. Noel (eds), *New Offerings, Ancient Treasures. Studies in Medieval Art for George Henderson*, Stroud, 2001, pp. 417–44. For Flawford, see Alexander and Binski, *Age of Chivalry*, nos 699, 700; the Boston figure has not been the subject of a detailed study.

42  L.M. Swinburn (ed.), *The Lanterne of Light*, EETS, original series, 151, 1917 (for 1915), p. 84.

43  Baxandall, *Limewood Sculptors*, pp. 166–8.

44  Vernacular version of the Latin prayer in H. Littlehales (ed.), *The Prymer or Lay Folks' Prayerbook*, EETS, original series 105, 1895 (reprinted 1996), p. 34.

45  This particular Cobham head may originally have been in the Lady Chapel (Marks, 'Altarpiece', p. 428). The Thomas More observation is cited in Aston, *Iconoclasts*, p. 107. For recent discussions of Gothic facial expression in sculpture, see P. Binski, 'The Angel Choir at Lincoln and the Poetics of the Gothic Smile', *Art History*, 20 no. 3 (1997), 350–74; R. Recht, *Le croire et le voir. L'art des cathédrales (XIIe-XVe siècle)*, Mayenne, 1999, pp. 315–16.

46  Bell, *Bedfordshire Wills 1484–1533*, pp. 59, 64, 128, nos 95, 104, 207; Beds. & Luton Archives, ABP/R3/64.

47  For censing, see below, Chapter Seven, pp. 161, 163. The Syon reference is quoted in D.R. Dendy, *The Use of Lights in Christian Worship*, Alcuin Club Collections, 41, 1959, p. 57.

48  Examples can be found from the twelfth century in Germany, France and Spain.

49  Belting, *Likeness and Presence*, p. 446, fig. 270. The English example is the mural of St Faith in Westminster Abbey (ibid., fig. 271). The famous Mailänder Madonna of Cologne Cathedral was originally displayed in an elaborate canopied niche analogous to the arrangements at Saint-Denis and Westminster; see U. Bergmann (ed.), *Verschwundenes Inventarium der Skulpturenfund im Kölner Domchor* (Cologne, Schnütgen Museum exhibition catalogue, 1984), pp. 11–18.

50  Bucks. RO, D/A/We3–47; S. Tymms (ed.), *Wills and Inventories from the Registers of the Commissary of Bury St Edmunds and the Archdeacon of Sudbury*, Camden Society, 49, 1850, p. 20.

51  John 14, v. 2.

52  Some of the paint and gilding applied to the Eaton Bray tabernacles and reredoses was still visible in 1831 (Pickford, *Bedfordshire Churches A–G*, p. 249).

53  Bell, *Bedfordshire Wills 1484–1533*, p. 58, no. 93; Beds. & Luton Archives, ABP/R3/82d, 117; ABP/R4/96d.

54  N. Poussin, *Lettres et propos sur l'art*, ed. A. Blunt, Paris, 1964, pp. 35–6: *afinque, en le considérant en toutes ses parties, les rayons de l'oeil soint retenus et non point épars au dehors, en recevant les espèces des autres objets voisins qui, venant pêle-mêle avec les choses dépeintes, confondent le jour?*

55  See P. Duro (ed.), *The Rhetoric of the Frame. Essays on the Boundaries of the Artwork*, Cambridge, 1996, especially L. Marin, 'The Frame of Representation and Some of its Figures', pp. 79–95.

56  M. McGregor (ed.), *Bedfordshire Wills Proved in the Prerogative Court of Canterbury 1383–1548*, BHRS, 58, 1979, p. 105, no. 85.

57  William Grene, 1533 (Beds. & Luton Archives, ABP/R3/102d).

58  Marks and Williamson, *Gothic*, no. 121.

59  W.A. Christian, *Person and God in a Spanish Valley*, Princeton, revised edn, 1989, p. 190.

60  The failure to take account of historical contexts has been a criticism levelled at David Freedberg's *Power of Images*; see the review by J.M. Nash, 'Art and Arousal', *Art History*, 13, no. 4 (1990), 566–70.

61  *Explicitam habent litterati et docti et devoti laici qui veraciter advertunt ymaginem nichil aliud esse quam lignum et lapidem. Unde ipsi nullo affectu vel reverencia moventur ad ipsum lignum, in quantum est materia ligna, vel in quantum est curiosa depicta. Nichil ponderant talia, sed utuntur ymaginibus velut recordacione, procumbentes coram ymaginibus, oblitis illis, preces emittunt ad Deum et ad sanctos eius. . . . Et si omnes fideles ita essent [roborati] et instructi per graciam sicut tales sunt, non foret necessarium ponere ymagines in ecclesiis* (Clark and Taylor, *Hilton's Latin Writings*, p. 205).

62  *. . . quia licet actualiter feratur mens eorum in ipsas ymagines quas vident, et non in Deum; sicut solent simplices facere quando vident pulcram ymaginem artificiose depictam et preciose ornatam: statim reverencia quadam carnali movetur mens eorum ad adoracionem cum humiliacione coporali faciend[am] illi ymagini magis quam alteri, et magis quam spiritualiter ipsi Deo eorum intellectus et affectus quasi occupantur in sensu exteriori* (Clark and Taylor, *Hilton's Latin Writings*, pp. 205–6).

63  Recht, *Le croire et le voir*, pp. 306–7. Recht is writing about the thirteenth century, but his remarks are applicable to fifteenth- and early sixteenth-century England.

64  Barnum, *Dives and Pauper*, 1, p. 86.

65  Ibid., pp. 102–9; see Aston, *Iconoclasts*, pp. 28–9, 47–61 and M. Camille, *The Gothic Idol. Ideology and Image-Making in Medieval Art*, Cambridge, 1989, pp. 203–41, for stimulating discussions of this issue.

66  For recent studies of the Gregorian topos, see M. Camille, 'Seeing and reading: some visual implications of medieval literacy and illiteracy', *Art History*, 8, no. 1 (1985), 26–49; L.G. Duggan, 'Was Art really the book of the illiterate?', *Word and Image*, 5 (1989), 227–51; C. Chazelle, 'Pictures, books and the illiterate, Pope Gregory I's letters to Serenius of Marseilles', *Word and Image*, 6 (1990), 138–53; M.H. Caviness, 'Biblical stories in windows: were they Bibles for the poor?', in B.S. Levy (ed.), *The Bible in the Middle Ages. Its Influence on Literature and Art*, Medieval and Renaissance Texts and Studies, 89, Binghamton, New York, 1992, pp. 103–47.

67  For a succinct discussion of this point, see A. Henry, *Biblia Pauperum. A Facsimile and Edition*, Aldershot, 1987, pp. 17–18.

68  Aston, *Iconoclasts*, p. 32. In discussing this question she has highlighted sagely the danger of reductive thinking on such matters: 'Human nature being what it is, for ever blending conscious and subconscious thought, blurring the

boundaries between representation and represented, it was possible for statues simultaneously both to be and not to be the saints they stood for' (ibid.).

69    R.C. Trexler, *Public Life in Renaissance Florence*, Ithaca and London, 1980, pp. 67–70, makes the point in respect of miracle-working images, but it also applies to images like those in Eaton Bray.

70    S. Fish, *Is There a Text in this Class? The Authority of Interpretive Communities*, Cambridge (Mass.) and London, 1980, pp. 13–17.

71    M. Mazower, *The Balkans*, London, 2001, p. 61.

72    A.K. McHardy (ed.), *Clerical Poll-Taxes of the Diocese of Lincoln 1377–1381*, Lincoln Record Society, 81, 1992, p. 81.

73    For the manorial descent, see VCH, *Bedfordshire*, 3, pp. 370–2; the Bray section has been superseded by M. Condon, 'From Caitiff and Villain to Pater Patriae: Reynold Bray and the Profits of Office', in M. Hicks (ed.), *Profit, Piety and the Professions in Later Medieval England*, Stroud, 1990, pp. 137–68. I am indebted to Margaret Condon for generously making available her unpublished researches on Bray's activities at Eaton Bray.

74    N. Lutt (ed.), *Bedfordshire Muster Lists 1539–1831*, BHRS, 71, 1992, p. 40.

75    The wills of Elizabeth Fox (1519), Alys Cooke (1521), Cuthbert Cutlat and John Collens (1528) all had Richard Broke as one of the witnesses. William Burre's (d. 1530) daughter was married to Richard Cooke. Cirket, *English Wills*, p. 60, no. 188 (Fox); Bell, *Bedfordshire Wills 1484–1533*, pp. 59, 128, 173, nos 95 (Cooke), 207 (Collens), 292 (Burre).

76    N.Z. Davis, 'From "Popular Religion" to "Religious Cultures"', in S. Ozment (ed.), *Reformation Europe: A Guide to Research*, St Louis, USA, 1982, p. 322. Among the numerous other discussions of 'popular religion', see especially L.E. Boyle, 'Popular Piety in the Middle Ages: What is Popular?', *Florilegium*, 4 (1982), 184–93; Brown, *Popular Piety*; Chartier, *Cultural History*, pp. 30–40; Christian, *Person and God*, pp. 81–8; Duffy, *Stripping*, pp. 2–3, 73–4, ch. 6; Scribner, *Simple Folk*, pp. 59, 95; Wandel, *Voracious Idols*.

77    P. Brown, *The Cult of the Saints. Its Rise and Function in Latin Christianity*, Chicago, 1982, p. 18.

78    PRO, PCC 26 Blamyr, 31 Adeane.

79    I am indebted to Margaret Condon for the chantry information and to the late Nicholas Bagshawe for access to his transcript of the fraternity register.

80    Stonyhurst College (Lancs.), MS 60; see J.J.G. Alexander, 'Katherine Bray's Flemish Book of Hours', *The Ricardian*, 8, no. 107 (December 1989), 308–17. Coincidentally, a richly illuminated fourteenth-century Book of Hours made for the Zouches of Harringworth, the previous overlords of Eaton Bray, has also survived (Oxford, Bodleian Library, MS Lat. liturg. E.41).

81    B. Spencer, *Pilgrim Souvenirs and Secular Badges. Medieval Finds from Excavations in London: 7*, Museum of London, London, 1998, pp. 16–18. Testators from Bilsby and Theddlethorpe St Helen (Lincs.) refer to St John's heads, in 1527 and 1531–2 respectively (C.W. Foster (ed.), *Early Lincoln Wills, vol. 2 AD 1505 to May, 1530*, Lincoln Record Society, 10, 1918, p. 52; idem, *Early Lincoln Wills, vol. 3 AD 1530 to 1532*, Lincoln Record Society, 24, 1930, p. 220).

82    Babington, *Repressor*, 1, pp. 214, 212–13.

83    The Sarum Primer of 1526 printed by Regnault includes such rubrics before the image of St Anne, the Virgin and Christ-Child (copy in Victoria & Albert Museum Library).

84    Clark and Taylor, *Hilton's Latin Writings*, p. 204.

85    PRO PCC 26 Blamyr; Bell, *Bedfordshire Wills 1484–1533*, p. 174, no. 292.

86    W. Lack, H.M. Stuchfield and P. Whittemore, *The Monumental Brasses of Bedfordshire*, The Monumental Brass Society, London, 1992, p. 36.

87    The inventory of Reynold Bray's possessions at the time of his death lists only three vestments under the chapel (PRO, E 154/2/10); for Lady Margaret Beaufort's chapel, see M.K. Jones and M.G. Underwood, *The King's Mother. Lady Margaret Beaufort Countess of Richmond and Derby*, Cambridge, 1992, p. 177.

88    For the significance of the 'dramatic close-up', see Ringbom, *Icon to Narrative*, pp. 39–71.

89    Christian made a clear distinction between the two: W.A. Christian Jr, *Local Religion in Sixteenth-Century Spain*, Princeton, 1981, p. 3.

# CHAPTER THREE

1    F. Bond, *Dedications & Patron Saints of English Churches. Ecclesiastical Symbolism. Saints and their Emblems*, Oxford, 1914, pp. 29–33.

2    I am indebted for the information about rededications to the unpublished researches of my colleague Dr Jane Hawkes.

3    VCH, *Bedfordshire*, 3, p. 374.

4    D. Kahn, 'The Romanesque Sculpture of the Church of St Mary at Halford, Warwickshire', *Journal of the British Archaeological Association*, 133 (1980), 64–73; her argument that the niches held an Annunciation rather than the

Virgin and St John is countered convincingly in S. Rickerby and D. Park, 'A romanesque "Visitatio Sepulchri" at Kempley', *Burlington Magazine*, 132 (1991), 27–31 (esp. 30–1).

5    *English Romanesque Art 1066–1200* (London, Arts Council exhibition catalogue, 1984), no. 115.

6    See M.P. Carroll, *The Cult of the Virgin Mary. Psychological Origins*, Princeton, 1986; M. Clayton, *The Cult of the Virgin Mary in Anglo-Saxon England*, Cambridge, 1990; L. Gambero, *Mary and the Fathers of the Church. The Blessed Virgin Mary in Patristic Thought*, San Francisco, 1999; G. Schiller, *Iconography of Christian Art*, I, London, 1971, pp. 26–125; M. Fassler, 'Mary's Nativity, Fulbert of Chartres, and the *Stirps Jesse*: Liturgical Innovation circa 1000 and its Afterlife', *Speculum*, 75 (2000), 389–434. For the early visual manifestations see *Mother of God. Representations of the Virgin in Byzantine Art* (Athens, Benaki Museum exhibition catalogue, 2001), pp. 10–12, 17–25.

7    J. Hawkes, 'Columban Virgins: Iconic Images of the Virgin and Child in Insular Sculpture', in C. Bourke (ed.), *Studies in the Cult of Saint Columba*, Dublin, 1997, pp. 107–35.

8    A. Binns, *Dedications of Monastic Houses in England and Wales, 1066–1216*, Woodbridge, 1989, pp. 22–32. Carroll, *Cult*, pp. 10–13, underestimates the importance of the Virgin in England. I am very grateful to Sandy Heslop for making available the section of his forthcoming monograph on English seals relating to the twelfth century.

9    I.H. Forsyth, *The Throne of Wisdom. Wood Sculptures of the Madonna in Romanesque France*, Princeton, 1972, pp. 7, 11, 70, 92–133. For the emergence of the three-dimensional image, see Schmitt, *Le corps des images*, pp. 167–98.

10   Hawkes, 'Columban Virgins', pp. 108–27; B.C. Raw, 'The Inglesham Virgin and Child', *Wiltshire Archaeological and Natural History Magazine*, 61 (1966), 43–6; I am indebted to Professor George Zarnecki and Dr Jane Hawkes for enlightening discussions about the Langridge figure.

11   Canterbury and Ely are documented in O. Lehmann-Brockhaus, *Lateinische Schriftquellen zur Kunst in England, Wales und Schottland vom Jahre 901 bis zum Jahre 1307*, 1, Munich, 1955, pp. 168 (no. 623), 419 (no. 1551); another eleventh-century example is noted at Coventry (Forsyth, *Throne of Wisdom*, p. 102).

12   A. Vauchez, *La spiritualité du Moyen Age occidental VIIIe-XIIIe siècle*, Paris, revised edn, 1994, p. 171; Rubin, *Corpus Christi*, pp. 54–63.

13   N. Morgan, 'Texts and Images of Marian Devotion in English Twelfth-Century Monasticism, and Their Influence on the Secular Church', in B. Thompson (ed.), *Monasteries and Society in Medieval Britain. Proceedings of the 1994 Harlaxton Symposium*, Harlaxton Medieval Studies 6, Stamford, 1999, p. 117.

14   Forsyth, *Throne of Wisdom*, p. 4 and passim. There is a useful collection of photographs in R. Laurentin and R. Oursel, *Vièrges romanes. Les vièrges assises*, Zodiaque, 1988.

15   Morgan, 'Texts and Images . . . Twelfth-Century', p. 131.

16   *English Romanesque Art*, nos 153, 161; A.W. Clapham, 'The York Virgin and its Date', *Archaeological Journal*, 105 (1948), 6–13; G. Zarnecki, 'A 12th-Century Column-figure of the Standing Virgin and Child from Minster-in-Sheppey, Kent', in idem, *Studies in Romanesque Sculpture*, London, 1979, ch. 14; P. Williamson, *Catalogue of Romanesque Sculpture (Victoria & Albert Museum)*, London, 1983, pp. 92–3, no. 42. There are also the fragmentary limestone Virgin of *c.* 1160–70 from St Mary's Abbey, York, which from its weathered surface was originally in an external location, and a fragment of *c.* 1200 from Cawood (Yorks.) (P. Williamson, *Gothic Sculpture 1140–1300*, Pelican History of Art, New Haven and London, 1995, p. 102, fig. 154). Both the St Mary's Abbey and the Cawood figures are in the Yorkshire Museum.

17   For example the Great Malvern, Abingdon and Reading monastic seals; for Malvern, see *English Romanesque Art*, no. 352.

18   *Ad ultimo vero ad b. virginis imaginem, ligno insculptam auroque et argento decenter ornatam, accesserunt, eaque gemmis et auro spoliata, cum puerum in matris gremio sedentem fugam maturando integrum avellere et asportare parassent, materque brachium utrumque porrectum, ut solet, in anteriora prius habeuerat, brachium dextrum ad puerum clausit et secum retinuit . . . usque in hodiernum autem in tanti miraculi signum brachio clauso mater filium amplexatur* (Lehmann-Brockhaus, *Schriftquellen*, 3, p. 195, no. 5862). The present church is dedicated to St Edith, not the Virgin, as stated by Giraldus. I do not share Camille's reading of this text as an attempt to explain stylistic changes in representations of the Virgin (*Gothic Idol*, p. 236).

19   For the *Shaftesbury Psalter* (BL MS Lansdowne 383), see M. Kauffmann, 'British Library, Lansdowne MS 383: the Shaftesbury Psalter?', in Binski and Noel, *New Offerings*, pp. 256–79.

20   The quotation is from P. Brown, *Society and the Holy in Late Antiquity*, London, 1982, p. 329. Nigel Morgan has observed that the kinds of empathy evident in later Marian pictorial images were initially confined to the words of writings produced in the cloister (idem, 'Texts and Images . . . Twelfth-Century', p. 118).

21   Forsyth, *Throne of Wisdom*, pp. 31–8, figs 90–4 (Orcival); Lehmann-Brockhaus, *Schriftquellen*, I, p. 13, no. 36.

22   E. Waterton, *Pietas Mariana Britannica. A History of English Devotion to the Most Blessed Virgin Marye Mother of God*, London, 1879, Book 2, pp. 148–9.

23   Forsyth, *Throne of Wisdom*, pp. 35–7, esp. n. 16. The author excludes the numerous copper and enamelled Virgin and Child images. For German images with cavities for relics, see U. Bergmann (ed.), *Schnütgen-Museum. Die Holzskulpturen des Mittelalters (1000–1400)*, Cologne, 1989, nos 14, 15, 32, 35, 73, 78.

24 Forsyth, *Throne of Wisdom*, pp. 156–203; see also the Madonnas from Viklau and Mo (A. Andersson and M. Rydbeck, *Medieval Wooden Sculpture in Sweden, vol. IV. The Museum Collection Catalogue*, Stockholm, 1975, pp. 52, 76–7).

25 The Virgin as *mater ecclesiae* will be discussed in Sandy Heslop's forthcoming book; Rickerby and Park, 'Kempley'; E.W. Tristram, *English Medieval Wall Painting. The Twelfth Century*, Oxford, 1944, pp. 24, 42–4, 98–9, 134–6.

26 E.W. Tristram, *English Medieval Wall Painting. The Thirteenth Century*, Oxford, 1950, p. 518.

27 Lehmann-Brockhaus, *Schriftquellen*, 1, p. 77, no. 290.

28 M. Blindheim, *Painted Wooden Sculpture in Norway* c. *1100–1250*, Oslo, Stockholm, Oxford and Boston, 1998, pp. 35, 61.

29 Forsyth, *Throne of Wisdom*, pp. 38–40; see also C. Klack-Eitzen, *Die thronenden Madonnen des 13.Jahrhunderts in Westfalen*, Denkmalpflege und Forschung in Westfalen, 6, Bonn, 1985, pp. 42–7, pls 33–5; the Carrières-Saint-Denis disposition has been questioned by Willibald Sauerländer (F. Baron, *Département des Sculptures du Moyen Age, de la Renaissance et des Temps Modernes. Sculpture Française 1 – Moyen Age*, Paris, 1996, p. 73).

30 H.T. Riley (ed.), *Gesta abbatum monasterii sancti Albani a Thoma Walsingham. The Chronicles and Memorials of Great Britain and Ireland during the Middle Ages, I: AD 793–1290*, Rolls Series, 28, London, 1867, p. 286; *English Romanesque Art*, no. 153. The possible translations of *supra* are discussed in B. Nilson, *Cathedral Shrines of Medieval England*, Woodbridge, 1998, p. 65.

31 P. Binski, 'The Murals in the Nave of St Albans Abbey', in D. Abulafia, M. Franklin and M. Rubin (eds), *Church and City 1000–1500: Essays in Honour of Christopher Brooke*, Cambridge, 1992, p. 263.

32 N. Morgan, 'Devotional Aspects of the Catalan Altar Frontals c. 1100–1350', in R. Archer and E. Martinell (eds), *Proceedings of the First Symposium on Catalonia in Australia (La Trobe University, Melbourne, 27–9 September 1996)*, Barcelona, 1998, pp. 101–22.

33 Forsyth, *Throne of Wisdom*, pp. 39–45; Riley, *Gesta abbatum*, I, p. 286 (*Cereum quoque quem floribus consuevimus redimire, constituit accendi ante nobilem Mariolam, diebus ac noctibus festorum praecipuorum, et in processione quae fit in commemoratione ejusdem*).

34 Henry III's image commissions are found in the *Calendar Liberate Rolls*; see also R.A. Brown, H.M. Colvin and A.J. Taylor (eds), *The History of the King's Works. 2: The Middle Ages*, London, 1963, pp. 731, 752, 760, 914, 915, 952, 957, 1013.

35 Williamson, *Gothic Sculpture*, p. 114, pl. 174. This is a revision of the dating of 1200–20 proposed by the same author in Alexander and Binski, *Age of Chivalry*, no. 249.

36 E.C. Rouse, 'Wall Paintings in Radnage Church, Bucks.', *Records of Buckinghamshire*, 15 (1947–52), 134–38.

37 The Upper Winchendon bracket may have supported the patronal image of St Mary Magdalen, but for the arguments already stated the Virgin is more likely at this period. The dimensions of the pedestal are 47cm × 35cm, compared with the Langham Virgin's width of 24.1cm.

38 Alexander and Binski, *Age of Chivalry*, no. 250. For the Scandinavian material and connections (also the Bristol figure), see A. Andersson, *English Influence in Norwegian and Swedish Figuresculpture in Wood 1220–1270*, Stockholm, 1949, pp. 108–18, 127–38; Blindheim, *Painted Wooden Sculpture*, p. 35; Williamson, *Gothic Sculpture*, pp. 114–17.

39 B. Kaland, 'Baldakin fra Hopperstad. Madonna fra Hove', *Årbok for Foreningen til Norske Fortidsminnesmerkers Bevaring*, 125 (1970), 85–98; see also Andersson, *Figuresculpture*, fig. 105, and Blindheim, *Painted Wooden Sculpture*, pp. 35, 61, pl. 28.

40 French framed Virgin and Child images can be seen on the *Porte romane* at Rheims Cathedral and the retable in the Louvre (referred to in n. 29 above), both of the second half of the twelfth century; see also Klack-Eitzen, *Thronenden Madonnen*, pp. 44–5, pls 36–7. As well as the manuscripts, see the Adoration of the Magi ivory in the Victoria & Albert Museum.

41 Riley, *Gesta abbatum*, I, p. 287; *Calendar Liberate Rolls Henry III. Vol. I: AD 1226–1240*, London, 1916, p. 350; ibid., *vol. II: AD 1240–1245*, London, 1930, p. 14.

42 J. Raine (ed.), *Testamenta Eboracensia. A Selection of Wills from the Registry at York, vol. II*, Surtees Society, 30, 1855, p. 257, no. CCI.

43 For example, D. Gillerman, *Enguerran de Marigny and the Church of Notre-Dame at Ecouis. Art and Patronage in the Reign of Philip the Fair*, Pennsylvania, 1994, pp. 91, 134; A. Vauchez, *Sainthood in the later Middle Ages* (trans. J. Birrell), Cambridge, 1997, p. 476.

44 Freedberg, *Power of Images*, p. 166.

45 See above, Chapter Two, p. 18.

46 Morgan, 'Texts and Images . . . Twelfth-Century', p. 119.

47 See Camille, *Gothic Idol*, pp. 232–41; the introduction to P. Whiteford (ed.), *The Myracles of Oure Lady, ed. from Wynkyn de Worde's edition*, Middle English Texts, 23, Heidelberg, 1990, pp. 10–18; V.F. Koenig (ed.), *Gautier de Coinci, Les Miracles de Nostre Dame*, 4 vols, Geneva, 1955–70.

48    London, British Library, MS Egerton 2849; N.J. Morgan, *Early Gothic Manuscripts 1190–1250. A Survey of Manuscripts Illuminated in the British Isles*, vol. 4, pt. 1, London, 1982, no. 56, ill. 202.

49    R. Cormack, *Byzantine Art*, Oxford, 2000, p. 182.

50    For a fuller discussion of the *Maria lactans*, see Chapter Six.

51    M. Warner, *Alone of All Her Sex. The Myth and Cult of the Virgin Mary*, London, 1990, pts 4 and 5.

52    See Morgan, 'Texts and Images . . . Twelfth-Century', pp. 122–3; idem, 'Texts and Images of Marian Devotion in Thirteenth-Century England', in W.M. Ormrod (ed.), *England in the Thirteenth Century. Proceedings of the 1989 Harlaxton Symposium*, Harlaxton Medieval Studies, 1, Stamford, 1991, pp. 69–103. See also P. Draper, 'Architecture and Liturgy', in Alexander and Binski, *Age of Chivalry*, pp. 83–91; for St Albans, see Riley, *Gesta abbatum*, I, pp. 284–5.

53    C. Donovan, *The de Brailes Hours. Shaping the Book of Hours in Thirteenth-Century Oxford*, London, 1991, esp. Chap. 4 and Appendix 3.

54    The woman may be reciting the *Ave* prayers to the Virgin which are written on the facing page (Morgan, 'Texts and Images . . . Twelfth-Century', p. 126).

55    Donovan, *Brailes Hours*, fig. 87.

56    N. Stratford, 'Glastonbury and two Gothic ivories in the United States', in F.H. Thompson (ed.), *Studies in Medieval Sculpture*, Society of Antiquaries Occasional Paper, new series 3, London, 1983, p. 216 n. 18 (for the Queen Eleanor reference). If a fine ivory Virgin and Child in Hamburg is of English craftsmanship, such images were already circulating in the second or third decades of the thirteenth century; see Alexander and Binski, *Age of Chivalry*, no. 248; P. Barnet (ed.), *Images in Ivory. Precious Objects of the Gothic Age* (Detroit Institute of Arts exhibition catalogue, 1997), no. 1, where a German origin is also suggested. For insight into the private devotional use of ivory statuettes of the Virgin by thirteenth-century German nuns, see Hamburger, *The Visual and the Visionary*, pp. 432–40.

57    Some base-metal thirteenth-century images of the Virgin were perhaps made for use by the humbler echelons of society; see M. Campbell, 'Medieval Metalworking and Bury St Edmunds', in A. Gransden (ed.), *Bury St Edmunds. Medieval Art, Architecture, Archaeology and Economy*, British Archaeological Association Conference Transactions, 20, 1998, p. 72, pl. XXVIIc.

58    The *Salve Regina* was in use in English Benedictine circles before the end of the twelfth century (Morgan, 'Texts and Images . . . Twelfth-Century', p. 125); see also idem, 'Texts and Images . . . Thirteenth Century', p. 74.

59    Inscriptions on brasses to laity sometimes include exhortations for prayers including the *Ave*, e.g. Brill (Bucks.).

60    For an important study of Marian pictorial cycles, see S. Cather, D. Park and R. Pender, 'Henry III's Wall Paintings at Chester Castle', in A. Thacker (ed.), *Medieval Archaeology, Art and Architecture at Chester*, British Archaeological Association Conference Transactions, 22, 2000, pp. 170–89; see also D. Park, 'The Duxford Master: a Thirteenth-century Painter in East Anglia', in Binski and Noel, *New Offerings*, pp. 312–24.

61    Camille, *Gothic Idol*, pp. 237–9.

62    H.F. Westlake, *The Parish Gilds of Mediaeval England*, London, 1919, p. 212; W. Sparrow Simpson, 'Visitation of Certain Churches belonging to the Dean and Chapter of St Paul's Cathedral in the years 1249–1252', *Camden Society Miscellany*, vol. 9, Camden Society, new series 53, 1895, pp. 20, 21, 32–3.

63    F.M. Powicke and C.R. Cheney (eds), *Councils and Synods with other documents relating to the English Church. II: AD 1205–1313*, Oxford, 1964, p. 1006. For the establishment of lay responsibilities see Mason, 'English Parishioner', 17–29, esp. 19–25.

64    *Calendar Liberate Rolls*, II, pp. 14–15.

65    The introduction of altarpieces on parish church high altars may also have been a factor in displacing the Virgin from this position.

66    Baker, 'Adoration of the Magi', 90–1.

67    For the association of Marian images and the Magi, see Forsyth, *Throne of Wisdom*, pp. 49–59; also E.A. Saxon, 'Aspects of the Eucharist: Theology and Iconography in French Romanesque Sculpture 1070–1150' (University College London, unpublished PhD thesis, 2001), pp. 167–71, 252, and Chapter Six below.

68    Tristram, *Thirteenth Century*, pp. 198, 509–10.

69    Sparrow Simpson, 'Visitation', pp. 3, 24.

70    F.Ll. Harrison, *Music in Medieval Britain*, London, 2nd ed., 1983.

## CHAPTER FOUR

1     For a version of this chapter, see R. Marks, 'The *Ymage Sancti Loci* in the English Medieval Parish Church. Its Status and Function in the Liturgy and Private Devotion', in A. Moraht-Fromm (ed.), *Kunst und Liturgie. Choranlagen des Spätmittelalters – Ihre Architektur, Ausstattung und Nutzung*, Ostfildern, 2003, pp. 31–58.

2    R.P. Hagerty, 'Peter de Wintonia, Parson of Crawley', *Records of Buckinghamshire*, 31 (1989), 93–104.

3    For Firmin, see E. Kirschbaum (ed.), *Lexikon der christlichen Ikonographie*, 6, Freiburg im Breisgau, 1974, cols 241–2.

4    There is a useful, if somewhat confusing, account in R.P. Hagerty, 'The Buckinghamshire Saints Reconsidered. 1: St Firmin of North Crawley', *Records of Buckinghamshire*, 27 (1985), 65–71.

5    Vauchez traces the replacement of relic by image to between the middle of the thirteenth and the middle of the fourteenth centuries: Vauchez, *Sainthood*, pp. 449–53; idem, *Saints, prophètes et visionnaires*, p. 81. As we shall see in this chapter, this may be valid in terms of the installation of images, but the evidence of church dedications suggest that relics were no longer present considerably earlier.

6    F. Arnold-Forster, *Studies in Church Dedications: or England's Patron Saints*, 3 vols, London, 1899; Bond, *Dedications*. I have not attempted to work my way through the continental literature on the subject, although M. Zender, *Räume und Schichten mittelalterlicher Heiligenverehrung in ihrer Bedeutung für die Volkskunde: Die Heiligen des mittleren Maaslander und der Rheinlande in Kultgeschichte und Kultverbreitung*, Cologne, 2nd edn, 1973, has been consulted.

7    Bond, *Dedications*, p. 17. Arnold-Foster's statistics are similar.

8    Orme, *Church Dedications*, p. 34.

9    A. Everitt, *Continuity and Colonization. The Evolution of Kentish Settlement*, Leicester, 1986, pp. 227, 257.

10    Orme, *Church Dedications*, pp. 19, 28–9. The same is true of Cornwall (also part of Exeter diocese): 'Little can be safely said about the dates when Cornish churches acquired their patron saints or which saints they originally acquired' (ibid., p. 12).

11    Everitt, *Continuity*, pp. 226–7, gives examples of altered dedications in Kent in medieval times. Nine or possibly ten Bedfordshire churches today have either completely or partly different dedications from those given in medieval wills and there are at least four in Buckinghamshire. There have been at least thirty dedication changes in Suffolk churches since the Reformation; see Northeast, 'Suffolk Churches', p. 101, n. 35.

12    Everitt, *Continuity*, pp. 230–9, also parts of ch. 10. His suggestion that the predominance of dedications to female saints in general and the Virgin in particular is connected with ancient pagan traditions may be going a little too far. See also Bond, *Dedications*, chs V and XVI.

13    J. Higgitt, 'The Dedication Inscription at Jarrow and its Context', *Antiquaries Journal*, 59 (1979), 343–74, esp. 368–70. For Saxon church dedications, see W. Levison, *England and the Continent in the Eighth Century*, Oxford, 1946, pp. 33–6, 259–65; L. Butler, 'Church dedications and the cults of Anglo-Saxon saints in England', in L.A.S. Butler and R.K. Morris (eds), *The Anglo-Saxon Church. Papers on history, architecture and archaeology in honour of Dr H.M. Taylor*, The Council for British Archaeology Research Report 60, 1986, pp. 44–50.

14    Binns, *Dedications*, p. 18.

15    Graham and Collingwood, 'Patron Saints of the Diocese of Carlisle', *Transactions of the Cumberland and Westmorland Antiquarian and Archaeological Society*, new series, 25 (1925), p. 14.

16    Orme, *Church Dedications*, pp. 37–40.

17    Christian, *Person and God*, p. 87.

18    The parochial histories are taken from the relevant Victoria County History volume for Bedfordshire.

19    J. Blair (ed.), *Minsters and Parish Churches. The Local Church in Transition 950–1200* (Oxford University Committee for Archaeology Monograph No. 17), Oxford, 1988, esp. pp. 7–10, 21–30.

20    Powicke and Cheney, *Councils and Synods*, II, p. 246; Orme, *Church Dedications*, pp. 5–6.

21    Orme, *Church Dedications*, p. 8; Powicke and Cheney, *Councils and Synods*, II, pp. 263–4.

22    D. Webb, *Patrons and Defenders. The Saints in the Italian City-States*, London and New York, 1996, pp. 3, 4, 6 and passim.

23    W. Sauerländer, 'Von der Glykophilousa zur "Amie Graciouse" . Uberlegungen und Fragen zur "Virgen Blanca" in der Kathedrale von Toledo', in *De la création à la restauration. Travaux d'histoire de l'art offerts à Marcel Durliat pour son 75e anniversaire*, Toulouse, 1992, p. 453. This may have been done even earlier, if the eleventh-century relief of St Michael formerly on the tower of Stinsford (Dorset) was *in situ*.

24    For the Auvergne relic-images, of which Ste-Foy at Conques is the *ne plus ultra*, see M. Aston, *Iconoclasts*, p. 25 and Forsyth, *Throne of Wisdom*, pp. 67–86.

25    Morgan, 'Catalan Altar Frontals'. The Fuentidueña apse is now in the Cloisters Collection, New York.

26    In the Westfälisches Landesmuseum, Münster.

27    M. Kupfer, *Romanesque Wall Painting in Central France. The Politics of Narrative*, New Haven and London, 1993.

28    Fonts at Cowlam, Hutton Cranswick and North Grimston.

29    A rare example is a wooden St Nicholas in the Landesmuseum, Bonn, of *c.* 1170.

30    W.G. Henderson (ed.), *Liber Pontificalis Chr. Bainbridge*, Surtees Society, 61, 1875, pp. 76–7; for earlier monastic dedication ceremonies, see Binns, *Dedications*, pp. 11–18.

31    Powicke and Cheney, *Councils and Synods*, II, p. 172: *Item, in ecclesiis dedicatis annus et dies dedicationis et nomen dedicantis et nomen sancti in cuius honore dedicata est ecclesia distincte et aperte scribantur circa maius altare, in loco ad hoc ydoneo. Idem fiat circa minora altaria.* See also J. Braun, *Der Christliche Altar in seiner geschichtlichen Ertwicklung*, Munich, 1924, I, pp. 720–30.

32    Lehmann-Brockhaus, *Schriftquellen*, 2, p. 77, no. 292.

33    Ibid., p. 483, no. 4064.

34    See Chapter Three, p. 61.

35    The very heavily restored paintings are based on original traces; see E.G. Bruton, 'The Recent Discovery of Wall-paintings on the Apse of Checkendon Church', *Oxfordshire Architectural and History Society Proceedings*, new series, 2 (1864–71), 75–8.

36    C. Wilson, D.E. O'Connor and M.A.J. Thompson, *St Giles Skelton. A Brief Guide*, 1978. It may be more than coincidental that both Alne and Skelton were manors held by the Treasurer of York Minster.

37    E.M. Elvey (ed.), *The Courts of the Archdeaconry of Buckingham 1483–1523*, Buckinghamshire Record Society, 19, 1975, p. 44; Bucks. RO, D/A/We3/50, 51.

38    Powicke and Cheney, *Councils and Synods*, II, p. 1006.

39    Michell Whitley, 'Visitations of Devonshire Churches' (passim).

40    G.G. Coulton, 'A Visitation of the Archdeaconry of Totnes in 1342', *English Historical Review*, 26 (1911), 108–24. These visitations may have had a pecuniary motivation as much as a pastoral one.

41    For example, Embleton (Northumberland) and St Ives (Cornwall). A variant at Stanton (Glos.) has the brackets located in the jambs of the chancel east window.

42    Little Wenham is dedicated to All Saints and the disposition of the murals suggests that it was originally dedicated to the Virgin; alternatively, the prescribed arrangement was not yet in force everywhere.

43    Marks, 'Altarpiece'; for Flawford, see Alexander and Binski, *Age of Chivalry*, nos 699–700.

44    Duncan and Hussey, *Testamenta* (East Kent), p. 340.

45    Bequests to the light of Our Lady at Stewkley do not specify whether it was in the nave or chancel, indicating that there was only one Marian image here (Elvey, *Courts*, p. 36; Bucks. RO, D/A/We2/57, We3/63).

46    Elvey, *Courts*, p. 343.

47    Morgan, 'Catalan Altar Frontals', p. 103.

48    A few early thirteenth-century wooden images of saints survive here and there in Belgium, Germany and Scandinavia.

49    Vauchez, *Saints*, pp. 81–2.

50    *Die Zeit der Staufer* (Stuttgart, Württembergisches Landesmuseum exhibition catalogue, 1977), no. 459.

51    H. Adrian and P. Grinder-Hansen, *Den Romanske Kirke – billede og betydning*, Copenhagen, Nationalmuseet, 1995, pp. 19–20; examples at Masterby and Tofta (Gotland).

52    Brown, *Cult of the Saints*, p. 100; see also idem, *Society and the Holy*, pp. 329–30, for the Virgin's significance for the individual from the twelfth century.

53    Vauchez, *Saints*, p. 81; idem, *Sainthood*, p. 453.

54    Duncan and Hussey, *Testamenta* (East Kent), p. 328.

55    Draper, 'Architecture and Liturgy', p. 88.

56    F.C. Hingeston-Randolph, *The Register of Edmund Stafford (AD 1395–1419), Bishop of Exeter*, London, 1886, p. 409. For Hunden's career, see A.B. Emden, *A Biographical Register of the University of Cambridge to 1500*, Cambridge, 1963, pp. 320–1.

57    Burgess, *The Pre-Reformation Records of All Saints', Bristol*, pp. 10–11.

58    The will is dated 1483; Raine, *Testamenta Eboracensia, III*, p. 288m, no. CXVII.

59    *Clavng' celor' & paule doctor populae interceder' p'me dignei' ad regem angelor.*

60    Powicke and Cheney, *Councils and Synods*, II, pp. 174, 297. The 1292 Statutes of Chichester decreed that only lords of the village, patrons of the church and their wives, and rectors and vicars could be buried within either church or chancel (ibid., p. 1117). Sepulchral monuments to gentry began to appear in chancels from at least the early fourteenth century; see N. Saul, *Death, Art and Memory in Medieval England. The Cobham family and their Monuments 1300–1500*, Oxford, 2001, pp. 75–6.

61    N.H. Nicolas (ed.), *Testamenta Vetusta*, II, London, 1826, p. 387.

62    McGregor, *Bedfordshire Wills*, pp. 86–7, no. 69.

63    T. Erbe (ed.), *Mirk's Festial: A Collection of Homilies by Johannes Mirkus (John Mirk)*, pt 1, EETS, extra series 96, 1905, pp. 241–2; for 'our dukes and leaders', see F.S. Ellis (ed.), *The Golden Legend or Lives of the Saints, as Englished by William Caxton*, 6, London, 1900, p. 98. The original Latin text is translated as 'our leaders and guides' in the most modern edition: Jacobus de Voragine, *The Golden Legend. Readings of the Saints*, trans. M.G. Ryan, Princeton, 1993, II, p. 274.

64    The saints are Edmund (Maids Moreton), Peter (19 locations including 8 jointly with St Paul), Dunstan (Monks Risborough), Nicholas (13 locations), Giles (5 locations), Botolph (Bradenham) and Martin (Fenny Stratford, Dunton).

65    Ellis, *Golden Legend*, 4, p. 73. An alabaster Magdalen statue in the Victoria & Albert Museum also has a crown; F. Cheetham, *English Medieval Alabasters*, Oxford, 1984, no. 58, p. 129.

66    P. Coss, *The Knight in Medieval England 1000–1400*, Stroud, 1993, pp. 72, 89–91.

67    For example, the glass of Stanford on Avon (Northants.) and the heraldic murals at Bedale (Yorks.).

68    Vauchez, *La spiritualité*, p. 192. Christian observed that in his Spanish villages devotion to the patronal saint (often Our Lady) was a compound of affection, pride, respect and obligation (*Person and God*, pp. 117, 175).

69    *Parochiani . . . debent invenire campanas et cordas campanarum, cruxifixum, cruces, et ymagines, et calicem argenteum, missale et casulam de sericio* (Powicke and Cheney, *Councils and Synods*, II, p. 513). For the establishment of lay responsibilities, see Mason, 'English Parishioner', 17–29, esp. 19–25.

70    *. . . reparationem navis ecclesie interius et exterius tam de iure quam de consuetudine tam in ymaginibus et precipue ymagine principale in cancello quam in altaribus et fenestris vitreis . . .* (Powicke and Cheney, *Councils and Synods*, 11, p. 1387).

71    This is apparent from Lyndewood's *Provinciale seu constitutiones Anglie Provinciale*, f. clxxxiii(r), note q, on the responsibilities of rectors and vicars. For an early sixteenth-century disagreement over responsibility for maintaining the chancel images, see Wood-Legh, *Kentish Visitations*, p. 274.

72    Bucks. RO, D/A/We2/57 (1525). Stewkley was dedicated to the Virgin in the later Middle Ages, not to St Michael as it is today.

73    Miller and Hatcher, *Medieval England*, p. 109.

74    Meech and Allen, *Book of Margery Kempe*, pp. 53, 207–8. Whether access to everyone was granted is questionable. Margaret Aston has drawn my attention to a complaint of the 1540s over church books being placed in the chancel 'where poor men durst not presume to come'.

75    Timmins, *Register of John Chandler*, pp. 79, 90, 92, 100, 104, 124, 128; Wood-Legh, *Kentish Visitations*, pp. 147, 273.

76    A. Hamilton Thompson (ed.), *Visitations in the Diocese of Lincoln 1517–1531*, Lincoln Record Society, vol. 1, 33, 1940, pp. 102–9, 113–17; vol. 2, 35, 1944, pp. 1–8.

77    Christian, *Local Religion*, p. 65.

78    '. . . there is little sign in the later Middle Ages of strong individual devotion to the parish patron' (Duffy, *Stripping*, p. 162); 'The patronal sculptures do not seem previously [before Mary I's reign] . . . to have attracted much attention' (Aston, *Iconoclasts*, p. 287).

79    Elvey, *Courts*, pp. 63, 276–7; Bucks. RO, D/A/We2/118, We3/133, 220.

80    Houghton Regis: Bell, *Bedfordshire Wills 1484–1533*, pp. 58, 69, nos 93, 113; Beds. & Luton Archives, ABP/R3/82d, 117, ABP/R4/96d. Luton: McGregor, *Bedfordshire Wills*, p. 37, no. 25; Cirket, *English Wills*, p. 68, no. 214; Beds. & Luton Archives, ABP/R4/29d. The length of time it took to complete the Houghton Regis tabernacle might equally be taken as evidence of a lack of enthusiasm among the parishioners.

81    A. Hussey, 'Hythe Wills', *Archaeologia Cantiana*, 50 (1938), 106–7; for a study of medieval ship-names in France, see G. and H. Brese, 'Les saints protecteurs des bateaux 1200–1460', *Ethnologie française*, 9 (1979), 161–78.

82    W.H. Frere (ed.), *The Use of Sarum*, vol. 1, Cambridge, 1898, pp. 29, 111, 213; F. Procter and C. Wordsworth (eds), *Breviarium ad Usum Insignis Ecclesiae Sarum Fasc.1 Kalendarium et Ordo Temporalis*, Cambridge, 1882, cols ix, lxvii.

83    G. Maxwell, *The Ten Pains of Death*, London, 1959, ch. 9; Brown, *Cult of the Saints*, pp. 98–102.

84    T. Milbourn, 'Church of St Stephen Walbrook', *Transactions of the London and Middlesex Architectural Society*, 5 (1876–80), 340, 363; *Letters and Papers Foreign and Domestic of the Reign of Henry VIII*, 18, pt 2, London, 1902, p. 297.

85    *Letters and Papers . . . Henry VIII*, 18, pt 2, p. 309.

86    C. Cotton, 'Churchwardens' Accounts of the Parish of St Andrew, Canterbury from AD 1485 to AD 1625', *Archaeologia Cantiana*, 32 (1917), 181–246, passim.

87    G. Rosser, *Medieval Westminster 1200–1540*, Oxford, 1989, pp. 271–3.

88    E. Freshfield, 'On the Parish Books of St Margaret-Lothbury, St Christopher-le-Stocks, and St Bartholomew-by-the-Exchange, in the City of London', *Archaeologia*, 45 (1880), 112. There were also sacred vessels here with representations of St Christopher and a reliquary.

89    I am grateful to Joanna Mattingley for drawing my attention to this West Country pattern; a manifestation is the commissioning in the early sixteenth century of St Neot's window in the Cornish church dedicated to him.

90    Duncan and Hussey, *Testamenta*, 'East Kent', p. 340.

91    For Wing, see Chapter Ten.

92    For the fortunes of the patronal image during the Reformation, see Chapter Ten.


# CHAPTER FIVE

1    Scribner, *Simple Folk*, p. 3.

2    Vauchez, *Saints, prophètes et visionnaires*, pp. 87–91.

3    Vauchez sees the years between 1250 and 1350 as the period when the devotional image replaced relics and took over the latter's supernatural functions (ibid., pp. 81–2).

4    Vauchez, *Sainthood*, p. 476.

5    See Chapter Three above. Such texts would only have been accessible to the most educated of the laity, hence the importance of their translation into pictorial form in murals like those at Chalfont St Giles. The *Legenda Aurea*

circulated mainly among the clergy, but it is also mentioned in late medieval lay wills (Middleton-Stewart, *Inward Purity*, p. 172).

6    R. Marks, *Stained Glass in England during the Middle Ages*, London, 1993, pp. 137–40.

7    *Calendar Liberate Rolls*, II, p. 15; see also Chapter Four above.

8    Sparrow Simpson, 'Visitation', pp. 3, 10, 24, 25.

9    W. Sparrow Simpson (ed.), *Visitations of Churches Belonging to St Paul's Cathedral in 1297 and in 1458*, Camden Society, new series 55, 1895, pp. 1–105 (passim).

10    Sparrow Simpson, 'Visitation', pp. 15, 24–5; idem, *Visitations . . . in 1297 and in 1458*, pp. 12, 14. There may have been some double-counting here.

11    *. . . ex dextra parte eiusdem crucis beate Virginis, Sanctorum Nicholai et Jacobi, et ex parte sinistra eiusdem ymagines Sancti Johanis Ewangeliste et ij ymagines beate Margarete. Item in quodam angulo ex parte sinistra ymagines Sanctarum Marie Magdalene et Katerine* (Sparrow Simpson, *Visitations . . . in 1297 and in 1458*, p. 45).

12    For the Worcester instruction, see above, Chapter Four.

13    *. . . altare sit ymago vel sculptura seu pictura vel scriptura expresse dignans et cuilibet intentui manifestans in cujus sancti nomen et honorem sit ipsum altare constructum*, quoted in J. Gardner, 'Altars, Altarpieces, and Art History: Legislation and Usage', in E. Borsook and F.S. Gioffredi (eds), *Italian Altarpieces 1250–1550. Function and Design*, Oxford, 1994, p. 11 n. 31. Charles Hope has suggested this edict was not widely adopted (idem, 'Altarpieces', p. 537).

14    Quoted in D. Webb, *Pilgrimage in Medieval England*, Hambledon, London and New York, 2000, p. 95.

15    *Que omnia diligenter per illum cui altare committitur, conserventur, qui eciam non permittat varias ymagines nec cereos apponi nec affigi circa altaria incomposite, ut fit in ecclesiis ruralibus, sed tantum ymagines sanctorum in quorum honore dedicantur . . .* (G. Oliver, *Monasticon Dioecesis Exoniensis*, Exeter and London, 1846, p. 270).

16    Apart from Fingringhoe (**IX**), examples may be seen at Hales (Norf.), and Reydon and Westhall (Suff.).

17    See, for example, Bergmann, *Holzskulpturen des Mittelalters*; H. Meurer, *Württembergisches Landesmuseum Stuttgart. Die mittelalterlichen Skulpturen, I Stein-und Holzskulpturen 800–1400*, Stuttgart, 1989.

18    *Item, parvam ymaginem Trinitatis, de alabastre. Item, parvam ymaginem Beate Marie de alabastre, vocatam Pyty. Item, j discum cum capite Johannis Baptiste. . . . Item j ymago Sancti Cristoforii, de alabastre. Item, ymago de Marie assumpcione, de alabastre. Item, j velum pictum, cum ymagine Sancti Michaelis. Item, j ymago Sancti Johannis Baptiste, cum j tabernacle. Item, j ymago Sancte Anne, cum j tabernacle. Item, j tabula, cum ymagine Sancti Erasmi. Item, j tabula, cum ymagine Sancti Cristofori.* See Hingeston-Randolph, *Register of Edmund Stafford*, p. 483.

19    Barnum, *Dives and Pauper*, 1, p. 81.

20    J. Catto, 'Religious Change under Henry V', in G.L. Harriss (ed.), *Henry V. The Practice of Kingship*, Oxford, 1985, pp. 97–115; Aston, *Iconoclasts*, pp. 25–6.

21    Milbourn, 'St Stephen Walbrook', 340–1, 343.

22    Eamon Duffy sees the early sixteenth century as a period when there was 'a flood of investments in building and ornaments, and the making of new images and the gilding, painting, and embellishing of old ones' (Duffy *Stripping*, p. 156). I do not dissent from the latter part of this statement, but remain unconvinced by his assessment of the scale of new image-provision in Henry VIII's reign. See below, Chapter Ten.

23    Most of these are discussed below. An early manifestation of St Brigitte's cult was the church dedicated to her in London's Fleet Street; in 1375 a gild was founded there to find a light before her image: Westlake, *Parish Gilds*, p. 182.

24    The prominence of many of these saints in the early sixteenth century is attested by their inclusion in the suffrages of printed Books of Hours, e.g. the York Primer has suffrages to SS Erasmus, George, Sebastian, Christopher, Roche and Anthony (C. Wordsworth (ed.), *Horae Eboracenses*, Surtees Society, 132, 1920, pp. 128–33).

25    The phrase, 'holie companie of Heven' is a common topos; this variant is taken from T. Astle (ed.), *The Will of King Henry VII*, London, 1775, pp. 2–3.

26    Ellis, *Golden Legend*, 6, p. 97.

27    While not denying their intercessory function, Vauchez also emphasizes the role of late medieval saints (especially females) as models for the faithful to follow (*Sainthood*, pp. 110, 212). See also K.A. Winstead, *Virgin Martyrs. Legends of Sainthood in Late Medieval England*, Ithaca and London, 1997, pp. 14, 15, 116–33, 178–80; she argues that there was a tendency in fifteenth-century devotional texts for gentle-born women and urban elites to emphasize the exemplary nature of the lives of female saints. The inimitable nature of saints is, however, stressed convincingly by Duffy (*Stripping*, pp. 170, 174–8) and in more detail by Brigitte Cazelles in *Le Corps de Sainteté*, Geneva, 1982, pp. 9, 17, 38–40, 44, 47, 139, 219. See also French, *People of the Parish*, pp. 194–206.

28    'S. Wilam Sanc price procures aydane' (*Gentleman's Magazine*, 26 (1756), 559–60).

29    J.E. Binney, *The Accounts of the Wardens of the Parish of Morebath, Devon 1520–1573*, Devon Notes and Queries, 1903–4, passim.

30    E. Mâle, *L'Art religieux de la fin du Moyen Age en France*, Paris, 1931, pp. 155, 157.

31    Duncan and Hussey, *Testamenta* (East Kent), pp. 29, 256; the brasses of John Stathum (d. 1453) and his son Sir Thomas (d. 1470) both feature St Christopher.

32    See above, Chapter Four.

33    The following figures for acreage and population are taken from the Victoria County History and Lutt, *Bedfordshire Muster Lists*.

34    Binney, *Wardens of Morebath*; Duffy, *Voices of Morebath*.

35    See, for example, N. Douglas, *Old Calabria*, London, 1983, ch. XXXI; C. Levi, *Christ Stopped at Eboli*, Harmondsworth, 1982, ch. 12; G. Maxwell, *The Ten Pains of Death*, London, 1959; Christian, *Person and God*.

36    Christian, *Person and God*, p. 77.

37    Meech and Allen, *Book of Margery Kempe*, pp. 111, 148.

38    K. Wrightson and D. Levine, *Poverty and Piety in an English Village. Terling, 1525–1700*, Oxford, 1995, pp. 76–9, table 4.1, fig. 4.1.

39    Bell, *Bedfordshire Wills 1484–1533*, pp. 21, 18–19, nos 30, 26.

40    For example, William Amere (1527/8) left 4*d* to St Peter's church and 3*s* 4*d* to St Cuthbert's as well as 12*d* to the high altar and 8*d* to the rood light of his own parish church of St Paul's (Bell, *Bedfordshire Wills 1484–1533*, pp. 47–8, no. 74).

41    Duffy *Stripping*, p. 179, quoting John Bale, *Comedy concerning thre lawes*.

42    Cheetham, *Medieval Alabasters*, p. 84, no. 13; A.F. Mata, *El retablo Gótico de Cartagena y los alabastros ingleses en España*, Madrid, 1999, fig. 22.

43    Some of these figures occur in murals, stained glass and screen-paintings. Everitt observed that, apart from Our Lady, local Anglo-Saxon saints and dedications associated with early Christianity in Kent formed a majority of titular saints (idem, *Continuity*, p. 228). His attempt to trace a connection between *pays* and the saints is problematic in terms of scope (no distinction is made between patronal saints and altar saints within parish churches) and chronological span (pp. 234–9).

44    See above, Chapter Two.

45    Also by the joint action of the two parishes in a dispute over grazing rights with the inhabitants of Houghton Regis in 1475/6; see F. Puttnam (ed.), 'Declaration of Common Rights: Eaton Bray and Totternhoe 1475', BHRS, 8, 1923, pp. 165–8.

46    L.W. Hepple and A.M. Doggett, *The Chilterns*, Chichester, 2nd edn, 1994, pp. 62, 83, 93, 125–6, pl. 44.

47    J. Godber, *History of Bedfordshire 1066–1888*, Bedfordshire County Council, 1969, pp. 98–9; E.B. Fryde, *Peasants and Landlords in Later Medieval England c. 1380–c. 1525*, Stroud, 1996, pp. 145–7.

48    Bell, *Bedfordshire Wills 1484–1533*, pp. 59–60, no. 95. For the growth of an upper echelon of peasantry in the late fifteenth century, see A. Jones, 'Bedfordshire: Fifteenth Century', in P.D.A. Harvey (ed.), *The Peasant Land Market in Fifteenth-Century England*, Oxford, 1984, p. 251.

49    Cirket, *English Wills*, pp. 54, 77–8, nos 170, 195, 246; Bell, *Bedfordshire Wills 1484–1533*, p. 64, no. 104. See also Chapter Two, p. 11.

50    Cirket, *English Wills*, p. 54, nos 170, 195.

51    Ellis, *Golden Legend*, 4, pp. 111–19; Tristram, *Fourteenth Century*, p. 115; see also Kirschbaum, *Lexikon*, 5, cols 496–508; H.C. Whaite, *St Christopher in English Mediaeval Wallpainting*, London, 1929.

52    For manuscripts, see the *Westminster Psalter* of *c.* 1250 (British Library, MS Royal 2 A. XXII. f. 220v) and the *Lambeth Apocalypse* of *c.* 1260–7 (London, Lambeth Palace Library, MS 209, f. 40). The mural at Little Hampden (Bucks.) is one of the earliest occurrences in this medium, pre-dating the well-known example in the south transept of Westminster Abbey.

53    *Christophori Sancti speciem quicunque tuetur; Illa nempe die nullo languore gravetur* (Tristram, *Fourteenth Century*, p. 115).

54    A. Hussey, 'Milton Wills (next Sittingbourne)–III', *Archaeologia Cantiana*, 46 (1934), 46. For the other Kent references, see Duncan and Hussey, *Testamenta* (East Kent), passim. Surprisingly, there are no bequests to St Christopher in Dunstable wills, although this town was situated on the busy Watling Street.

55    Burgess, *Pre-Reformation Records of All Saints', Bristol*, p. 14. The primer was stolen twice. The first time it was recovered at Compostella.

56    F.H. Thompson, 'Norton Priory, near Runcorn, Cheshire', *Archaeological Journal*, 123 (1966), p. 67, pl. XII; R. Deacon and P. Lindley, *Image and Idol: Medieval Sculpture* (London, Tate Gallery exhibition catalogue, 2001), p. 46.

57    Ellis, *Golden Legend*, 5, pp. 1–12 (quote on p. 12); see also Wordsworth, *Horae Eboracenses*, p. 131, n. 1; Kirschbaum, *Lexikon*, 8, cols 275–8; Bottisford's will is in the Beds. & Luton Archives, ABP/R3/102.

58    Cheetham, *Medieval Alabasters*, p. 147, no. 76; Mata, *El retablo Gótico*, fig. 118. Apart from Totternhoe, the other Bedfordshire examples were at Eversholt, Luton, Shillington and Sharnbrook.

59    N. Orme, 'A Letter of Saint Roche', *Devon and Cornwall Notes and Queries*, 36 (1987–91), 153–9; see also F.H. Dickinson (ed.), *Missale ad Usum Insignis et Praeclare Ecclesiae Sarum*, Burntisland, 1861–83, cols 900★–903★.

60    Other (fragmentary) alabaster figures of St Anthony exist at Oscott College, Barling Magna (Essex), East Rudham (Norf.) and Preston (E. Yorks.) and possibly at Bushmead Priory (Beds.); a painted cycle of St Anthony is on the back of the choirstalls of Carlisle Cathedral. For St Anthony, see Kirschbaum, *Lexikon*, 7, cols 205–17.

61 R.M. Serjeantson and H. Isham Longden, 'The Parish Churches and Religious Houses of Northamptonshire: Their Dedications, Altars, Images and Lights', *Archaeological Journal*, 70 (1913), 268. The most famous depiction of St Anthony as patron of the sick (and as 'founder' of the Antonine Order) is in Grünewald's altarpiece painted for Isenheim: see A. Hayum, *The Isenheim Altarpiece. God's Medicine and the Painter's Vision*, Princeton, 1989. Locality also might affect his representation. The fourteenth-century murals at Longthorpe Tower near Peterborough include what may be a very rare St Anthony miracle connected with basket-making, of which craft he was patron saint; see E.C. Rouse and D. Baker, 'The Wall-Paintings at Longthorpe Tower near Peterborough, Northants.', *Archaeologia*, 96 (1955), 49. This is a precocious image and the birds in a tree suggest that the saint is more likely to be Francis.

62 William Tevett bequeathed a measure of barley to her light at Totternhoe: P. Bell (ed.), *Bedfordshire Wills 1480–1519*, BHRS, 45, 1966, p. 66, no. 139.

63 Webb, *Pilgrimage*, p. 152.

64 For St Sitha, see Kirschbaum, *Lexikon*, 8, cols 640–1; T. Turville-Petre, 'A Middle English Life of St Zita', *Nottingham Medieval Studies*, 35 (1991), 102–5; J. Franks, 'St Zita, St Sythe and St Osyth', *Nottingham Medieval Studies*, 36 (1992), 148–50; S. Sutcliffe, 'The Cult of St Sitha in England: an introduction', *Nottingham Medieval Studies*, 37 (1993), 83–9. For the spread of the cult in Italy, see Vauchez, *Sainthood*, pp. 210, 240–1. Despite their proximity to Aylesbury, the saint represented by images in the Bedfordshire villages, as elsewhere, was the Lucchese servant, not the English St Osyth.

65 M. Goodich, *Ancilla Dei: 'The Servant as Saint'*, in J. Kirshner and S.F. Wemple (eds), *Women of the Medieval World. Essays in Honor of John H. Mundy*, Oxford, 1985, pp. 119–36 (esp. 128–30).

66 See P. Cullum and J. Goldberg, 'How Margaret Blackburn taught her Daughters; Reading Devotional Instruction in a Book of Hours', in J. Wogan-Browne *et al.* (eds), *Medieval Women: Texts and Contexts in Late Medieval Britain. Essays for Felicity Riddy*, Turnhout, 2000, pp. 225–8.

67 Raine, *Testamenta Eboracensia, I*, p. 287, no. CCVIII.

68 York Minster Library, MS Additional 2, f. 40v; F.W. Cheetham, *Medieval English Alabaster Carvings in the Castle Museum Nottingham*, Nottingham, rev. edn, 1973, pp. 50–1. A fourteenth-century mural in St Albans Abbey has been identified as St Sitha, but the attributes are unclear: E. Roberts, *The Wall Paintings of Saint Albans Abbey*, St Albans, 1993, pp. 19–20.

69 H.N. MacCracken (ed.), *The Minor Poems of John Lydgate*, pt I, EETS, extra series 107, 1911 (for 1910), p. 137.

70 C. Welch (ed.), *The Churchwardens' Accounts of the Parish of Allhallows, London Wall*, London, 1912, pp. 59–61; Duncan and Hussey, *Testamenta* (East Kent), p. 30.

71 Ellis, *Golden Legend*, 3, p. 262. For the iconography of St Eligius, see Kirschbaum, *Lexikon*, 6, cols 122–7. For pilgrim badges, see D. Bruna, *Musée National du Moyen Age – Thermes de Cluny. Enseignes de Pèlerinage et Enseignes Profanes*, Paris, 1996, pp. 131–4.

72 M. Rubin, *Corpus Christi. The Eucharist in Late Medieval Culture*, Cambridge, 1991, p. 262.

73 A. Hanham (ed.), *The Cely Letters 1472–1488*, EETS, original series 273, 1975, p. 48, no. 52.

74 For Chagford and the Exeter farriers, see R. Whiting, *The Blind Devotion of the People. Popular Religion and the English Reformation*, Cambridge, 1989, pp. 50, 72, 110. The Derby churchwardens' accounts are quoted in J.C. Cox, *Churchwardens' Accounts*, London, 1913, p. 164. Notable equine events take place in Provence on the feast of St Eligius, also one of the famous Breton Pardons; see E. Brisbois, *Pardons et pèlerinages en Bretagne et Normandie*, Paris, 1994, pp. 93–4.

75 For a list, see Cheetham, *Medieval Alabasters*, p. 99. However, a mural in the remote parish church at Shorthampton (Oxon.) appears to represent him as a layman.

76 An observation made in Hope, 'Altarpieces', p. 547.

77 St Eligius is also carved on the roof of St Paul's church in Bedford.

78 Bell, *Bedfordshire Wills 1484–1533*, p. 64, no. 104.

79 Kirschbaum, *Lexikon*, 6, cols 156–8; Ellis, *Golden Legend*, 7, pp. 267–73; Dickinson, *Missale*, cols 899*–900*.

80 A. Raine, *Mediaeval York. A topographical survey based on original sources*, London, 1955, p. 191.

81 Brown, *Popular Piety*, p. 215, citing Bishop Langton's Register of 1485–93.

82 C. Eveleigh Woodruff, 'The Sacrist's Rolls of Christ Church, Canterbury', *Archaeologia Cantiana*, 48 (1936), 42, 67ff.

83 C. Horstmann (ed.), *Sammlung Altenglischer Legenden*, Heilbronn, 1878, pp. 198–203; see also the Suffrage in Wordsworth, *Horae Eboracenses*, pp. 128–9.

84 P. Tudor-Craig, 'Fragment of panel painting of the Flagellation in the possession of Canterbury Cathedral and the Martyrdom of St Erasmus belonging to the Society of Antiquaries', *Antiquaries Journal*, 54 (1974), 289–90; Marks and Williamson, *Gothic*, no. 285. There is an early sixteenth-century stained glass representation at Lullingstone, also in Kent. For other examples, see Cheetham, *Medieval Alabasters*, p. 100.

85 Duffy *Stripping*, p. 180.

86 A. Hussey, 'Milton Wills (next Sittingbourne) – II, *Archaeologia Cantiana*, 45 (1933), 25.

87 I am most grateful to Charles Phythian-Adams for drawing my attention to the significance of the Weald for timber used in ship-building.

88   Bell, *Bedfordshire Wills 1480–1519*, p. 96, no. 190; idem, *Bedfordshire Wills 1484–1533*, p. 91, no. 152.

89   Southfleet, Strood, Rochester, Wade, Sholden, Oxney, Dover, Newington and New Romney; see Everitt, *Continuity*, pp. 232–3; for St Nicholas, see Kirschbaum, *Lexikon*, 8, cols 45–58.

90   Dickinson, *Missale*, cols 665–6.

91   See above, Chapter Two.

92   Ellis, *Golden Legend*, 2, pp. 118–19.

93   A. Vere Woodman, 'The Accounts of the Churchwardens of Wing', *Records of Buckinghamshire*, 16 (1953–60), 314; R. Hutton, *The Rise and Fall of Merry England. The Ritual Year 1400–1700*, Oxford, 1994, pp. 10–12.

94   Ellis, *Golden Legend*, 3, p. 133.

95   The literature on St George is expanding. The most recent substantial addition is S. Riches, *St George. Hero, Martyr and Myth*, Stroud, 2000; see also the observations in French, *People of the Parish*, pp. 204–6.

96   L.L. Duncan, 'The parish churches of West Kent, their dedications, altars, images, and lights', *Transactions of the St Paul's Ecclesiological Society*, 3 (1895), p. 261.

97   Lutt, *Bedfordshire Muster Lists*, p. 40 (Swanson is transcribed as 'Water Swarston'). Cutlat also appears on the Muster Roll (his will is in Beds. & Luton Archives, ABP/R1544/11/39d); for Lord Bray, see G.E. Cokayne, *The Complete Peerage*, 2, new edn, revised by V. Gibbs, London, 1912, p. 287.

98   D. Wilkins, *Concilia Magnae Britanniae et Hiberniae*, London, 1737, 3, p. 824.

99   A mounted George occurs on the brass of Sir Hugh Hastings (d. 1347) at Elsing (Norf.). The saint is also mounted on several Romanesque tympana.

100  C. Richmond, 'Three Suffolk Pieces', in S. Ditchfield (ed.), *Christianity and Community in the West. Essays for John Bossy*, Aldershot, 2001, p. 55.

101  Marks and Williamson, *Gothic*, nos 58, 84.

102  J.T. Fowler, *Memorials of the Church of SS. Peter and Wilfrid, Ripon, vol. IV*, Surtees Society, 115, 1908, pp. 294–6; for further discussion of the Ripon contract, see Chapter Nine below. C. Kerry, *A History of the Municipal Church of St Lawrence, Reading*, Reading, 1883, p. 40; A.V. Peatling and C.L. Kingsford (eds), *Surrey Wills (Archdeaconry Court, Spage Register)*, Surrey Record Society, 5 1921, p. 39, no. 131; J.W. Clay (ed.), *North Country Wills*, Surtees Society, 116, vol. ii, 1908, p. 109, no. LXXX.

103  Marks and Williamson, *Gothic*, no. 284.

104  R.F.B. Hodgkinson (trans.), *The Account Books of the Gilds of St George and of St Mary in the Church of St Peter Nottingham*, Thoroton Society Record Series, 7, 1939; M. Grace (ed.), *Records of the Gild of St George in Norwich, 1389–1547*, Norfolk Record Society, 9, 1937.

105  Hodgkinson, *Account Books*, pp. 49, 72; Duffy *Stripping*, pp. 440–1.

106  The detachable arm of a wooden George in the Visby Museum (Gotland, Sweden) evokes the Ripon image.

107  Grace, *Gild of St George*, pp. 16–17; *The Norwich Snapdragon*, Norfolk Museum Services Information Sheet, Norfolk Museums Service, 1984. For the Norwich and other George processions, see R. Hutton, *The Stations of the Sun. A History of the Ritual Year in Britain*, Oxford, 1997, pp. 214–17.

108  Fowler, *Memorials*, pp. 294–6; Bishop Hobhouse (ed.), *Churchwardens' Accounts*, Somerset Record Society, 4, 1890, pp. 29, 30, 32. Hobhouse's claim (p. 32, n. 1) that the outlay was not just for the image but for the entire chapel of St George on the north side of the chancel is debatable when the costs of the Ripon image are considered.

109  Bassingbourn churchwardens' accounts, ff. 80, 121–4, 127, 131 (Roberts transcript in Cambridge University Library, MS Add. 2792); wills of John Hubard (1518) and Giles Ashwell (1521) (Cambs. RO. C8:11, WR 1★4029).

110  For a survey, see J. Svanberg and A. Qwarnström, *Sankt Göran och draken*, Stockholm, revised edn, 1998 (the list of Finnish and Swedish Georges was omitted from the English edition).

111  Kerry, *St Lawrence, Reading*, p. 45; Hodgkinson, *Account Books*, pp. 28–72; H.B. Walters, *London Churches at the Reformation with an Account of their Contents*, London, 1939, pp. 215, 467–8, 581.

112  Hodgkinson, *Account Books*, p. 29 (1470–1).

113  . . . *ad laicorum et omnium illuc adventantium aedificationem, et consolationem saecularium*: Riley, *Gesta abbatum*, 1, p. 287; Burgess, *Pre-Reformation Records of All Saints', Bristol*, p. 10. For the formulaic 'excite people to devotion' see Chapter Two above.

114  For Wynch, see Bell, *Bedfordshire Wills 1484–1533*, p. 68, no. 111.

# CHAPTER SIX

1    L. Forgeard, *L'Age d'Or de la Vièrge et l'Enfant. Le XIVe siècle en Seine-et-Marne*, Paris, 1995.

2    See, for example, the fourteenth-century Swedish material studied in C. Jacobsson, *Höggotisk träskulptur i gamla Linköpings stift*, Visby, 1995.

3    For the history of the church, see VCH, *Bedfordshire*, 3, London, 1912, pp. 311–13; G. Odell, *The Church of St Mary the Virgin, Marston Moreteyne*, Ampthill, 1982; C. Pickford (ed.), *Bedfordshire Churches in the Nineteenth Century. Part II. Parishes H to R*, BHRS, 77, 1998, pp. 463–72. I am also indebted to Mr John Kempton, one of the churchwardens, for sharing his knowledge of the church fabric and history. A grandson of Thomas Reynes, also named Thomas, was the (well-connected) rector of Marston Moreteyne between 1505 and 1524/5.

4    H. Jenkinson and G.H. Fowler, 'Some Bedfordshire Wills at Lambeth and Lincoln', BHRS, 14, 1931, p. 115; Cirket, *English Wills*, pp. 9, 11, 13, 19, 29, 36, 37, 49, 71, nos 21d, 23, 23d, 34, 42d, 55d, 76d, 96d, 97, 97d, 150, 225; McGregor, *Bedfordshire Wills*, p. 121, no. 97; Bell, *Bedfordshire Wills 1484–1533*, pp. 106, 147, 170, nos 173, 244, 285; Beds. & Luton Archives, ABP/R3/75d, 92d, 126d; ABP/R4/180d.

5    Summaries of the history of the *Pietà* are in Schiller, *Iconography*, pp. 179–81, and Kirschbaum, *Lexikon*, 4, cols 450–6. More detailed studies include W. Passarge, *Das deutsche Vesperbild im Mittelaltar*, Cologne, 1924, and E. Reiners-Ernst, *Das freudvolle Vesperbild und die Anfänge der Pietà-Vorstellung*, Munich, 1939.

6    For the *Pietà* in England, see R. Marks, 'Viewing Our Lady of Pity', in *Magistro et Amico. Amici discipulique Lechowi Kalinowskiemu w osiemdziesięciolecie urodzin*, Cracow, 2002, pp. 101–21. This section of the chapter is a revised version of this article. The only other detailed study of the English image in literature and art is M.J. Power, 'The *Pietà* in Medieval England' (University of York unpublished MA dissertation, 1980/1).

7    M.B. Parkes (comp.), *The Medieval Manuscripts of Keble College Oxford*, London, 1979, pp. 216–18, pl. 122. Nigel Morgan cites an earlier English occurrence in the *Taymouth Hours* (London, British Library MS Yates Thompson 13, f. 123v), of c. 1330–40, where it appears below the Deposition in a sequence of Passion miniatures; see N. Morgan, 'Texts and Images of Marian Devotion in Fourteenth-Century England', in N. Rogers (ed.), *England in the Fourteenth Century. Proceedings of the 1991 Harlaxton Symposium*, Harlaxton Medieval Studies 3, Stamford, 1993, p. 54. The representation's uniqueness (for its date) and presence in a narrative sequence suggest that it was not viewed as an iconic *Pietà*.

8    An English origin has also been suggested for a small walnut *Pietà* of c. 1370–1400; see P. Williamson, *Northern Gothic Sculpture 1200–1450 (Victoria & Albert Museum)*, London, 1988, pp. 142–5, no. 40.

9    The Hornton *Pietà* and an accompanying mural of St George both have the Prince of Wales's feathers and scroll for a motto, associating them with Edward the Black Prince (d. 1376); the figure-style and armour of St George, however, suggest a date a few years later.

10   Waterton, *Pietas Mariana Britannica*, Book 1, London, 1879, p. 127.

11   Meech and Allen, *Book of Margery Kempe*, p. 148.

12   R. Woolf, *The English Religious Lyric in the Middle Ages*, Oxford, 1968, p. 257.

13   Cirket, *English Wills*, p. 78, no. 247d; Bell, *Bedfordshire Wills 1484–1533*, pp. 75, 78, nos 122, 127.

14   See also Chapter Nine for a general discussion of polychromy.

15   C. Prigent, *Les sculptures anglaises d'albâtre au musée national du Moyen Age*, Thermes de Cluny, Paris, 1998, p. 59, no. 1; Marks and Williamson, *Gothic*, no. 344.

16   The quotations are from Nicholas Love's popular translation; see J. Hogg and L.F. Powell (eds), *Nicholas Love, The Mirrour of the Blessed Lyf of Jesu Christ*, Analecta Cartusiana, 91, 1989, 1, p. 47; 2, p. 237. Given the Franciscan provenance of the *Meditationes*, it is not unexpected to find that Our Lady's kerchief was one of the prize relics of Assisi, where it was venerated by Margery Kempe (Meech and Allen, *Book of Margery Kempe*, p. 79).

17   For the poem, see MacCracken, *John Lydgate*, pp. 268–79.

18   D. Gray, *Themes and Images in the Medieval English Religious Lyric*, London and Boston, 1972, p. 88; see also pp. 88–90.

19   Morgan, 'Text and Images . . . Fourteenth-Century', pp. 41–2, 47, discusses the rose symbolism. German examples are examined in W. Krönig, 'Ein Vesperbild im Schnütgen-Museum zu Köln mit einem Exkurs über die Bedeutung der Rosetten', *Wallraf-Richartz Jahrbuch*, 31 (1969), 7–24.

20   The subjects with their verse equivalents are discussed in Woolf, *English Religious Lyric*, pp. 395–7; see also C. Woodforde, *The Norwich School of Glass-Painting in the Fifteenth Century*, Oxford, 1950, Chapter VII; Morgan, 'Text and Images . . . Fourteenth-Century', pp. 55–6.

21   W.H. Forsyth, *The Pietà in French Late Gothic Sculpture. Regional Variations*, New York, 1995, pp. 123–4, 167, fig. 169.

22   W. Krönig, *Rheinische Vesperbild*, Münchengladbach, 1967; Forsyth, *Pietà*. For a critique of Forsyth's methodology, see the review by Phillip Lindley in *Burlington Magazine*, 140, no. 1149 (December 1998), 834–5. For alabaster image-production, see Chapter Nine.

23   Duncan and Hussey, *Testamenta* (East Kent), p. 72.

24   For the Virgin as co-Redemptrix, see B. Williamson, 'The Virgin *Lactans* as Second Eve: Image of the *Salvatrix*', *Studies in Iconography*, 19 (1998), 105–38.

25   Morgan, 'Text and Images . . . Fourteenth-Century', p. 52. The Thame reference is taken from F.G. Lee, *History and Antiquities of the Prebendal Church of the Blessed Virgin Mary of Thame*, London, 1883, col. 25. Lee had examined the churchwardens' accounts and asserted that the altar of Our Lady of Pity stood on the north side of the roodscreen, rather than on the south side where the mural is located (ibid., col. 21). However, only an altar of Our Lady or Our Lady in Gesyn is mentioned in Julia Carnwath's study, 'The Churchwardens' Accounts of

Thame, Oxfordshire, *c.* 1443–1524', in D.J. Clayton, R.G. Davies and P. McNiven (eds), *Trade, Devotion and Governance. Papers in Later Medieval History*, Stroud, 1994, p. 187.

26    S. Badham, 'Status and Salvation: The Design of Medieval English Brasses and Incised Slabs', *Monumental Brass Society Transactions*, 15, pt. 5 (1997), 437, fig. 13.

27    Duncan, 'West Kent', 292; F.E. Warren, 'A Pre-Reformation Village Gild', *Proceedings of the Suffolk Institute of Archaeology*, 11 (1901), 142–3.

28    MacCracken, *John Lydgate*, p. 269.

29    N.P. Tanner (ed.), *Heresy Trials in the Diocese of Norwich, 1428–31*, Camden Society, Fourth Series, 20, 1977, pp. 89–90.

30    R.T. Davies (ed.), *Medieval English Lyrics. A Critical Anthology*, Northwestern University Press, 1964, p. 211.

31    Duncan, 'West Kent', 7.

32    Gendered aspects of devotion are considered further in Chapter Seven.

33    The prayer is discussed in R.S. Wieck, *Painted Prayers. The Book of Hours in Medieval and Renaissance Art*, New York, 1997, pp. 86–90; Duffy *Stripping*, pp. 262–4, 318.

34    Wordsworth, *Horae Eboracenses*, p. 66, n. 3 (citing the *Sarum Hours*). For examples of this indulgence in continental Hours, see V. Reinburg, 'Hearing Lay People's Prayer', in B.B. Diefendorf and C. Hesse (eds), *Culture and Identity in Early Modern Europe (1500–1800). Essays in Honor of Natalie Zemon Davis*, University of Michigan Press, Ann Arbor, 1993, pp. 27–9, esp. n. 31.

35    Freshfield, 'On the Parish Books', 119.

36    A graveyard image was at Erith (Kent) (Duncan, 'West Kent', 267); an example of a funerary pall with the *Pietà* is that belonging to the Vintners' Company.

37    Duncan and Hussey, *Testamenta* (East Kent), p. 120.

38    For the will and brass, see L.L. Duncan, 'Notes on the Topography of Cranbrook Church', *Archaeologia Cantiana*, 37 (1925), 25.

39    M.R. James and W.T. Bensly, *The Sculptured Bosses in the Roof of the Bauchun Chapel of Our Lady of Pity in Norwich Cathedral*, Norwich, 1908; B. Dodwell, 'William Bauchun and his Connection with the Cathedral Priory at Norwich', *Norfolk Archaeology*, 36 (1974–7), 111–18; J.R. Shinners Jr, 'The Veneration of Saints at Norwich Cathedral in the Fourteenth Century', *Norfolk Archaeology*, 40 (1987–9), 133–44. My interpretation differs in some details from that of the other two authors.

40    The Consistory Court was the bishop's court and its jurisdiction encompassed cases which had to be tried according to canon law. These included probate matters, marriage disputes, cases against those claiming clerical privilege and those who had transgressed against church discipline and religion (except in matters of doctrine and liturgy).

41    MacCracken, *John Lydgate*, p. 268.

42    W. Dugdale, *The History of St Paul's Cathedral in London, from its foundation . . . to the year 1658* (with continuations and additions by H. Ellis), London, 1818, pp. 21–2. Roger, who probably died in 1336, was a figure of some importance. His devotion to the Virgin is attested by the multiple miniatures in a miscellany he owned which depict him venerating Our Lady, albeit not in childbed; see L.F. Sandler, *Omne Bonum. A Fourteenth-Century Encyclopedia of Universal Knowledge*, London, 1996; for his career, see A.B. Emden, *A Biographical Register of the University of Oxford to A.D. 1500*, 3, Oxford, 1959, pp. 1974–5.

43    The dimensions are 1.50 × 0.81m. The panel seems to have escaped the notice of students of medieval sculpture, although it is illustrated in N. Pevsner, *The Buildings of England. Derbyshire*, Harmondsworth, 2nd edn, 1978, p. 92, pl. 23. I am indebted to Allan Barton for drawing my attention to the Newark panel.

44    G. Kaftal, *Saints in Italian Art. Iconography of the Saints in Central and South Italian Schools of Painting*, Florence, 1965, p. 479, fig. 546; idem, *Saints in Italian Art. Iconography of the Saints in the Painting of North East Italy*, Florence, 1978, p. 331, fig. 393; Van Os, *Art of Devotion*, pp. 99–100.

45    Vauchez, *La Spiritualité*, p. 141. For the Gesyn, see Kirschbaum, *Lexikon*, 4, cols 535–6; E. Klinge, 'Eine "Muttergottes im Wochenbett" aus dem 14. Jahrhundert', in M. Lisner and R. Becksmann (eds), *Kunstgeschichtliche Studien für Kurt Bauch zum 70. Geburtstag von seinen Schülern*, Munich and Berlin, 1967, pp. 51–6. I have not consulted the dissertation by J. Schewe, *Unserer Lieben Frau Kindbett. Ikonographische Studien zur Marienminne des Mittelalters* (University of Kiel, 1958).

46    See Meurer, *Die mittelalterlichen Skulpturen . . . 800–1400*, no. 92, pp. 173–6; this also lists other German examples. The reception of this image in a German convent is discussed in Hamburger, *The Visual and the Visionary*, pp. 445–6. For two French Gesyn images of *c.* 1330–40, see M. Blanc, *La collection du Musée des Arts Décoratifs. Retables*, Paris, 1998, pp. 134–6.

47    Woolf, *English Religious Lyric*, pp. 148–57.

48    Cirket, *English Wills*, p. 18, no. 53.

49    VCH, *Bedfordshire*, 3, London, 1912, p. 311.

50    Duncan and Hussey, *Testamenta* (East Kent), pp. 84, 88, 120–1, 189, 201 (Chislet, Cranbrook, Faversham, Lenham, Lydd); Duncan, 'West Kent', 273, 278, 284, 288 (Hoo All Hallows, Rochester Cathedral, Snodland, West Malling).

51    Serjeantson and Isham Longden, 'Northamptonshire', 276, 290, 310, 382, 415 (Blakesley, Bugbrooke, Daventry, Long Buckby, Northborough and Thorpe Mandeville).

52    Part of a Gesyn/Nativity of *c.* 1320 is painted on the south transept west wall of Winchester Cathedral, but it is not known whether it formed part of a larger Christological cycle; D. Park and P. Welford, 'The Medieval Polychromy of Winchester Cathedral', in J. Crook (ed.), *Winchester Cathedral. Nine Hundred Years 1093–1993*, Chichester, 1993, p. 123, fig. 10.1.

53    M.F. Bond (ed.), *The Inventories of St George's Chapel Windsor Castle 1384–1667 (Historical Monographs relating to St George's Chapel Windsor Castle)*, Windsor, 1947, pp. 52–3.

54    The totals include surviving images of the Gesyn/Nativity which from their oblong shape are unlikely to have formed part of a Christological or Life of the Virgin series of panels from an altarpiece. The distinction, however, might be a fine one.

55    Kerry, *St Lawrence, Reading*, pp. 33–5, engraving between pp. 34 and 35. Ten are listed in Cheetham, *Medieval Alabasters*, p. 42, nn. 218, 219.

56    Assuming, of course, that such artefacts were exported prior to the Reformation.

57    Duncan and Hussey, *Testamenta* (East Kent), pp. 120–1.

58    F.W. Weaver (ed.), *Somerset Medieval Wills*, Somerset Record Society, 16 (1901), p. 361.

59    G.M. Gibson, *The Theater of Devotion. East Anglian Drama and Society in the Late Middle Ages*, Chicago and London, 1989, ch. 3.

60    H.M. Chew (ed.), *Hemingby's Register*, Wiltshire Archaeological and Natural History Society, Records Branch, 18, 1962, p. 108, no. 159 (1341), p. 151, no. 275 (1336); C. Wordsworth (ed.), *Ceremonies and Processions of the Cathedral Church of Salisbury*, Cambridge, 1901, pp. 305–6 (no. xxvii). An altar to the Gysine was still in existence in 1461.

61    The location can be fixed by a document of 1365; see D.M. Owen (ed.), *The Making of King's Lynn. A Documentary Survey*, Records of Social and Economic History, new series, 9, London, 1984, no. 163, p. 149; H. Harrod, *Report on the Deeds and Records of the Borough of King's Lynn*, King's Lynn and London, 1874, pp. 14–15.

62    Meech and Allen, *Book of Margery Kempe*, p. 19.

63    The wills of rectors Papley (1419–20) and William Marshall (1535) both expressed the wish for burial in the chancel of the Assumption of our Blessed Mary: Odell, *Marston Moreteyne*, p. 5.

64    Catto, 'Religious Change', p. 109; Spencer, *Pilgrim Souvenirs and Secular Badges, Salisbury Museum Medieval Catalogue Part 2*, Salisbury & South Wiltshire Museum, 1990, pp. 29–30. For the Assumption, see Kirschbaum, *Lexikon*, 2, cols 276–83.

65    A fine and reasonably securely dated example is the large alabaster panel above the tomb of Richard Herbert (d. 1510) and his wife at Abergavenny (Monmouths.).

66    For a range of iconographical variations, see Cheetham, *Medieval Alabasters*, pp. 199–207, nos 126–34; Prigent, *Les sculptures*, pp. 68–71, nos 9–11.

67    For the early cult of St Anne, see W. Scase, 'St Anne and the Education of the Virgin: Literary and Artistic Traditions and their Implications', in N. Rogers (ed.), *England in the Fourteenth Century. Proceedings of the 1991 Harlaxton Symposium*, Harlaxton Medieval Studies 3, Stamford, 1993, pp. 81–96; Morgan, 'Texts and Images . . . Fourteenth-Century', p. 44; P. Sheingorn, '"The Wise Mother": The Image of St Anne teaching the Virgin Mary', *Gesta*, 32 (1993), 69–80; K. Ashley and P. Sheingorn (eds), *Interpreting Cultural Symbols. Saint Anne in Late Medieval Society*, Athens (Georgia) and London, 1990. Many of the surviving images in various media are listed in C. Norton, D. Park and P. Binski, *Dominican Painting in East Anglia: The Thornham Parva Retable and the Musée de Cluny Frontal*, Woodbridge, 1987, pp. 51–3.

68    Sparrow Simpson, *Visitations . . . in 1297 and in 1458*, pp. 25, 55.

69    J. Evans, 'An English alabaster at Montpezat', *Antiquaries Journal*, 37 (1957), 73, pl. XIX; other alabaster versions are listed in Cheetham, *Medieval Alabasters*, p. 74. For Kersey, see S. Boldrick, D. Park and P. Williamson, *Wonder. Painted Sculpture from Medieval England* (Leeds, Henry Moore Institute exhibition catalogue, 2002), no. 12.

70    Cheetham, *Medieval Alabasters*, p. 74, no. 3.

71    For the *Anna Selbdritt* and related Holy Kinship images, see P. Sheingorn, 'Appropriating the Holy Kinship: Gender and Family History', in Ashley and Sheingorn, *Interpreting Cultural Symbols*, pp. 169–98.

72    Duncan and Hussey, *Testamenta* (East Kent), p. 121.

73    For this image, see especially Williamson, 'The Virgin *Lactans*', 105–38; idem, 'The Virgin *Lactans* and the Madonna of Humility: Image and Devotion in Italy, Metz and Avignon in the Thirteenth and Fourteenth Centuries', University of London (Courtauld Institute of Art) PhD thesis, 1996; this paragraph is heavily indebted to these excellent studies. See also Morgan, 'Texts and Images . . . Thirteenth-Century', pp. 93–7.

74    For a number of French statues with this iconography, see *Les Fastes du Gothique. Le siècle de Charles V* (Paris exhibition catalogue, 1981). The link between Incarnation and Passion is made explicit in an Italian panel painting attributed to the Master of the Casale fresco and showing the Virgin wrapping her veil around Christ's body:

M. Davies, *National Gallery Catalogues: The Early Italian Schools before 1400*, revised by D. Gordon, London, 1988, no. 565 (p. 74, Pl. 53). For the *tunica humanitatis*, see C.W. Bynum, *Holy Feast and Holy Fast. The Religious Significance of Food to Medieval Women*, Berkeley and London, 1987, p. 265.

75  Morgan, 'Texts and Images . . . Thirteenth-Century', pp. 95–7.

76  Jenkinson and Fowler, 'Some Bedfordshire Wills', pp. 104–5. The other examples were at Stoke (West Kent) and Immingham and Sutterton (Lincs.). The Shillington image may have been identical with Our Lady of Grace in the same location.

77  Williamson, *Gothic Sculpture*, 1995, p. 241, fig. 359; Sauerländer, 'Glykophilousa', esp. pp. 449–61. See also G. Huard in *Bulletin de la Société nationale des Antiquaires de France* (1938), 95–103; *Fastes du Gothique*, p. 113, no. 60 (b).

78  Unfortunately, none of the Blunham wills refers to this image, so its medieval appellation is unknown.

79  Relevant textual sources are given in Sauerländer, 'Glykophilousa', pp. 454, 456; R. Kroos, '"Gotes tabernakel". Zu Function und Interpretation von Schreinmadonnen', *Zeitschrift für Schweizerische Archäologie und Kunstgeschichte*, 43 (1986), 62.

80  Recht, *Le croire et le voir*, pp. 323–4.

# CHAPTER SEVEN

1  For the history of the parish, see VCH, *Bedfordshire*, 2, London, 1908, pp. 348–75; the advowson was worth more than £66 in 1291 and in 1544 the rectorial tithes were valued at £92 (p. 374).

2  The principal accounts of the church are H. Cobbe, *Luton Church. Historical and Descriptive*, London and Bedford, 1899, esp. pp. 289–367, and C. Pickford (ed.), *Bedfordshire Churches in the Nineteenth Century. Part II: Parishes H to R*, BHRS, 77, 1998, pp. 437–60. For the Luton guild, see R. Marks, 'Two Illuminated Guild Registers from Bedfordshire', in M.P. Brown and S. McKendrick (eds), *Illuminating the Book. Makers and Interpreters. Essays in Honour of Janet Backhouse*, London and Toronto, 1998, pp. 120–41.

3  Knowledge of all these images is derived from wills in the Beds. & Luton Archives, some published by the BHRS, some still unpublished.

4  A brief, but helpful, recent study of the relationship between images and liturgy is E. Palazzo, *Liturgie et société au Moyen Age*, Mayenne, 2000, ch. VII; see also idem, 'Iconographie et liturgie dans les études médiévales aujourd-hui: un éclairage méthodologique', *Cahiers de civilisation médiévale*, 41 (1998), 65–9.

5  See R.W. Pfaff, 'Prescription and Reality in the Rubrics of Sarum Rite Service Books', in L. Smith and B. Ward (eds), *Intellectual Life in the Middle Ages. Essays Presented to Margaret Gibson*, London, 1992, pp. 197–205. For the diffusion of the Sarum Rite, see N. Morgan, 'The Introduction of the Sarum Calendar into the Dioceses of England in the Thirteenth Century', in M. Prestwich, R. Britnell and R. Frame (eds), *Thirteenth Century England. VIII. Proceedings of the Durham Conference 1999*, Woodbridge, 2001, pp. 179–206.

6  For accounts of the liturgical year, see Duffy *Stripping*, ch. 1, and Hutton, *Merry England*, chs 1 and 2; the German equivalent is discussed in stimulating fashion in R.W. Scribner, *Popular Culture and Popular Movements in Reformation Germany*, London and Ronceverte, 1987, chs 1 and 2.

7  Scribner, *Popular Culture*, p. 1.

8  Boyle, 'Popular Piety', 186.

9  The importance of intimate contact with the sacred in late medieval religious practice was pointed out to me by Dr Margaret Aston.

10  Babington, *Repressor*, 1, pp. 170–1.

11  Dendy, *The Use of Lights*. This will be superseded by Catherine Vincent's forthcoming *Un monde enluminé: Lumière et luminaires dans la vie religieuse en Occident du XIIe siècle au début XVIe siècle*; in the interim, see her 'Une scène urbaine méconnue: les "chandelières" aux portes des églises', in P. Lardin and J.-L. Roch (eds), *La Ville médiévale en-deçà et au-delà de ses murs. Mélanges Jean-Pierre Leguay*, Rouen, 2000, pp. 205–15. I am indebted to Professor Vincent for sending me her publications and for discussions about lights and images.

12  Beds. & Luton Archives, ABP/R3/44d.

13  Duncan and Hussey, *Testamenta* (East Kent), p. 134.

14  McGregor, *Bedfordshire Wills*, p. 37, no. 25.

15  Frere, *Use of Sarum I*, pp. 4–6.

16  Beds. & Luton Archives, ABP/R3/114d (1533).

17  P. Bell, *Bedfordshire Wills 1484–1533*, p. 17 no. 23.

18  Frere, *Use of Sarum I*, pp. 44, 114, 183, 312–13. The English quotation is from Barnum, *Dives and Pauper*, 1, p. 111 (the practice is discussed on pp. 110–13); see also Babington, *Repressor*, 1, p. 169. Image-censing, together with kneeling and making oblations, is proscribed in the 1536 Articles (C. Lloyd (ed.), *Formularies of Faith Put Forth by Authority During the Reign of Henry VIII*, Oxford, 1825, p. 14).

19    W.G. Henderson (ed.), *Processionale ad usum insignis ac praeclarae ecclesiae Sarum*, Leeds, 1882, pp. 136, 137, 148, 158, 159, 161. Strictly speaking, altars were consecrated to God, in honour and memory of certain saints.

20    Dickinson, *Missale*, cols 979–83.

21    Erbe, *Mirk's Festial*, esp. p. 201.

22    Ibid., pp. 276–7.

23    See Chapter Four for details of patronal feasts.

24    Duffy *Stripping*, pp. 15–22; Hutton, *Stations of the Sun*, pp. 139–45; Erbe, *Mirk's Festial*, pp. 61–2; see also Scribner, *Popular Culture*, pp. 3–4, 6, 32.

25    C. Hole, *A Dictionary of British Folk Customs*, Oxford, 1995, pp. 113–14; C.E. Prior, 'Dedications of churches, with some Notes as to Village Feasts and Old Customs in the Deaneries of Islip and Bicester', *Oxfordshire Archaeological Society Reports for the year 1903* (1904), 22–3.

26    D. Dymond and C. Paine, *The Spoil of Melford Church. The Reformation in a Suffolk Parish*, Ipswich, 1992, p. 14; Walters, *London Churches*, passim.

27    Duncan and Hussey, *Testamenta* (East Kent), pp. 274–5.

28    See T. Lentes, 'Die Gewänder der Heiligen. Ein Diskussionsbetrag zum Verhältnis von Gebet, Bild und Imagination', in G. Kerschner (ed.), *Hagiographie und Kunst. Der Heiligenkult in Schrift, Bild und Architektur*, Berlin, 1993, pp. 120–51; Griffiths, *Certain Sermons*, p. 275.

29    J.M. Cowper, 'Accounts of the Churchwardens of St Dunstan's, Canterbury AD 1484–1580', *Archaeologia Cantiana*, 16 (1886), 299.

30    Information from the church guide. The 'grimr' suggestion was made to the parish by Margaret Bolton.

31    Barnum, *Dives and Pauper*, 1, p. 100.

32    R. Lloyd, *An Account of the Altars, Monuments, and Tombs, existing AD 1428 in Saint Alban's Abbey*, St Albans, 1873, p. 25; W. Sparrow Simpson, 'Inventory of the Vestments, Plate and Books Belonging to the Church of St Peter Cheap, in the City of London, in the Year 1431', *JBAA*, 24 (1868), 158; Freshfield, 'On the Parish Books', 117; McGregor, *Bedfordshire Wills*, pp. 24–5, no. 16.

33    F.R. Mercer (trans.), *Churchwardens' Accounts at Betrysden 1515–1573*, Kent Archaeological Society Records Branch, 5, 1928, p. 61.

34    Duncan, 'West Kent', 292; for the covering and uncovering of images during Lent, see Frere, *Use of Sarum I*, pp. 138–9, 144.

35    Bell, *Bedfordshire Wills 1484–1533*, pp. 23, 140, 171, nos 34, 230, 288; see also above, Chapter Two for Eaton Bray.

36    Beds. & Luton Archives, ABP/R4/90d. Richard Brother left small bequests to Our Lady of Pity and St Christopher as well as the rood (Bell, *Bedfordshire Wills 1480–1519*, p. 71, no. 147).

37    McGregor, *Bedfordshire Wills*, p. 128, no. 102.

38    Ibid., p. 37, no. 25; Cobbe, *Luton Church*, p. 351.

39    S. Delany (ed.), *A Legend of Holy Women. A Translation of Osbern Bokenham's Legends of Holy Women*, Notre Dame and London, 1992, p. 79.

40    Cirket, *English Wills*, pp. 53–4, no. 170; Beds. & Luton Archives, ABP/R5/18d.

41    Christian, *Person and God*, p. 81.

42    Duncan and Hussey, *Testamenta* (East Kent), p. 178.

43    Westlake, *Parish Gilds*, p. 194.

44    Ibid., pp. 191, 229.

45    Bell, *Bedfordshire Wills 1484–1533*, p. 83, no. 136; Vere Woodman, 'Churchwardens of Wing', 307–29; Mercer, *Betrysden*, pp. 50, 60–5. The Bethersden light-keepers' accounts are quite detailed.

46    E. Peacock (ed.), *Myrc's Instructions for Parish Priests*, EETS, original series 31, 1888, p. 31.

47    Scribner, *Popular Culture*, ch. 2.

48    The literature on this subject is extensive. See especially K.P.F. Moxey, 'Sebald Beham's church anniversary holidays: festive peasants as instruments of repressive humour', *Simiolus*, 12 (1981/2), 107–30; M.D. Carroll, 'Peasant Festivity and Political Identity in the Sixteenth Century', *Art History*, 10 (1987), 289–314.

49    Bell, *Bedfordshire Wills 1484–1533*, pp. 9, 22, nos 9, 33; *Tong Church Guide*, pp. 6–7. A variant of this custom, with a bunch of roses put on the tomb effigy of Isabella Pembrugge (d. 1446), was still practised at Tong on this festival in the eighteenth century.

50    Aston, *Iconoclasts*, pp. 152, n. 91, 226.

51    For a survey, see L. Gougaud, *Devotional and Ascetic Practices in the Middle Ages*, London, 1927.

52    The quotation is from Virginia Reinburg's postscript (p. 149) to J. Bossy, 'Christian Life in the Later Middle Ages: Prayers', *Transactions of the Royal Historical Society*, 6th series, I (1991), 137–48 (comments by Reinburg on pp. 148–50). For medieval prayer attitudes, see also Van Os, *Art of Devotion*, pp. 63–4, figs 19–21.

53    These are based on the distinctions made in Christian, *Person and God*, pp. 114–21. John Bossy also distinguishes between 'social' (relating to one's neighbour), 'devotional' (concerned with the individual's relations with a

supernatural power) and 'me-prayers' (prayers for the prayer-maker). These categories are criticized by Reinburg (see n. 52).

54 Bell, *Bedfordshire Wills 1484–1533*, p. 68, no. 111. The phrase 'dedes of pitie' occurs in John Bowstred of Luton's will (1523) in reference to 'sum ornament' for his parish church and other good works he wished his executors to perform (ibid., p. 33, no. 52).

55 See Chapter Six. For Brother's will, see Bell, *Bedfordshire Wills 1480–1519*, p. 71, no. 147.

56 Serjeantson and Isham Longden, 'Northamptonshire', 310.

57 Whiting, *Blind Devotion*, pp. 60–1.

58 Tanner, *Heresy Trials*, pp. 89–90; see Chapter Six above.

59 Christian, *Person and God*, p. 115.

60 Erbe, *Mirk's Festial*, p. 216.

61 A. Rapoport, 'Systems of activities and systems of settings', in S. Kent (ed.), *Domestic Architecture and the Use of Space. An interdisciplinary cross-cultural study*, Cambridge, 1990, pp. 13, 18.

62 Duncan, 'West Kent', 245–6; Duncan and Hussey, *Testamenta* (East Kent), p. 265.

63 Duncan, 'West Kent', p. 273; Duncan and Hussey, *Testamenta* (West Kent), p. 39.

64 Cirket, *English Wills*, p. 8, no. 21.

65 An elaborate example of *c.* 1350–1400 is at New College, Oxford (Alexander and Binski, *Age of Chivalry*, p. 473, no. 609).

66 Hobhouse, *Churchwardens' Accounts*, pp. 64–5.

67 See P. Binski, *Medieval Death. Ritual and Representation*, London, 1996, pp. 71–7; C. Daniell, *Death and Burial in Medieval England 1066–1550*, London and New York, 1997, ch. 4; C. Wilson, 'The Medieval Monuments', in P. Collinson, N. Ramsay and M. Sparks (eds), *A History of Canterbury Cathedral*, Oxford, 1995, pp. 451–510, esp. pp. 452–3.

68 Saul, *Death, Art and Memory*, 2001, pp. 75–6.

69 Powicke and Cheney, *Councils and Synods*, II, p. 1117; Daniell, *Death and Burial*, pp. 96–7.

70 The Luton totals are taken from the published wills, antiquarian sources and the brasses and indents of brasses. For the last two categories, see Cobbe, *Luton Church*, pp. 318–57; Lack et al., *Monumental Brasses*, pp. 63–72. In the case of the monuments only the adults and not the children are included. There may be some double-counting between the number of interments in the nave and those requested by testators merely in the church. In at least one instance an individual who stipulated burial in the churchyard is commemorated on a brass within the building. My formulation differs slightly from those outlined in Daniell, *Death and Burial*, pp. 95–103, and V. Harding, 'Burial choice and burial location in late medieval London', in S. Bassett (ed.), *Death in Towns. Urban Responses to the Dying and the Dead, 100–1600*, Leicester, London and New York, 1992, pp. 119–35. See also Middleton-Stewart, *Inward Purity*, pp. 68–72.

71 R. Paul, 'The Plan of the Church and Monastery of St Augustine, Bristol', *Archaeologia*, 63 (1911–12), 238–9.

72 Beds. & Luton Archives, ABP/R4/90d; McGregor, *Bedfordshire Wills*, p. 105, no. 85.

73 Duncan, 'West Kent', 278; Duncan and Hussey, *Testamenta* (East Kent), p. 121.

74 Lack et al., *Monumental Brasses*, p. 70.

75 Raine, *Testamenta Eboracensia, IV*, Surtees Society, 53, 1868, p. 210, no. CXIII. The diminutive alabaster *Pietà* at Wood Ditton (Cambs.) may have been a sepulchral image.

76 See also the alabaster tombs at Youlgreave (Derbys.) and Abergavenny (Monmouths.), where the families of the deceased kneel before the Virgin.

77 E.A. Greening Lamborn, *The Lovel Tomb at Minster*, Shipston-on-Stour, n.d.

78 R.C. Trexler, *Public Life in Renaissance Florence*, Ithaca and London, 1980, p. 94.

79 The concept of the social frame is formulated in Trexler, *Public Life*, pp. 92–6. Michael Baxandall's description of Italian Renaissance paintings as 'deposits of social relationships' is similar (*Painting and Experience in Fifteenth-Century Italy*, Oxford, 2nd edn, 1988, p. 1).

80 Serjeantson and Isham Longden, 'Northamptonshire', 286.

81 McGregor, *Bedfordshire Wills*, p. 37, no. 25.

82 Waterton, *Pietas Mariana Britannica*, bk 2, pp. 72–3, citing Dugdale, *St Paul's*.

83 H.S. London, *The Life of William Bruges, the First Garter King of Arms*, Harleian Society, 111, 112, 1959–60, London, 1970, pp. 86–7.

84 Duncan, 'West Kent', 293; Burgess, *Pre-Reformation Records of All Saints', Bristol*, pp. 10–11, 41.

85 PRO, PCC wills 14 Fettiplace. I am indebted to Peter Northeast for a transcript.

86 Prowte left the cost of making the pillar in his will (Duncan and Hussey, *Testamenta* (East Kent), p. 44).

87 For kneeling as a gesture of subordination, see C. Bell, *Ritual Theory, Ritual Practice*, Oxford, 1992, pp. 99–100.

88 There must have been examples of English images bearing commemorative inscriptions with the donor's name and date of the gift and sometimes inviting prayers. Several French images preserve such texts. Quite a detailed

example is the inscription on a fourteenth-century marble Virgin and Child known as *Notre-Dame la Blanche* at Huerta, near Pamplona in northern Spain: AN.DNI.MCCCXLIX FECIT MARTINUS DUARDI MERCATOR DE PAMPELONE TRANSFERRE HANC IMAGINEM DE VILLA PARISIEN. IN ECCLESIAM ISTAM ET DEDIT ILLAM IN HONORE BEATE MARIE VIRGINIS ORATE PRO EO (*Les Fastes du Gothique*, p. 113, no. 60 (b) (ill.); see also pp. 94, 121, nos 38, 69).

89  See Trexler, *Public Life*, p. 94.

90  Marks, 'Two Illuminated Guild Registers', p. 131.

91  Bucks RO D/A/We3/138; for Kent examples see Duncan and Hussey (East Kent), pp. 136, 359. For a general discussion, see K.L. French, 'Maidens' Lights and Wives' Stores: Women's Parish Guilds in Late Medieval England', *Sixteenth-Century Journal*, 29 (1998), 399–425.

92  See also Chapter Six in respect of Marian images.

93  Duncan and Hussey, *Testamenta* (East Kent), pp. 255, 359.

94  Christian, *Person and God*, pp. 133–4. This production *versus* reproduction model has been criticized on the grounds that anthropologists expected to find it and therefore did so.

95  Brown, *Popular Piety*, p. 215.

96  Griffiths, *Certain Sermons*, pp. 277–8.

97  C. Peters, 'Women and the Reformation: Social Relations and Attitudes in Rural England *c.* 1470–1570' (unpublished DPhil dissertation, University of Oxford, 1992). A critical survey of the sources available for an earlier period is P. Biller, 'The Common Woman in the Western Church in the Thirteenth and Early Fourteenth Centuries', in W.J. Sheils and D. Wood (eds), *Women in the Church, Studies in Church History*, 27, 1990, pp. 127–57.

98  Peters,'Women and the Reformation', p. 160.

99  Hussey, 'Hythe Wills', pp. 49, 51–2. The extent of male bequests of apparel and rings may have been underestimated. Sometimes these may still have been women's artefacts, like the two wedding rings and his wife's beads which John Hickenson of Beckenham left to an image of Our Lady (Duncan, 'West Kent', 255).

100  Cirket, *English Wills*, pp. 8, 36, nos 21, 96d; Raine, *Mediaeval York*, p. 268.

101  For this aspect of female devotion, see Peters, 'Women and the Reformation', pp. 249–50.

102  See Chapter Six.

103  Duncan and Hussey, *Testamenta* (West Kent), pp. 39, 40.

104  Dickinson, *Missale*, col. 849*. In the 1549 edition of the Book of Common Prayer, the ceremony was to take place at the entrance to the choir. The 1552 edition brought the ceremony closer to the most sacred place in the church, stating that the woman should kneel 'nighe unto the place where the table standeth': *The First and Second Prayer Books of King Edward the Sixth*, Everyman Edition, London, 1910, pp. 278, 428; see also W. Coster, 'Purity, Profanity and Puritanism: the Churching of Women, 1500–1700', in Sheils and Wood, *Women in the Church*, pp. 377–87. For a critical account of churching in the modern Catholic Church, see Christian, *Person and God*, p. 154.

105  Duffy *Stripping*, p. 435; Duncan and Hussey, *Testamenta* (East Kent), p. 211.

106  Rosser, *Medieval Westminster*, p. 273.

107  L. Keen and C. Taylor, *St Catherine's Chapel at Abbotsbury and the Legend of the Saint*, Abbotsbury, 1999, pp. 21–2.

108  French, 'Maidens' Lights'; Vere Woodman, 'Churchwardens of Wing', 314.

# CHAPTER EIGHT

1  See K. Köster, 'Gemalte Kollektionen von Pilgerzeichen und Religiösen Medaillen in flämischen Gebet- und Stundenbüchern des 15. und frühen 16. Jahrhunderts. Neue Funde in Handschriften der Gent-Brügger Schule', in F. Vanwijngaerden (ed.), *Liber Amicorum Herman Liebaers*, Brussels, 1984, pp. 485–535. Lady Bray's manuscript was apparently unknown to this author. See also Chapter Two above for this book.

2  N.H. Nicolas (ed.), *Privy Purse Expenses of Elizabeth of York: Wardrobe Accounts of Edward the Fourth: with a memoir of Elizabeth of York*, London, 1830, pp. 3–4, 50.

3  Wills of Alice Cooke of Horstead and Gregory Clerk (1517) of Norwich; I am grateful to Dr Simon Cotton for the transcripts. Cooke's will is partly printed in R. Hart, 'The Shrines and Pilgrimages of the County of Norfolk', *Norfolk Archaeology*, 6 (1864), 277. Clerk did not mention any of the Norwich cults, presumably because there was no merit to be gained from posthumous pilgrimage to somewhere on the doorstep. For Mintlyn and Caister's tomb in Norwich, see Meech and Allen, *Book of Margery Kempe*, pp. 200, 147.

4  Raine, *Testamenta Eboracensia, III*, pp. 200–1, no. LVII; *IV*, p. 257, no. CXLVIII. For wills mentioning pilgrimage sites in the west of England, see Webb, *Pilgrimage*, p. 199.

5  For the concept of liminality, see V. Turner and E. Turner, *Image and Pilgrimage in Christian Culture. Anthropological Perspectives*, Oxford, 1978, ch. 1; for critiques, see S. Coleman and J. Elsner, 'Contesting Pilgrimage: Current Views

and Future Directions', *Cambridge Anthropology*, 15, pt 3 (1991), 63–73; idem, *Pilgrimage Past and Present*, London, 1995, pp. 6, 196–220; idem, 'Pilgrimage to Walsingham and the Re-Invention of the Middle Ages', in J. Stopford (ed.), *Pilgrimage Explored*, York, 1999, pp. 191–4; R.J. Maniura, 'Image and Pilgrimage. The Cult of the Virgin of Częstochowa in the Late Middle Ages' (Courtauld Institute of Art unpublished PhD thesis, 1998), ch. 1.

6   Turner and Turner, *Image and Pilgrimage*, p. 202.

7   C. Rawcliffe, 'Caring bodies and healing souls: pilgrimage and the sick in medieval East Anglia', in C. Morris and P. Roberts (eds), *Pilgrimage. The English Experience from Becket to Bunyan*, Cambridge, 2002, pp. 108–40.

8   Christian, *Person and God*, p. 44; see also idem, *Local Religion*, ch. 3 and app. B.

9   N. Orme (ed.), *Nicholas Roscarrock's Lives of the Saints: Cornwall and Devon*, Devon and Cornwall Record Society, new series, 35, 1992, p. 139; R.C. Finucane, *Miracles and Pilgrims. Popular Beliefs in Medieval England*, London, 1995, p. 193.

10   Meech and Allen, *Book of Margery Kempe*, passim.

11   Köster, 'Religiöse Medaillen'; Turner and Turner, *Image and Pilgrimage*, pp. 181–2.

12   Finucane, *Miracles*, pp. 166–9, 173–88.

13   The evidence can be distorted by sites where favourable environmental conditions have ensured the preservation of pilgrim badges; the occurrence of St Sidwell in the glass at All Souls College, Oxford was not due to the strength of her cult in Oxford but to the Exeter connections of the supervisor of the works (Marks, *Stained Glass*, p. 63, fig. 44).

14   The visual evidence is rendered problematic by the fact that her iconography is very similar to that of St Sidwell. Orme, *Roscarrock's Lives*, pp. 137–9; M. Gill, 'Late Medieval Wall-Painting in England: Content and Context (*c.* 1330–*c.* 1530)' (Courtauld Institute of Art unpublished PhD thesis, 2001), pp. 482–6.

15   The architectural setting is discussed in Maniura, 'Image and Pilgrimage', ch. 5.

16   The major shrines and their emplacement are discussed in Nilson, *Cathedral Shrines*, ch. 3; a recent survey is Webb, *Pilgrimage*; see also T. Tatton-Brown, 'Canterbury and the architecture of pilgrimage shrines in England', in Morris and Roberts, *Pilgrimage. The English Experience*, pp. 90–107 (esp. 101–7).

17   The principal studies are S. Robertson, 'The Crypt of Canterbury Cathedral: Part II', *Archaeologia Cantiana*, 13 (1913), 525–46, and C.E. Woodruff, 'The Chapel of Our Lady in the Crypt of Canterbury Cathedral', *Archaeologia Cantiana*, 38 (1926), 153–71.

18   Spencer, *Pilgrim Souvenirs: London*, pp. 131–3, nos 136, 136a, 136b, 137, 137a.

19   Robertson, 'Crypt', 525. The murals were destroyed in the 1893 restoration.

20   Robertson, 'Crypt', 526–8; Woodruff, 'Our Lady in the Crypt', 160, 168; Spencer, *Pilgrim Souvenirs: London*, pp. 132–3; Nilson, *Cathedral Shrines*, pp. 149, 154; D. Erasmus, *Peregrinatio religionis ergo*, in C.R. Thompson (trans.), *The Collected Works of Erasmus. Colloquies*, Toronto, 1997, pp. 645, 647.

21   Find-sites of the pilgrim badges just described include London and King's Lynn (Norf.) (Spencer, *Pilgrim Souvenirs: London*, p. 132.

22   Woodruff, 'Our Lady in the Crypt', 166–8.

23   Erasmus, *Peregrinatio* (trans. Thompson), pp. 642–5.

24   For the screens, see Wilson, 'The Medieval Monuments', p. 494.

25   Robertson, 'Crypt', 535–8, and for the candelabrum and bowl, Woodruff, 'Our Lady in the Crypt', 161. For medieval mirror-magic, see Spencer, *Pilgrim Souvenirs: London*, pp. 17–18, 258–9. For the Marian iconography, see Morgan, 'Texts and Images . . . Thirteenth-Century', pp. 88–9; Warner, *Alone of All Her Sex*, pp. 255–69.

26   Woodruff, 'Our Lady in the Crypt', 161–2, 170.

27   Robertson, 'Crypt', 527, 532–5, 539–41. His attribution of the screenwork to the Black Prince is challenged convincingly in Woodruff, 'Our Lady in the Crypt', 153–71 (cf. pp. 156–7). For the monuments, see Wilson, 'The Medieval Monuments', pp. 485–6, 494–5, 507–8.

28   C. Green and A.B. Whittingham, 'Excavations at Walsingham Priory, Norfolk, 1961', *Norfolk Archaeology*, 125 (1968), 255–90. There is an excellent account of the workings of the cult in Spencer, *Pilgrim Souvenirs: London*, pp. 135–48; see also J.C. Dickinson, *The Shrine of Our Lady of Walsingham*, Cambridge, 1956. For the modern pilgrimage, see Coleman and Elsner, 'Walsingham', pp. 189–214.

29   W. de G. Birch, *Catalogue of Seals in the Department of Manuscripts in the British Museum, I*, London, 1887, pp. 788–9.

30   For the pilgrimage, see J.H. Harvey (ed.), *William Worcestre: Itineraries*, Oxford, 1969, pp. 174–5; Erasmus, *Peregrinatio* (trans. Thompson), pp. 628–41; Dickinson, *Walsingham*, pp. 14–19.

31   Webb, *Pilgrimage*, ch. 6.

32   The sequence as set out here follows Erasmus, *Peregrinatio* (trans. Thompson), p. 631.

33   Will of John Benett of Raunds (1531); see Serjeantson and Isham Longden, 'Northamptonshire', 263.

34   Appropriate because of the Eucharistic overtones of the *Maria lactans*; see Chapter Six above.

35   Harvey, *William Worcestre*, pp. 174–5; Erasmus, *Peregrinatio* (trans. Thompson), p. 629.

36 Marks, *Stained Glass*, pp. 209–19. The excavated glass fragments from Walsingham (in the care of Norfolk Museums Service, Norwich), are too de-vitrified for any conclusions about the design to be drawn.

37 Erasmus, *Peregrinatio* (trans. Thompson), pp. 629–30, 634; C. Lewis (ed.), *The Commonplace Book of Robert Reynes of Acle. An Edition of Tanner MS 407*, New York and London, 1980, p. 323. In 1439 Isabella Beauchamp, Countess of Warwick, requested that a silver tabernacle based on the wooden tabernacle enclosing Our Lady of Caversham be made for the Walsingham image (Dickinson, *Walsingham*, p. 37).

38 For the rich offerings of royalty and nobility, see Dickinson, *Walsingham*, pp. 18–19, 21, 35–47; D.J. Hall, *English Mediaeval Pilgrimage*, London, 1966, Chapter V.

39 Erasmus, *Peregrinatio* (trans. Thompson), p. 630. For the chantry Masses and burials, see Dickinson, *Walsingham*, pp. 35–47.

40 E.C. Rouse, 'Bradwell Abbey and the Chapel of St Mary', *Milton Keynes Journal of Archaeology and History*, 2 (1973), 34–8; D.C. Mynard, 'Excavations at Bradwell Abbey', *Milton Keynes Journal of Archaeology and History*, 3 (1974), 31–66 (including App.: 'Bradwell Priory Chapel' by S.E. Rigold and P. Woodfield).

41 Rouse, 'Bradwell Abbey', 36–7.

42 J.T. Fowler (ed.), *Rites of Durham*, Surtees Society, 107, 1902, p. 30. The image is discussed in Camille, *Gothic Idol*, pp. 230–1. For this kind of image see M.-M.E. Marcos, *La Escultura de Marfil en España. Romanica y Gótica*, Madrid, 1984, pp. 128–46; Kroos, 'Gotes tabernakel', 58–64; G. Radler, *Die Schreinmadonna 'Vièrge ouvrante', von den bernhardinischen Anfängen bis zur Frauenmystik im Deutschordensland*, Frankfurt am Main, 1990; K. Holbert, 'The Vindication of a Controversial Early Thirteenth-Century *Vièrge Ouvrante* in the Walters Art Gallery', *Journal of the Walters Art Gallery*, 55/6 (1997–8), 101–21.

43 Camille, *Gothic Idol*, pp. 231–2; see also *Iconoclasme. Vie et mort de l'image médiévale*, no. 129; Schmitt, *Le corps des images*, p. 161.

44 For the Galilee chapel, see Fowler, *Rites of Durham*, pp. 42–51.

45 Ibid., p. 113.

46 Ibid., p. 30.

47 Orme, *Roscarrock's Lives*, p. 139; see also above, pp. 189.

48 B. Cherry and N. Pevsner, *The Buildings of England. Devon*, Harmondsworth, 2nd edn, 1991, p. 259.

49 R. Marks, 'Images of Henry VI', in J. Stratford (ed.), *The Lancastrian Court. Proceedings of the 2001 Harlaxton Symposium*, Harlaxton Medieval Studies X, Stamford, 2003, pp. 111–24; idem, 'A Late Medieval Pilgrimage Cult: Master John Schorn of North Marston and Windsor', in L. Keen and E. Scarff (eds), *Windsor. Medieval Archaeology, Art and Architecture of the Thames Valley*, British Archaeological Association Conference Transactions 25, 2002, pp. 192–207.

50 In this respect the image approximated to the localized shrines found in Spain; see Christian, *Local Religion*, ch. 3 and app. B; idem, *Person and God*, pp. 50–80, 99–101.

51 C. Paine, 'The Building of Long Melford Church', in Long Melford PCC, *A Sermon in Stone. The 500th anniversary book of Long Melford Church*, Lavenham, 1984, pp. 9–18 (esp. pp. 15–17). For the 1459 will see Northeast, *Wills of the Archdeaconry of Sudbury*, p. 422, no. 1237.

52 Paine, 'Building of Long Melford Church', pp. 15, 17.

53 D. Dymond and C. Paine, *Spoil of Melford Church. The Reformation in a Suffolk Parish*, Ipswich, 1992, pp. 13–14.

54 E.M. Beloe, *The Red Mount, King's Lynn with the Chapels thereon*, King's Lynn, 1925; N. Pevsner and B. Wilson, *The Buildings of England. Norfolk 2. North-West and South*, Harmondsworth, 2nd edn, 1999, pp. 472–4. The structure and documentation of the building have been studied in detail by Michael Begley and David Pitcher. I am indebted to them for access to their unpublished researches and for conducting me round the chapel. The income figures are taken from R.N. Swanson, 'Urban Rectories and Urban Fortunes in Late Medieval England. The Evidence of Bishop's Lynn', in T.R. Slater and G. Rosser (eds), *The Church in the Medieval Town*, Aldershot, 1998, p. 117.

55 The design of the upper chapel is attributed to Wastell in J. Harvey, *English Mediaeval Architects. A Biographical Dictionary down to 1550*, Gloucester, rev. edn, 1984, p. 325.

56 J. Penninck, *De Jeruzalemkerk te Brugge*, Bruges, 1986.

57 For the well and cult see Hall, *Mediaeval Pilgrimage*, ch. II; the building is described in C. David, *St Winefride's Well. A History and Guide*, Llandysul, new edn, 2002, and E. Hubbard, *The Buildings of Wales. Clwyd*, Harmondsworth and the University of Wales, 1986, pp. 371–3.

58 St Winifred is depicted in two major 'Lancastrian' artefacts, the east window of the Beauchamp Chapel at Warwick and her life is illustrated in *The Bedford Breviary* (Paris, Bibliothèque nationale, MS lat. 17294, ff. 630–5); she also appears among the ranks of carved saints in Henry VII's Chapel, Westminster Abbey and in the east window tracery of Llandyrnog church (Clwyd).

59 Nicolas, *Testamenta Vetusta*, I, p. 240.

60 Jones and Underwood, *The King's Mother*, p. 150.

61 This description of modern pilgrim behaviour is based on personal observation and the instructions in T. Charles-Edwards, *Saint Winefride and her Well. The Historical Background*, Holywell, n.d., p. 23.

62 Marks, 'Schorn', p. 201.

63 The relic–image relationship has been addressed in several studies, but the subject merits more attention. See Belting, *Likeness and Presence*, pp. 301–3; A. Dupront, 'Pèlerinage et lieux sacrés', in *Mélanges en l'honneur de Fernand Braudel: Méthodologie de l'Histoire et des sciences humaines*, Paris, 1972–3, 2, pp. 189–206 (esp. pp. 196–7); Schmitt, *Le corps des images*, pp. 273–94 (esp. pp. 279–85).

64 Woodruff, ' Our Lady in the Crypt', 163.

65 An observation made by Camille in *Gothic Idol*, pp. 223–4; for the emergence of three-dimensional images, see Forsyth, *Throne of Wisdom*, pp. 31–8.

66 Babington, *Repressor*, 1, pp. 184–5, 188.

67 L. Sousa, S. Poole and J. Lockhart (eds and trans), *The Story of Guadalupe. Luis Laso de la Vega's* Huei tlamahuiçoltica *of 1649*, UCLA Latin American Studies, 84 (Nahuatl Studies Series no. 5), Los Angeles, 1998, p. 121.

68 Quoted from Freedberg, *Power of Images*, p. 110.

69 Webb, *Pilgrimage*, p. 100 (for Ipswich).

70 Christian, *Local Religion*, pp. 75–91.

71 The account in VCH, *A History of the County of York. East Riding* volume 2, Oxford, 1974, pp. 187, 207, has been clarified in Webb, *Pilgrimage*, pp. 147–8. See also Kamerick, *Popular Piety*, pp. 107–12.

72 *acsi in eadem plus quam in aliis similibus imaginibus aliquid numinis appararet.*

73 A. Vauchez, *Saints*, p. 90.

74 See Maniura, 'Image and Pilgrimage', pp. 214–21. For the Sablon image, see also below, Chapter Nine, n. 86.

75 For Walsingham, see Waterton, *Pietas Mariana Britannica*, bk 2, pp. 155–220; Ketsby is discussed briefly in Spencer, *Pilgrim Souvenirs: Salisbury 2*, pp. 55–6.

76 Dickinson, *Walsingham*, p. 17; C. Paine, 'The Chapel and Well of Our Lady of Woolpit', *Proceedings of the Suffolk Institute of Archaeology*, 38 (1993–6), 8; Robertson, 'Crypt', 525–6; C.L. Kingsford, 'Our Lady of the Pew. The King's Oratory or Closet in the Palace of Westminster', *Archaeologia*, 68 (1917), 1–20; F. Haslewood, 'Our Lady of Ipswich', *Proceedings of the Suffolk Institute of Archaeology*, 10 (1898–1900), 53.

77 After the loss of Acre in 1291 perhaps no more than three hundred English pilgrims annually made the journey to the Holy Land via Venice, with a few more taking other routes (C. Morris, 'Pilgrimage to Jerusalem in the late Middle Ages', in Morris and Roberts, *Pilgrimage. the English Experience*, p. 142.

78 The differing clienteles for local and major sites is suggested in P.J.P. Goldberg, 'Pilgrims and Pilgrimage: Some Late Medieval Evidence', *Medieval Yorkshire*, 21 (1992), 2–6.

79 Serjeantson and Isham Longden, 'Northamptonshire', 264; Cirket, *English Wills*, p. 34.

80 Spencer, *Pilgrim Souvenirs: London*, pp. 131–3; idem, *Medieval Pilgrim Badges from Norfolk*, Norfolk Museums Service, 1980, p. 10.

81 A.W. Morant, 'Notices of the Church of St Nicholas, Great Yarmouth', *Norfolk Archaeology*, 7 (1872), 228; C.J. Bettey, 'Late Medieval Bristol: from town to city', *The Local Historian*, 28, no. 1 (February 1998), 5–6.

82 *Letters and Papers . . . Henry VIII*, 13, pt.2, p. 143, no. 367 (citing British Library, MS Cleopatra E.iv, f. 225); also p. 143, no. 368 (British Library, MS Cleopatra E. iv, f. 226).

83 U.M. Radford, 'The Wax Images found in Exeter Cathedral', *Antiquaries Journal*, 29 (1949), 164–8. For discussions of *ex-votos*, see Freedberg, *Power of Images*, ch. 7, and L. Kriss-Rettenbeck, *Ex Voto. Zeichen, Bild und Abbild im christlichen Votivbrauchtum*, Zürich and Freiburg-im-Breisgau, 1972. Many *ex-voto* painted panels have found their way to museums and have been the subject of special exhibitions, for example *Votivbilder aus dem Freiburgerland* (Fribourg (Switzerland)), Musée de l'art et d'histoire, 1978).

84 Bettey, 'Late Medieval Bristol', 6.

85 Babington, *Repressor*, 1, pp. 237–8.

86 Freedberg, *Power of Images*, p. 153, citing Kriss-Rettenbeck, *Ex-Voto*, p. 155.

87 J. Gairdner (ed.), *The Paston Letters, 2*, London, 1904, p. 55, no. 47. Life-size wax images can still be seen in Mediterranean churches, for example in the former Lampadistis monastery in Cyprus.

88 Dickinson, *Walsingham*, p. 36; Marks, *Stained Glass*, p. 61; the *Goldenes Rössel* of Altötting in Bavaria provides some idea of the magnificence of Ufford's offering.

89 Babington, *Repressor*, 1, p. 238.

90 Erasmus, *Peregrinatio* (trans. Thompson), p. 647.

91 C. Grössinger, *North-European Panel Paintings. A Catalogue of Netherlandish and German Paintings before 1600 in English Churches and Colleges*, London, 1992, pp. 131–3, no. 33.

92 Haslewood, 'Our Lady of Ipswich', 54.

93 Brown, *Cult of the Saints*, pp. 5, 23–49, 88. There is a succinct discussion of the controversies over burial within churches, and especially interment in proximity to saints' shrines, in Wilson, 'The Medieval Monuments', pp. 451–3. See also Chapter Seven above.

94 English translation of the Latin in Paine, 'Building of Long Melford Church', p. 17.

95 Coleman and Elsner, 'Pilgrimage to Walsingham', p. 193, applies the element of choice to large structures but not to the smaller sites.

96 A. Martindale, 'The Wall-paintings in the Chapel of Eton College', in C. Barron and N. Saul (eds), *England and the Low Countries in the Late Middle Ages*, Stroud, 1995, pp. 133–52; M. Williamson, '*Pictura et scriptura*: the Eton Choirbook in its iconographical context', *Early Music*, 28 (2000), 359–80; for the image and cult, see Spencer, *Pilgrim Souvenirs: Salisbury 2*, pp. 29–30.

97 The experience of looking is addressed in Maniura, 'Image and Pilgrimage', ch. 5.

98 Erasmus, *Peregrinatio* (trans. Thompson), p. 639.

99 Camille, *Gothic Idol* p. 233.

100 Freedberg, *Power of Images*, pp. 117–18.

101 Whiteford, *Myracles*, pp. 71–2.

102 The literature on this image and its accoutrements is extensive. For the crown, see H. Lepie, *Die Domschatzkammer zu Aachen. Katalog*, Aachen, 6th edn, 1990, p. 54; H. van der Velden, *The Donor's Image. Gerald Loyet and the Votive Portraits of Charles the Bold*, Brepols, 2000, pp. 215–17; Marks and Williamson, *Gothic*, no. 11. For the image, see W. Christ and G. Minkenberg, *Gemälde und Skulpturen des Aachener Domes im Blickfeld von Konservierung und Restaurierung. 30 Jahre Restaurierungswerkstatt für Gemälde und Skulpturen am Dom zu Aachen*, Karlsverein Schriftenreihe, 1, 1995, pp. 24–9; W. Hübner, M. Paredis-Vroon and G. Minkenberg, *Der Schatz des Gnadenbildes im Dom zu Aachen, Domschatzkammer Aachen*, Aachen, 1996. Only the head and right hand of the Virgin and the head of the Christ-Child from the original early fourteenth-century oak statue survived a fire in 1676.

103 Hall, *Mediaeval Pilgrimage*, p. 112; Woodruff, 'Our Lady in the Crypt', 160; Brown, *Popular Piety*, p. 85.

104 Cited in Bond, *Inventories of St George's Chapel*, p. 286; T. Cranmer, *A Short Instruction into Christian Religion (1548)*, reprinted Oxford, 1829, p. 23.

105 Erasmus referred to grilles as security for the treasures and watchmen patrolled the crypt on the eve and feast of Becket's translation; traces of their emplacement remain (Woodruff, 'Our Lady in the Crypt', 154, 155). For touching, see Maniura, 'Image and Pilgrimage', p. 237.

106 Spencer, *Pilgrim Souvenirs: London*, pp. 16–18; also Freedberg, *Power of Images*, pp. 128–35.

107 Hobhouse, *Churchwardens' Accounts*, p. 64.

108 Tymms, *Wills and Inventories*, p. 83.

109 Belting, *Likeness and Presence*, p. 441.

110 Spencer, *Norfolk*, p. 28, no. 122.

111 Raine, *Mediaeval York*, p. 105; Duncan and Hussey, *Testamenta* (East Kent), p. 232. The wills refer to lights, but must have burned before images.

112 Freedberg, *Power of Images*, pp. 112–28, makes this point in relation to small-scale, personal replicas.

113 For this image, see Duffy *Stripping*, p. 166; A.W. Morant, 'Notices of the Church of St Nicholas, Great Yarmouth', *Norfolk Archaeology*, 7 (1872), 215–48; H. Swinden, *The History and Antiquities of the Ancient Burgh of Great Yarmouth in the County of Norfolk*, Norwich, 1772, pp. 807–20.

114 S. Vandenberghe and W.P. Dezutter, 'Trois insignes de pèlerinage du 15e siècle de Notre-Dame d'Aardenburg', *Berichten van de Rijksdienst voor het Oudheidkundig Bodemonderzoek*, 33 (1983), 455–9.

115 Harvey, *William Worcestre*, pp. 182–3.

116 Meech and Allen, *Book of Margery Kempe*, p. 60.

117 J.T. Fowler, 'On a Window representing the Life and Miracles of S. William of York', *Yorkshire Archaeological Journal*, 3 (1875), 294–5; T. French, *York Minster. The St William Window* (Corpus Vitrearum Medii Aevi Great Britain, Summary Catalogue 5), Oxford, 1999, p. 89.

118 Spencer, *Norfolk*, pp. 10–11, nos 1–6; idem, *Pilgrim Souvenirs: London*, pp. 136–7, nos 137, 138 (see also pp. 233–5 for examples of French pilgrim badges based on Romanesque seals). Some small bronze Virgin and Child images may also be replicas of Our Lady of Walsingham; see Campbell, 'Medieval Metalworking', 72, pl. XXVIIc.

119 Spencer, *Pilgrim Souvenirs: London*, pp. 131–3, nos 136, 136a, 136b, 137, 137a.

120 Spencer, *Norfolk*, p. 18, no. 50; idem, *Pilgrim Souvenirs: Salisbury*, pp. 29–30, figs 59, 60, 65.

121 Spencer, *Norfolk*, p. 28, no. 122.

122 Belting, *Likeness and Presence*, pp. 438–42; Freedberg, *Power of Images*, pp. 124–8; Maniura, 'Image and Pilgrimage', ch. 8.

123 For example, the Baroque copies of the famous cult image of the Virgin at Einsiedeln Abbey, Switzerland, which were blessed by the abbot; see *Iconoclasme. Vie et mort de l'image médiévale*, no. 102.

124 See above, p. 209.

125 Lehmann-Brockhaus, *Schriftquellen*, I, pp. 37–8.

126 Owst, *Literature and the Pulpit*, pp. 140–1; see also Kamerick, *Popular Piety*, pp. 118–19.

127 Babington, *Repressor*, 1, pp. 183–4.

128 The principal modern account is A. Neame, *The Holy Maid of Kent. The Life of Elizabeth Barton, 1506–1534*, London, 1971. The story is put into wider context in D. MacCulloch, *Thomas Cranmer. A Life*, London and New

Haven, 1996, pp. 102–9, 115, 125 and passim. For the chapel, see F.C. Elliston Erwood, 'Notes on the Architecture of Aldington Church, Kent and the Chapel at Court-at-Street, called "Bellirica"', *Archaeologia Cantiana*, 41 (1928), 143–51.

129  The local repercussions of the Maid of Kent affair were protracted. In the early 1540s the vicar of Chilham was believed to have concealed the Court-at-Street image in his house. See *Letters and Papers . . . Henry VIII*, 18, pt 2, pp. 303, 319.

130  The best account is Aston, *Iconoclasts*, pp. 105, 107, 158, 192, 237, 300–1, 429.

131  Tanner, *Heresy Trials*, p. 142.

132  A. Hudson (ed.), *Selections from English Wycliffite Writings*, Cambridge, 1978, p. 87; Tanner, *Heresy Trials*, p. 148.

133  Aston, *Iconoclasts*, p. 136.

134  Ibid., p. 234.

135  Orme, *Roscarrock's Lives*, p. 138.

136  Marks, 'Schorn', pp. 204–5; Hall, *Mediaeval Pilgrimage*, pp. 34–44.

# CHAPTER NINE

1  Quoted in full in Chapter Five, p. 90; Milbourn, 'St Stephen Walbrook', 340–3.

2  F.W. Weaver (ed.), *Somerset Medieval Wills*, II, Somerset Record Society, 19, 1903, p. 167.

3  J. Munby, 'Wood', in J. Blair and N. Ramsay (eds), *English Medieval Industries. Craftsmen, Techniques, Products*, London, 1991, ch. 15; L.F. Salzman, *Building in England down to 1540: a Documentary History*, Oxford, reprinted 1967, ch. XVI; H. Swanson, *Building Craftsmen in Late Medieval York*, University of York Borthwick Paper no. 63, York, 1983, p. 14.

4  N. Ramsay, 'Alabaster', in Blair and Ramsay, *Industries*, ch. 2, esp. pp. 30–2; Cheetham, *Medieval Alabasters*, pp. 11–17, 41–9; R.J. Firman, 'A geological approach to the history of English alabaster', *The Mercian Geologist*, 9, no. 3 (March 1984), 161–78.

5  Waterton, *Pietas Mariana Britannica*, bk 2, p. 262, citing Archbishop Zouche's register, f. 335.

6  For Kersey, see Boldrick, Park and Williamson, *Wonder*, no. 12; T.B. Dilks (ed.), *Bridgwater Borough Archives*, Somerset Record Society, 48, 1933, p. 191 (*iii ymaginariis de alabaustro provenientibus ex legacione Alicie Plumpton*).

7  Hingeston-Randolph, *Register of Edmund Stafford*, p. 483 (see above, Chapter Five, p 89)

8  For medieval quarries, see Salzman, *Building*, ch. VII.

9  This image was found in 1880 on the site of the holy well chapel of St Cohan and was subsequently housed in Merther, in which parish Tresillian is located.

10  Alabaster images of the Virgin and Child, a prelate and another figure survive at Crannock, on the north Cornish coast, also a Gesine at Treslothan, a fragmentary martyrdom of St Lawrence panel at Lantoglos-by-Fowey and a St Christopher at St Ive.

11  *The Statutes of the Realm*, IV, London, Record Commission, 1819, pt 1, p. 111.

12  N.J. Moore, 'Brick', in Blair and Ramsay, *Industries*, pp. 218–20; A.P. Baggs, 'Sixteenth-Century Terra-Cotta Tombs in East Anglia', *Archaeological Journal*, 125 (1968), 296–301. For the terracotta work of Da Maiano and Torrigiano for Wolsey and the Crown, see P.G. Lindley, 'Playing check-mate with royal majesty? Wolsey's patronage of Italian Renaissance Sculpture', in S.J. Gunn and P.G. Lindley (eds), *Cardinal Wolsey. Church, State and Art*, Cambridge, 1991, p. 284; P. Lindley, *Gothic to Renaissance. Essays on Sculpture in England*, Stamford, 1995, chs VI and VII.

13  Cheetham, *Medieval Alabasters*, p. 50, fig. 30. The remains of a similar plaque also in the Castle Museum were excavated from a site at Pottergate in Norwich (reg. no. 149N/1295); the finds date from before a fire in 1507. Cheetham also mentions a terracotta Betrayal panel in the Victoria & Albert Museum (A60-1930), which closely resembles English alabaster altarpieces.

14  J. Leeuwenberg, 'Die Ausstrahlung Utrechter Tonplastik', in *Studien zur Geschichte der Europäischen Plastik. Festschrift Theodor Müller*, Munich, 1965, pp. 151–66. Recent excavations have modified some of Leeuwenberg's conclusions; see C. Perier-D'Ieteren and A. Born (eds), *Retables en Terre Cuite des Pays-Bas (XVe - XVIe siècles). Etude Stylistique et Technologique*, Brussels, 1992. Several pipeclay statuettes found in London are in the Museum of London; see Marks and Williamson, *Gothic*, no. 221.

15  See above, Chapter Three, pp. 55, 58.

16  A. MacGregor, 'Antler, Bone and Horn', in Blair and Ramsay, *Industries*, pp. 376–8; N. Stratford, 'Gothic Ivory Carving in England', in Alexander and Binski, *Age of Chivalry*, pp. 107–13; M.H. Longhurst, *English Ivories*, London, 1926.

17  *Unum tabernaculum eburn' cum diversis imaginibus de ebore in uno coffino, Unum tabernaculum parvum cum imaginibus de eburn' in uno coffino* as well as *Imago beate Marie de eburn' cum tabernaculo eburn' in uno coffino*. See P. Williamson, 'Ivory Carvings in English Treasuries before the Reformation', in D. Buckton and T.A. Heslop (eds), *Studies in Medieval Art and Architecture presented to Peter Lasko*, Stroud, 1994, pp. 197, 200. Ivory images were widely

NOTES

distributed; see, for example, the will of Sir William Vavasour of Haslewood (Yorks.) (1311): *Item Domino Willielmo de Nunny unam ymaginem Beatae Virginis de yvor* (J. Raine and W. Greenwell (eds), *Wills and Inventories . . . of the Northern Counties of England . . . Part 1*, Surtees Society, 2, 1835, p. 14).

18   Alexander and Binski, *Age of Chivalry*, no. 248 (with qualifications); Stratford, 'Glastonbury and Two Gothic Ivories', pp. 208–16; P. Williamson, 'An English ivory tabernacle wing of the thirteenth century', *Burlington Magazine*, 132 (1990), 863–6; idem, 'Symbiosis across Scale: Gothic Ivories and Sculpture in Stone and Wood in the Thirteenth Century', in Barnet, *Images in Ivory*, pp. 38–45.

19   Tymms, *Wills and Inventories*, p. 15. John of Bridlington was canonized in 1401.

20   Waterton, *Pietas Mariana Britannica*, bk 2, p. 222; Raine, *Mediaeval York*, p. 46.

21   H. Littlehales (trans. and ed.), *The Medieval Records of a London City Church (St Mary at Hill) AD 1420–1559*, EETS, original series,125 and 128, 1904–5, p. 45.

22   Binney, *Wardens of Morebath*, pp. 12, 14, 16, 18, 19, 22, 25, 28, 32, 33, 35–8, 42, 43, 47, 49, 50, 52, 59, 61, 70, 72, 77, 94, 103. For the history of the parish in this period, see Duffy, *Voices of Morebath*.

23   Baxandall, *Limewood Sculptors*, pp. 102–6; Marks, *Stained Glass*, p. 22.

24   The vogue for monumental St George tableaux is discussed in Chapter Five above.

25   Fowler, *Memorials*, pp. 294–6.

26   Harvey, *English Mediaeval Architects*, p. 37; J.S. Purvis, 'Ripon Carvers and the Lost Choir-Stalls of Bridlington Priory', *Yorkshire Archaeological Journal*, 29 (1927–9), 157–201.

27   H. Harrod, 'Some Particulars relating to the History of the Abbey Church of Wymondham in Norfolk', *Archaeologia*, 43 (1871), 271.

28   Salzman, *Building*, pp. 18–20.

29   Baxandall, *Limewood Sculptors*, pp. 102–22; see also idem, *Painting and Experience in Fifteenth-Century Italy*, Oxford, 2nd edn, 1988, ch. I.

30   C. Richmond, 'The English Gentry and Religion, *c.* 1500', in C. Harper-Bill (ed.), *Religious Belief and Ecclesiastical Careers in Late Medieval England. Proceedings of the Conference Held at Strawberry Hill, Easter 1989*, Woodbridge, 1991, p. 124.

31   Weaver, *Somerset Wills*, I, 16, 1901, p. 94; J. Nichols, *Illustrations of the Manners and Expenses of Antient Times in England*, London, 1797, p. 186.

32   Richard Bramston, 1516 (PRO, PCC wills, 25 Holder); I am indebted to Peter Northeast for a transcript.

33   Kerry, *St Lawrence, Reading*, p. 68; Baxandall, *Limewood Sculptors*, pp. 105–6.

34   S. Ringbom, 'Devotional Images and Imaginative Devotions. Notes on the Place of Art in Late Medieval Private Piety', *Gazette des Beaux-Arts*, series 6, 73 (1969), 165; C. Harbison, 'Visions and meditations in early Flemish painting', *Simiolus*, 15 (1985), 113.

35   For the argument that form was governed in the thirteenth century by theological formulations, see J. Wirth, 'L'Apparition du surnaturel dans l'art du Moyen Age', in F. Dunand, J.-M. Speiser and J. Wirth (eds), *L'Image et la Production du Sacré, Actes du colloque de Strasbourg (20–1 January, 1988) organisé par le Centre d'Histoire de Religion de l'Université de Strasbourg*, II, Paris, 1991, pp. 139–64 (esp. pp. 154–61).

36   Riley, *Gesta abbatum*, I, p. 281.

37   Marks and Williamson, *Gothic*, no. 84; P. Nelson, 'Some additional specimens of English alabaster carvings', *Archaeological Journal*, 84 (1927), 116–17, pl. opp. p. 115.

38   During the second half of the fifteenth century the craftsman's skill rather than the materials used becomes more prominent in Italian artists' contracts (Baxandall, *Painting*, pp. 14–27).

39   Duffy *Stripping*, p. 436.

40   Suffolk County Record Office (Bury St Edmunds): Thomas Swayn, 1506 (PCC 12 Adeane; Peter Northeast transcript).

41   For the issue of form, see Wirth, 'L'Apparition'; Recht, *Le croire et le voir*, chs 5 and 6; Schmitt, *Le corps des images*, pp. 51–4.

42   Marks, 'Altarpiece', pp. 417–44.

43   Belting, *Likeness and Presence*, chs 19, 20; for a critique of Belting's views, see Schmitt, *Le corps des images*, pp. 51–4.

44   Brown, *Popular Piety*, p. 86.

45   Bassingbourn Churchwardens' Accounts, f. 61 (Cambs. Record Office); transcript by Alfred Roberts, Cambridge University Library MS Add. 2792).

46   Hussey, 'Hythe Wills', 110–11; Bell, *Bedfordshire Wills 1480–1519*, p. 98, no. 194.

47   E. Peacock, 'Churchwardens' Accounts of Saint Mary's, Sutterton', *Archaeological Journal*, 39 (1882), 62; Kerry, *St Lawrence, Reading*, p. 67.

48   London, *The Life of William Bruges*, pp. 86–7.

49   Barnum, *Dives and Pauper*, 1, p. 94.

50   See above, Chapter Three.

51    For example the images from Dal (Oslo, Universitets Oldsamling) and Hove (Bergen Historisk Museum); see Andersson, *English Influence*, pp. 127–38; M. Blindheim, *Painted Wooden Sculpture*, p. 35; Boldrick, Park and Williamson, *Wonder*, no. 3; Kaland, 'Baldakin fra Hopperstad', pp. 85–98.

52    See also above, Chapter Two, pp. 23–4.

53    J.J. Wilkinson (ed.), 'Receipts and Expenses in the Building of Bodmin Church, AD 1469 to 1472', Camden Society, Camden Miscellany, 7, 1875, p. 27.

54    Hobhouse, *Churchwardens' Accounts*, p. 126.

55    The Wing tabernacle was made in the same year for 19s 6d; see Vere Woodman, 'Churchwardens of Wing', 316, incl. n. 16; A. Hussey, 'Sittingbourne Wills', *Archaeologia Cantiana*, 43 (1931), 69.

56    For Barbour's will, see PRO, PCC wills, 14 Fettiplace (transcript by Peter Northeast); Rosser, *Medieval Westminster*, p. 272.

57    Littlehales, *St Mary at Hill*, p. 142.

58    Tabernacles for the Trinity, St Katherine and St Anthony (Oakley); for St Thomas (Sandy) and St Margaret (Shillington).

59    Rosser, *Medieval Westminster*, p. 272.

60    Dymond and Paine, *Spoil of Melford Church*, p. 1.

61    Cheetham, *Medieval Alabasters*, pp. 29–30.

62    J. Browne, *The History of the Metropolitan Church of St Peter, York*, London, 1847, p. 270.

63    Littlehales, *St Mary at Hill*, pp. 219–20.

64    Duncan, 'West Kent', 297; Rosser, *Medieval Westminster*, p. 272; P. Northeast (ed.), *Boxford Churchwardens' Accounts 1530–1561*, Suffolk Records Society, 23, 1982, pp. 11, 14.

65    Hudson, *Wycliffite Writings*, p. 84.

66    S.S. Doree (ed.), *Early Churchwardens' Accounts of Bishops Stortford 1431–1558*, Hertfordshire Record Publications, 10, 1994, p. 287; W.J. Lightfoot, 'Notes from the Records of Hawkhurst Church 1. Extracts from the Churchwardens' Account-Book 1515 to 1714', *Archaeologia Cantiana*, 5 (1862–3), 57, 58, 62.

67    For an overview, see Boldrick, Park and Williamson, *Wonder*.

68    Baxandall, *Painting*, p. 81.

69    W.O. Ross (ed.), *Middle English Sermons*, EETS, original series, 209, 1940, p. 283.

70    P. Binski, *Medieval Craftsmen. Painters*, London, 1991, p. 25; N.J. Morgan, *The Lambeth Apocalypse. Manuscript 209 in Lambeth Palace Library: A Critical Study*, London, 1990, pp. 50–1.

71    Cheetham, *Alabaster Carvings in the Castle Museum Nottingham*, pp. 18–25.

72    Babington, *Repressor*, 2, p. 193.

73    Swinburn, *Lanterne of Light*, p. 84; Hudson, *Wycliffite Writings*, pp. 84–5. Contemporary criticism of gilding in particular is discussed in M. Aston, 'Gold and Images', in W.J. Sheils and D. Wood (eds), *The Church and Wealth, Studies in Church History*, 24, 1987, pp. 189–209.

74    Browne, *York*, p. 259.

75    Kerry, *St Lawrence, Reading*, p. 70.

76    Bell, *Bedfordshire Wills 1484–1533*, pp. 58, 69, nos 93, 113; Beds. & Luton Archives, nos ABP/R3/82d, 117; ABP/R4/96d.

77    The case against the linking of the unpainted retable with the Reformation is made by Hartmut Krohm, 'The Sources of Riemenschneider's Art', in *Tilman Riemenschneider Master Sculptor of the Late Middle Ages* (National Gallery of Art, Washington and The Metropolitan Museum of Art, New York exhibition catalogue), New Haven and London, 1999, pp. 63–6 (with bibliography).

78    Marks, 'Altarpiece', pp. 417–44.

79    See above, Chapter Six, pp. 129, 154–6.

80    Barnum, *Dives and Pauper*, 1, pp. 100–1.

81    *Letters and Papers . . . Henry VIII*, 13, pt 2, p. 143, no. 367.

82    W.H. St John Hope, *Windsor Castle. An Architectural History*, 2, London, 1913, pp. 374, 395 n. 6; Bond, *Inventories of St George's Chapel*, p. 166 (the 1534 Inventory).

83    Walters, *London Churches*, pp. 91–2, 107, 201, 341, 395, 410, 413, 418, 432, 447, 457, 502, 545, 596, 602; for a sexual reading of robing images, see R.C. Trexler, 'Habiller et déshabiller les images: ésquisse d'une analyse', in Dunand, Speiser and Wirth, *L'Image et la Production*, pp. 195–231.

84    J. Edwards, 'Some Murals in North-East Oxfordshire', *Oxoniensia*, 58 (1993), 242; E.J. Tench, 'The Church of Saint James, Great Ellingham', *Norfolk Archaeology*, 22 (1926), pl. opp. p. 341; for All Saints' Bristol, see above, Chapter Four, p. 79.

85    Littlehales, *St Mary at Hill*, p. 306.

86    Timmins, *Register of John Chandler*, p. 92. The legend of Our Lady of Sablon, an image of the Virgin which an elderly woman was ordered by the Virgin in a vision to restore and which then became miracle-working, would have encouraged such practices. The legend is depicted, *inter alia*, on a set of four Brussels tapestries made for the

funerary chapel of a high Burgundian official in the church of Our Lady of Sablon in Brussels; see A. Van Ruymbeke, 'La légende de Notre-Dame de Sablon', in *Tapisseries bruxelloises de la pre-Rénaissance* (Brussels, Musées Royaux d'Art et d'Histoire exhibition catalogue, 1976), pp. 85–99.

87 Bergmann, *Holzskulpturen des Mittelalters*, pp. 321–3, cat. 91.

88 Coulton, 'Visitation', 116, 123; Duncan and Hussey, *Testamenta* (East Kent), p. 374.

89 Duffy *Stripping*, p. 186, argues that the replacement of images at Morebath shows the parishioners were aware of the distinction; the opposite line is taken in R.C. Trexler, 'Florentine Religious Experience: The Sacred Image', *Studies in the Renaissance*, 19 (1972), 7–41 (esp. 20–1).

90 See M. Caviness, '*De convenientia et cohaerentia antiqui et novi operis*: Medieval conservation, restoration, pastiche and forgery', *Intuition und Kunstwissenschaft. Festschrift für Hanns Swarzenski zum 70. Geburtstag*, Berlin, 1973, pp. 205–21.

91 R.A. Shoaf (ed.), *Thomas Usk, The Testament of Love*, Kalamazoo, 1998, bk 2, ll. 460–1.

92 A. Hudson (ed.), *Two Wycliffite Texts*, EETS, original series, 301, 1993, p. 58; E.A. Bond (ed.), *Chronica Monasterii de Melsa*, Rolls Series, 43, London, 1868, vol. 3, p. 35; discussed in Camille, *Gothic Idol*, pp. 212–13.

93 Salzman, *Building*, p. 31.

94 Lehmann-Brockhaus, *Schriftquellen*, 2, pp. 364, 402, nos 3596, 3905; Riley, *Gesta abbatum*, I, p. 286.

95 *Calendar Liberate Rolls*, 1, p. 51.

96 Salzman, *Building*, pp. 31–2: the term 'graver' was used by Wycliffe (Aston, *Iconoclasts*, p. 109) and was often applied to carvers in East Anglia, like Sterlyng and Bale of Wymondham.

97 Harvey, *English Mediaeval Architects*, pp. 199–200; for the All Souls' figures and the Beauchamp effigy, see Marks and Williamson, *Gothic*, nos 36, 99, 87.

98 Harvey, *English Mediaeval Architects*, p. 207; for Peter Kerver, see A. Hanham (ed.), *Churchwardens' Accounts of Ashburton 1479–1580*, Devon and Cornwall Record Society, new series, 15, 1969, passim.

99 The chief source used is Harvey, *English Mediaeval Architects*.

100 F. Collins (ed.), *Register of the Freemen of the City of York from the City Records, vol. 1 1272–1558*, Surtees Society, 96, 1896, passim.

101 Swanson, *Building Craftsmen*, pp. 16–17; idem, *Medieval Artisans. An Urban Class in Late Medieval England*, Oxford, 1989, p. 86.

102 As for example, in Lindley, *Gothic to Renaissance*, p. 30. In any case guild control did not necessarily mean sterility and could provide an effective quality assurance mechanism, as in the case of Netherlandish carved retable production; see L.F. Jacobs, *Early Netherlandish Carved Altarpieces, 1380–1550. Medieval Tastes and Mass Marketing*, Cambridge, 1998, esp. pp. 234–5.

103 N. Rogers, 'Regional Production', in Marks and Williamson, *Gothic*, pp. 94–7; Marks, *Stained Glass*, p. 198.

104 Suffolk Record Office (Bury St Edmunds): Osbern 160 (Myldenhale), Hawlee 55v (Aleyn). Photocopies and transcripts of the Bury wills provided by Peter Northeast.

105 Suffolk Record Office (Bury St Edmunds): Hawlee 118.

106 Suffolk Record Office (Bury St Edmunds): Howlee 287 (Cosyn). For Wolsey, see Harvey, *English Mediaeval Architects*, p. 345.

107 Suffolk Record Office (Bury St Edmunds): Bury wills, Mason 2v.

108 Suffolk Record Office (Bury St Edmunds): Bury wills, Mason 23 (Belamy).

109 Kerry, *St Lawrence, Reading*, p. 67.

110 M. Sellers (ed.), *York Memorandum Book Part II (1388–1493)*, Surtees Society, 125, 1915, pp. 281–2.

111 Harvey, *English Mediaeval Architects*, p. 14.

112 K.L. Wood-Legh, *Perpetual Chantries in Britain*, Cambridge, 1965, p. 300; Doree, *Bishops Stortford*, p. 12.

113 For accounts of the alabaster trade, see Cheetham, *Medieval Alabasters*, pp. 11–17, 41–9; Ramsay, 'Alabaster', in Blair and Ramsay, *Medieval Industries*, ch. 2.

114 Collins, *Freemen*, 1, pp. 177, 183, 185, 187, 194, 213, 246.

115 J.F. Williams (ed.), *The Early Churchwardens' Accounts of Hampshire*, Winchester and London, 1913, p. 22.

116 Cambs. Record Office, Consistory Court of Ely Probate Records C8: 29. She also made a bequest of 20d to gild the Trinity; Marion Symond (1497) left a flaxen sheet to the altar and image of Our Lady of Pity (C4: 113).

117 Other concentrations of alabaster are at Wood Ditton (Cambs.) and East Rudham (Norf.).

118 Cheetham, *Medieval Alabasters*, pp. 28, 31.

119 Ibid., pp. 26–7 and 56–7, app. IV, for an analysis of pigments used on English alabasters; for other framed alabasters, see ibid., cat. no. 94, col. pl. IV, figs 16, 17, 33. Other results of pigment analyses are in L. Flavigny and C. Jablonski-Chauveau, *D'Angleterre en Normandie. Sculptures d'albâtre du Moyen Age* (Rouen and Evreux exhibition catalogue, 1998), pp. 78–9, 99–100; C. Prigent, *Les sculptures anglaises d'albâtre au musée national du Moyen Age, Thermes de Cluny*, Paris, 1998, pp. 36–7.

120 Kerry, *St Lawrence, Reading*, p. 38; Cambs. Record Office, Bassingbourn Churchwardens' Accounts, f. 64 (1507–8) (Roberts transcript in Cambridge University Library, MS Add. 2792).

121     Cheetham, *Medieval Alabasters*, p. 42; see also above, Chapter Six.

122     H.H.S. Croft (ed.), *The Boke of the Gouernour deuised by Sir Thomas Elyot, Knight*, London, 1883, 1, pp. 139–40.

123     This affair is discussed by T.A. Heslop, 'Attitudes to the Visual Arts: The Evidence from Written Sources', in Alexander and Binski, *Age of Chivalry*, p. 26.

124     Overviews are provided by C. Reynolds, 'England and the Continent: Artistic Relations' and K. Woods, 'Immigrant Craftsmen and Imports', in Marks and Williamson, *Gothic*, pp. 76–85, 91–4.

125     See especially D.R. Ransome, 'The struggle of the Glaziers' Company with the foreign glaziers, 1500–1550', *Guildhall Miscellany*, 2, no. 1 (September 1960), 12–20; Marks, *Stained Glass*, pp. 227–8; S. Foister, 'The Production and Reproduction of Holbein's Portraits', in K. Hearn (ed.), *Dynasties. Painting in Tudor and Jacobean England 1530–1630* (London, Tate Gallery exhibition catalogue, 1995), p. 21.

126     Jacobs, *Early Netherlandish Carved Altarpieces*, pp. 156, 159–60.

127     P.G. Lindley, 'The Great Screen at Winchester Cathedral, II', *Burlington Magazine*, 135 (1993), 796–807; J. Evans and N. Cook, 'A Statue of Christ from the Ruins of Mercers' Hall', *Archaeological Journal*, 111 (1954), 168–80; soon afterwards the Mercers ordered a retable for the high altar of their chapel from the Antwerp carver Walter van Dale (Woods, 'Immigrant Craftsmen', p. 93). Nonetheless, the hybrid nature of the Winchester figures and the statuary in Henry VII's Chapel, Westminster Abbey, makes it impossible to identify the country of origin of the carvers.

128     Summaries of these and other likely alien carvers are in Harvey, *English Mediaeval Architects*, pp. 69–70, 78, 100, 105, 130–1, 143, 201, 216, 231, 232, 275, 305.

# CHAPTER TEN

1     Lollards are also recorded in the area at Dunstable and Drayton Beauchamp in the early fifteenth century; for these and their successors, see J.A.F. Thomson, *The Later Lollards 1414–1520*, Oxford, 1965, ch. III. The movement was not eradicated in the Chilterns by the early sixteenth-century episcopal persecutions, but it was severely weakened by them (C. Haigh, *English Reformations. Religion, Politics, and Society under the Tudors*, Oxford, 1993, pp. 51–5).

2     Ringbom, 'Devotional Images', 163; Harbison, 'Visions and meditations', 113; Recht, *Le croire et le voir*, pp. 252–5, 401.

3     For Fitzralph's sermon, see Owst, *Literature and the Pulpit*, pp. 140–1. The best discussion of these texts is Aston, *Iconoclasts*, ch. 4; see also Kamerick, *Popular Piety*, chs 1 and 2.

4     Ringbom, 'Devotional Images', 165; C. Harbison, 'Visions and meditations', 113. For the *Vièrges ouvrantes*, see Chapter Eight above, pp. 198–9. The criticisms of Gerson and also of Archbishop Antonin of Florence (1450) are discussed in Schmitt, *Le corps des images*, pp. 158–61.

5     Lyndwood's *Provinciale*, f. clxxxiii(r), note b: *Imaginem principalem f. illi' – sancti ad cuius honorem ecclesia consecrata est q[uo]d intellige ubi talis imago est imaginabilis. Nam ubi talis ecclesia fundata est in honore o[mn]i[u]m sanctoru[m] ɔ puto posse unam imaginem fieri omnes sanctos representatem, sed aut oportet plures fieri aut nullam.* For the imagery of All Saints, see P. Sheingorn, 'The Bosom of Abraham Trinity: A Late Medieval All Saints Image', in D. Williams (ed.), *England in the Fifteenth Century, Proceedings of the 1986 Harlaxton Symposium*, Woodbridge, 1987, pp. 273–95.

6     Barnum, *Dives and Pauper*, 1, p. 81.

7     Aston, *Iconoclasts*, pp. 25–6.

8     Catto, 'Religious Change', pp. 97–115.

9     For Lollards and images, see Aston, *Iconoclasts*, ch. 4; W.R. Jones, 'Lollards and Images. The Defence of Religious Art in England', *Journal of the History of Ideas*, 34 (1973), 27–50; A. Hudson, *The Premature Reformation. Wycliffite Texts and Lollard History*, Oxford, 1988, esp. pp. 92–4, 165–7, 301–9; idem, *Wycliffite Writings*, pp. 19–27, 83–8, 179–81; idem, *Two Wycliffite Texts*. An important contemporary response to the Lollards is Walter Hilton's *De Adoracione Ymaginum*; see Clark and Taylor, *Hilton's Latin Writings*, pp. 175–214; the text is discussed in J.M. Russell-Smith, 'Walter Hilton and a Tract in Defence of the Veneration of Images', *Dominican Studies*, 7 (1954), 180–214 and Clark, 'Walter Hilton in Defence of the Religious Life', 1–25.

10     See *Iconoclasme. Vie et mort de l'image médiévale*, no. 127.

11     Aston, *Iconoclasts*, pp. 133–43. For Bergh Apton, see Tanner, *Heresy Trials*, p. 218. For the images, see F.W. Cheetham, 'A Medieval English Alabaster Figure of St Paul', *Norfolk Archaeology*, 35 (1970), 143–4.

12     Haigh, *English Reformations*, pp. 51–7, 60–7; S. Brigden, *London and the Reformation*, Oxford, 1989, ch. II.

13     Clapham, 'The York Virgin', 6–13; *English Romanesque Art*, no. 153; see also Chapter Three above.

14     J. Wirth, 'Théorie et pratique de l'image sainte à la veille de la Réforme', *Bibliothèque d'Humanisme et Renaissance*, 48 (1986), 343, 350.

15     Freshfield, 'On the Parish Books', 119; Raine, *Testamenta Eboracensia, V*, p. 74, no. LXIII.

16     See especially the essays by Jean Wirth, Beat Hodler and Olivier Christin in *Iconoclasme. Vie et mort de l'image médiévale*, pp. 28–37, 52–6, 57–66.

17 The most comprehensive accounts of the official pronouncements on images are Aston, *Iconoclasts*, ch. 6 and Duffy *Stripping*, pt II.

18 Bucks. RO, PR 234/5/1; they have been partly transcribed (Bucks. RO, AR 65/72) and in Vere Woodman, 'Churchwardens of Wing', 307–29.

19 Apart from the Coronations, all of this imagery was recorded by the antiquary Browne Willis in the early eighteenth century (Oxford, Bodleian Library, MS Willis 34, ff. 83r, 84r).

20 See above, Chapter Five, p. 114.

21 See the relevant archdeaconry registers in the Beds. & Luton Archives and the Bucks. Record Office.

22 See above, Chapter Nine, p. 234.

23 Vere Woodman, 'Churchwardens of Wing', 313–16; Bucks. RO, D/A/We3/213.

24 Baxandall, *Limewood Sculptors*, pp. 78–93; Duffy *Stripping*, p. 355; see also Trexler, *Public Life*, pp. 85–111.

25 M. Aston, 'Iconoclasm at Rickmansworth, 1522: Troubles of Churchwardens', *Journal of Ecclesiastical History*, 40 (1989), 524–52; see also idem, *Iconoclasts*, pp. 210–19 and Brigden, *London and the Reformation*, pp. 288–93.

26 C. Lloyd (ed.), *Formularies of Faith Put Forth by Authority During the Reign of Henry VIII*, Oxford, 1825, pp. 13–14.

27 W.H. Frere and W.M. Kennedy (eds), *Visitation Articles and Injunctions of the Period of the Reformation vol. II 1536–1558*, Alcuin Club Collections, 15, 1910, pp. 5–6.

28 Bucks. RO, D/A/We3/373; Whiting, *Blind Devotion*, p. 65.

29 For Our Lady of Bradwell, see above, Chapter Eight, pp. 197–8.

30 Marks, 'Schorn', pp. 192–207. North Marston had at least twelve other images in the early sixteenth century, excluding the rood and St Sunday.

31 Frere and Kennedy, *Visitation Articles, II*, p. 38.

32 See Aston, *Iconoclasts*, pp. 226–8, for a discussion of the 1538 Injunctions.

33 Bucks. RO, D/A/W/159 (Adam), D/A/We6/94 (Buckmaster).

34 Brown, *Popular Piety*, p. 226 (Table 16).

35 Beds. & Luton Archives, ABP/R 1545: 11/55d. In 1989 a large stone tomb, probably that of William Ashwell, was found under the floor in the space before these brackets and the respond.

36 I owe this reference to the kindness of Dr Simon Cotton.

37 Aston, *Iconoclasts*, pp. 257–8; Wandel, *Voracious Idols*; *Iconoclasme. Vie et mort de l'image médiévale*, pp. 34–6, 75–103.

38 Frere and Kennedy, *Visitation Articles, II*, pp. 115–16. The Injunctions are analysed in Aston, *Iconoclasts*, pp. 254–8.

39 Aston, *Iconoclasts*, pp. 256–7; Frere and Kennedy, *Visitation Articles, II*, pp. 105, 107.

40 Barnum, *Dives and Pauper*, 1, p. 100; A.G. Dickens, 'Robert Parkyn's Narrative of the Reformation', in idem, *Reformation Studies*, London, 1982, p. 295.

41 J.E. Cox (ed.), *Miscellaneous Writings and Letters of Thomas Cranmer*, Parker Society, 18, 1846, pp. 509–11.

42 *The Statutes of the Realm, IV*, London, Record Commission, 1819, pt 1, p. 111; the date when the Virgin and Child was removed from the Parker brass illustrated in plate **172** is not known.

43 R.B. Bond (ed.), *Certain Sermons or Homilies (1547) and A Homily against Disobedience and Wilful Rebellion (1570)*, Toronto, Buffalo and London, 1987.

44 For all these events, see Vere Woodman, 'Churchwardens of Wing', 319–21.

45 *The First and Second Prayer Books of King Edward the Sixth*, p. 378; compare with the First Prayer Book (ibid., pp. 212–13).

46 For Sir Robert's will, see London, PRO wills, PCC Powell 26; no pious bequests are made. For Lady Jane, see Vere Woodman, 'Churchwardens of Wing', 307.

47 Vere Woodman, 'Churchwardens of Wing', 329, n. 26.

48 Bucks. RO, D/A/We6/162 (Holden); D/A/We6/240 (Fountain).

49 Dickens, 'Parkyn', pp. 295, 297.

50 W.H. Godfrey (ed.), *Sussex Wills Vol. I*, Sussex Record Society, 41, 1935, p. 278; idem, *Vol. IV*, Sussex Record Society, 45, 1940/1, p. 423.

51 Among the proponents of this view, see Duffy *Stripping*, ch. 16, and Haigh, *English Reformations*, ch. 12.

52 *Statutes of the Realm, IV*, pt 1, pp. 202, 246–54.

53 Vere Woodman, 'Churchwardens of Wing', 322–4.

54 Frere and Kennedy, *Visitation Articles, II*, pp. 388, 397, 408, 424; W. Sharp and L.E. Whatmore (trans.), *Archdeacon Harpsfield's Visitation, 1557*, Catholic Record Society, 45, 1950; L.E. Whatmore (trans.), *Archdeacon Harpsfield's Visitation, 1557, together with Visitations of 1556 and 1558*, Catholic Record Society, 46, 1951.

55 For example the rood and attendant figures at Ludham (Norf.) are painted not carved (Duffy *Stripping*, pl. 137).

56 Sharp and Whatmore, *Harpsfield*, p. 133 (Newendon); Mercer, *Betrysden*, pp. 114–15; F. Haslewood, 'Notes from the Records of Smarden Church', *Archaeologia Cantiana*, 9 (1874), 231–2; H.R. Plomer (trans.), *The Churchwardens' Accounts of St Nicholas, Strood*, Kent Archaeological Society Records Branch, 5, 1927, p. 8.

57 A. Hanham (ed.), *Churchwardens' Accounts of Ashburton 1479–1580*, Devon and Cornwall Record Society, new series, 15, 1969, p. 134; Lee, *Prebendal Church of the Blessed Virgin Mary of Thame*, cols 73–4.

58    Littlehales, *St Mary at Hill*, pp. 94, 401; a further 18*s* 4*d* was spent on painting the patronal image, 'Reffreshynge' the tabernacle and colouring the reverse of the rood cross.

59    See Aston, *Iconoclasts*, p. 287; Duffy *Stripping*, pp. 525–6, 563–4.

60    Duffy *Stripping*, pp. 540, 542.

61    Bucks. RO, D/A/Wf2/319 (Mayne); We12/167 (Bate); D/A,We10/4 (Wells).

62    Bucks. RO, D/A/Wf/3/78 (Daulton). For accounts of the difficulties in using wills as a barometer of religious allegiance see Duffy *Stripping*, ch. 15 and Haigh, *English Reformations*, pp. 199–202.

63    Vere Woodman, 'Churchwardens of Wing', 324. The altar stone was not broken up but laid down in the church floor until it was removed during the Victorian restoration.

64    Ibid., 326.

65    Aston, *Iconoclasts*, pp. 302–3; A.G. Dickens, 'The First Stages of Romanist Recusancy in Yorkshire, 1560–1590', in idem, *Reformation Studies*, p. 163; see also Haigh, *English Reformations*, pp. 245–6.

66    Aston, *Iconoclasts*, pp. 317–20.

67    E.R.C. Brinkworth (ed.), *South Newington Churchwardens' Accounts 1553–1684*, Banbury History Society, 6 (1964), p. 6.

68    Collins, *Register of the Freemen of the City of York I, II*, passim; Marks, *Stained Glass*, p. 234.

69    Whatmore, *Harpsfield*, p. 188. Presumably the carver was hostile to the restoration of the Catholic faith.

70    Aston, *Iconoclasts*, p. 291, quoting J.O. Halliwell (ed.), *Tarlton's Jests and News out of Purgatory*, Shakespeare Society, London, 1844, pp. 86–7.

71    L. Stone, *Sculpture in Britain. The Middle Ages*, Harmondsworth, 2nd edn, 1972, p. 233.

72    It seems that the children of Robert Dormer were baptised into the Catholic faith in the parish church as the parish register bears a cross against their names (Vere Woodman, 'Churchwardens of Wing', 328, n. 3).

73    The lack of weathering on the St Faith statue suggests that it was originally set up inside the church. Details of the discovery of the Stewkley figures are given in *St Michael's Stewkley Buckinghamshire* (church guide book), Aspley Guise, 1972.

74    P. Bell (ed.), *Episcopal Visitations in Bedfordshire 1706–1720*, BHRS, 81, 2002, p. 29.

75    For Morebath, see Duffy, *Voices of Morebath*, p. 143; Binney, *Wardens of Morebath*, p. 185; Serjeantson and Isham Longden, 'Northamptonshire', 403, n. 3.

76    This extract from the 1571 diocesan visitation is taken from D. Beevers, R. Marks and J. Roles, *Sussex Churches and Chapels*, Brighton, 1989, p. 19.

77    See also the evidence of religious imagery in Elizabethan households: S. Foister, 'Paintings and other works of art in sixteenth-century English inventories', *Burlington Magazine*, 123, no. 938 (May 1981), 273–82.

78    See above, p. 257.

79    I am indebted to Mr Ron Gray and Mrs Pat Gray, who discovered the buried image, for the description of the site.

80    Marks, 'Altarpiece', pp. 417–44; Aston, *Iconoclasts*, p. 267; D. Freedberg, 'The Structure of Byzantine and European Iconoclasm', in A. Bryer and J. Herrin (eds), *Iconoclasm (Papers given at the Ninth Spring Symposium of Byzantine Studies, University of Birmingham, 1975)*, Birmingham, 1977, p. 169.

81    Marks and Williamson, *Gothic*, no. 280.

82    Little Shelford, Milton (now in the Cambridge University Museum of Archaeology and Anthropology), Toft, Whittlesford and Wood Ditton.

83    See B. Thordeman, *Medieval Wooden Sculpture in Sweden Vol. 1. Attitudes to the heritage*, Stockholm, 1964, pp. 7–15; M. Blindheim, 'The Cult of Medieval Wooden Sculptures in Post-Reformation Norway', *Universitetes Oldsaksamling Årbok* (1995/6), 139–51.

84    See above, n. 19.

85    Aston, *Iconoclasts*, pp. 361–2, 368.

86    Godber, *Bedfordshire*, p. 190.

87    RCHM, *Buckinghamshire, vol. 2*, London, 1913, p. 194. The text is now almost illegible.

88    Rouse, 'Wall Paintings in Radnage Church', 134–8. Neither of the two extant pre-Reformation wills from Radnage identifies any images (Bucks. RO, D/A/We3/101, 105).

89    Latimer's actual wording is 'The founding of monasteries argued purgatory to be; so the putting down of them argueth it not to be': G.E. Corrie (ed.), *Sermons and Remains of Hugh Latimer*, Parker Society, 23, 1845, p. 249.

90    Dickinson, *Missale*, cols 664–7; Vere Woodman, 'Churchwardens of Wing', 314; Hutton, *Stations of the Sun*, pp. 100–3. See also Chapter Five above.

91    *The First and Second Prayer-Books of King Edward the Sixth*, pp. 378, 430. The extracts are from the 1552 book. The Decalogue and Commination prayers are discussed in Aston, *Iconoclasts*, ch. 7.

92    Fowler, *Rites of Durham*, p. 30; Orme, *Roscarrock's Lives*; Martin's account is transcribed in Dymond and Paine, *Spoil of Melford Church*, pp. 1–9; Duffy, *Voices of Morebath*.

93    An observation made in Lucy Wooding's review of Duffy, *Voices of Morebath*, in A. Shepherd (ed.), *Reviews in History* (ashepher@ihr.sas.ac.uk).

# BIBLIOGRAPHY

## MANUSCRIPTS AND UNPUBLISHED DOCUMENTS

Bedfordshire & Luton Archives and Records Service, Bedford: ABP/R3, R4, R5 (Archdeaconry of Bedford Probate Records)

Bodleian Library, Oxford: MS Willis 34

British Library, London: Cotton MS Tiberius A VII (Deguileville, *Pilgrimage of the Soul*)
    Lansdowne MS 874 (*Pontifical*)
    Lansdowne MS 383 (*Shaftesbury Psalter*)
    Yates Thompson MS 2, f. 29

Buckinghamshire Record Office, Aylesbury: D/A/We2, We3, We6, We10, We12, Wf2, Wf3 (Archdeaconry of Aylesbury Probate Records); RO PR 234/5/1 (Wing churchwardens' accounts; partly transcribed in AR 65/72)

Cambridge University Library, Cambridge: MS Add. 2792, Bassingbourn churchwardens' accounts, transcript by Alfred Roberts

Cambridgeshire Record Office, Cambridge: Consistory Court of Ely Probate Records etc., and Bassingbourn churchwardens' accounts (C4:113, C8:11, 29:WRI *4029)

Norfolk Records Service, Norwich: Register Spurlyng (Diocese of Norwich Probate Records)

Public Record Office, London: Prerogative Court of Canterbury (PCC), Probate Records

Society of Antiquaries of London: W. Lyndewood, *Provinciale seu constitutiones Anglie Provinciale* (early sixteenth-century printed copy)

Stonyhurst College (Lancs.): MS 60 (Lady Katherine Bray's *Book of Hours*)

Suffolk County Record Office, Bury St Edmunds: Probate Records

## PRINTED SOURCES

Alberti, *De re aedificatoria*, J. Leoni, ed. J. Ryckwert (trans.), London, reprinted 1955

Astle, T. (ed.), *The Will of King Henry VII*, London, 1775

Babington, C. (ed.), *The Repressor of Over Much Blaming of the Clergy by Reginald Peacock D.D.* , 2 vols, Rolls Series, London, 1860

Barnum, P.H. (ed.), *Dives and Pauper*, vol. 1, pt 1, Early English Text Society, original series, 275, 1976

Blackley, F.D. and Hermansen, G. (trans.), *The Household Book of Queen Isabella of England, for the fifth regnal year of Edward II, 8th July 1311 to 7th July 1312*, Alberta (Canada), 1971

Bokenham, O. see under Delany, S.

Bond, R.B. (ed.), *Certain Sermons or Homilies* (1547) and *A Homily against Disobedience and Wilful Rebellion (1570)*, Toronto, Buffalo and London, 1987

*Calendar Liberate Rolls Henry III Vol. I 1226–1240*, London, 1916, *Vol. II 1240–1245*, London, 1930

Clark, J.P.H. and Taylor, C. (eds), *Walter Hilton's Latin Writings*, 2 vols, Analecta Cartusiana, 124, 1987

Clay, J.W. (ed.), *North Country Wills*, Surtees Society, 116, vol. ii, 1908

Coinci, Gautier de – see under Koenig, V.F.

Corrie, G.E. (ed.), *Sermons and Remains of Hugh Latimer*, Parker Society, 23, 1845

Cox, J.E. (ed.), *Miscellaneous Writings and Letters of Thomas Cranmer*, Parker Society, 18, 1846

Cranmer, T., *A Short Instruction into Christian Religion* (1548), reprinted Oxford, 1829

Cranmer, T. – see also under Cox, J.E.

Croft, H.H.S. (ed.), *The Boke of the Gouernuor deuised by Sir Thomas Elyot, Knight*, 2 vols, London, 1883

Davies, R.T. (ed.), *Medieval English Lyrics. A Critical Anthology*, Northwestern University Press, 1964

Delany, S. (ed.), *A Legend of Holy Women. A Translation of Osbern Bokenham's Legends of Holy Women*, Notre Dame and London, 1992

Dickinson, F.H. (ed.), *Missale ad Usum Insignis et Praeclare Ecclesiae Sarum*, Burntisland, 1861–83

Ellis, F.S. (ed.), *The Golden Legend or Lives of the Saints, as Englished by William Caxton*, 7 vols, London, 1900; see also under Jacobus de Voragine

Elyot, Sir. T. – see under Croft, H.H.S.

Erasmus, D., *Peregrinatio religionis ergo*, in C.R. Thompson (trans.), *The Collected Works of Erasmus. Colloquies*, Toronto, 1997, pp. 619–74.

Erbe, T. (ed.), *Mirk's Festial: A Collection of Homilies by Johannes Mirkus (John Mirk)*, pt 1, Early English Text Society, extra series, 96, 1905

*The First and Second Prayer Books of King Edward the Sixth* (Everyman Edition), London, 1910

Frere, W.H. (ed.), *The Use of Sarum*, 2 vols, Cambridge, 1898–1901

—— and Kennedy, W.M. (eds), *Visitation Articles and Injunctions of the Period of the Reformation*, Alcuin Club Collections, vols 14 and 15, 1910

Gairdner, J. (ed.), *The Paston Letters*, London, 1904

Griffiths, J. (ed.), *Certain Sermons or Homilies Appointed to be Read in Churches in the Time of Queen Elizabeth of Famous Memory*, London, 1864

Halliwell, J.O. (ed.), *Tarlton's Jests and News out of Purgatory*, Shakespeare Society, London, 1844

Hanham, A. (ed.), *The Cely Letters 1472–1488*, Early English Text Society, original series, 273, 1975

Harrod, H., *Report on the Deeds and Records of the Borough of King's Lynn*, King's Lynn and London, 1874

Harvey, J.H. (ed.), *William Worcestre: Itineraries*, Oxford, 1969

Henderson, W.G. (ed.), *Liber Pontificalis Chr. Bainbridge*, Surtees Society, 61, 1875

—— (ed.), *Processionale ad usum insignis ac praeclarae ecclesiae Sarum*, Leeds, 1882

Henry, A., *Biblia Pauperum. A Facsimile and Edition*, Aldershot, 1987

Hilton, W. – see under Clark, J.P.H. and Taylor, C.

Hogg, J. and Powell, L.F. (eds), *Nicholas Love, The Mirrour of the Blessed Lyf of Jesu Christi*, Analecta Cartusiana, 91 (1989)

Horstmann, C. (ed.), *Sammlung Altenglischer Legenden*, Heilbronn, 1878

Hudson, A. (ed.), *Selections from English Wycliffite Writings*, Cambridge, 1978

——, *Two Wycliffite Texts*, Early English Text Society, original series, 301, 1993

Jacobus de Voragine, *The Golden Legend. Readings of the Saints*, trans. W.G. Ryan, 2 vols, Princeton, 1993; see also under Ellis, F.S.

Kempe, M. – see under Meech, S.B. and Allen, E.A.

Koenig, V.F. (ed.), *Gautier de Coinci, Les Miracles de Nostre Dame*, 4 vols, Geneva, 1955–1970

Latimer, H. – see under Corrie, G.E.

Lehmann-Brockhaus, O., *Lateinische Schriftquellen zur Kunst in England, Wales und Schottland vom Jahre 901 bis zum Jahre 1307*, 5 vols, Munich, 1955–60

*Letters and Papers Foreign and Domestic of the Reign of Henry VIII*, 34 parts, London, 1862–1932

Lewis, C. (ed.), *The Commonplace Book of Robert Reynes of Acle. An Edition of Tanner MS 407*, New York and London, 1980

Littlehales, H. (ed.), *The Prymer or Lay Folks' Prayerbook*, Early English Text Society, original series, 105, 1895 (reprinted 1996)

Lloyd, C. (ed.), *Formularies of Faith Put Forth by Authority During the Reign of Henry VIII*, Oxford, 1825

Louth, A. (trans.), *St John of Damascus, Three Treatises On the Divine Images*, New York, 2003

Love, N. – see under Hogg, J. and Powell, L.F.

Lydgate, J. – see under MacCracken, H.N.

Lyndewood, W., – see under Manuscripts, Society of Antiquaries

MacCracken, H.N. (ed.), *The Minor Poems of John Lydgate Part I*, Early English Text Society, extra series, 107, 1911 (for 1910)

Meech, S.B. and Allen, E.H. (eds), *The Book of Margery Kempe*, Early English Text Society, original series, 212, 1940 (reprinted 1997)

Mirk/Myrc, J. – see under Erbe, T., Peacock, E.

Morgan, N.J., *The Lambeth Apocalypse. Manuscript 209 in Lambeth Palace Library: A Critical Study*, London, 1990

Nichols, J., *Illustrations of the Manners and Expenses of Antient Times in England*, London, 1797

Nicolas, N.H. (ed.), *Privy Purse Expenses of Elizabeth of York: Wardrobe Accounts of Edward the Fourth: with a memoir of Elizabeth of York*, London, 1830

——, *Testamenta Vetusta*, 2 vols, London, 1826

Oliver, G., *Monastican Dioecesis Exoniensis*, Exeter, 1846

Parsons, J. Carmi (ed.), *The Court and Household of Eleanor of Castile in 1290*, Toronto, 1977

Peacock, E. (ed.), *Myrc's Instructions for Parish Priests*, Early English Text Society, original series, 31, 1888

Pecock, R. – see under Babington, C.

Poussin, N., *Lettres et propos sur l'art*, ed. A. Blunt, Paris, 1964

Powicke, F. M. and Cheney, C.R. (eds), *Councils and Synods with other documents relating to the English Church. II. AD 1205–1313*, Oxford, 1964

Procter, F. and Wordsworth, C. (eds), *Breviarium ad Usum Insignis Ecclesiae Sarum*, 3 vols, Cambridge, 1879–1886

Raine, J. and Greenwell, W. (eds), *Wills and Inventories . . . of the Northern Counties of England . . . part 1*, Surtees Society, 2, 1835

Reynes, R. – see under Lewis, C.

Ross, W.O. (ed.), *Middle English Sermons*, Early English Text Society, original series, 209, 1940

Shoaf, R.A. (ed.), *Thomas Usk, The Testament of Love*, Kalamazoo, 1998

Simmons, T.F. (ed.), *The Lay Folks Mass Book or the Manner of Hearing Mass with Rubrics and Devotions for the People*, Early English Text Society, original series, 71, 1879

*The Statutes of the Realm, IV*, London, Record Commission, 1819, pt 1

Sousa, L., Poole, S., and Lockhart, J. (eds and trans), *The Story of Guadelupe: Luis Laso de la Vega's* Huei tlamahuiçoltica *of 1649*, UCLA Latin American Studies, 84 (Nahuati Studies Series no. 5), Los Angeles, 1998

Stratford, J., *The Bedford Inventories. The Worldly Goods of John, Duke of Bedford, Regent of France (1389–1435)*, Report of the Research Committee of the Society of Antiquaries of London no. 49, London, 1993

Swinburn, L.M. (ed.), *The Lanterne of Light*, Early English Text Society, original series, 151, 1917 (for 1915)

Usk. T. – see under Shoaf, R.A.

Whiteford, P. (ed.), *The Myracles of Oure Lady ed. from Wynkyn de Worde's edition*, Middle English Texts, 23, Heidelberg, 1990

Wilkins, D., *Concilia Magnae Britanniae et Hiberniae*, London, 1737

Worcestre, W. – see under Harvey, J.H.

Wordsworth, C. (ed.), *Horae Eboracenses*, Surtees Society, 132, 1920

—— (ed.), *Ceremonies and Processions of the Cathedral Church of Salisbury*, Cambridge, 1901


*Bedfordshire*

Note: BHRS: Bedfordshire Historical Record Society

Bell, P. (ed.), *Bedfordshire Wills 1480–1519*, BHRS, 45, 1966

—— (ed.), *Bedfordshire Wills 1484–1533*, BHRS, 76, 1997

—— (ed.), *Episcopal Visitations in Bedfordshire 1706–1720*, BHRS, 81, 2002

Cirket, A.F. (ed.), *English Wills, 1498–1526*, BHRS, 37, 1957

Jenkinson, H. and Fowler, G.H., 'Some Bedfordshire Wills at Lambeth and Lincoln', BHRS, 14, 1931, pp. 79–132

Lutt, N. (ed.), *Bedfordshire Muster Lists 1539–1831*, BHRS, 71, 1992

McGregor, M. (ed.), *Bedfordshire Wills Proved in the Prerogative Court of Canterbury 1383–1548*, BHRS, 58, 1979

Pickford, C. (ed.), *Bedfordshire Churches in the Nineteenth Century. Parts I–III*, BHRS, 73, 1994; 77, 1998; 79, 2000

Puttnam, F. (ed.), 'Declaration of Common Rights: Eaton Bray and Totternhoe: 1475', BHRS, 8, 1923, 165–8


*Berkshire*

Bond, M.F. (ed.), *The Inventories of St. George's Chapel Windsor Castle 1384–1667 (Historical Monographs Relating to St George's Chapel Windsor Castle)*, Windsor, 1947

See also under *Salisbury Diocese*


*Bristol* (see also under *Somerset*)

Burgess, C. (ed.), *The Pre-Reformation Records of All Saints' Bristol: Part 1*, Bristol Record Society Publications, 46, 1995

Masters, B.R. and Ralph, E., *The Church Book of St Ewen's Bristol 1454–1584*, Bristol & Gloucestershire Archaeological Society Records Society, 6, 1967


*Buckinghamshire*

Chibnall, A.C. and Vere Woodman, A. (eds), *Subsidy Roll for the County of Buckingham Anno 1524*, Buckinghamshire Record Society, 8, 1944

Elvey, E.M. (ed.), *The Courts of the Archdeaconry of Buckingham 1483–1523*, Buckinghamshire Record Society, 19, 1975

Vere Woodman, A., 'The Accounts of the Churchwardens of Wing', *Records of Buckinghamshire*, 16 (1953–60), 307–29


*Cambridgeshire*

Foster, J.E. (ed.), *Churchwardens' Accounts of St Mary the Great, Cambridge, from 1504 to 1635*, Cambridge Antiquarian Society, 35, 1905


*Devon and Cornwall*

Binney, J.E. (ed.), *The Accounts of the Wardens of the Parish of Morebath, Devon 1520–1573*, Devon Notes and Queries, 1903–4

Coulton, G.G., 'A Visitation of the Archdeaconry of Totnes in 1342', *English Historical Review*, 26 (1911), 108–24

Hanham, A. (ed.), *Churchwardens' Accounts of Ashburton 1479–1580*, Devon and Cornwall Record Society, new series, 15, 1969

Hingeston-Randolph, F.C. (ed.), *The Register of Walter de Stapledon, Bishop of Exeter (AD 1307–1326)*, London and Exeter, 1892

———, *The Register of Edmund Stafford (AD 1395–1419), Bishop of Exeter*, London, 1886

Orme, N., 'A Letter of Saint Roche', *Devon and Cornwall Notes and Queries*, 36 (1987–91), 153–9

———, *Nicholas Roscarrock's Lives of the Saints: Cornwall and Devon*, Devon and Cornwall Record Society, new series, 35, 1992

Michell Whitley, H., 'Visitations of Devonshire Churches', *Reports and Transactions of the Devonshire Association*, 42 (1910), 446–74

Roscarrock, N. – see under Orme, N.

Wilkinson, J.J. (ed.), 'Receipts and Expenses in the Building of Bodmin Church, 1469 to 1472', Camden Society, Camden Miscellany, 7, 1875


*County Durham*

Fowler, J.T. (ed.), *The Rites of Durham*, Surtees Society, 107, 1903


*Dorset*

See under *Salisbury Diocese*


*Hampshire*

Williams, J.F. (ed.), *The Early Churchwardens' Accounts of Hampshire*, Winchester and London, 1913

See also under *Salisbury Diocese*


*Hereford Diocese*

Bannister, A.T., 'Visitation Returns of the Diocese of Hereford in 1397', *English Historical Review*, 44 (1929), 279–89, 444–53; 45 (1930), 92–101, 444–63


*Hertfordshire*

Doree, S.S. (ed.), *Early Churchwardens' Accounts of Bishops Stortford 1431–1558*, Hertfordshire Record Publications, 10, 1994

Flood, S. (ed.), *St Albans Wills 1471–1500*, Hertfordshire Record Publications, 9, 1993

Lloyd, R., *An Account of the Altars, Monuments, and Tombs, existing A.D. 1428 in Saint Alban's Abbey*, St Albans, 1873

Luard, H.R. (ed.), *Gesta Abbatum Monasterii Sancti Albani*, Rolls Series, 1, London, 1870

Munby, L.M. (intro), *All My Worldly Goods*, Bricket Wood Society, 1991

Riley, H.T. (ed.), *Gesta abbatum monasterii Sancti Albani a Thoma Walsingham. The Chronicles and Memorials of Great Britain and Ireland during the Middle Ages, vol. I: 793–1290, vol. 2: 1290–1349, vol. 3: 1349–1411*, Rolls Series, 28, London, 1867–9


*Kent*

Cotton, C., 'Churchwardens' Accounts of the Parish of St Andrew, Canterbury from AD 1485 to AD 1625', *Archaeologia Cantiana*, 32 (1917), 181–246

Cowper, J.M., 'Accounts of the Churchwardens of St Dunstan's, Canterbury AD 1484–1580', *Archaeologia Cantiana*, 16 (1886), 289–321

Duncan, L.L., 'The parish churches of West Kent, their dedications, altars, images, and lights', *Transactions of the St Paul's Ecclesiological Society*, 3 (1895), 241–98

———, 'Ecclesiological Notes respecting the Deanery of Shoreham, Kent', *Archaeologia Cantiana*, 23 (1898), 134–49

——— and Hussey, A. (eds), *Testamenta Cantiana: A Series of Extracts from Fifteenth and Sixteenth Century Wills*, Kent Archaeological Society (Kent Records), Extra Volume (1907)

Eveleigh Woodruff, C., 'The Sacrist's Rolls of Christ Church, Canterbury', *Archaeologia Cantiana*, 48 (1936), 38–80

———, 'Some Early Kentish Wills', *Archaeologia Cantiana*, 46 (1934), 28–35

Haslewood, F., 'Notes from the Records of Smarden Church', *Archaeologia Cantiana*, 9 (1874), 224–35

Hussey, A., 'Milton Wills (next Sittingbourne)', *Archaeologia Cantiana*, 44 (1932), 79–102; 45 (1933), 13–30; 46 (1934), 36–51

———, 'Sittingbourne Wills', *Archaeologia Cantiana*, 43 (1931), 49–71

———, 'Hythe Wills', *Archaeologia Cantiana*, 49 (1938), 127–56; 50 (1938), 87–121; 51 (1939), 27–65

Lightfoot, W.J., 'Notes from the Records of Hawkhurst Church 1. Extracts from the Churchwardens' Account-Book 1515 to 1714', *Archaeologia Cantiana*, 5 (1862–3), 55–86

Mercer, F.R. (trans.), *Churchwardens' Accounts at Betrysden 1515–1573*, Kent Archaeological Society Records Branch, 5, 1928

Plomer, H.R. (trans.), *The Churchwardens' Accounts of St Nicholas, Strood*, Kent Archaeological Society Records Branch, 5, 1927

Sharp, W. and Whatmore, L.E. (trans.), *Archdeacon Harpsfield's Visitation, 1557*, Catholic Record Society, 45, 1950

Tanner, N. (ed.), *Kent Heresy Proceedings 1511–1512*, Kent Archaeological Society, Kent Records, 26, 1997

Whatmore, L.E. (trans.), *Archdeacon Harpsfield's Visitation, 1557, together with Visitations of 1556 and 1558*, Catholic Record Society, 46, 1951

Wood-Legh, K.L. (ed.), *Kentish Visitations of Archbishop Warham and his Deputies, 1511–1512*, Kent Archaeological Society, Kent Records, 24, 1984


*Lincoln Diocese*

Clark, A. (ed.), *Lincoln Diocese Documents 1450–1544*, Early English Text Society, original series, 149, 1914

Hamilton Thompson, A. (ed.), *Visitations in the Diocese of Lincoln 1517–1531*, Lincoln Record Society, vol. 1, 30, 1940; vol. 2, 35, 1944

Hill, R.M.T. (ed.), *The Rolls and Register of Bishop Oliver Sutton 1280–1299*, vols V and VI, Lincoln Record Society, 60, 1965; 64, 1969

McHardy, A.K. (ed.), *Clerical Poll-Taxes of the Diocese of Lincoln 1377–1381*, Lincoln Record Society, 81, 1992


*Lincolnshire*

Foster, C.W. (ed.), *Early Lincoln Wills, vol. 1 AD 1271 to 1526*, Lincoln Record Society, 5, 1914; *vol. 2 AD 1505 to May 1530*, Lincoln Record Society, 10, 1918; *vol. 3 AD 1530 to 1532*, Lincoln Record Society, 24, 1930

Peacock, E., 'Churchwardens' Accounts of Saint Mary's, Sutterton', *Archaeological Journal*, 39 (1882), 53–63

See also under *Lincoln Diocese*


*London*

Littlehales, H. (trans. and ed.), *The Medieval Records of a London City Church (St Mary at Hill) AD 1420–1559*, Early English Text Society, original series, 125 and 128, 1904–5

Overall, W.H. (ed.), *The Accounts of the Churchwardens of the Parish of St Michael, Cornhill, in the City of London, from 1456 to 1608*, privately printed, 1871

Sparrow Simpson, W., 'Inventory of the Vestments, Plate and Books Belonging to the church of St Peter, West Cheap, in the City of London, in the year 1431', *Journal of the British Archaeological Association*, 24 (1868), 150–60

——, 'Visitation of Certain Churches belonging to the Dean and Chapter of St Paul's Cathedral in the years 1249–1252', *Camden Society Miscellany*, vol. 9, Camden Society, new series, 53 (1895), pp. 1–38

——, *Visitations of Churches Belonging to St Paul's Cathedral in 1297 and in 1458*, Camden Society Miscellany, new series, Camden Society, 55 (1895), pp. 1–105

Walters, H.B., *London Churches at the Reformation: with an Account of their Contents*, London, 1939

Welch, C. (ed.), *The Churchwardens' Accounts of the Parish of Allhallows, London Wall*, London, 1912

See also Freshfield, E. and Milbourn, T. under SECONDARY WORKS


*Norfolk*

Grace, M. (ed.), *Records of the Gild of St George in Norwich, 1389–1547*, Norfolk Record Society, 9, 1937

Morant, A.W., 'Notices of the Church of St Nicholas, Great Yarmouth', *Norfolk Archaeology*, 7 (1872), 215–48

Owen, D.M. (ed.), *The Making of King's Lynn. A Documentary Survey*, Records of Social and Economic History, new series, 9, London, 1984

Tanner, N.P. (ed.), *Heresy Trials in the Diocese of Norwich, 1428–31*, Camden Society, Fourth Series, 20, 1977

Watkin, Dom Aelred (trans.), *Inventory of Church Goods, temp. Edward III (1368)*, Norfolk Record Society, 19, pt I, 1947; pt II, 1948


*Nottinghamshire*

Hodgkinson, R.F.B. (trans.), *The Account Books of the Gilds of St George and of St Mary in the Church of St Peter, Nottingham*, Thoroton Society Record Series, 7, 1939


*Oxfordshire*

Anon., 'Churchwardens' Presentments, 1520', *Reports of the Oxfordshire Archaeological Society*, 70 (1925), 75–117

Brinkworth, E.R.C. (ed.), *South Newington Churchwardens' Accounts 1553–1684*, Banbury History Society, 6 (1964)


*Salisbury Diocese*

Timmins, T.C.B. (ed.), *The Register of John Chandler, Dean of Salisbury 1404–17*, Wiltshire Record Society, 39, 1984

——, *The Register of John Waltham Bishop of Salisbury 1388–1395*, The Canterbury and York Society, 80, 1994

*Somerset*

Dilks, T.B. (ed.), *Bridgwater Borough Archives*, Somerset Record Society, 48, 1933

Hobhouse, Bishop (ed.), *Churchwardens' Accounts*, Somerset Record Society, 4, 1890

Weaver, F.W. (ed.), *Somerset Medieval Wills, vols 1–3*, Somerset Record Society, 16, 19, 21, 1901–5


*Suffolk*

Northeast, P. (ed.), *Boxford Churchwardens' Accounts 1530–1561*, Suffolk Records Society, 23, 1982

——, *Wills of the Archdeaconry of Sudbury 1439–1474. Wills from the Register 'Baldewyne'. Pt I: 1439–1461*, Suffolk Records Society, 44, 2001

Tymms, S. (ed.), *Wills and Inventories from the Registers of the Commissary of Bury St Edmunds and the Archdeacon of Sudbury*, Camden Society, 49, 1850


*Surrey*

Drew, C. (ed.), *Lambeth Churchwardens' Account, 1504–1645 and Vestry Book 1610*, Surrey Record Society, 40, 1940

Peatling, A.V. and Kingsford, C.L. (eds), *Surrey Wills (Archdeaconry court, Spage Register)*, Surrey Record Society, 5, 1921


*Sussex*

Godfrey, W.H. (ed.), *Sussex Wills. Vols 1–4*, Sussex Record Society, 41, 1935; 42, 1937; 43, 1938; 45, 1940–1


*Wiltshire*

Chew, H.M. (ed.), *Hemingby's Register*, Wiltshire Archaeological & Natural History Society, Records Branch, 18, 1962

See also under *Salisbury Diocese*


*Yorkshire*

Bond, E.A. (ed.), *Chronica Monasterii de Melsa*, Rolls Series 43, 3 vols, London, 1866–81

Clay, J.W. (ed.), *Testamenta Eboracensia. A Selection of Wills from the Registry at York, vol. VI*, Surtees Society, 106, 1902. See also Raine, J.

Collins, F. (ed.), *Register of the Freemen of the City of York: from the City Records, vol. 1 1272–1558*, Surtees Society, 96, 1896; *vol. 2 1559–1579*, Surtees Society, 1889, 102.

——, *Wills and Administrations from the Knaresborough Court Rolls, vol. 1*, Surtees Society, 104, 1900

Fowler, J.T., *Memorials of the Church of SS Peter and Wilfrid, Ripon, vol. IV*, Surtees Society, 115, 1908

Greatrex, J., 'The Dispute Between the Carmelite Friars and the Rector of St Crux, York, 1350', in D.M. Smith (ed.), *The Church in Medieval York: Records edited in honour of Professor Barrie Dobson*, Borthwick Texts and Calendars, 24 (1999), 69–73

Raine, J. (ed.), *Testamenta Eboracensia. A Selection of Wills from the Registry at York*, 5 vols, Surtees Society, 4, 1836; 30, 1855; 45, 1864; 53, 1868; 79, 1884. See also Clay, J.W.

——, *Wills and Inventories from the Registry of the Archdeaconry of Richmond, Extending over the Counties of York, Westmorland, Cumberland and Lancaster*, Surtees Society, 26, 1853

Sellers, M. (ed.), *York Memorandum Book Part II (1388–1493)*, Surtees Society, 125, 1915

Webb, C.C. (ed.), *The Churchwardens' Accounts of St Michael, Spurriergate, York, 1518–1548*, Borthwick Texts and Calendars, 20 (1997)

# UNPUBLISHED DISSERTATIONS

Ford, J., 'A Study of Wills and Will-making in the Period 1500–1533 with Special Reference to the Copy Wills in the Probate Registers of the Archdeacon of Bedford, 1489–1533', Open University, Faculty of Arts (History) PhD thesis, 1992

Gill, M., 'Late Medieval Wall-Painting in England: Content and Context (*c.* 1330–*c.* 1530)', University of London (Courtauld Institute of Art) PhD thesis, 2001

Maniura, R.J., 'Image and Pilgrimage. The Cult of the Virgin of Częstochowa in the Late Middle Ages', University of London (Courtauld Institute of Art) PhD thesis, 1998

Peters, C., 'Women and the Reformation: Social Relations and Attitudes in Rural England *c.* 1470–1570', Oxford University DPhil thesis, 1992

Power, M.J., 'The *Pietà* in Medieval England', University of York MA thesis, 1980/1

Saxon, E.A., 'Aspects of the Eucharist: Theology and Iconography in French Romanesque Sculpture 1070–1150', University College London PhD thesis, 2001

Williamson, B., 'The Virgin *Lactans* and the Madonna of Humility: Image and Devotion in Italy, Metz and Avignon in the Thirteenth and Fourteenth Centuries', University of London (Courtauld Institute of Art) PhD thesis, 1996

Wilson, T.H., 'Saint George in Tudor and Stuart England', University of London (Warburg Institute) unpublished MPhil. dissertation, 1976

# SECONDARY WORKS

Adrian, H. and Grinder-Hansen, P., *Den Romanske Kirke – billede og betydning*, Copenhagen, Nationalmuseet, 1995

Alexander, J.J.G., 'Katherine Bray's Flemish Book of Hours', *The Ricardian*, 8, no. 107 (December 1989), 308–17

Alexander, J. and Binski, P. (eds.), *Age of Chivalry. Art in Plantagenet England 1200–1400* (London, Royal Academy of Arts exhibition catalogue, 1987)

Allison, K.J., *The Victoria History of the County of York, East Riding*, II, Oxford, 1974

Andersson, A., *English Influence in Norwegian and Swedish Figuresculpture in Wood 1220–1270*, Stockholm, 1949

—— and Rydbeck, M., *Medieval Wooden Sculpture in Sweden, vol. IV: The Museum Collection Catalogue*, Stockholm, 1975

Arnold-Forster, F., *Studies in Church Dedications: or England's Patron Saints*, 3 vols, London, 1899

Ashley, K. and Sheingorn, P. (eds), *Interpreting Cultural Symbols. Saint Anne in Late Medieval Society*, Athens (Georgia) and London, 1990

Aston, M., *England's Iconoclasts, vol. I. Laws Against Images*, Oxford, 1988

——, 'Gold and Images', in W.J. Sheils and D. Wood (eds), *The Church and Wealth*, Studies in Church History, 24 (1987), pp. 189–209

——, 'Iconoclasm at Rickmansworth, 1522: Troubles of Churchwardens', *Journal of Ecclesiastical History*, 40 (1989), 524–52

——, *Lollards and Reformers: Images and Literacy in Late Medieval Religion*, London, 1984

Avril, F. and Stirnemann, P.D., *Manuscrits Enluminés d'origine insulaire VIIe–XXe Siècle*, Bibliothèque Nationale Département des Manuscrits, Centre de Recherche sur les Manuscrits Enluminés, Paris, 1987

Badham, S., 'Status and Salvation: The Design of Medieval English Brasses and Incised Slabs', *Monumental Brass Society Transactions*, 15, pt 5 (1997), 413–65

Baggs, A.P., 'Sixteenth-Century Terra-Cotta Tombs in East Anglia', *Archaeological Journal*, 125 (1968), 296–301

Baker, C., review of H. Van Os, *The Art of Devotion*, in *Art History*, 18 no. 4 (December 1995), 599–602

Baker, E., 'The Adoration of the Magi at Shelfanger Church, Norfolk', *Norfolk Archaeology*, 34 (1966–9), 90–1

Baker, M., 'De l'église au musée: les monuments du XVIIIe siècle (fonctions, significations, et histoire)', in *Sculptures hors contexte, actes du colloque international organisé au musée du Louvre par le service culturel le 29 Avril 1994*, Paris Documentation Française, Louvre conférences et colloques, Paris, c. 1996, pp. 73–92

Barnet, P. (ed.), *Images in Ivory. Precious Objects of the Gothic Age* (Detroit Institute of Arts exhibition catalogue, 1997)

Baron, F., *Département des Sculptures du Moyen Age, de la Renaissance et des Temps Modernes. Sculpture Français 1 – Moyen Age*, Paris, 1996

Barthes, R., 'Le *Guide bleu*', in idem, *Mythologies (Oeuvres complètes, I, 1942–1965)* , ed. E. Marty, Paris, 1993, pp. 637–9

Baxandall, M., *The Limewood Sculptors of Renaissance Germany*, London and New Haven, 1980

——, *Painting and Experience in Fifteenth-Century Italy*, Oxford, 2nd edn, 1988

——, *South German Sculpture 1480–1530*, Victoria & Albert Museum, London, 1974

Bayliss, J., 'Richard Parker "The Alabasterman"', *Church Monuments*, 5 (1990), 39–56

——, 'Richard and Gabriel Royley of Burton-upon-Trent, Tombmakers', *Church Monuments*, 6 (1991), 21–41

Beevers, D., Marks, R. and Roles, J., *Sussex Churches and Chapels*, Brighton, 1989

Bell, C., *Ritual Theory, Ritual Practice*, Oxford, 1992

Beloe, E.M., *The Red Mount, King's Lynn with the Chapels thereon*, King's Lynn, 1925

Belting, H., *The Image and Its Public in the Middle Ages. Form and Function of Early Paintings of the Passion* (trans. M. Bartusis and R. Meyer), New York, 1990

——, *Likeness and Presence. A History of the Image before the Era of Art* (trans. E. Jephcott), Chicago and London, 1994

Bengston, J., 'Saint George and the Formation of English Nationalism', *Journal of Medieval and Early Modern Studies*, 27 (1997), 317–40

Bergmann, U. (ed.), *Verschwundenes Inventarium der Skulpturenfund im Kölner Domchor* (Cologne, Schnütgen Museum exhibition catalogue, 1984)

—— (ed.), *Schnütgen-Museum. Die Holzskulpturen des Mittelalters (1000–1400)*, Cologne, 1989

Bettey, C.J., 'Late Medieval Bristol: from town to city', *Local Historian*, 28, no. 1 (February 1998), 3–13

Biller, P., 'The Common Woman in the Western Church in the Thirteenth and Early Fourteenth Centuries', in W.J. Sheils and D. Wood, *Women in the Church*, Studies in Church History, 27, 1990, pp. 127–57

Binns, A., *Dedications of Monastic Houses in England and Wales, 1066–1216*, Woodbridge, 1989

Binski, P., *Medieval Craftsmen. Painters*, London, 1991

——, *Medieval Death. Ritual and Representation*, London, 1996

——, 'The Murals in the Nave of St Albans Abbey', in D. Abulafia, M. Franklin and M. Rubin (eds), *Church and City 1000–1500: Essays in Honour of Christopher Brooke*, Cambridge, 1992, pp. 249–78

——, 'The 13th-century English altarpiece', in *Norwegian Medieval Altar Frontals and Related Material: Papers from the Conference in Oslo, 16th to 19th December 1989*, Acta ad Archaeologiam et Artivm Historiam Pertinentia, 11 (1995), Rome, pp. 47–57

——, 'The Angel Choir at Lincoln and the Poetics of the Gothic Smile', *Art History*, 20, no. 3 (1997), 350–74

Birch, W. de G., *Catalogue of Seals in the Department of Manuscripts in the British Museum*, 6 vols, London, 1887–1900

Blair, J. (ed.), *Minsters and Parish Churches. The Local Church in Transition 950–1200* (Oxford University Committee for Archaeology Monograph no. 17), Oxford, 1988

—— and Ramsay, N. (eds), *English Medieval Industries: Craftsmen, Techniques, Products*, London, 1991

Blanc, M., *La collection du Musée des Arts Décoratifs. Retables*, Paris, 1998

Blindheim, M., 'The Cult of Medieval Wooden Sculptures in Post-Reformation Norway', *Universitetes Oldsaksamling Årbok* (1995/1996), 139–51

——, *Painted Wooden Sculpture in Norway c. 1100–1250*, Oslo, Stockholm, Oxford and Boston, 1998

Boldrick, S., Park, D. and Williamson, P., *Wonder. Painted Sculpture from Medieval England* (Leeds, Henry Moore Institute exhibition catalogue, 2002)

Bond, F., *Dedications & Patron Saints of English Churches. Ecclesiastical Symbolism. Saints and their Emblems*, Oxford, 1914

Borenius, T., 'The cycle of images in the palaces and castles of Henry III', *Journal of the Warburg and Courtauld Institutes*, 6 (1943), 40–50

Bossy, J., 'Blood and Baptism: Kinship, Community and Christianity in Western Europe from the Fourteenth Century–Seventeenth Century', in D. Baker (ed.), *Sanctity and Secularity. The Church and the World*, Studies in Church History, 10, 1973, pp. 129–43

——, 'The Mass as a Social Institution 1200–1700', *Past and Present*, 100 (1983), 29–61

——, 'Christian Life in the Later Middle Ages: Prayers', *Transactions of the Royal Historical Society*, 6th series, I (1991), 137–48

Boyle, L.E., 'Popular Piety in the Middle Ages: What is Popular?', *Florilegium*, 4 (1982), 184–93

Braun, J., *Der Christliche Altar in seiner geschichtlichen Entwicklung*, 2 vols, Munich, 1924

Brese, G. and H., 'Les saints protecteurs des bateaux 1200–1460', *Ethnologie française*, 9 (1979), 161–78

Brigden, S., *London and the Reformation*, Oxford, 1989

Brisbois, E., *Pardons et pèlerinages en Bretagne et Normandie*, Paris, 1994

Brown, A.D., *Popular Piety in Late Medieval England. The Diocese of Salisbury 1250–1550*, Oxford, 1995

Brown, P., *The Cult of the Saints. Its Rise and Function in Latin Christianity*, Chicago, 1982

——, *Society and the Holy in Late Antiquity*, London, 1982

Brown, R.A., Colvin, H.M. and Taylor, A.J. (eds), *The History of the King's Works, 2: The Middle Ages*, London, 1963

Browne, J., *The History of the Metropolitan Church of St Peter, York*, London, 1847

Bruna, D., *Musée National du Moyen Age – Thermes de Cluny. Enseignes de Pèlerinage et Enseignes Profanes*, Paris, 1996

Bruton, E.G., 'The Recent Discovery of Wall-paintings on the Apse of Checkendon Church', *Oxfordshire Architectural and History Society Proceedings*, new series 2 (1864–71), 75–8

Burgess, C.R., '"By Quick and by Dead": wills and pious provision in late medieval Bristol', *English Historical Review*, 305 (1987), 837–58

——, 'Late Medieval Wills and Pious Convention: Testamentary Evidence Reconsidered', in M. Hicks (ed.), *Profit, Piety and the Professions in Later Medieval England*, Stroud, 1990, pp. 14–33

Butler, L., 'Church dedications and the cults of Anglo-Saxon saints in England', in L.A.S. Butler and R.K. Morris (eds), *The Anglo-Saxon church. Papers on history, architecture, and archaeology in honour of Dr H.M. Taylor*, Council for British Archaeology Research Report 60, 1986, pp. 44–50.

Bynum, C.W., *Holy Feast and Holy Fast. The Religious Significance of Food to Medieval Women*, Berkeley and London, 1987

Camille, M., *Gothic Art. Vision and Revelations of the Medieval World*, London, 1996

——, *The Gothic Idol. Ideology and Image-making in Medieval Art*, Cambridge, 1989

——, 'Seeing and reading: some visual implications of medieval literacy and illiteracy', *Art History*, 8, no. 1 (1985), 26–49

Campbell, M., 'Medieval Metalworking and Bury St Edmunds', in A. Gransden (ed.), *Bury St Edmunds Medieval Art, Architecture, Archaeology and Economy*, British Archaeological Association Conference Transactions, 20, 1998, pp. 69–80

Carnwath, J., 'The Churchwardens' Accounts of Thame, Oxfordshire, c. 1443–1524', in D.J. Clayton, R.G. Davies and P. McNiven (eds), *Trade, Devotion and Governance. Papers in Later Medieval History*, Stroud, 1994, pp. 177–97

Carpenter, C., 'The Religion of the Gentry of Fifteenth-Century England', in D. Williams (ed.), *England in the Fifteenth Century*, Proceedings of the 1986 Harlaxton Symposium, Woodbridge, 1987, pp. 53–74

Carroll, M.D., 'Peasant Festivity and Political Identity in the Sixteenth Century', *Art History*, 10 (1987), 289–314

Carroll, M.P., *The Cult of the Virgin Mary. Psychological Origins*, Princeton, 1986

Carruthers, M.J., *The Book of Memory. A Study of Memory in Medieval Culture*, Cambridge, 1990

Cather, S., Park, D. and Pender, R., 'Henry III's Wall Paintings at Chester Castle', in A. Thacker (ed.), *Medieval Archaeology, Art and Architecture at Chester*, British Archaeological Association Conference Transactions, 22, 2000, pp. 170–89

Catto, J., 'Religious Change under Henry V', in G.L. Harriss (ed.), *Henry V. The Practice of Kingship*, Oxford, 1985, pp. 97–115

Caviness, M.H., '*De convenientia et cohaerentia antiqui et novi operis*: Medieval conservation, restoration, pastiche and forgery', *Intuition und Kunstwissenschaft. Festschrift für Hanns Swarzenski zum 70. Geburtstag*, Berlin, 1973, pp. 205–21

——, 'Biblical stories in windows: were they Bibles for the poor?', in B.S. Levy (ed.), *The Bible in the Middle Ages. Its Influence on Literature and Art*, Medieval and Renaissance Texts and Studies, 89, Binghamton (New York), 1992, pp. 103–47

Cazelles, B., *Le Corps de Sainteté*, Geneva, 1982

Charles-Edwards, T., *Saint Winefride and her Well. The Historical Background*, Holywell, n.d.

Chartier, R., *Cultural History. Between Practices and Representations* (trans. L.G. Cochrane), Cambridge, 1988

Chazelle, C., 'Pictures, books and the illiterate, Pope Gregory I's letters to Serenius of Marseilles', *Word and Image*, 6 (1990), 138–53

Cheetham, F., *English Medieval Alabasters*, Oxford, 1984

——, 'A Medieval English Alabaster Figure of St Paul', *Norfolk Archaeology*, 35 (1970), 143–4

——, *Medieval English Alabaster Carvings in the Castle Museum Nottingham*, Nottingham, rev. edn, 1973

Christ, W. and Minkenberg, G., *Gemälde und Skulpturen des Aachener Domes im Blickfeld von Konservierung und Restaurierung. 30 Jahre Restaurierungswerkstatt für Gemälde und Skulpturen am Dom zu Aachen*, Karlsverein Schriftenreihe, 1, 1995

Christian Jr., W.A., *Local Religion in Sixteenth-Century Spain*, Princeton, 1981

——, *Person and God in a Spanish Valley*, Princeton, rev. edn, 1989

*The Church of St Mary and St Michael, Stoke Charity*, church guide, 1998

Clapham, A.W., 'The York Virgin and its Date', *Archaeological Journal*, 105 (1948), 6–13

Clark, J.P.H., 'Walter Hilton in Defence of the Religious Life and of the Veneration of Images', *Downside Review*, 103 (1985), 1–25

Clark, P., *English Provincial Society from the Reformation to the Revolution: Religion, Politics and Society in Kent 1500–1640*, Hassocks, Sussex, 1977

Clay, R., 'Saint-Sulpice de Paris: Art, Politics and Sacred Space in Revolutionary Paris 1789–1795', *Object*, 1 (October 1998), 5–22

Clayton, M., *The Cult of the Virgin Mary in Anglo-Saxon England*, Cambridge, 1990

Cobbe, H., *Luton Church. Historical and Descriptive*, London and Bedford, 1899

Cokayne, G.E., *The Complete Peerage*, 14 vols, London, 1910–98

Coleman, S. and Elsner, J., 'Contesting Pilgrimage: Current Views and Future Directions', *Cambridge Anthropology*, 15 pt 3 (1991), 63–73

——, *Pilgrimage Past and Present*, London, 1995

——, 'Pilgrimage to Walsingham and the Re-Invention of the Middle Ages', in J. Stopford (ed.), *Pilgrimage Explored*, York, 1999, pp. 189–214

Condon, M., 'From Caitiff and Villain to Pater Patriae: Reynold Bray and the Profits of Office', in M. Hicks (ed.), *Profit, Piety and the Professions in Later Medieval England*, Stroud, 1990, pp. 137–68

Cormack, R., *Painting the Soul: Icons, Death Masks and Shrouds*, London, 1997

——, *Byzantine Art*, Oxford, 2000

Coss, P., *The Knight in Medieval England 1000–1400*, Stroud, 1993

Coster, W., 'Purity, Profanity and Puritanism: the Churching of Women, 1500–1700', in W.J. Sheils and D. Wood (eds), *Women in the Church*, Studies in Church History, 27, 1990, pp. 377–87

Cox, J.C., *Churchwardens' Accounts*, London, 1913

Cullum, P. and Goldberg, J., 'How Margaret Blackburn taught her Daughters; Reading Devotional Instruction in a Book of Hours', in J. Wogan-Browne *et al.* (eds), *Medieval Women: Texts and Contexts in Late Medieval Britain. Essays for Felicity Riddy*, Turnhout, 2000, pp. 217–36

Daniell, C., *Death and Burial in Medieval England 1066–1550*, London and New York, 1997

David, C., *St Winefride's Well. A History and Guide*, Llandysul, new edn, 2002

Davies, M. (ed.), *National Gallery Catalogues: The Early Italian Schools before 1400*, rev. by D. Gordon, London, 1988

Davis, J.F., *Heresy and Reformation in the South-East of England 1520–1559*, Royal Historical Society Studies in History, 34, London, 1983

Davis, N.Z., 'Some Tasks and Themes in the Study of Popular Religion', in C. Trinkhaus and H.A. Oberman (eds), *The Pursuit of Holiness in Late Medieval and Renaissance Religion*, Leiden, 1974, pp. 307–36

——, *Society and Culture in Early Modern France*, London, 1975

——, 'From "Popular Religion" to "Religious Cultures"', in S. Ozment (ed.), *Reformation Europe: A Guide to Research*, St Louis, USA, 1982, pp. 321–41

Deacon, R. and Lindley, P., *Image and Idol: Medieval Sculpture* (London, Tate Gallery exhibition catalogue, 2001)

Dendy, D.R., *The Use of Lights in Christian Worship*, Alcuin Club Collections, 41, 1959

Derrida, J., *The Truth in Painting* (trans. G. Bennington and I. McLeod), Chicago, 1987

Dickens, A.G., 'The First Stages of Romanist Recusancy in Yorkshire, 1560–1590', in idem (ed.), *Reformation Studies*, London, 1982, pp. 159–84

——, 'Robert Parkyn's Narrative of the Reformation', in idem (ed.), *Reformation Studies*, London, 1982, pp. 287–312

Dickinson, J.C., *The Shrine of Our Lady of Walsingham*, Cambridge, 1956

Dimmick, J., Simpson, J. and Zeeman, N. (eds), *Images, Idolatry and Iconoclasm in Late Medieval England: Textuality and the Visual Image*, Oxford, 2002

Dodwell, B., 'William Bauchun and his Connection with the Cathedral Priory at Norwich', *Norfolk Archaeology*, 36 (1974–7), 111–18

Dodwell, C.R., *Anglo-Saxon Art: A New Perspective*, Manchester, 1982

Donovan, C., *The de Brailes Hours. Shaping the Book of Hours in Thirteenth-Century Oxford*, London, 1991

Douglas, N., *Old Calabria*, London, 1983

Dow, H.J., *The Sculptural Decoration of the Henry VII Chapel*, Edinburgh, 1992

Draper, P., 'Architecture and Liturgy', in J. Alexander and P. Binski (eds), *Age of Chivalry. Art in Plantagenet England 1200–1400* (London, Royal Academy exhibition catalogue, 1987), pp. 83–91

Duffy, E., *The Stripping of the Altars. Traditional Religion in England c. 1400–c. 1580*, New Haven and London, 1992

——, 'Morebath 1520–1570: A Rural Parish in the Reformation', in J. Devlin and R. Fanning (eds), *Religion and Rebellion*. Historical Studies, 20, Papers read before the 22nd Irish Conference of Historians, Dublin, 1997, pp. 17–39

——, 'The Parish, Piety, and Patronage in Late Medieval East Anglia: The Evidence of Rood Screens', in K.L. French, G.A. Gibbs and B.A. Kumin (eds), *The Parish in English Life 1400–1600*, Manchester and New York, 1997, pp. 133–62

——, *The Voices of Morebath. Reformation and Rebellion in an English Village*, New Haven and London, 2001

Dugdale, W., *The History of St Paul's Cathedral in London, from its Foundation . . . to the year 1658* (with continuations and additions by H. Ellis), London, 1818

Duggan, L.G., 'Was Art really the book of the illiterate?', *Word and Image*, 5 (1989), 227–51

Dunand, F., Speiser, J.-M. and Wirth, J. (eds), *L'Image et la Production du Sacré*, Actes du colloque de Strasbourg (20–21 January, 1988) organisé par le Centre d'Histoire de Religion de l'Université de Strasbourg, II, Paris, 1991

Duncan, L.L., 'Notes on the Topography of Cranbrook Church', *Archaeologia Cantiana*, 37 (1925), 21–31

Dupront, A., 'Pèlerinage et lieux sacrés', in *Mélanges en l'honneur de Fernand Braudel: Méthodologie de l'Histoire et des sciences humaines*, 2, Paris, 1972–3, pp. 189–206

Duro, P. (ed.), *The Rhetoric of the Frame. Essays on the Boundaries of the Artwork*, Cambridge, 1996

Dyer, C., *Standards of Living in the Later Middle Ages. Social Change in England c. 1200–1520*, Cambridge, 1993

Dymond, D. and Paine, C., *The Spoil of Melford Church. The Reformation in a Suffolk Parish*, Ipswich, 1992

Edwards, J., 'Some Murals in North-East Oxfordshire', *Oxoniensia*, 58 (1993), 240–51

Elliston Erwood, F.C., 'Notes on the Architecture of Aldington Church, Kent and the Chapel at Court-at-Street, called "Bellirica"', *Archaeologia Cantiana*, 41 (1928), 143–51

Emden, A.B., *A Biographical Register of the University of Cambridge to 1500*, Cambridge, 1963

——, *A Biographical Register of the University of Oxford to AD 1500*, Oxford, 3 vols, 1957–9

*English Romanesque Art 1066–1200* (London, Arts Council exhibition catalogue, 1984)

Evans, J., *English Art, 1307–1461*, Oxford History of English Art, V, Oxford, 1949

——, 'An English Alabaster at Montpezat', *Antiquaries Journal*, 37 (1957), 73

—— and Cook, N., 'A Statue of Christ from the Ruins of Mercers' Hall', *Archaeological Journal*, 111 (1954), 168–80

Everitt, A., *Continuity and Colonization. The Evolution of Kentish Settlement*, Leicester, 1986

Farmer, H., 'The Vision of Orme', *Analecta Bollandia*, 75 (1957), 72–82

Fassler, M., 'Mary's Nativity, Fulbert of Chartres, and the *Stirps Jesse*: Liturgical Innovation circa 1000 and its Afterlife', *Speculum*, 75 (2000), 389–434

*Les Fastes du Gothique. Le siècle de Charles V* (Paris, exhibition catalogue, 1981)

Finucane, R.C., *Miracles and Pilgrims. Popular Beliefs in Medieval England*, London, 1995

Firman, R.J., 'A geological approach to the history of English alabaster', *The Mercian Geologist*, 9, no. 3 (March 1984), 161–78

Fish, S., *Is There a Text in this Class? The Authority of Interpretive Communities*, Cambridge (Mass.) and London, 1980

Fisher, T., *Monumental Remains and Antiquities in Bedfordshire*, London, 1828

Flavigny, L. and Jablonski-Chauveau, C., *D'Angleterre en Normandie. Sculptures d'albâtre du Moyen Age* (Rouen and Evreux exhibition catalogue, 1998)

Fleming, F., 'Charity, Faith, and the Gentry of Kent 1422–1529', in T. Pollard (ed.), *Property and Politics: Essays in Later Medieval English History*, Gloucester, 1984, pp. 36–58

Fleming, P., *Family and Household in Medieval England*, Basingstoke and New York, 2001

Foister, S., 'Paintings and other works of art in sixteenth-century English inventories', *Burlington Magazine*, 123, no. 938 (May 1981), 273–82

——, 'The Production and Reproduction of Holbein's Portraits', in K. Hearn (ed.), *Dynasties. Painting in Tudor and Jacobean England 1530–1630* (London, Tate Gallery exhibition catalogue, 1995), pp. 21–6

Forgeard, L., *L'Age d'Or de la Vièrge et L'Enfant. Le XIVe siècle en Seine-et-Marne*, Paris, 1995

Forsyth, I.H., *The Throne of Wisdom. Wood Sculptures of the Madonna in Romanesque France*, Princeton, 1972

Forsyth, W.H., *The Pietà in French Late Gothic Sculpture. Regional Variations*, New York, 1995

Forville, R., 'Manifestations de Lollardisme à Exeter en 1421', *Le Moyen Age*, 69, Series 4, no. 18 (1963), 691–706

Fowler, J.T., 'On a Window representing the Life and Miracles of S. William of York', *Yorkshire Archaeological Journal*, 3 (1875), 198–348

Franks, J., 'St Zita, St Sythe and St Osyth', *Nottingham Medieval Studies*, 36 (1992), 148–50

Freedberg, D., 'The Structure of Byzantine and European Iconoclasm', in A. Bryer and J. Herrin (eds), *Iconoclasm (Papers given at the Ninth Spring Symposium of Byzantine Studies, University of Birmingham, 1975)*, Birmingham, 1977, pp. 165–77

——, *The Power of Images. Studies in the History and Theory of Response*, Chicago and London, 1989

French, K.L., 'Maidens' Lights and Wives' Stores: Women's Parish Guilds in Late Medieval England', *Sixteenth-Century Journal*, 29 (1998), 399–425

——, *The People of the Parish. Community Life in a Late Medieval English Diocese*, Philadelphia, 2001

French, T., *York Minster. The St William Window* (Corpus Vitrearum Medii Aevi Great Britain, Summary Catalogue 5), Oxford, 1999

Freshfield, E., 'On the Parish Books of St Margaret-Lothbury, St Christopher-le-Stocks, and St Bartholomew-by-the-Exchange, in the City of London', *Archaeologia*, 45 (1880), 57–123

Fryde, E.B., *Peasants and Landlords in Later Medieval England c. 1380–c. 1525*, Stroud, 1996

Gambero, L., *Mary and the Fathers of the Church. The Blessed Virgin Mary in Patristic Thought*, San Francisco, 1999

Gardner, A., *English Medieval Sculpture*, Cambridge, rev. edn, 1951

Gardner, J., 'Altars, Altarpieces and Art History: Legislation and Usage', in E. Borsook and F.S. Gioffredi (eds), *Italian Altarpieces 1250–1550, Function and Design*, Oxford, 1994, pp. 5–19

Geary, P.J., *Furta Sacra. Thefts of Relics in the Central Middle Ages*, Princeton, 1978

*The Gentleman's Magazine*, 26 (1756), 559–60

Gibson, G.M., *The Theater of Devotion. East Anglian Drama and Society in the Late Middle Ages*, Chicago and London, 1989

Gillerman, D., *Enguerran de Marigny and the Church of Notre-Dame at Ecouis. Art and Patronage in the Reign of Philip the Fair*, Pennsylvania, 1994

Ginzburg, C., *The Cheese and the Worms: The Cosmos of a Sixteenth-Century Miller*, Harmondsworth, 1992

Godber, J., *History of Bedfordshire 1066–1888*, Bedfordshire County Council, 1969

Goldberg, P.J.P., introductory essay in idem (ed.), *Woman is a Worthy Wight. Women in English Society c. 1200–1500*, Stroud, 1992, pp. ix–xvii

——, 'Pilgrims and Pilgrimage: Some Late Medieval Evidence', *Medieval Yorkshire*, 21 (1992), 2–6

Goodich, M., '*Ancilla Dei*: The Servant as Saint', in J. Kirshner and S.F. Wemple (eds), *Women of the Medieval World. Essays in Honor of John H. Mundy*, Oxford, 1985, pp. 119–36

Gougaud, L., *Devotional and Ascetic Practices in the Middle Ages*, London, 1927

Graham, T.H.B. and Collingwood, W.G., 'Patron Saints of the Diocese of Carlisle', *Transactions of the Cumberland and Westmorland Antiquarian and Archaeological Society*, new series, 25 (1925), 1–27

Graves, C.P., 'Social Space in the English Parish Church', *Economy and Society*, 18, no. 3 (1990), 297–322

Gray, D., *Themes and Images in the Medieval English Religious Lyric*, London and Boston, 1972

Green, C. and Whittingham, A.B., 'Excavations at Walsingham Priory, Norfolk, 1961', *Norfolk Archaeology*, 125 (1968), 255–90

Greening Lamborn, E.A., *The Lovel Tomb at Minster*, Shipston-on-Stour, n.d

Grössinger, C., *North-European Panel Paintings. A Catalogue of Netherlandish and German Paintings before 1600 in English Churches and Colleges*, London, 1992

Guillot de Suduiraut, S., *Gregor Erhart Sainte Marie-Madeleine*, The Louvre, Paris, 1997

Hagerty, R.P., 'The Buckinghamshire Saints Reconsidered 1: St Firmin of North Crawley', *Records of Buckinghamshire*, 27 (1985), 65–71

——, 'Peter de Wintonia, Parson of Crawley', *Records of Buckinghamshire*, 31 (1989), 93–104

Haigh, C., *English Reformations. Religion, Politics, and Society under the Tudors*, Oxford, 1993

Hall, D.J., *English Mediaeval Pilgrimage*, London, 1966

Hamburger, J.F., *The Visual and the Visionary. Art and Female Spirituality in Late Medieval Germany*, New York, 1998

Harbison, C., 'Visions and meditations in early Flemish painting', *Simiolus*, 15 (1985), 87–118

Harding, V., 'Burial choice and burial location in late medieval London', in S. Bassett (ed.), *Death in Towns. Urban Responses to the Dying and the Dead, 100–1600*, Leicester, London and New York, 1992, pp. 119–35

Harrison, F.Ll., *Music in Medieval Britain*, London, 2nd edn., 1983

Harrod, H., 'Some Particulars relating to the History of the Abbey Church of Wymondham in Norfolk', *Archaeologia*, 43 (1871), 264–72

Hart, R., 'The Shrines and Pilgrimages of the County of Norfolk', *Norfolk Archaeology*, 6 (1864), 277–94

Harvey, J., *English Mediaeval Architects. A Biographical Dictionary down to 1550*, Gloucester, rev. edn, 1984

Haslewood, F., 'Our Lady of Ipswich', *Proceedings of the Suffolk Institute of Archaeology*, 10 (1898–1900), 53–5

Hawkes, J., 'Columban Virgins: Iconic Images of the Virgin and Child in Insular Sculpture', in C. Bourke (ed.), *Studies in the Cult of Saint Columba*, Dublin, 1997, pp. 107–35

Hayum, A., *The Isenheim Altarpiece. God's Medicine and the Painter's Vision*, Princeton, 1989

Hearn, K. (ed.), *Dynasties. Painting in Tudor and Jacobean England 1530–1630* (London, Tate Gallery exhibition catalogue, 1995)

Hepple, L.W. and Doggett, A.M., *The Chilterns*, Chichester, 2nd edn, 1994

Heslop, T.A., 'Attitudes to the Visual Arts: The Evidence from Written Sources', in J. Alexander and P. Binski (eds), *Age of Chivalry. Art in Plantagenet England 1200–1400* (London, Royal Academy of Arts exhibition catalogue, 1987), pp. 26–32

Higgitt, J., 'The Dedication Inscription at Jarrow and its Context', *Antiquaries Journal*, 59 (1979), 343–74

Hildburgh, W.L., 'Miscellaneous notes concerning English alabaster carvings', *Archaeological Journal*, 88 (1931), 228–46

Hillen, H.J., *The History of King's Lynn*, Borough of Norwich, 1907

Holbert, K., 'The Vindication of a Controversial Early Thirteenth-Century *Vierge Ouvrante* in the Walters Art Gallery', *Journal of the Walters Art Gallery*, 55/56 (1997–8), 101–21

Hole, C., *English Shrines and Sanctuaries*, London, 1954

——, *A Dictionary of British Folk Customs*, Oxford, 1995

Hope, C., 'Altarpieces and the Requirements of Patrons', in T. Verdon and J. Henderson (eds), *Christianity and the Renaissance. Image and Religious Imagination in the Quattrocento*, New York, 1990, pp. 535–71

Huard, G., in *Bulletin de la Société nationale des Antiquaires de France* (1938), 95–103

Hubbard, E., *The Buildings of Wales: Clwyd*, Harmondsworth and the University of Wales, 1986

Hubner, W., Paredis-Vroon, M. and Minkenberg, G., *Der Schatz des Gnadenbildes im Dom zu Aachen, Domschatzkammer Aachen*, Aachen, 1996

Hudson, A., *The Premature Reformation. Wycliffite Texts and Lollard History*, Oxford, 1988

Huth, H., *Kunstler und Werkstatt der Spätgotik*, Darmstadt, 1977

Hutton, R., *The Rise and Fall of Merry England. The Ritual Year 1400–1700*, Oxford, 1994

——, *The Stations of the Sun. A History of the Ritual Year in Britain*, Oxford, 1997

*Iconoclasme. Vie et mort de l'image médiévale* (Berne, Musée d'histoire and Strasbourg, Musée de L'Oeuvre Notre-Dame exhibition catalogue, 2001)

Jacobs, L.F., *Early Netherlandish Carved Altarpieces, 1380–1550. Medieval Tastes and Mass Marketing*, Cambridge, 1998

Jacobsson, C., *Höggotisk träskulptur i gamla Linköpings stift*, Visby, 1995

James, H.M., 'Excavations on the Site of Flawford Church, Ruddington, Nottinghamshire', *Transactions of the Thoroton Society of Nottinghamshire*, 98 (1994), 134–6

James, M.R. and Bensly, W.T., *The Sculptured Bosses in the Roof of the Bauchun Chapel of Our Lady of Pity in Norwich Cathedral*, Norwich, 1908

Jones, A., 'Bedfordshire: Fifteenth Century', in P.D.A. Harvey (ed.), *The Peasant Land Market in Medieval England*, Oxford, 1984, pp. 178–251

Jones, F., *The Holy Wells of Wales*, Cardiff, 1954 and 1992

Jones, M.K. and Underwood, M.G., *The King's Mother. Lady Margaret Beaufort, Countess of Richmond and Derby*, Cambridge, 1992

Jones, W.R, 'Lollards and Images. The Defence of Religious Art in England', *Journal of the History of Ideas*, 34 (1973), 27–50

Kaftal, G., *Saints in Italian Art*, 4 vols, Florence, 1952–85

——, *St Dominic in Early Italian Painting*, Oxford, 1948

Kahn, D., 'The Romanesque Sculpture of the Church of St Mary at Halford, Warwickshire', *Journal of the British Archaeological Association*, 133 (1980), 64–73

Kaland, B., 'Baldakin fra Hopperstad. Madonna fra Hove', *Årbok for Foreningen til Norske Fortidsminnesmerkers Bevaring*, 125, 1970, pp. 85–98

Kamerick, K., *Popular Piety and Art in the Late Middle Ages. Image Worship and Idolatry in England 1350–1500*, New York and Basingstoke, 2002

Kauffmann, M., 'British Library, Lansdowne MS 383: the Shaftesbury Psalter?', in P. Binski and W. Noel (eds), *New Offerings, Ancient Treasures. Studies in Medieval Art for George Henderson*, Stroud, 2001, pp. 256–79

Kay, S. and Rubin, M. (eds), *Framing Medieval Bodies*, Manchester and New York, 1994

Keen, L. and Taylor, C., *St Catherine's Chapel at Abbotsbury and the Legend of the Saint*, Abbotsbury, 1999

Kerry, C., *A History of the Municipal Church of St Lawrence, Reading*, Reading, 1883

Kingsford, C.L., 'Our Lady of the Pew. The King's Oratory or Closet in the Palace of Westminster', *Archaeologia*, 68 (1917), 1–20

Kingsford, H.S., *Illustrations of the Occasional Offices of the Church in the Middle Ages from Contemporary Sources*, Alcuin Club Collections, 24, 1921

Kirschbaum, E. (ed.), *Lexikon der christlichen Ikonographie*, 8 vols, Freiburg im Breisgau, 1968–1976

Klack-Eitzen, C., *Die thronenden Madonnen des 13. Jahrhunderts in Westfalen*, Denkmalpflege und Forschung in Westfalen, 6, Bonn, 1985

Klinge, E., 'Eine "Muttergottes im Wochenbett" aus dem 14. Jahrhundert', in M. Liner and R. Becksmann (eds), *Kunstgeschichtliche Studien für Kurt Bauch zum 70. Geburtstag von seinen Schülern*, Munich and Berlin, 1967, pp. 51–6

Kollwitz, J., 'Bild und Bildertheologie im Mittelalter', in *Das Gottesbild im Abendland*, Witten and Berlin, 1959, pp. 109–38

Köster, K., 'Religiöse Medaillen und Wallfahrts-Devotialien in der flämischen Buchmalerei des 15. und frühen 16. Jahrhunderts', in *Buch und Welt. Festschrift für Gustav Hoffmann zum 65. Geburtstag dargebracht*, Wiesbaden, 1965, pp. 459–504

——, 'Gemalte Kollektionen von Pilgerzeichen und Religiösen Medaillen in flämischen Gebet- und Stundenbüchern des 15. und frühen 16. Jahrhunderts. Neue Funde in Handschriften der Gent-Brügger Schule', in F. Vanwijngaerden (ed.), *Liber Amicorum Herman Liebaers*, Brussels, 1984, pp. 485–535.

Kriss-Rettenbeck, L., *Ex Voto. Zeichen, Bild und Abbild im christlichen Votivbrauchtum*, Zürich and Freiburg, 1972

Krohm, H., 'The Sources of Riemenschneider's Art', in *Tilman Riemenschneider Master Sculptor of the Late Middle Ages* (National Gallery of Art, Washington and The Metropolitan Museum of Art, New York exhibition catalogue), New Haven and London, 1999, pp. 45–68

Krönig, W., 'Ein Vesperbild im Schnütgen-Museum zu Köln mit einem Exkurs über die Bedeutung der Rosetten', *Wallraf-Richartz-Jahrbuch*, 31 (1969), 7–24

——, *Rheinische Vesperbilder*, Mönchengladbach, 1967

Kroos, R., '"Gotes tabernakel". Zu Funktion und Interpretation von Schreinmadonnen', *Zeitschrift für Schweizerische Archäologie und Kunstgeschichte*, 43 (1986), 58–64

Kümin, B.A., *The Shaping of a Community. The Rise & Reformation of the English Parish c. 1400–1560*, Aldershot, 1996

Kupfer, M., *Romanesque Wall Painting in Central France. The Politics of Narrative*, New Haven and London, 1993

Lack, W., Stuchfield, H.M. and Whittemore, P., *The Monumental Brasses of Bedfordshire*, The Monumental Brass Society, London, 1992

Lang, J., *Corpus of Anglo-Saxon Stone Sculpture, vol. 3: York and Eastern Yorkshire*, Oxford, 1991

Langdon, J., *Horses, Oxen, and Technological Innovation in English Farming from 1066 to 1500*, Cambridge, 1986

Laurentin, R. and Oursel, R., *Vierges romanes. Les vierges assises*, Zodiaque, 1988

Lee, F.G., *History and Antiquities of the Prebendal Church of the Blessed Virgin Mary of Thame*, London, 1883

Leeuwenberg, J., 'Die Ausstrahlung Utrechter Tonplastik', in *Studien zur Geschichte der europäischen Plastik. Festschrift Theodor Müller*, Munich, 1965, pp. 151–66

Lentes, T., 'Die Gewänder der Heiligen. Ein Diskussionsbetrag zum Verhältnis von Gebet, Bild und Imagination', in G. Kerschner (ed.), *Hagiographie und Kunst. Der Heiligenkult in Schrift, Bild und Architektur*, Berlin, 1993, pp. 120–51

Lepie, H., *Die Domschatzkammer zu Aachen, Katalog*, Aachen, 6th edn, 1990

Levi, C., *Christ Stopped at Eboli*, Harmondsworth, 1982

Levison, W., *England and the Continent in the Eighth Century*, Oxford, 1946

Lindley, P.G., *Gothic to Renaissance. Essays on Sculpture in England*, Stamford, 1995

——, 'The Great Screen at Winchester Cathedral, II', *Burlington Magazine*, 135 (1993), 796–807

——, 'Playing Check-Mate with Royal Majesty? Wolsey's Patronage of Italian Renaissance Sculpture', in S.J. Gunn and P.G. Lindley (eds), *Cardinal Wolsey. Church, State and Art*, Cambridge, 1991, pp. 261–85

——, review of W.H. Forsyth, *The Pietà in French Late Gothic Sculpture. Regional Variations* in *Burlington Magazine*, 140, no. 1149 (December 1998), 834–5

London, H.S., *The Life of William Bruges, the First Garter King of Arms*, Harleian Society, 111, 112, 1959–60, London, 1970

Longhurst, M.H., *English Ivories*, London, 1926

Lutton, R., 'Connections between Lollards, Townsfolk and Gentry of Tenterden in the Late Fifteenth and Early Sixteenth Centuries', in M. Aston and C. Richmond (eds), *Lollards and the Gentry in the Late Middle Ages*, Stroud, 1997, pp. 199–229

MacCulloch, D., *Thomas Cranmer. A Life*, London and New Haven, 1996

MacGregor, A., 'Antler, Bone and Horn', in J. Blair and N. Ramsay (eds), *English Medieval Industries: Craftsmen, Techniques, Products*, London, 1991, pp. 376–8

MacGregor, N., *A Victim of Anonymity. The Master of the St Bartholomew Altarpiece*, London, 1993

Mâle, E., *L'Art religieux de la fin du Moyen Age en France*, Paris, 1931

Mango, C.A., *The Art of the Byzantine Empire 312–1453. Sources and Documents*, New Jersey, 1972

Maniura, R., review of H. Belting, *Likeness and Presence*, in *Burlington Magazine*, 137 (1995), 62–3

Marcos, M.-M.E., *La Escultura de Marfil en España Romanica y Gótica*, Madrid, 1984

Marin, L., 'The Frame of Representation and Some of its Figures', in P. Duro (ed.), *The Rhetoric of the Frame. Essays on the Boundaries of the Artwork*, Cambridge, 1996, pp. 79–95

Marks, R., *Stained Glass in England during the Middle Ages*, London, 1993

——, 'The Glazing of Henry VII's Chapel, Westminster Abbey', in B. Thompson (ed.), *The Reign of Henry VII. Proceedings of the 1993 Harlaxton Symposium*, Harlaxton Medieval Studies 5, Stamford, 1995, pp. 157–74

——, 'Two Illuminated Guild Registers from Bedfordshire', in M.P. Brown and S. McKendrick (eds), *Illuminating the Book. Makers and Interpreters. Essays in Honour of Janet Backhouse*, London and Toronto, 1998, pp. 120–41

——, 'Altarpiece, Image and Devotion: Fourteenth-Century Sculpture at Cobham, Kent', in P. Binski and W. Noel (eds), *New Offerings, Ancient Treasures. Studies in Medieval Art for George Henderson*, Stroud, 2001, pp. 417–44

——, 'A Late Medieval Pilgrimage Cult: Master John Schorn of North Marston and Windsor', in L. Keen and E. Scarff (eds), *Windsor. Medieval Archaeology, Art and Architecture of the Thames Valley*, British Archaeological Association Conference Transactions, 25, 2002, pp. 192–207

——, 'Viewing Our Lady of Pity', in *Magistro et Amico. Amici discipulique Lechowi Kalinowskiemu w osiemdziesięciolecie urodzin*, Cracow, 2002, pp. 101–21

——, 'Images of Henry VI', in J. Stratford (ed.), *The Lancastrian Court. Proceedings of the 2001 Harlaxton Symposium*, Harlaxton Medieval Studies X, Stamford, 2003, pp. 111–24

——, 'The *Ymage Sancti Loci* in the English Medieval Parish Church. Its Status and Function in the Liturgy and Private Devotion', in A. Moraht-Fromm (ed.), *Kunst und Liturgie. Choranlagen des Spätmittelaltersihre Architektur, Ausstatung und Nutzung*, Ostfildern, 2003, pp. 31–58

—— and Williamson, P. (eds), *Gothic. Art for England 1400–1547* (London, Victoria & Albert Museum exhibition catalogue, 2003)

Marrow, J.H., 'Symbol and Meaning in Northern European Art of the Late Middle Ages and early Renaissance', *Simiolus*, 16 (1986), 150–69

Martindale, A., 'The Wall-paintings in the Chapel of Eton College', in C. Barron and N. Saul (eds), *England and the Low Countries in the Late Middle Ages*, Stroud, 1995, pp. 133–52

Mason, E., 'The Role of the English Parishioner, 1100–1500', *Journal of Ecclesiastical History*, 27 (1976), 17–29

Mata, A.F., *El retablo Gótico de Cartagena y los alabastros ingleses en España*, Madrid, 1999

Maxwell, G., *The Ten Pains of Death*, London, 1959

Mayr-Harting, H., 'Functions of a Twelfth-Century Recluse', *History*, 60 (1975), 337–52

Mazower, M., *The Balkans*, London, 2001

Meurer, H., *Württembergisches Landesmuseum Stuttgart. Die mittelalterlichen Skulpturen, I Stein- und Holzskulpturen 800–1400*, Stuttgart, 1989

Micklethwaite, J.T., 'Notes on the Imagery of Henry the Seventh's Chapel, Westminster', *Archaeologia*, 47 (2) (1883), 361–79

Middleton-Stewart, J., *Inward Purity and Outward Splendour. Death and Remembrance in the Deanery of Dunwich, Suffolk, 1370–1547*, Woodbridge, 2001

Milbourn, T., 'Church of St Stephen Walbrook', *Transactions of the London and Middlesex Archaeological Society*, 5 (1876–80), 327–402

Miles, M.R., *Image as Insight: Visual Understanding in Western Christianity and Secular Culture*, Boston (Mass.), 1985

Miller, E. and Hatcher, J., *Medieval England. Rural Society and Economic Change 1086–1348*, London and New York, 1978

Moore, N.J., 'Brick' in J. Blair and N. Ramsay (eds), *English Medieval Industries: Craftsmen, Techniques, Products*, London, 1991, pp. 211–36

Morant, A.W., 'Notices of the Church of St Nicholas, Great Yarmouth', *Norfolk Archaeology*, 7 (1872), 215–48

—— and L'Estrange, J., 'Notices of the Church of Randworth', *Norfolk Archaeology*, 7 (1872), 178–212

Morgan, N.J., *Early Gothic Manuscripts 1190–1250. A Survey of Manuscripts Illuminated in the British Isles*, 4, pt 1, London, 1982

——, *Early Gothic Manuscripts 1250–1285. A Survey of Manuscripts Illuminated in the British Isles*, 4, pt 2, London, 1988

——, 'Texts and Images of Marian Devotion in English Twelfth-Century Monasticism, and Their Influence on the Secular Church', in B. Thompson (ed.), *Monasteries and Society in Medieval Britain. Proceedings of the 1994 Harlaxton Symposium*, Harlaxton Medieval Studies 6, Stamford, 1999, pp. 117–36

——, 'Texts and Images of Marian Devotion in Thirteenth-Century England', in W.M. Ormrod (ed.), *England in the Thirteenth Century. Proceedings of the 1989 Harlaxton Symposium*, Harlaxton Medieval Studies 1, Stamford, 1991, pp. 69–103

——, 'Texts and Images of Marian Devotion in Fourteenth-Century England', in N. Rogers (ed.), *England in the Fourteenth Century. Proceedings of the 1991 Harlaxton Symposium*, Harlaxton Medieval Studies 3, Stamford, 1993, pp. 34–57

——, 'Devotional Aspects of the Catalan Altar Frontals *c*. 1100–1350', in R. Archer and E. Martinell (eds), *Proceedings of the First Symposium on Catalonia in Australia (La Trobe University, Melbourne, 27–9 September 1996)*, Barcelona, 1998, pp. 101–22

——, 'The Introduction of the Sarum Calendar into the Dioceses of England in the Thirteenth Century', in M. Prestwich, R. Britnell and R. Frame (eds), *Thirteenth Century England. VIII. Proceedings of the Durham Conference 1999*, Woodbridge, 2001, pp. 179–206

Morris, C., 'Pilgrimage to Jerusalem in the late Middle Ages' in C. Morris and P. Roberts (eds), *Pilgrimage. the English Experience from Becket to Bunyan* Cambridge, 2002, pp. 141–63

*Mother of God. Representations of the Virgin in Byzantine Art* (Athens, Benaki Museum exhibition catalogue, 2001)

Moxey, K.P.F., 'Sebald Beham's church anniversary holidays: festive peasants as instruments of repressive humour', *Simiolus*, 12 (1981–2), 107–30

Munby, J., 'Wood', in J. Blair and N. Ramsay (eds), *English Medieval Industries: Craftsmen, Techniques, Products*, London, 1991, pp. 379–405

Mynard, D.C., 'Excavations at Bradwell Abbey', *Milton Keynes Journal of Archaeology and History*, 3 (1974), 31–66 (including Appendix: 'Bradwell Priory Chapel' by S.E. Rigold and P. Woodfield)

Nash, J.M., 'Art and Arousal' (review of D. Freedberg, *The Power of Images. Studies in the History and Theory of Response*, Chicago, 1989), in *Art History*, 13, no. 4 (1990), 566–70

Neame, A., *The Holy Maid of Kent. The Life of Elizabeth Barton, 1506–1534*, London, 1971

Nelson, P., 'Some additional specimens of English alabaster carvings', *Archaeological Journal*, 84 (1927), 114–24

Netzer, N., 'Collecting, Re/Collecting, Contextualizing and Recontextualizing: Devotion to Fragments of the Middle Ages', in N. Netzer and V. Reinburg (eds), *Fragmented Devotion. Medieval Objects from the Schnütgen Museum Cologne* (McMullen Museum of Art, Boston College USA exhibition catalogue, 2000), pp. 17–30

Nilson, B., *Cathedral Shrines of Medieval England*, Woodbridge, 1998

Northeast, P., 'Suffolk Churches in the Later Middle Ages: The Evidence of Wills', in C. Harper-Bill, C. Rawcliffe and R. Wilson (eds), *East Anglia's History: Studies in Honour of Norman Scarfe*, Woodbridge, 2002, pp. 93–106

Norton, C., Park, D. and Binski, P., *Dominican Painting in East Anglia: The Thornham Parva Retable and the Musée de Cluny Frontal*, Woodbridge, 1987

*The Norwich Snapdragon*, Norfolk Museums Services information sheet, Norfolk, 1984

Odell, G., *The Church of St Mary the Virgin, Marston Moreteyne*, Ampthill, 1982

Orme, N., *Unity and Variety. A History of the Church in Cornwall and Devon*, Exeter, 1991

——, *English Church Dedications with a Survey of Cornwall and Devon*, Exeter, 1996

Ousterhout, R. and Brubacker, L. (eds), *The Sacred Image, East and West*, Urbana and Chicago, 1995

Owst, G.R., *Literature and the Pulpit in Medieval England*, Oxford, 2nd edn, 1961

Page, W. (ed.), *The Victoria History of the County of Bedford*, 3 vols, London, 1904–72

Paine, C., 'The Chapel and Well of Our Lady of Woolpit', *Proceedings of the Suffolk Institute of Archaeology*, 38 (1993–6), 8–11

——, 'The Building of Long Melford Church', in Long Melford PCC, *A Sermon in Stone. The 500th anniversary book of Long Melford Church*, Lavenham, 1984, pp. 9–18

Palazzo, E., 'Iconographie et liturgie dans les études médiévales aujourd'hui: un éclairage méthodologique', *Cahiers de civilisation médiévale*, 41 (1998), 65–9

——, *Liturgie et société au Moyen Age*, Mayenne, 2000

Panofsky, E., '*Imago Pietatis*: Ein Beitrag zur Typengeschichte des "Schmerzensmanns" und der "Maria Mediatrix"', *Festschrift für Max J. Friedländer zum 60. Geburtstag*, Leipzig, 1927, pp. 261–308

Park, D., 'The "Lewes Group" of Wall Paintings in Sussex', *Anglo-Norman Studies, The Proceedings of the Battle Conference*, 6, 1983, pp. 200–35

——, 'The Duxford Master: a Thirteenth-century Painter in East Anglia', in P. Binski and W. Noel (eds), *New Offerings, Ancient Treasures. Studies in Medieval Art for George Henderson*, Stroud, 2001, pp. 312–24

—— and Welford, P., 'The Medieval Polychromy of Winchester Cathedral', in J. Crook (ed.), *Winchester Cathedral. Nine Hundred Years 1093–1993*, Chichester, 1993, pp. 123–66

Parker, W., *The History of Long Melford*, London, 1873

Parkes, M.B. (comp.), *The Medieval Manuscripts of Keble College Oxford*, London, 1979

Passarge, W., *Das deutsche Vesperbild im Mittelalter*, Cologne, 1924

Paul, R., 'The Plan of the Church and Monastery of St Augustine, Bristol', *Archaeologia*, 63 (1911–12), 231–50

Peacock, E., 'Owr Lady of Pity', *Archaeological Journal*, 48 (1891), 111–16

Penninck, J., *De Jeruzalemkerk te Brugge*, Bruges, 1986

Perdrizet, P., *La Vièrge de Miséricorde: étude d'un thème iconographique*, Paris, 1908

Perier-D'Ieteren, C. and Born, A. (eds), *Retable en Terre Cuite des Pays-Bas (Xve–XVIe siècles). Etude Stylistique et Technologique*, Brussels, 1992

Pevsner, N., *The Buildings of England. Bedfordshire and the County of Huntingdon and Peterborough*, Harmondsworth, 1968

——, *The Buildings of England. Derbyshire*, Harmondsworth, 2nd edn, 1978

—— and Cherry, B., *The Buildings of England. Devon*, Harmondsworth, 2nd edn, 1991

—— and Wilson, B., *The Buildings of England. Norfolk 2. North-West and South*, Harmondsworth, 2nd edn, London, 1999

Pfaff, R.W., 'Prescription and Reality in the Rubrics of Sarum Rite Service Books', in L. Smith and B. Ward (eds), *Intellectual Life in the Middle Age. Essays Presented to Margaret Gibson*, London, 1992, pp. 197–205

Phythian-Adams, C., *Local History and Folklore: a New Framework*, Standing Conference for Local History, London, 1975

——, *Rethinking English Local History*, University of Leicester, Department of English Local History Occasional Papers, Fourth Series, no. 1, Leicester, 1987

Prigent, C., *Les sculptures anglaises d'albâtre au musée national du Moyen Age, Thermes de Cluny*, Paris, 1998

Prior, C.E., 'Dedications of Churches with Some Notes as to Village Feasts and Old Customs in the Deaneries of Islip and Bicester', *Oxfordshire Archaeological Society Reports for the Year* 1903 (1904), 20–42

Purvis, J.S., 'The Ripon Carvers and the Lost Choir-Stalls of Bridlington Priory', *Yorkshire Archaeological Journal*, 29 (1927–9), 157–201

Radford, U.M., 'The Wax Images Found in Exeter Cathedral', *Antiquaries Journal*, 29 (1949), 164–8

Radler, G., *Die Schreinmadonna 'Vièrge ouvrante', von den bernhardinischen Anfängen bis zur Frauenmystik im Deutschordensland*, Frankfurt am Main, 1990

Raine, A., *Mediaeval York. A topographical survey based on original sources*, London, 1955

Ramsay, N., 'Alabaster', in J. Blair and N. Ramsay (eds), *English Medieval Industries: Craftsmen, Techniques, Products*, London, 1991, ch. 2

Ransome, D.R., 'The struggle of the Glazier's Company with the foreign glaziers, 1500–1550', *Guildhall Miscellany*, 2, no. 1 (September 1960), 12–20

Rapoport, A., *The Meaning of the Built Environment. A Nonverbal Communication Approach*, Tucson, 1990

——, 'Systems of activities and systems of settings', in S. Kent (ed.), *Domestic Architecture and the Use of Space. An interdisciplinary cross-cultural study*, Cambridge, 1990

Raw, B.C., 'The Inglesham Virgin and Child', *Wiltshire Archaeological and Natural History Magazine*, 61 (1966), 43–6

Rawcliffe, C., 'Caring bodies and healing souls: pilgrimage and the sick in medieval East Anglia', in C. Morris and P. Roberts (eds), *Pilgrimage. The English Experience From Becket to Bunyan*, Cambridge, 2002, pp. 108–40

Recht, R., *Le croire et le voir. L'art des cathédrales (XIIe–XVe siècle)*, Mayenne, 1999

Reinburg, V., 'Hearing Lay People's Prayer', in B.B. Diefendorf and C. Hesse (eds), *Culture and Identity in Early Modern Europe (1500–1800). Essays in Honor of Natalie Zemon Davis*, University of Michigan Press, Ann Arbor, 1993, pp. 19–39

Reiners-Ernst, E., *Das freudvolle Vesperbild und die Anfänge der Pieta-Vorstellung*, Munich, 1939

Reiss, A., *The Sunday Christ. Sabbatarianism in English medieval wall-painting*, British Archaeological Reports, British Series, 292, Oxford, 2000

Reynolds, C., 'England and the Continent: Artistic Relations', in R. Marks and P. Williamson (eds), *Gothic. Art for England 1400–1547* (London, Victoria & Albert Museum exhibition catalogue, 2003), pp. 76–85

Riches, S., *St George. Hero, Martyr and Myth*, Stroud, 2000

Richmond, C., 'The English Gentry and Religion, c. 1500', in C. Harper-Bill (ed.), *Religious Belief and Ecclesiastical Careers in Late Medieval England*, Proceedings of the Conference Held at Strawberry Hill, Easter 1989, Woodbridge, 1991, pp. 121–50

——, *The Paston Family in the Fifteenth Century. Endings*, Manchester, 2000

——, 'Three Suffolk Pieces', in S. Ditchfield (ed.), *Christianity and Community in the West. Essays for John Bossy*, Aldershot, 2001, pp. 44–58

Rickerby, S. and Park, D., 'A romanesque "Visitatio Sepulchri" at Kempley', *Burlington Magazine*, 132 (1991), 27–31

Ringbom, S., *Icon to Narrative. The Rise of the Dramatic Close-Up in Fifteenth-Century Devotional Painting*, Åbo, 1965

——, 'Devotional Images and Imaginative Devotions. Notes on the Place of Art in Late Medieval Private Piety', *Gazette des Beaux-Arts*, series 6, 73 (1969), 159–70

Roberts, E., *The Wall-Paintings of Saint Albans Abbey*, St Albans, 1993

Robertson, S., 'The Crypt of Canterbury Cathedral: Part II', *Archaeologia Cantiana*, 13 (1913), 500–46

Rogers, N., 'Regional Production', in R. Marks and P. Williamson (eds), *Gothic. Art for England 1400–1547* (London, Victoria & Albert Museum exhibition catalogue, 2003), pp. 94–7

Rosser, G., *Medieval Westminster 1200–1540*, Oxford, 1989

Rouse, E.C., 'Wall-Paintings in Radnage Church, Bucks.', *Records of Buckinghamshire*, 15 (1947–52), 134–8

——, 'Bradwell Abbey and the Chapel of St Mary', *Milton Keynes Journal of Archaeology and History*, 2 (1973), 34–8

—— and Baker, D., 'The Wall-Paintings at Longthorpe Tower near Peterborough, Northants.', *Archaeologia*, 96 (1955), 1–57

Royal Commission on Historical Monuments (England), *Buckinghamshire*, 2 vols, London, 1912–13

Rubin, M., *Corpus Christi. The Eucharist in Late Medieval Culture*, Cambridge, 1991

Russell-Smith, J.M., 'Walter Hilton and a Tract in Defence of the Veneration of Images', *Dominican Studies*, 7 (1954), 180–214

St John Hope, W.H., *Windsor Castle. An Architectural History*, 2 vols, London, 1913

*St Michael's Stewkley Buckinghamshire* (church guidebook), Aspley Guise, 1972

Salzman, L.F., *Building in England down to 1540: a Documentary History*, Oxford, repr. 1967

Sandler, L.F., *Omne Bonum. A Fourteenth-Century Encyclopedia of Universal Knowledge*, London, 1996

——, *Gothic Manuscripts 1285–1385. A Survey of Manuscripts Illuminated in the British Isles*, 5, 2 vols, Oxford, 1986

Sauerländer, W., *Gothic Sculpture in France 1140–1270*, London, 1972

——, 'Von der Glykophilousa zur "Amie Gracieuse". Überlegungen und Fragen zur "Virgen Blanca" in der Kathedrale von Toledo', in *De la création à la restauration. Travaux d'histoire de l'art offerts à Marcel Durliat pour son 75e anniversaire*, Toulouse, 1992, pp. 449–61

Saul, N., *Death, Art and Memory in Medieval England. The Cobham Family and their Monuments 1300–1500*, Oxford, 2001

Scase, W., 'St Anne and the Education of the Virgin: Literary and Artistic Traditions and their Implications', in N. Rogers (ed.), *England in the Fourteenth Century. Proceedings of the 1991 Harlaxton Symposium*, Harlaxton Medieval Studies 3, Stamford, 1993, pp. 81–96

Schiller, G., *Iconography of Christian Art*, 2 vols, London, 1971–2

Schmitt, J.-C., *Le corps des images. Essais sur la culture visuelle au Moyen Age*, Paris, 2002

Scholz, H., 'Hans Wild und Hans Kamensetzer – Hypotheken der Ulmer und Strassburger Kunstgeschichte des Spätmittelalters', *Jahrbuch der Berliner Museen*, Neue Folge, 36 (1994), 93–140

Scott, K.L., *Later Gothic Manuscripts 1390–1490. A Survey of Manuscripts Illuminated in the British Isles*, 6, 2 vols, London, 1996

Scribner, R.W., *For the Sake of Simple Folk. Popular Propaganda for the German Reformation*, Oxford, 2nd edn, 1994

——, *Popular Culture and Popular Movements in Reformation Germany*, London and Ronceverte, 1987

Serjeantson, R.M. and Isham Longden, H., 'The Parish Churches and Religious Houses of Northamptonshire: Their Dedications, Altars, Images and Lights', *Archaeological Journal*, 70 (1913), 217–452

Sheingorn, P., 'The Bosom of Abraham Trinity: A Late Medieval All Saints Image', in D. Williams (ed.), *England in the Fifteenth Century. Proceedings of the 1986 Harlaxton Symposium*, Woodbridge, 1987, pp. 273–95

——, 'Appropriating the Holy Kinship: Gender and Family History', in K. Ashley and P. Sheingorn (eds), *Interpreting Cultural Symbols. St Anne in Late Medieval Society*, Athens (Georgia) and London, 1990, pp. 169–98

——, '"The Wise Mother": The Image of St Anne teaching the Virgin Mary', *Gesta*, 32 (1993), 69–80

Shinners Jr, J.R., 'The Veneration of Saints at Norwich Cathedral in the Fourteenth Century', *Norfolk Archaeology*, 40 (1987–9), 133–44

Silver, L., 'The State of Research in Northern European Art of the Renaissance Era', *Art Bulletin*, 68 (1986), 518–35

Spencer, B., *Medieval Pilgrim Badges from Norfolk*, Norfolk Museums Service, 1980

——, *Pilgrim Souvenirs and Secular Badges, Salisbury Museum Medieval Catalogue, pt 2*, Salisbury & South Wiltshire Museum, 1990

——, *Pilgrim Souvenirs and Secular Badges. Medieval Finds from Excavations in London: 7*, Museum of London, London, 1998

*Spiegel der Seligkeit. Privates Bild und Frömmigkeit im Spätmittelaltar* (Nuremberg, Germanisches Nationalmuseum exhibition catalogue, 2000)

Sprigath, G., 'Sur Le Vandalisme Révolutionnaire (1792–1794)', *Annales Historiques de la Révolution Française*, 52 (1980), 510–35

Stone, L., *Sculpture in Britain. The Middle Ages*, Harmondsworth, 2nd edn, 1972

Stratford, N., 'Glastonbury and Two Gothic Ivories in the United States', in F.H. Thompson (ed.), *Studies in Medieval Sculpture*, Society of Antiquaries of London, occasional paper, new series, 3 (1983), pp. 208–16

——, 'Gothic Ivory Carvings in England', in J. Alexander and P. Binski (eds.), *Age of Chivalry. Art in Plantagenet England 1200–1400* (London, Royal Academy exhibition catalogue, 1987), pp. 107–13

Sumption, J., *Pilgrimage. An Image of Mediaeval Religion*, London, 1975

Sussmann, V., 'Maria mit dem Schutzmantel', *Marburger Jahrbuch für Kunstwissenschaft*, 5 (1929), 285–351

Sutcliffe, S., 'The Cult of St Sitha in England: an introduction', *Nottingham Medieval Studies*, 37 (1993), 83–9

Svanberg, J. and Qwarnström, A., *Sankt Göran och draken*, Stockholm, rev. edn, 1998

——, *St George in the Art of Sweden and Finland*, Stockholm, 1998

Swanson, H., *Building Craftsmen in Late Medieval York*, University of York Borthwick Paper no. 63, York, 1983

——, *Medieval Artisans. An Urban Class in Late Medieval England*, Oxford, 1989

Swanson, R.N., 'Urban Rectories and Urban Fortunes in Late Medieval England. The Evidence of Bishop's Lynn', in T.R. Slater and G. Rosser (eds), *The Church in the Medieval Town*, Aldershot, 1998, pp. 100–30

Swinden, H., *The History and Antiquities of the Ancient Burgh of Great Yarmouth in the County of Norfolk*, Norwich, 1772

Tatton-Brown, T., 'Canterbury and the architecture of pilgrimage shrines in England', in C. Morris and P. Roberts (eds), *Pilgrimage. The English Experience from Becket to Bunyan*, Cambridge, 2002, pp. 101–7

Tench, E.J., 'The Church of St James, Great Ellingham', *Norfolk Archaeology*, 22 (1926), 341–9

Thompson, F.H., 'Norton Priory, near Runcorn, Cheshire', *Archaeological Journal*, 123 (1966), 62–8

Thomson, J.A.F., *The Later Lollards 1414–1520*, Oxford, 1965

Thordeman, B., *Medieval Wooden Sculpture in Sweden Vol. 1. Attitudes to the heritage*, Stockholm, 1964

Toussaert, J., *Le Sentiment religieux en Flandre à la fin du Moyen-Age*, Paris, 1960

Trexler, R.C., 'Florentine Religious Experience: The Sacred Image', *Studies in the Renaissance*, 19 (1972), 7–41

——, *Public Life in Renaissance Florence*, Ithaca and London, 1980

——, 'Habiller et déshabiller les images: ésquisse d'une analyse', in F. Dunand, J.-M. Speiser and J. Wirth (eds), *L'Image et la Production du Sacré*, Actes du colloque de Strasbourg (20–21 January, 1988) organisé par le Centre d'Histoire de Religion de l'Université de Strasbourg, II, Paris, 1991, pp. 195–231

Tristram, E.W., *English Medieval Wall Painting. The Twelfth Century*, Oxford, 1944

——, *English Medieval Wall Painting. The Thirteenth Century*, Oxford, 1950

——, *English Wall Painting of the Fourteenth Century*, London, 1955

Tudor-Craig, P., 'Fragment of panel painting of the Flagellation in the possession of Canterbury Cathedral and the Martyrdom of St Erasmus belonging to the Society of Antiquaries', *Antiquaries Journal*, 54 (1974), 289–90

Turner, V. and Turner, E., *Image and Pilgrimage in Christian Culture. Anthropological Perspectives*, Oxford, 1978

Turville-Petre, T., 'A Middle English Life of St Zita', *Nottingham Medieval Studies*, 35 (1991), 102–5

Vandenberghe, S. and Dezutter, W.P., 'Trois insignes de pèlerinage du 15e siècle de Notre-Dame d'Aardenburg', *Berichten van de Rijksdienst voor het Ouheidkundig Bodemonderzoek*, 33 (1983), 455–9

Van der Velden, H., *The Donor's Image. Gerald Loyet and the Votive Portraits of Charles the Bold*, Brepols, 2000

Van Os, H., *The Art of Devotion in the Late Middle Ages in Europe 1300–1500*, London, 1994

Van Ruymbeke, A., 'La légende de Notre-Dame de Sablon', in *Tapisseries bruxelloises de la pre-Rénaissance* (Brussels, Musées royaux d'Art et d'Histoire exhibition catalogue, 1976), pp. 85–8

Vauchez, A., *La spiritualité du Moyen Age occidental VIIIe–XIIIe siècle*, Paris, rev. edn, 1994

——, *Sainthood in the later Middle Ages* (trans. J. Birrell), Cambridge, 1997

——, *Saints, prophètes et visionnaires. Le pouvoir surnaturel au Moyen Age*, Paris, 1999

*Victoria County Histories*

Vincent, P., 'Une scène urbaine méconnue: les "chandelières" aux portes des églises', in P. Lardin and J.-L. Roch (eds), *La Ville médiévale en-deçà et au-delà de ses murs. Mélanges Jean-Pierre Leguay*, Rouen, 2000, pp. 205–15

——, *Un monde enluminé: Lumière et luminaires dans la vie religieuse en Occident du XIIe siècle au début XVIe siècle* (forthcoming)

*Votivbilder aus dem Freiburgerland* (Fribourg (Switzerland) Musée de l'art et d'histoire exhibition catalogue, 1978)

Walters, H.B., *London Churches at the Reformation with an Account of their Contents*, London, 1939

Wandel, L.P., *Voracious Idols and Violent Hands. Iconoclasm in Reformation Zurich, Strasbourg and Basel*, Cambridge, 1995

Warner, M., *Alone of All Her Sex. The Myth and Cult of the Virgin Mary*, London, 1990

Warren, F.E., 'A Pre-Reformation Village Gild', *Proceedings of the Suffolk Institute of Archaeology*, 11 (1901), 134–47

Waterton, E., *Pietas Mariana Britannica. A History of English Devotion to the Most Blessed Virgin Marye Mother of God*, London, 1879

Watson, N., '*Et que est huius ydoli materia? Tuipse*: Idols and Images in Walter Hilton', in J. Dimmick, J. Simpson and N. Zeeman (eds), *Images, Idolatry, and Iconoclasm in Late Medieval England: Textuality and the Visual Image*, Oxford, 2002, pp. 95–111

Wayment, H.G., 'The Stained Glass of the Chapel of the Vyne and the Chapel of the Holy Ghost, Basingstoke', *Archaeologia*, 107 (1982), 141–52

Webb, D., *Patrons and Defenders. The Saints in the Italian City-States*, London and New York, 1996

——, *Pilgrimage in Medieval England*, Hambledon, London and New York, 2000

Weissmann, R.F.E., 'Reconstructing Renaissance Sociology: The "Chicago School" and the Study of Renaissance Society', in R.C. Trexler (ed.), *Persons in Groups: Social Behavior as Identity Formation in Medieval and Renaissance Europe*, Papers of the Sixteenth Annual Conference of the Center for Medieval and Early Renaissance Studies, Binghamton, New York, 1985, pp. 39–46

Westlake, H.F., *The Parish Gilds of Mediaeval England*, London, 1919

Whaite, H.C., *St Christopher in English Mediaeval Wall-painting*, London, 1929

Whiting, R., *The Blind Devotion of the People. Popular Religion and the English Reformation*, Cambridge, 1989

Wieck, R.S., *Painted Prayers. The Book of Hours in Medieval and Renaissance Art*, New York, 1997

Williamson, B., 'The Virgin *Lactans* as Second Eve: Image of the *Salvatrix*', *Studies in Iconography*, 19 (1998), 105–38

Williamson, M., '*Pictura et scriptura*: the Eton Choirbook in its iconographical context', *Early Music*, 28 (2000), 359–80

Williamson, P., *Catalogue of Romanesque Sculpture (Victoria & Albert Museum)*, London, 1983

——, *Northern Gothic Sculpture 1200–1450 (Victoria & Albert Museum)*, London, 1988

——, 'An English ivory tabernacle wing of the thirteenth century', *Burlington Magazine*, 132 (1990), 863–6

——, 'Ivory Carvings in English Treasuries before the Reformation', in D. Buckton and T.A. Heslop (eds), *Studies in Medieval Art and Architecture presented to Peter Lasko*, Stroud, 1994, pp. 187–202

——, *Gothic Sculpture 1140–1300*, Pelican History of Art, New Haven and London, 1995

——, 'Symbiosis across Scale: Gothic Ivories and Sculpture in Stone and Wood in the Thirteenth Century', in P. Barnet (ed.), *Images in Ivory. Precious Objects of the Gothic Age* (Detroit Institute of Arts exhibition catalogue, 1997), pp. 38–45

Wilson, C., 'The Medieval Monuments', in P. Collinson, N. Ramsay and M. Sparks (eds), *A History of Canterbury Cathedral*, Oxford, 1995, pp. 451–510

——, O'Connor, D.E. and Thompson, M.A.J., *St Giles Skelton. A Brief Guide*, 1978

Winstead, A., *Virgin Martyrs. Legends of Sainthood in Late Medieval England*, Ithaca and London, 1997

Wirth, J., 'Théorie et pratique de l'image sainte à la veille de la Réforme', *Bibiliothèque d'Humanisme et Renaissance*, 48 (1986), 319–58

——, *L'image médiévale: naissance et développments VIe–XVe siècle*, Paris, 1989

——, 'L'Apparition du surnaturel dans l'art du Moyen Age', in F. Dunand, J.-M. Speiser and J. Wirth (eds), *L'Image et la Production du Sacré*, Actes du colloque de Strasbourg (20–21 January, 1988) organisé par le Centre d'Histoire de Religion de l'Université de Strasbourg, II, Paris, 1991, pp. 139–64

——, 'Faut-il adorer les images? La théorie du culte des images jusqu'au concile de Trente', in *Iconoclasme. Vie et mort de l'image médiévale* (Berne, Musée d'histoire and Strasbourg, Musée de l'Oeuvre Notre-Dame exhibition catalogue, 2001), pp. 28–37

Woodforde, C., *The Norwich School of Glass-Painting in the Fifteenth Century*, Oxford, 1950

Wood-Legh, K.L., *Perpetual Chantries in Britain*, Cambridge, 1965

Woodruff, C.E., 'The Chapel of Our Lady in the Crypt of Canterbury Cathedral', *Archaeologia Cantiana*, 38 (1926), 153–72

Woods, K., 'Immigrant Craftsmen and Imports', in R. Marks and P. Williamson (eds), *Gothic. Art for England 1400–1547* (London, Victoria & Albert Museum exhibition catalogue, 2003), pp. 91–4

Woolf, R., *The English Religious Lyric in the Middle Ages*, Oxford, 1968

Wrightson, K. and Levine, D., *Poverty and Piety in an English Village. Terling, 1525–1700*, Oxford, 1995

Wrigley, R., 'Breaking the Code: Interpreting French Revolutionary Iconoclasm', in A. Yarrington and K. Everest (eds), *Reflections on Revolution: Images of Romanticism*, London, 1993, pp. 182–95

Zarnecki, G., 'A 12th Century Column-figure of the Standing Virgin and Child from Minster-in-Sheppey, Kent', in idem, *Studies in Romanesque Sculpture*, London, 1979, ch. 14

*Die Zeit der Staufer. Geschichte, Kunst, Kultur* (Stuttgart, Württembergisches Landesmuseum exhibition catalogue, 1977)

Zender, M., *Räume und Schichten mittelalterlicher Heiligenverehrung in ihrer Bedeutung für die Volkskunde: Die Heiligen des mittleren Maaslandes und Rheinlande in Kulturgeschichte und Kultverbreitung*, Cologne, 2nd edn, 1973

Ziegler, J.E., *Sculpture of Compassion. The Pieta and the Beguines in the Southern Low Countries c. 1300–c. 1600*, Brussels and Rome, 1992

# INDEX